THE MILWAUKEE BRAVES

A Baseball Eulogy

Bob Buege

Douglas American Sports Publications

1988

The author gratefully acknowledges the invaluable assistance of Don Bolanowski, Vic Boll, Dawn Hass, Paula Haubrich, Mark Iczkowski, Mike Ploszay, Bob Ramstack, Wally Rank, Marge Skare, and Chris Wilson.

Copyright © 1988 by Robert D. Buege

Published by Douglas American Sports Publications
P.O. Box 21619, Milwaukee, WI 53221-0619

Publisher's Cataloging in Publication Data

Buege, Bob
    The Milwaukee Braves
    A baseball eulogy
        1. Baseball—History.
        2. Baseball Clubs—U.S.
        3. Milwaukee Braves [Baseball team].
        I. Title
GV875.M5B83 1988   796.357′64′09   88-070552
ISBN 0-929134-26-5 Softcover
ISBN 0-929134-34-6 Hardcover

Manufactured in the United States of America

Milwaukee Braves Roster

Hank Aaron 1954-1965
Tommie Aaron 1962-63, 65
Joe Adcock 1953-62
Sandy Alomar 1964-65
Felipe Alou 1964-65
Johnny Antonelli 1953, 61
Ken Aspromonte 1962
Toby Atwell 1956
Bobby Avila 1959
Ed Bailey 1964
Jim Beauchamp 1965
Howie Bedell 1962
Gus Bell 1962-64
Vern Bickford 1953
Ethan Blackaby 1962
Johnny Blanchard 1965
Wade Blasingame 1963-65
Frank Bolling 1961-65
Ray Boone 1959-60
Bob Boyd 1961
John Braun 1964
George Brunet 1960-61
Bill Bruton 1953-60
Bob Buhl 1953-62
Lew Burdette 1953-63
Paul Burris 1953
Cecil Butler 1962
Sammy Calderone 1954
Clay Carroll 1964-65
Rico Carty 1963-65
Neil Chrisley 1961
Gino Cimoli 1961
Ty Cline 1963-65
Tony Cloninger 1961-65
Dave Cole 1953
Dick Cole 1957
Gene Conley 1954-58
Jim Constable 1962
Walker Cooper 1953
Chuck Cottier 1959-60
Wes Covington 1956-61
Billy Cowan 1965
Del Crandall 1953-63
Ray Crone 1954-57
George Crowe 1953, 55
Jack Curtis 1962

Alvin Dark 1960
Mike de la Hoz 1964-65
John DeMerit 1957-59, 61
Don Dillard 1963
Jack Dittmer 1953-56
Dick Donovan 1953
Moe Drabowsky 1961
John Edelman 1955
Dave Eilers 1964-65
Hank Fischer 1962-65
Terry Fox 1960
Frank Funk 1963
Len Gabrielson 1960, 63-64
Bob Giggie 1959-60
Jesse Gonder 1965
Sid Gordon 1953
Charlie Gorin 1954-55
Eddie Haas 1958
Harry Hanebrink 1953, 57-58
Bob Hartman 1959
Bob Hazle 1957-58
Bob Hendley 1961-63
Earl Hersh 1956
Billy Hoeft 1964
Joey Jay 1953-55, 57-60
Virgil Jester 1953
Ernie Johnson 1953-58
Ken Johnson 1965
Lou Johnson 1962
Dave Jolly 1953-57
Mack Jones 1961-63, 65
Nippy Jones 1957
Dick Kelly 1964-65
Billy Klaus 1953
Lou Klimchock 1962-65
Gary Kolb 1964-65
Joe Koppe 1958
Dave Koslo 1954-55
Mike Krsnich 1960
Norm Larker 1963
Frank Lary 1964
Charlie Lau 1960-61
Denny Lemaster 1962-65
Don Liddle 1953
Dick Littlefield 1958
Johnny Logan 1953-61

Stan Lopata 1959-60
Ken MacKenzie 1960-61
Bobby Malkmus 1957
Felix Mantilla 1956-61
Billy Martin 1961
Eddie Mathews 1953-65
Lee Maye 1959-65
Don McMahon 1957-62
Roy McMillan 1961-64
Denis Menke 1962-65
Catfish Metkovich 1954
Seth Morehead 1961
Joe Morgan 1959
Bubba Morton 1963
Red Murff 1956-57
Chet Nichols 1954-56
Phil Niekro 1964-65
Don Nottebart 1960-62
Johnny O'Brien 1959
Danny O'Connell 1954-57
Billy O'Dell 1965
Gene Oliver 1963-65
Chi Chi Olivo 1961, 64-65
Dan Osinski 1965
Andy Pafko 1953-59
Phil Paine 1954-57
Jim Pendleton 1953-56
Taylor Phillips 1956-57
Ron Piche 1960-63
Jim Pisoni 1959
Juan Pizarro 1957-60
Billy Queen 1954
Merritt Ranew 1964
Claude Raymond 1961-63
Del Rice 1955-59
Mel Roach 1953-54, 57-61
Humberto Robinson 1955-56, 58
Phil Roof 1961
Bob Roselli 1955-56, 58
Bob Rush 1958-60
Bob Sadowski 1963-65
Amado Samuel 1962-63

Carl Sawatski 1957-58
Dan Schneider 1963-64
Red Schoendienst 1957-60
Bob Shaw 1962-63
Ray Shearer 1957
Sibby Sisti 1953-54
Enos Slaughter 1959
Lou Sleater 1956
Roy Smalley 1954
Jack Smith 1964
Bill Southworth 1964
Warren Spahn 1953-64
Al Spangler 1959-61
Ebba St. Claire 1953
Max Surkont 1953
Chuck Tanner 1955-57
Bennie Taylor 1955
Hawk Taylor 1957-58, 61-63
Frank Thomas 1961
Bobby Thomson 1954-57
Bob Thorpe 1953
Bobby Tiefenauer 1963-65
Frank Torre 1956-60
Joe Torre 1960-65
Bob Trowbridge 1956-59
Bob Uecker 1962-63
Arnie Umbach 1964
Roberto Vargas 1955
Mickey Vernon 1959
Charlie White 1954-55
Sammy White 1961
Carl Willey 1958-62
Jim Wilson 1953-54
Casey Wise 1958-59
Woody Woodward 1963-65

Managers
Bobby Bragan 1963-65
Charlie Dressen 1960-61
Charlie Grimm 1953-56
Fred Haney 1956-59
Birdie Tebbetts 1961-62

FOREWORD

I don't think any city has ever gone as crazy over a baseball team as the city of Milwaukee did when the Braves arrived there in 1953. Actually, it wasn't just the city of Milwaukee. It was the state of Wisconsin, the state of Iowa, the state of Minnesota—even the people from Chicago. It was unreal!

I mean, we were drawing over two million fans a year in a fairly small ballpark. And the way the fans treated us—I can't even describe it. We were getting cars loaned to us, free gasoline, free drycleaning, gifts of every kind. This went on throughout the fifties. We were taken into people's homes. It was just like one big happy family. There'll never be anything like it again.

The team we had in Boston in 1952, my rookie year, was a very poor ballclub. We were very inexperienced, we finished in seventh place, and we didn't draw any fans. They kind of had taken a bunch of young kids up there that weren't quite ready for the big leagues. They just sacrificed that year, but the experience all of us got made us ready to be a pennant contender the following season. When we got to Milwaukee in spring of 1953, the difference was like night and day.

I had played in Milwaukee before that, but not for long. When I got out of the service in 1951, I joined the minor league Brewers in old wooden Borchert Field. I pinch hit once for the Brewers—and hit a grand slam home run—but they sent me down to the double-A club in Atlanta right after that. I finished out the season down there.

Nineteen fifty-three, though, was different. Everything seemed to jell, and we all had a great season—the players and the fans. It was exciting for me because, even though I was still just 22 years old, I was able to contribute to our second-place finish. In fact, 1953 was my best year. I led the league with 47 home runs, and I was selected to the National League All-Star team. I'll never forget that All-Star Game because I faced Satchel Paige. He got me to hit into a double play. He was 47 years old then, but he threw a little harder than I thought he did.

I had so many memorable moments in my Milwaukee Braves career. This book captures a lot of them. One of the greatest, of course, was when we won our first pennant in 1957. Another one was the home run I hit at County Stadium in the tenth inning of the fourth game of the 1957 World Series. That homer tied the Series at two games each, and we went on to win it in seven games. That home run meant a lot to me. I was having a good Series, defensively and offensively, and that just kind of climaxed it. Winning the '57 Series was a big thrill because it was the first for most of us—not Spahnie, but most of us were still fairly young, and it was a super thrill. County Stadium was full of thrills.

As far as the Braves' move to Atlanta, I think most of us had reservations about it. We pretty well had put our roots into the Milwaukee area. Most of us were living there, raising our kids there, and when the guys from Chicago bought the club, it just seemed we lost a lot. When Lou Perini and John Quinn had the ballclub, we were like a family. We were over there for Christmas parties and things like that. I knew Atlanta—I had played there in 1950 and part of '51, and I had friends there—but, truthfully, I didn't feel it would be another Milwaukee.

Getting back to the subject of thrills, certainly my induction into the Baseball Hall of Fame in Cooperstown was the climax of my career. I don't want to say it was the ultimate thrill, because I had a lot of enjoyment. Being associated with the great names in the Hall of Fame—the greatest ballplayers who ever lived—is a nice way to be remembered, though. I'd also like to be remembered as a ballplayer that went out there and gave one hundred percent every time I went out—and that I enjoyed every minute of it.

If there's anything lacking in today's ballplayers, that would be it—I'm sorry to say that I don't think they have as much fun as we did. They don't enjoy it as much. They're too worried about jumping teams and going to where there's a little more money to be made. And to me there's a lack of loyalty, a lack of feeling, and that's too bad. We totally enjoyed baseball. Readers of this book will see ballplayers that played for the love of the game. Sure, we tried to get as much as we could, but it wasn't floating around like it is today, and we weren't worried about the money. There's certain ballplayers today that are as good as we were in the fifties, but I'd like to see them produce a little more for what they make.

So here then is the story of the Milwaukee Braves. It's a story that is long overdue. The Milwaukee Braves were a good ballclub—a unique ballclub. In a way it surprises me that no one until now has told our story, but then again, Milwaukee is not New York or Los Angeles. Ballplayers and teams in the Midwest never did get the publicity that those cities got. It's an exciting story, though, a story so unusual that, if you weren't there, if you didn't experience it, it's hard to believe. It was fantastic.

For fans who were part of it, this book will bring back a flood of wonderful memories. For those who were too young to be a part of it, this book will introduce you to one of the greatest chapters in baseball history. This book will be a treat for baseball fans everywhere, but especially for the fans in Wisconsin. I still think they're the best.

Eddie Mathews
Milwaukee Braves, 1953-1965
Hall of Fame, 1978

Milwaukee Journal Photo

Eddie Mathews swung a big bat for the Milwaukee Braves.

*Lloyd Park, 16th and Lloyd St., home of Milwaukee's minor league
clubs from 1895 to 1904*

Prologue

"If you build it, he will come."

—W.P. Kinsella, *Shoeless Joe*

Milwaukee has always been a baseball town. Back in 1878, when Rutherford B. Hayes was President of the United States and just two years after the telephone was invented, Milwaukee had a team in the fledgling National League. Six years later, the short-lived Union Association claimed Milwaukee among its members. In 1891, when the American Association was big-league, the Cincinnati club moved to Milwaukee during the season. And in 1901, when the American League was formed, Milwaukee was a charter member.

In addition to providing teams for the major leagues, Milwaukee sent some of its native sons to big-league stardom: hard-hitting "Unser Choe" Hauser, who once hit 69 homers in the minors in one year and who hit 27 for Connie Mack's A's; Ken Keltner, who stopped the great DiMaggio's hitting streak at 56 games; and Hall of Famer "Bucketfoot" Al Simmons, nee Aloysius Szymanski, the "Duke of Mitchell Street" and the pride of Milwaukee's south side. Throughout the first half of the twentieth century, though, Milwaukee baseball meant the minor league Milwaukee Brewers.

The people of Milwaukee loved the Brewers, and why not? The Brewers offered a diversion from the Great Depression and from several wars, and they gave Beertown a chance to know some of baseball's most fascinating characters—some on the ascent to the majors, some on the decline, some going nowhere—but all heroes to the Wisconsin faithful. Brewer fans followed the exploits of major league footnote/minor league star Antonio Bordetzki, whom they and several generations of sandlot youngsters were to know as Bunny Brief. They marveled at the awesome power of rising star Rudy York, and they cheered Ted Gullic, a popular outfielder who once hit a home run through his own living room window. They witnessed the managerial genius of Casey Stengel in the pupa stage, and they rejoiced in the madcap entrepreneurial maneuverings of Bill Veeck, who scheduled early morning swing-shift games to accommodate factory workers and served them bowls of corn flakes. It was minor-league baseball, but it was big-league entertainment.

The setting for this entertainment was Athletic Park, later purchased by and renamed for Otto Borchert. It was a ramshackle wooden rectangle encompassing one square block, long since demolished and paved over for Interstate 43. Borchert Field was a neighborhood ballpark with no parking, splintered seats, little-league distances down the foul lines, and grandstands that jutted out to the foul lines and obscured flyballs from spectators. The grandstand caught fire more than once, and it was decapitated by wind during the mid-40's. Borchert Field was substandard even

Milwaukee Sentinel Photo
"Borchert Orchard," home of the Milwaukee Brewers

10

Preparing Borchert for its last opener, April, 1952

by minor league standards, a fact recognized early in its existence, but a replacement was a long time in coming.

As far back as 1909, Charles B. Whitnall, called the father of Milwaukee County's park system, thought the area around Story quarry would be a perfect site for a public stadium. No one really disagreed, but neither did anyone act upon the suggestion. In 1931 the Milwaukee Common Council discussed the idea of a 50,000-seat municipal stadium, but the idea died. Then in 1936 County Supervisor Raymond J. Moore asked for an opinion on the legality of paying for the construction of a baseball stadium with Public Works Administration funds. The construction was ruled legal, and on October 27, 1936, the County Board adopted a resolution calling for the building of a stadium. By that time, however, no PWA money was available, and the project was shelved for two years.

In 1938 the board authorized the selection of a suitable site for a half-million dollar, publicly-financed stadium. There the project sat for nearly nine years until February 24, 1947, when the board finally voted to build the stadium. The site chosen was the former Story quarry. Senator Alexander Wiley introduced a bill in Congress to allow 120 acres of the Soldiers' Home grounds, adjacent to the stadium site, to be sold to the county for parking, and in September, 1949, President Truman signed the bill into law. The newly-acquired land proved more desirable as a stadium location, so the site was moved. Ground was finally broken for the county's new ballpark on October 19, 1950, at the site west of 44th Street and south of the Speedrail interurban line.

Construction of the stadium began, only to be halted by a shortage of steel. Because of the Korean War, federal regulations limited new construction using steel. Wisconsin's representatives were able to obtain the necessary approval by showing that the stadium project was already underway, so construction proceeded, and by March, 1953, the new public ballpark was nearly ready for occupancy by the Milwaukee Brewers.

The Brewers of 1951 and 1952 had been among the most talented minor league clubs ever assembled. The 1951 team won its league playoff and the Little World Series, and the 1952 team included two-time Minor League Player of the Year Gene Conley, Dick Donovan, Don Liddle, Billy Bruton, Billy Klaus, George Crowe, Jack Dittmer, and Johnny Logan. With a winning tradition and a new stadium, the Milwaukee Brewers promised to be great in 1953.

And then it all changed. Milwaukee officials had hoped that their new stadium might someday attract a big-league franchise, perhaps Bill Veeck's perennial losers, the St. Louis Browns. Veeck wanted to move the club, and he had always said Milwaukee was a good baseball town, but the American League owners would not let him leave St. Louis and stave off bankruptcy. Instead Lou Perini, owner of the Brewers' parent club, the Boston Braves, announced on Friday, March 13, 1953, his intention to petition National League owners for permission to move the Braves to Milwaukee. It seemed doubtful that such a shift would be approved, considering Veeck's lack of success and considering that opening day was just a month away. Nevertheless, Milwaukee fans were hopeful.

On Sunday afternoon, March 15th, the new stadium was opened to the public for the first time. People had been driving past and admiring the huge stadium for months, but now they were allowed inside their coliseum. The weather was lousy, cold and drizzly, but more than 10,000 people attended, gazing in awe and dreaming of a team they barely knew. Friday the 13th had

12

Borchert Field demolition, March, 1953—free kindling

Construction of Milwaukee County Stadium, 1952

been a lucky day for Milwaukee baseball fans—if Wednesday the 18th proved as lucky and the National League owners granted their approval, the major league Braves would be theirs.

The big news story of Tuesday, March 17, was an atomic explosion in the Nevada desert. The 33rd atomic device ever detonated by man was exploded atop a 300-foot tower at Yucca Flat as a test of the new U.S. atomic capability. Milwaukeeans, like citizens throughout the nation, were awed and somewhat chilled by photographs of the event. Almost before the dust had settled from the blast, however, another shock-wave struck Milwaukee, this one centered on the Vinoy Park Hotel in St. Petersburg, Florida. At 1:33 the following afternoon, Milwaukee time, Wednesday, March 18, 1953, the National League owners voted 8-0 to allow Lou Perini to move his Boston Braves to Milwaukee—and Milwaukee went crazy.

Mayor Frank Zeidler immediately announced a week of celebration to welcome the new heroes, including a parade and a public rally. Local businesses bought advertisements welcoming the Braves and offered free merchandise and services: free cleaning of the team's uniforms, free cases of beverages, complimentary use of automobiles. Fans from all around Wisconsin began sending requests for tickets, and team officials speculated wildly that attendance might surpass one-million in the first year. The strangers from Beantown were instantly taken to heart by the adoring Milwaukee fans— sight unseen.

But who were these guys? Of course Charlie Grimm had managed the Brewers, and several of the players had apprenticed at Borchert Field before making the big club: men like Vern Bickford, Ernie Johnson, Johnny Logan, and several others. Nevertheless, the club Milwaukee was adopting was leaving Boston because it had been failing miserably, both on the field and at the turnstiles. The 1952 Braves had lured only 281,000 fans into decrepit Braves Field, and the team had finished in 7th place, 32 full games behind Brooklyn.

In fact, the Boston Braves' losing tradition extended back to the turn of the century. Through more than a half century, the Braves (also called, at various times, the Beaneaters and the Bees) had managed only two pennants, the 1914 "miracle" and the 1948 "Spahn and Sain and pray for rain" fluke. In that 52-year span, the pathetic Braves managed to win more games than they lost in only eleven seasons; they lost more games than any other National League team except the Philadelphia Phillies; they won fewer pennants than anyone except the Phillies, who also won two, but the Phillies finished second four times, while the Braves were second only once; they finished no higher than fourth place for thirty consecutive years, 1917-1946; and they finished in either last or second-last place 24 times. They came by their losing reputation honestly.

The Braves team that closed Boston was very much in the tradition. Their team batting average was an anemic .233, second lowest in the major leagues. They ranked next to last in the National League in runs scored, slugging percentage, and double plays, and they were third worst in runs allowed, errors, fielding percentage, and team earned run average. In other words, they could not hit, pitch, or catch. They summoned manager Grimm (an apt name for the skipper of this team) from the minors in May, but his guidance led the Braves nowhere. They were a team without a .300 hitter (or a .290 hitter, for that matter) or a pitcher with a winning record in more than 100 innings. And now they were Milwaukee-bound.

The team that reached Milwaukee on April 8, 1953, did not, however, resemble the one that had fled Boston. The ugly ducklings became glorious swans the moment they arrived at the Chicago & Northwestern Railroad station near Milwaukee's lakefront. New sluggers like Wisconsin native Andy Pafko and powerful Joe Adcock had been obtained in winter trades; minor league speedsters Jim Pendleton (obtained in the Adcock trade) and Billy Bruton had been promoted to the majors; and promising youngsters Del Crandall, Johnny Antonelli, and Bob Buhl had completed military service and were ready to play ball. Alongside the new faces were proven veterans like Warren Spahn, Sid Gordon, and Max Surkont, plus second-year slugger Eddie Mathews, former Brewer Johnny Logan, and several other quality ballplayers. Baseball-hungry Milwaukee fans would have embraced losers and stumblebums just to be in the big leagues, but as it turned out, they did not have to. This was an exciting team with a bright future.

At the train depot, 12,000 sign-waving, cheering fans turned out to welcome their team. The ensuing parade attracted 60,000 people, and the next night the official civic reception at the Arena drew more than 6000 despite a driving rainstorm. The next day the Braves made their debut at County Stadium before a crowd of nearly 10,000 brave souls (the pun is intentional) in an exhibition game against the Boston Red Sox, but the game had to be postponed because of freezing rain after only two innings. The game was rescheduled for the following day, but Wisconsin's April climate again refused to cooperate. The game had to be canceled because of cold weather, delaying the Braves' home

15

debut yet another time. The season opener was only two days away, on Monday, April 13, in Cincinnati, with the home opener the day after.

So it was that Milwaukee rejoined the big leagues. They had a new (in fact, unfinished) stadium, a host of new ballplayers, a new schedule traded from Pittsburgh (reluctantly, by Branch Rickey), and a new community spirit bordering on mania. Major league baseball's first franchise shift in over fifty years was now accomplished and ready for judgment by a skeptical baseball establishment. Many people doubted the wisdom of the move to Milwaukee, including some National League owners who had voted to allow it. But the situation in Boston had become so desperate that in 1952, as Boston sportswriter John Gillooly wrote, "The Braves had the worst franchise in the history of baseball—a $600,000 bouncing check. The National League wants Perini to get out of Boston." Milwaukee was not Perini's first choice—years later he revealed publicly that he actually would have preferred Toronto—but it was his territory, having his minor league club, and it offered a new stadium. The other owners gave their blessing; Baseball Commissioner Ford Frick offered his typical contribution ("If I had the power I would have stopped them. But I can't."); and Perini moved. The only professional sports franchise destined never to suffer a losing season had been born.

Time Capsule - April 14, 1953

"This was a wonderful example of Milwaukee gemuetlichkeit."

—Owner Louis Perini

Everything that happened in this game represented a first. It was the first major league game in Milwaukee in 52 years; the first National League game in 75 years; the initial game in new Milwaukee County Stadium. Solly Hemus of the St. Louis Cardinals was the first batter in the new stadium; he also received the first base on balls. Red Schoendienst made the first out, a pop foul to Johnny Logan. Stan Musial hit the first fair ball, a fly to Andy Pafko in rightfield. Enormous Steve Bilko was the first batter to strike out. Cardinal Del Rice got the first extra-base hit. Vern Benson of St. Louis was the first pinch runner. And so on.

A sellout crowd of 34,357 had turned out to cheer their first-place Braves, conquerors of Cincinnati's Redlegs the day before in the National League's season inaugural. Many fans knew little about their new team, but they came out of civic pride, a sense of history, and the exhilaration of being in the big leagues. These people were unfettered by big-city sophistication—they cheered both teams, though somewhat louder for their own. They cheered for foul balls, called strikes, the ground crew, a hit batsman, and every fielding play. These were children attending their first circus.

The starting pitcher for Milwaukee was, of course, lefthander Warren Spahn. The high-kicking veteran was among the league's finest, possessor of 122 victories and a four-time 20-game winner in Boston. Spahn was certainly the player best-known by Milwaukee's new fans. His mound counterpart was Cardinal ace Gerry Staley, a seasoned righthander with 36 wins in the previous two campaigns. The Cardinals had finished a strong third in 1952 and recorded the highest team batting average in the league, led by six-time batting champ Stan "The Man" Musial.

Spahn walked Hemus to start the game, then retired the next three batters. In the home first Billy Bruton flied to Musial, and Johnny Logan and Eddie Mathews fanned. The Cardinals went down in order in the second, as did the first two Braves, Sid Gordon and Andy Pafko. Joe Adcock then registered the first base hit in County Stadium, a single to left. Del Crandall topped a slow roller toward Ray Jablonski at third, and when Jablonski's throw eluded first baseman Bilko, Adcock scored the first run. Jack Dittmer grounded out to Bilko unassisted, but the Braves led 1-0.

The third and fourth innings produced no hits by either team; Spahn, in fact, had a no-hitter going into the fifth. He walked Enos Slaughter to start that inning, though, and when Spahn's pickoff attempt got away from Adcock, Slaughter moved to second. He promptly scored on Jablonski's single to right, tying the score. Rip Repulski singled to left, with Jablonski advancing to second and still no outs. Del Rice hit a fly to Sid Gordon in left. Gordon caught it and threw out Jablonski trying to tag and go to third. Spahn then retired Staley to end the threat. Milwaukee got the leadoff man on base when Adcock walked, but after Del Crandall sacrificed, Staley got Dittmer and Spahn, and the score was tied 1-1 after five innings.

St. Louis threatened again in the sixth, but the Braves escaped with the help of a strange double play. Hemus led off with his second walk (the base on balls was Hemus' forte— although just a .273 lifetime hitter, and no slugger, he had walked more times in 1952 than Joe DiMaggio, Willie Mays, Henry Aaron, or Roger Maris ever did in a season). After Red Schoendienst sacrificed, Stan Musial bounced to Logan at short. Hemus was caught in a rundown, finally tagged by Logan, and Musial was out trying to reach second.

Bruton led off the Braves' sixth with a single, but Milwaukee again failed to score. Neither team scored in the seventh, but in the eighth St. Louis put runners on first and third with nobody out. Del Rice doubled down the leftfield line, Vern Benson ran for him, and Staley laid down a bunt. Spahn fielded the ball and tried to throw to third, but his foot slipped, the throw was late, and both men were safe. Spahn got Hemus to ground to Adcock, who threw to Crandall to trap Benson. As Benson was run down and tagged, Staley went to third, Hemus to second. With the infield drawn in, Schoendienst grounded to Logan, and the runners had to hold. The next batter, Stan Musial, blasted a line

18

Milwaukee Journal Photo

Solly Hemus takes the first pitch in County Stadium, ball one, from Warren Spahn.

drive to right-centerfield, destined for extra bases. Somehow the streaking Bruton caught up to the ball and speared it in his glove as the crowd erupted.

Rookie Bruton was rapidly becoming a Milwaukee favorite. The previous day in Cincinnati he had scored the first (winning) run for the Braves and had made three incredible catches in centerfield to protect Max Surkont's shutout victory. Even before that, Milwaukee fans had cheered Bruton's fielding, batting, and base-stealing heroics at Borchert Field in 1952 during his (and the Brewers') final minor league season.

In the bottom of the eighth, with two out and nobody on base, Bruton further enhanced his reputation by lining a long triple, into the wind, over Enos Slaughter in right. The next batter, Logan, was hit by a pitch. Mathews, having struck out three straight times in an inauspicious home debut, walked to load the bases. Clean-up hitter Sid Gordon topped a slow roller down the third base line; Staley fielded the ball but could not make a throw, so Bruton scored to make it 2-1. Pafko then grounded into a force play to end the inning.

In the ninth Spahn got both Slaughter and Bilko on routine flies to Pafko in right. In anticipation of imminent victory, the standing-room fans beyond the centerfield fence began moving toward the exits. Umpire Jocko Conlan had the stadium announcer ask the crowd to remain in place until the game ended so they would not distract the batters; the fans obeyed. Jablonski singled, pitcher Harvey Haddix ran for him, and pinch hitter Peanuts Lowrey, batting for Repulski, tied the game with a long double to the fence in left.

Spahn retired the side, the Braves failed to score in the ninth, and Spahn held the Cardinals again in the top of the tenth. By now the crowd was growing tense, fearful of losing what had looked like a sure win. Spahn was due to lead off the Milwaukee tenth; manager Charlie Grimm disdained a pinch hitter and sent Spahn up to bat. He grounded weakly to Staley for the first out. The next batter was Billy Bruton.

Bruton was a fine fielder and runner but not much of a threat to hit one out of the park. In the minors he had never hit more than five homers in a season. However, in a testament to the power of the adrenal glands, the slender outfielder smacked a long drive to right, against a stiff breeze, that glanced off Slaughter's outstretched mitt and dropped over the fence for a home run. Umpire Lon Warneke (a Chicago Cubs teammate of Charlie Grimm in the 1930's, an all-star pitcher known as "The Arkansas Humming Bird") thought the ball had bounced over the fence and signalled Bruton back to second. Grimm charged out of the dugout, bellowing, and a moment later the decision was overruled and Bruton was motioned home with the winning run. It was to be Bruton's only home run until July 5, 1954.

1953

"This is only the beginning of good times for Milwaukee."

—Commissioner Ford Frick

Opening Day in Cincinnati foreshadowed the entire season, as it turned out. The Braves won, as they would do with surprising frequency, and they won with superior pitching—in this case a three-hit, no-walk performance by chunky veteran Max Surkont, a 30-year-old Clydesdale at the peak of his skills. The 2-0 victory, though, belonged as much to rookie centerfielder Billy Bruton as to Surkont. Bruton not only singled, stole second, and scored the first Milwaukee Braves' run in the first inning, but also saved the game for his team with several excellent catches in the field. Like his centerfield predecessor Sam Jethroe, Bruton was a speedster who could lead off, steal bases (he led the National League in 1953 with 26), and run down anything hit to center. To top it off, he was a former Milwaukee Brewer and therefore an immediate favorite of Braves fans.

The next day was the County Stadium inaugural, and 34,357 delirious fans were on hand to welcome major league baseball back to Milwaukee after a 52-year absence. They overflowed the available seating, with thousands standing behind the rightfield fence and anywhere else they could get a vantage point. In fact, more fans stood for this game than had attended the 1952 opener in Boston when the Braves and Dodgers attracted a cozy gathering of 4,694. Naturally a new team in a new stadium would draw a large crowd, but the outpouring of emotion from the Milwaukee fans was to become a year-long event. Fans stood and cheered foul balls and applauded called strikes. County Stadium was a wild scene, later characterized by a writer as "an insane asylum with bases."

21

The Braves responded to this avalanche of fan support with a thrilling, ten-inning victory over the Cardinals, 3-2, winning on Billy Bruton's home run [see Time Capsule]. With the season just two days old, the Braves were undefeated and atop the National League standings. Cold rain forced postponement the next day, followed by an off-day to travel to Cincinnati, so the season was five days old before the Braves tasted defeat, a loosely-played 10-9 slugfest with the Reds. Snow postponed the next game in St. Louis before the Cardinals beat the Braves on consecutive days, 4-3 and 9-4. Then in Chicago the Braves displayed their muscle for the first time, pounding the Cubs, 15-6, behind Eddie Mathews' two homers and a double, giving Surkont his second win. The next day, April 23, the Cubs beat Milwaukee, 6-2, putting the Braves below the .500 mark for the second, and last, time of the 1953 season, despite another Mathews home run.

Returning home, and following another rainout, the Braves belted Cincinnati, 8-4, led by Mathews' two home runs, giving him five in three games and six for the year. Sunday the 26th was to be the initial County Stadium doubleheader, but rain and cold washed away both contests, making five postponements in two weeks and leaving the Braves at 4-4 as they embarked on their first eastern trip.

At New York's Polo Grounds, Surkont gained his third straight victory, 4-1, and the following day, April 29, the Braves made history. Warren Spahn beat the Giants, 3-2, but the historic moment belonged to Joe Adcock, who clubbed a ball 475 feet into the stands in dead center, the first home run ever hit to dead center in that mammoth old park. Adcock's blast was merely a precursor of the historic batting feats he would achieve in the nation's largest city, but it marked him at once as a slugger of epic proportions. It also pointed up the one trait that would prevent him from destroying all home run records—he was basically a straightaway hitter, and many of his best hits were merely loud flyouts to the deepest part of the ballpark.

After Sal "The Barber" Maglie outdueled Vern Bickford in the series finale, winning 1-0 on Bobby Thomson's ninth-inning homer, the Braves moved on to Philadelphia, where Adcock, Jim Wilson, and Andy Pafko hit home runs in support of Wilson's complete-game pitching to win, 5-2. The next day they were again rained out before moving on to Brooklyn to meet the Boys of Summer for the first time in a scheduled three-game series.

The Dodgers were the defending league champions, and deservedly so. They had only mediocre pitching from such famous names as Carl Erskine, Russ Meyer, Billy Loes, Johnny Podres,

*County Stadium inaugural, with Governor Walter Kohler, Mayor
Frank Zeidler, NL president Warren Giles, and umpire*

Joe Black, and Preacher Roe (Don Newcombe was in military
service), but they possessed one of the most fearsome batting
lineups ever assembled. The 1953 Dodgers led the league in team
batting average by twelve points over their nearest rival, and they
led in slugging by fifty points. Their starting lineup boasted five
.300 hitters, including the league batting champ, Carl Furillo, at
.344, and their starting outfield hit a collective .336. They easily
led the league in home runs with 208, paced by Duke Snider with
42 and Roy Campanella with 41, and they had eight home-run
hitters in double figures. They outscored their nearest rivals by
nearly 200 runs, and they dominated the RBI leaders with top
man Campanella driving in 142, Snider 126, and Gil Hodges 122.
They also led the National League in stolen bases, nearly double
their closest competitor, and to complete the picture, they led the
league in fielding. They were a formidable team.

In the Braves' first meeting with the Dodgers, on May 3, Billy
Loes beat Milwaukee, 4-3, thanks mainly to the base-running of

Jackie Robinson. The Braves won the next contest, 9-4, with a good long-relief job by Lew Burdette, but the final game of the series was rained out, as were the next two in Pittsburgh, giving the Braves a record through May 7 of eight wins, six losses, and nine rainouts (or snowouts). They returned to Milwaukee eager to play some ballgames and gain some ground.

Thanks to their marvelous pitching, they did gain some ground. In the next ten days, all at home, the Braves took three of four from the Cubs, two straight from the Giants, two in a row from the Pirates, and one of two from the Phillies. In that ten-game stretch, their pitchers threw two shutouts and allowed just fifteen runs as Charlie Grimm's club moved into a tie for the National League lead.

Johnny Antonelli began the homestand by shutting out the Cubs, 2-0; the next day the Cubs returned the favor, beating Jim Wilson, 2-0. On May 10 the Braves swept the Cubs in the Stadium's first doubleheader, winning 6-2 behind Max Surkont and 4-1 behind Don Liddle's two-hitter in his first major league start. Two days later rookie Bob Buhl matched the feat with a two-hitter against the Giants in his first start, winning 8-1 on a frigid evening better suited to ice-fishing. Then Lew Burdette beat the Giants with a seven-inning relief job, his second long-relief win in nine days. On May 14 the Braves climbed into a first-place tie as Jim Wilson stopped the Pirates, 3-2, with his teammates scoring twice in the ninth, winning on Jack Dittmer's hit. The next night Surkont, rapidly becoming a Milwaukee institution, won his fifth game without a defeat, beating the Pirates, 4-3, and keeping the Braves tied for first.

On May 16 the Braves suffered a temporary setback against the Phillies and Curt Simmons. Billy Bruton led off the bottom of the first with a lined single to center. Simmons, the Phils' star lefty, then retired the next 27 batters in order to saddle Don Liddle with a 3-0 loss. Simmons struck out ten, expanding his league-leading total to 45, and stayed ahead of the hitters and in total command throughout the game. Only Bruton's hit deprived Simmons of a perfect game.

The following day the scheduled doubleheader was rained out, the Braves' second Sunday washout, but on Monday Buhl hurled a 4-0 shutout at the Phillies in his second major league start, again drawing Milwaukee into a first-place tie. Besides the Braves regaining a share of the lead, the May 18 game is noteworthy for two reasons. First, under the National League rules of the time, the final game of a series could not be played at night without the permission of the visiting manager. The double rainout of the previous day necessitated a makeup game for Monday, but without a pre-sale of tickets, the game might have been played in semi-privacy had Phillies manager Steve O'Neill not consented to play in the evening. He did, and the second noteworthy event occurred—the Braves' ticketsellers sold 22,237 tickets between 9:00 in the morning and game-time.

The next night the Brooklyn Dodgers made their first County Stadium appearance, and their arrival drew a Milwaukee record 36,439 fans to the game. The Dodgers spoiled the party by beating Jim Wilson, 4-1, pushing the hometown heroes back into second place. The following afternoon they repeated the insult by belting Vern Bickford, 7-2. Even in defeat, though, Milwaukee achieved satisfaction. On May 20, in only their thirteenth home date, they surpassed the attendance of the Braves' entire 1952 season in Boston.

Moving on to Chicago, the Braves won two of three (they also experienced their twelfth rainout), then returned home and swept three from the Redlegs and one from the Cubs. On May 28 they hit the road (actually, the rails) with a 22-11 record and a game and a half lead over their nearest rivals. They faced a crucial test of their readiness to contend for the pennant—between May 29 and June 15 they would play 22 games in six cities in 18 days, appearing in every rival ballpark except Chicago's Wrigley Field. This longest road trip of the season was a stern challenge to the upstart Milwaukee team, especially the pitching staff, with added pressure placed on them by having five doubleheaders during that span. On May 24 and 25, and again on May 30 and 31, they played back-to-back doubleheaders, each in a different city, and from June 12 through June 16, including their first day back in Milwaukee, they played three doubleheaders in five days, with single games sandwiched in between.

The road trip turned out to be a huge success—Milwaukee won fifteen and lost seven, helped by three doubleheader sweeps—and the Braves won the series in each city except Cincinnati, where they split a pair. The Braves had lost their slender lead and now trailed the Dodgers by percentage points, but they showed they could win consistently away from home.

Back in Milwaukee on June 16 the Braves quickly regained first by sweeping a doubleheader from the Phillies. Between games, burly Max Surkont, a local favorite, especially among those sharing his Polish ancestry, was honored with a Max Surkont Night on the occasion of his 31st birthday. Surkont responded to the honor by hurling his ninth victory in ten decisions in the nightcap. Unfortunately, his popularity may have

In the segregated South of 1953, Braves' black players roomed above a garage during spring training.

Black players' lodging, spring, 1953, with their hosts

contributed to his downfall. He made no secret of his love for Polish sausage, so his fans sent him huge quantities of it. He obligingly consumed the gifts, and his already substantial weight increased steadily to near 240 pounds, with the predictable effect on his pitching. After winning nine games in the first two months of the season, he failed to win his next game for more than a month, finally earning his tenth victory on July 19 in a game shortened to five innings by darkness. Five days later he pitched poorly but won as his teammates pounded the Dodgers for eleven runs, but after that he never won another game for the Braves. The day after Christmas he was traded to the Pittsburgh Pirates. He never had another winning season.

After beating Philadelphia again, the Braves led the league on June 17 by two and a half games with an amazing 40-18 record. Their renaissance was clearly evident in the won-lost records of their top pitchers: Max Surkont was 9-1, Lew Burdette was 6-0, Warren Spahn was 8-1, Johnny Antonelli was 6-2, and Bob Buhl was 5-2. The Braves were on top of the world, not to mention the National League standings, but there were serious forebodings.

For one thing, the Braves were tired. They may not even have realized it, but they were. The heady feeling of winning, of leading the league after years of wallowing in the muck of the second division, had made them oblivious to the fatigue of 32 games in 26 days, but the fatigue was genuine, and the schedule would not soon relent—the spate of early-season postponements would eventually exact its toll in makeup games. For another thing, despite winning 37 of 51 games, the Braves had been unable to pull away from the talent-laden Dodgers.

June 19 may have been the pivotal point of the Braves' 1953 season. The afternoon temperature in Milwaukee soared to 100 degrees as the Braves prepared to host the New York Giants in an evening contest at the Stadium. Back in the Giants' home state, at Sing Sing prison, less than an hour before game time, convicted atomic spies Julius and Ethel Rosenberg died, one after the other, in the electric chair. At County Stadium, 34,348 baseball zealots sought relief from the oppressive heat and the oppressive Cold War by turning out to cheer their league-leading Braves as they tried to extend their two and a half game lead. Rookie Bob Buhl was Milwaukee's starting hurler, opposing the Giants' Sal Maglie, but the night belonged to Maglie. He throttled the Braves with a four-hitter and drove in four runs on three hits as New York embarrassed the Braves, 15-1. Milwaukee's only run scored on a homer by relief pitcher Dave Cole in the sixth, and by that time the score was 12-0. Of course it was only one loss, but it stung the

Braves and began a skid that took them out of first place for good.

The Braves did beat the Giants the next afternoon, but they lost their next eight games in a row. By the end of the streak, on June 30, they had seen the last of first place. They played good baseball during the losing streak, but fate was against them. After losing 5-0 to the Giants in the first game of a doubleheader to begin the streak, the Braves fought from behind to tie, 6-6, in the nightcap. Unfortunately, darkness prevented the completion of the game because league rules at that time prohibited the use of lights in a Sunday ballgame.

The next three games were disappointing losses to cellar-dwelling Pittsburgh. First the Pirates won, 1-0, despite a two-hit, twelve-strikeout performance by Warren Spahn. Then Vern Bickford was belted for a 10-1 trouncing. Finally the Braves failed to hold a 4-1 ninth inning lead and lost in ten innings, 6-4. Yet even after being swept by the Pirates, the Braves still led by two games when the Dodgers came to town for a three-game series.

The series opener on June 26 was a heartbreaker for Max Surkont, who was 9-0 against the rest of the league but lost his second game to Brooklyn, 4-3. The next day was even more disappointing, a ten-inning loss by the same score that dropped the Braves into a first-place tie with the Dodgers. In the finale the Bums simply unloaded on Spahn, 11-1, extending his career-long jinx against them. The great lefty had been 13-21 against the Dodgers while he played in Boston; in 1952 he had been 0-5 against them. Now he was 0-1 as a Milwaukee Brave, and the Braves had tumbled out of first place.

The Braves continued to flirt with first place for another two weeks, up until the All-Star break, thanks mainly to the pitching of Spahn and the slugging of third baseman Eddie Mathews. Those two Milwaukee heroes represented the Braves in the All-Star classic on July 14 in Cincinnati, an honor richly deserved by both. Spahn was 11-3, leading the league in earned run average; Mathews was setting the pace with 27 home runs. In the National League's 5-1 All-Star victory, Mathews scored the first run for his team, and Spahn pitched three strong innings to record the win.

The Braves were a game and a half behind the Dodgers at the All-Star break, but they quickly began to slide out of contention. They won four of eight games but fell five and a half games behind the red-hot Dodgers. The Braves arrived at Ebbets Field on July 24 for a four-game series with the leaders, needing at least three wins to get back in the race. They won the opener in a

28

slugfest, 11-6, behind Surkont's final win as a Brave, but were whitewashed 7-0 in game two. That set the stage for a Sunday doubleheader that was clearly the Braves' last chance, barring a miracle.

So important was this doubleheader that 33,421 Dodger fans packed Ebbets Field, an occurrence that would have been unremarkable at County Stadium but which represented the largest Brooklyn turnout since 1951. The rabid, vocal Dodger fans were legendary, but usually from a distance. In the largest borough of the nation's most populous city, the Dodgers frequently drew crowds under 10,000. This pair of contests, however, piqued their interest, and their heroes rewarded them with a sweep. They beat Johnny Antonelli in the opener, 3-2, then edged Lew Burdette in the nightcap, 2-1. This game marked Burdette's first start as a Milwaukeean, and although he lost, he so impressed Charlie Grimm that he immediately took his place in the starting rotation.

The losses pushed Grimm's club seven and a half games behind, ending the Braves' pennant drive even though two months of the season remained. The frustration of the double loss to the Dodgers, in which the Braves received excellent pitching but no hitting, manifested itself that evening in a restaurant on New York's 42nd Street. Teammates Johnny Logan and Vern Bickford, both fierce competitors, staged a knock-down, drag-out fight which, according to eyewitnesses, began inside the restaurant, moved onto the sidewalk, then moved back inside. A wire service report said the brawl lasted 30 minutes; Logan and Bickford downplayed it, insisting it was a one-punch fight. Whichever account was accurate, it was the most hitting the Braves did that day.

Back in Milwaukee the next night, the Braves took out their frustrations on the Giants. Eddie Mathews blasted two home runs and Warren Spahn fired his third shutout of the season to overwhelm New York, 13-0. The next night Bob Buhl also blanked the Giants, 2-0, although the big story of the night was the gift of a fishnet for catching foul balls to Braves announcers Earl Gillespie and Blaine Walsh, given by a Waukesha radio station during Waukesha County Night ceremonies. (Thus was born one of the most familiar phrases on Braves broadcasts— "Blainer, get the net!")

Two days later Burdette blanked the Giants, completing a four-game series in which the Giants scored three runs and were shut out three times. The following night, July 31, in a doubleheader during which Sid Gordon was honored, Max Surkont whitewashed the Phillies through ten innings of a scoreless nightcap ended by rain. The following day Warren Spahn climaxed an incredible seven-game, five-shutout stretch by Milwaukee pitchers with a near-perfect one-hit masterpiece against the Phillies [see Time Capsule].

During August the Braves continued to play good baseball and win consistently, but they still could not gain on the Dodgers. After splitting a four-game series with Brooklyn between August 3 and August 6, leaving them eight and a half games behind, the Braves won six straight, then lost once, won two, lost once, then won eight in a row. And after this amazing stretch, winning sixteen of eighteen games, they did not gain even one game in the standings. During that span Spahn won four games, Burdette won four, Mathews smashed five home runs, Andy Pafko hit three homers and extended a hitting streak to 20 games, and the Braves played solid, sometimes outstanding baseball. Fans continued to flock to the games, including a new Stadium record 37,243 on August 21 for Andy Pafko Night, but the team could not catch, or even approach, the Dodgers. In this season, the Bums from Brooklyn were unbeatable.

September saw the Braves solidify their hold on second place and set records on the field and at the box-office. On September 4 they surpassed the all-time Braves attendance record set in the pennant year of 1948. On September 11 the Dodgers arrived in Milwaukee needing one win to clinch the pennant. A tenth-inning home run by Pafko delayed the inevitable, but the next day Carl Erskine outpitched Bob Buhl to put Brooklyn officially back in the World Series. In the home finale on September 20, 36,011 fans helped the Braves set an all-time National League attendance record of 1,826,397, shattering the record set by the Brooklyn Dodgers in 1947. Milwaukee's new record was set in just 64 home dates, in an uncompleted stadium, with no opportunity for a season-ticket sales promotion.

Also in the home finale, 18-year-old bonus baby Joey Jay, the first Little Leaguer to reach the majors, shut out the Redlegs, 3-0, to record his first victory. Two days later in a doubleheader in St. Louis, Eddie Mathews had a home run, a double, a single, four walks, and was hit by a pitch, in addition to committing four errors. The home run was his 47th, tops in the major leagues, and it established a new Braves record. He also set team records for runs batted in (135), and extra base hits (86); he established a National League record of 30 home runs on the road; he tied the major league record of 157 games played by a third baseman; he tied for the league lead in slugging percentage at .627; and on the

30

Speedy Bill Bruton was Milwaukee's first hero.

negative side, he led league third basemen with 30 errors.

On September 27 in Cincinnati, the Braves closed out their initial season of Milwaukee affiliation by beating the Redlegs, 8-2, behind Warren Spahn. As was the case all year, Spahn was brilliant—both Cincinnati runs were undeserved, and one was officially unearned. The high-kicking southpaw finished the season 23-7, tying Robin Roberts for most wins, and Spahn's 2.10 ERA led the league by far. His nearest rival, Roberts, was at 2.75, and the only other league hurler under 3.00 was Bob Buhl at 2.97. The victory in the finale also gave Milwaukee a 92-62 record, the club's best showing since the Miracle Boston Braves of 1914.

And so, despite finishing thirteen games behind the Dodgers, the first edition of the Milwaukee Braves could point with pride to an outstanding season, a season surpassing even the wildest dreams of their fans or their owner. They had shattered attendance records and climbed from near the cellar to second place.

They were, with a few notable exceptions, a young team with power, speed, and the finest pitching staff in the National League. It was a great time to be a baseball fan in Milwaukee.

Milwaukee Journal Photo

Milwaukee receives the good news, March 18, 1953.

1953 Nemesis - Billy Loes

"Oh, hell, if you win twenty games they want you to do it every year."

—Billy Loes

The 1953 Brooklyn Dodgers were tough for everyone to beat, winning 105 games, the most in the league since World War II. The Milwaukee Braves won only 9 of 22 games against them, but there was a more telling statistic. Brooklyn pitcher Billy Loes beat the Braves five times before the Fourth of July.

Loes was a temperamental but talented, hard-throwing righthander who won 50 games for Brooklyn from 1952 through 1955 while losing 26. He was primarily a starter, sometimes a spot reliever, never the Dodgers' big winner but among them for those four years. In 1953 he won fourteen games, his highest total ever, and lost eight, even though his earned run average was a hefty 4.54. Against the Braves, though, he was Cy Young.

The first game ever played between the Milwaukee Braves and the Brooklyn Dodgers was won by Billy Loes. On May 3, 1953, in Ebbets Field, Loes pitched a three-hitter against the Braves and beat them, 4-3. On May 20 in Milwaukee, Loes hurled a six-hit complete game in beating Vern Bickford, 7-2. Then on June 4 in Brooklyn, Loes needed relief help and heavy hitting support but administered Max Surkont's first defeat after six wins, beating the portly pitcher, 10-5.

After leading the National League through most of June, the Braves began a fatal losing streak on June 21. On June 26 in Milwaukee, they lost their fifth game in a row, 4-3, to the Dodgers. The game marked Max Surkont's second loss, against nine wins, and the winner, in relief, was Billy Loes. He worked just two-thirds of an inning in the game, and he did it with one pitch—a double-play ball to Joe Adcock. The next day the Dodgers beat the Braves again, 4-3 in ten innings, dropping Milwaukee into a tie for first place, their final taste of the league's top spot that season. The winner, pitching the ninth and tenth innings and getting the victory on a Pee Wee Reese home run, was Billy Loes.

The Braves and Surkont got a small measure of revenge against Loes on July 24, knocking him out in the fifth inning of an 11-6 triumph, Surkont's last win as a Brave. By then, though, the Braves were five and a half games back and dropping out of contention. Milwaukee would never again beat Loes—he beat them twice the next year without a loss, and three times without defeat in 1955. Early in 1956 Brooklyn traded him to the Baltimore Orioles, for whom he pitched four years before returning to the National League in 1960 with the transplanted Giants in San Francisco. He beat the Braves twice more, in a one-inning relief job on June 12, 1960, and in a memorable complete game on April 30, 1961, memorable not for Loes' effort but for Willie Mays' four home runs in the game. Loes finished his career with 80 victories, twelve against Milwaukee while losing just one, and five of the wins against the Braves were recorded in a span of less than two months in 1953.

Time Capsule - May 25, 1953

"I was just sitting in the dugout, praying that it would stop raining."

—Max Surkont

Before he ate himself out of a job, Max Surkont was the most successful pitcher the Milwaukee Braves had. He had been the winning pitcher in the Braves' season opener in Cincinnati, tossing a 2-0 shutout. At the start of the doubleheader with the Redlegs on May 25 he was 5-0, with five complete-game victories. He had only a mediocre fastball, but his control was good and he was a fierce competitor.

The Braves entered the evening's games atop the National League standings, one-half game ahead of the St. Louis Cardinals. They had played, and split, a doubleheader in Chicago the day before; tonight's twin-bill at County Stadium was necessitated by Milwaukee's soggy April weather, which had rained out four games. On this night the weather was cool and drizzly, with a threat of a thunderstorm. Undeterred by the possibility of another rainout, 24,445 fans were on hand, hopeful of a double victory.

In the first game rookie Don Liddle, in his third big-league start, his first since losing to Curt Simmons' near-perfect game on May 16, shut down the Redlegs on three hits and won, 5-1. Liddle kept the game interesting by walking six batters, but the Cincinnati hitters could do nothing to drive the runners home as Liddle celebrated his 28th birthday with his second major league win. The Braves only managed five hits themselves, but a wild pickoff attempt by Reds' catcher Andy Seminick sent the winning run home, and a two-run triple by Johnny Logan in the seventh put the game out of reach.

The second game matched Surkont against the Reds' Harry Perkowski, a tall lefthander who had won twelve games in 1952.

35

This clearly was not Perkowski's night—he faced six batters but retired none, walking one and allowing five hits, including a three-run home run by Eddie Mathews. The Braves took a six-run lead in the first inning, so the only suspense was whether the rain would hold off long enough to make the game official. Surkont struck out Perkowski's relief man, Herman Wehmeier, to end the second inning, then struck out the side in the third, fanning Rocky Bridges, Bobby Adams, and Gus Bell.

In the fourth the rain began. The Redlegs, trailing by a big margin and hoping for a rainout, started to move as if in slow motion. They took their time getting into the batter's box, and they stepped out frequently to clean their spikes. Surkont kept his concentration and struck out Willard Marshall, Bob Borkowski, and Grady Hatton to run his string of whiffs to seven. With the strikeout of Hatton, Surkont tied the post-1900 major league record for consecutive strikeouts, set in 1908 by Hooks Wiltse (brother of Snake Wiltse) of the Giants and tied by Dodgers Dazzy Vance and Van Lingle Mungo, in 1924 and 1936 respectively.

Surkont led off the Braves' half of the fourth inning, with Reds' pitcher Wehmeier obviously stalling. The rain was now nearly a downpour, and after Surkont took a strike, time was called by umpire Bill Engeln. Fans scrambled for cover, then nervously waited out a 33-minute delay. After the ground crew removed the tarpaulins to let the game resume, Wehmeier casually took his warmup pitches while the crowd lustily booed his dilatory tactics. Surkont quickly struck out when play resumed, then ran to the bullpen to warm up his arm from the long delay. The Braves were retired in the fourth in a light rain, and as the Milwaukee players scurried to their positions, Andy Seminick strolled to the plate.

Working quickly, Surkont got Seminick in the hole at one ball, two strikes. His fourth pitch to the Reds' catcher was an inside fastball that veered across the plate and past Seminick for the third strike. Surkont now owned the modern strikeout record, but only if the game could be completed. Immediately following the eighth strikeout the rain fell harder, and the umpire called time. It appeared he had signalled that the game was cancelled, but after Grimm protested and the umpires conferred, play continued. Surkont retired Roy McMillan, bringing third pitcher Ernie Nevel to the plate with one more out necessary for an official ballgame. In a steady rain, Nevel was called back to the dugout after reaching the batter's box. The crowd again booed its condemnation, incensed by the continuing delay tactics of Cincinnati manager Rogers Hornsby. Finally pinch hitter Bob Marquis made the final out of the fifth inning, and the game and the record were assured.

Time was again called as the rain cascaded down, necessitating a 40-minute intermission, but now it made no difference. Stadium announcer Art Truss informed the crowd of Surkont's record, and the fans screamed their approval. After the second delay Surkont returned to the mound and completed the game, finishing with thirteen strikeouts and a 10-3 win. He had earned his sixth season victory and a place in the record books. Herman Wehmeier, Rocky Bridges, Bobby Adams, Gus Bell, Willard Marshall, Bob Borkowski, Grady Hatton, and Andy Seminick: the names may not have the luster of the men Carl Hubbell struck out consecutively in the 1934 All-Star Game (Ruth, Gehrig, Foxx, Simmons, and Cronin); nevertheless, Surkont's achievement set the major league standard between Smiling Mickey Welch's nine straight in 1884 and Tom Seaver's ten in a row in 1970.

1953 Feat of Clay

"Baseball is very big with my people. It's the only time we can get to shake a bat at a white man without starting a riot."

—Dick Gregory, *From the Back of the Bus*

On the warm, humid night of August 3, 1953, the league-leading Brooklyn Dodgers arrived at County Stadium to begin a four-game series with the second-place Braves. A boisterous, near-capacity throng of 32,739 had gathered to see their heroes do battle with the defending champions. The crowd was hopeful of witnessing their club's first home victory over the Bums, after five straight failures, and of watching their team decrease the seven and one-half game advantage the visitors currently enjoyed.

The opposing pitchers for the contest were Brooklyn's Russ Meyer, a ten-game winner already boasting three wins against Milwaukee, and the Braves' newest starter, Lew Burdette, 8-1 on the season, starting just his third game since being promoted from the bullpen eight days before in Brooklyn. On this night both pitchers were sharp; through six innings the game was scoreless. Then in the top of the seventh, with runners on first and second, Meyer bounced a ball up the middle off Jack Dittmer's glove, scoring pinch runner Don Thompson from second and giving the Dodgers the lead.

Meyer retired the first two batters in the bottom of the seventh. Then with one strike on Del Crandall, the game was delayed by rain. After play resumed, the Braves failed to score.

In the top of the eighth, Duke Snider led off with a home run into the centerfield bullpen. Burdette retired Gil Hodges, bringing catcher Roy Campanella to the plate. Burdette threw a pitch in the vicinity of the batter's head, and Campanella hit the dirt. Very shortly another high inside pitch sent the Dodger backstop

Milwaukee Journal Photo

Dodger Roy Campanella, after being beaned

sprawling. Obviously shaken, Campanella then struck out. It was one of baseball's time-honored traditions—a frustrated pitcher venting his anger after a home run by playing "chin music" on a subsequent hitter. The national pastime was often spiced with moments of brutality and intimidation.

This one, however, had deeper implications. Roy Campanella was a baseball pioneer, the second black ballplayer (" Negro" at that time) in the National League. His roommate, Jackie Robinson, had been the first major league player to "break the color line" in 1947. The civil rights movement had not yet been born; the Supreme Court had not yet rendered its decision in Brown vs. Topeka Board of Education; Martin Luther King, Jr., had not yet become pastor of the Dexter Avenue Baptist Church in Montgomery. When Roy Campanella was "dusted" by Burdette, Campanella's perception of the event involved more than baseball ritual. It included his recollection of angry words between Burdette and Robinson in Boston in September, 1952, and further words and menacing gestures between the two just eight days previous in Brooklyn.

After he struck out, the enraged Campanella charged toward Burdette, bat in hand. Both dugouts emptied onto the field. Carl Furillo managed to wrestle the bat away from Campanella as players from both teams restrained the irate catcher. During the fracas heated words were exchanged—according to Jackie Robinson, Burdette called Campanella "a dirty nigger." Eventually order was restored and the game continued. When Campanella returned to his position for the bottom of the eighth, he was greeted by cushions and other objects hurled by local partisans.

By now the game was nearly anticlimactic. After two Milwaukee batters were retired, the game was halted by rain again. The downpour abated after a short time, but by now the field, especially the outfield, was a quagmire. Braves President Lou Perini walked onto the field, signalled the ground crew, and the game was over—called because of rain. Snider's home run was washed away, and the final score read Brooklyn 1, Milwaukee 0.

The bitterness between the teams, of course, was not so easily expunged. Two days short of a year later, in Ebbets Field, the day after Joe Adcock hit four home runs and a double, Dodger Russ Meyer made Adcock hit the dirt in the third inning. In the fourth Clem Labine threw a high pitch behind Adcock, striking him solidly on the head and knocking him down. In the ensuing near-brawl, the principal antagonists were Burdette, Mathews, and Robinson. No blows were struck, but neither were any friendships cemented. Major league baseball was still coming to grips with racial diversity just six years after Jackie Robinson created it. In 1953 only three National League teams had ever had a black player on their roster—the Dodgers, the Giants, and the Braves. For the Philadelphia Phillies, desegregation was still five years in the future.

Time Capsule - August 1, 1953

"It probably could have been called either way, but as long as he was safe, he had to get a hit."

—Warren Spahn

No accomplishment in baseball is so revered as the perfect game—one pitcher retiring each batter to face him during nine innings. From the creation of the National League in 1876 until the matriculation of the Milwaukee Braves in 1953, only two N.L. pitchers, Lee Richmond and Monte Ward, had accomplished that lofty task—each of them born before the Civil War, and each performing the feat during baseball's age of reptiles, in 1880, pitching for the teams from Worcester and Providence, respectively. In 1953, within a span of two and a half months, fans at County Stadium twice came within a whisker of witnessing a perfect game. On May 16 Curt Simmons of the Phillies allowed a leadoff single to Billy Bruton, then retired 27 batters in a row. On August 1 it was Warren Spahn's turn to flirt with perfection.

The Braves had ended July with a Friday night doubleheader against Philadelphia, designated Sid Gordon Night in honor of the veteran leftfielder. The third-place Phillies had beaten the local favorites in the opener behind Robin Roberts, who won his league-leading eighteenth game. In the nightcap Max Surkont pitched shutout ball for ten innings (his last strong performance with the Braves) but could not win; his teammates could not score either, and after ten innings the game was rained out. The loss and tie left the Braves eight games behind the leading Dodgers.

Spahn entered Saturday's ballgame with a 13-4 record after shutting out the Giants, 13-0, in his previous outing, his 30th career shutout. Against the Phillies he breezed through the first

41

inning by setting down the side in order. His first victim was Eddie Waitkus, a singles-hitting first baseman who in June of 1949 had been shot by a deranged female admirer but who had recovered to help lead the Phillies' "Whiz Kids" to the 1950 pennant. Next Spahn retired speedy centerfielder Richie Ashburn, then got rightfielder Johnny Wyrostek.

In their half the Braves produced the only run Spahn would need this day. Jim Pendleton, ordinarily a reserve outfielder but playing this day at shortstop, singled to left with one out, then scored on Andy Pafko's double to right with two out. Spahn retired the side in order in the second, but two of the three hard-hit balls the Phillies would manage occurred in this inning. Powerful Del Ennis led off with a high fly to Sid Gordon in deep left, and the next batter, Granny Hamner, hit a long fly that Bruton snagged on the warning track in center. Spahn then got Stan Lopata for the third out. In the third inning he put down Puddin' Head Jones, Ted Kazanski, and pitcher Jim Konstanty consecutively.

The Braves padded their lead in the bottom of the third. Bruton led off with a single and moved to third on Pendleton's double. Mathews struck out, but Pafko, batting clean-up for the first time since his days with the Cubs, delivered a single to drive in both runners and make it 3-0 for Milwaukee. In the next inning Spahn sent in a run with a drive off the rightfield fence, and in the eighth Mathews produced the Braves' final run with a home run, his 33rd, over the centerfield fence. The key play of the game, however, was not produced by the Braves' offense—it occurred with the Phillies at bat in the fourth. In fact, it could be argued that the key play of this afternoon's game had occurred the night before.

In Friday night's second game, Milwaukee shortstop Johnny Logan had injured his hand while putting a tag on Richie Ashburn at second base. Logan was replaced on Saturday by Jim Pendleton, a rookie outfielder obtained from the Dodgers' farm system in the four-team deal that brought Joe Adcock to Milwaukee. Pendleton had played shortstop in the minors but never before in the majors. His lack of experience at that position became significant when, with one out in the fourth, Ashburn hit a high bouncing ball to shortstop. Pendleton fielded the ball cleanly but seemed to have trouble getting the ball out of his glove and making the throw. On a very close play at first, Ashburn was called safe. First baseman Adcock argued the call, but it stood. With Spahn pitching well and leading 3-0, the play appeared inconsequential, but it became important when Spahn retired the next seventeen batters. Ashburn was the only Phillie of the game to reach base.

"The play was very close," first base umpire Larry Goetz said afterwards. "Pendleton hesitated just a little too long before he threw to first." If regular shortstop Logan had been playing, Ashburn would very likely have been out. Logan was an experienced shortstop and in fact led National League shortstops in fielding percentage in 1953.

Spahn's masterpiece was his finest of the season, if not his career. The Philadelphia team he handled with ease was a first division team, one that had arrived in Milwaukee boasting five .300 hitters. Spahn's performance surpassed his effort of June 23 when, despite pitching a two-hitter and striking out twelve, he was defeated by the Pittsburgh Pirates, 1-0, also at County Stadium. And in 1951 he had hurled a one-hitter against St. Louis, losing his no-hit bid on a bloop single in the seventh by Cardinal pitcher Alpha Brazle.

With the victory the Braves stayed eight games out of first place and moved two games ahead of the Phillies. Spahn's shutout was the Milwaukee pitching staff's fifth in its past seven games, beginning with Spahn's whitewash of the Giants. In a 64-inning span, the Braves blanked their opponents in 60 of them. And of Spahn's brilliant near-perfect game, the worst that can be said is that it merely postponed his baseball immortality.

Time Capsule - August 30, 1953

"It tops any home run hitting in my experience in the big leagues."

—Charlie Grimm

The Braves' month of August, 1953, began with the finest display of pitching their young franchise had produced— Warren Spahn's near-perfect game. The team's month ended with the greatest display of home run hitting the National League had ever seen—eight Milwaukee homers in one game, twelve homers in a doubleheader, and a pair of lopsided victories, 19-4 and 11-5.

Trailing Brooklyn by ten and a half games, the second-place Braves visited the Pirates in cavernous Forbes Field for a one-day, two-game final season appearance. The home club was convincingly mired in the slough of last place, 51 and 1/2 games behind the Dodgers and twelve and a half behind the seventh-place Chicago Cubs. The Pirates had lost their previous seven games and had earned their cellar residency by merit. They not only had the worst hitting team in the league, but they also had the league's worst pitching staff. This doubleheader would once again clearly demonstrate that fact.

The starting pitchers in the first game were a study in contrasts. Johnny Antonelli of the Braves was a 23-year-old southpaw; Johnny Lindell of the Pirates was a righthander pitching on his 37th birthday. Antonelli was a rising star, a youngster returning to baseball after two years of military service who made the big leagues at 18 and never played in the minors; until this season Lindell had not pitched in the majors since 1942, having broken in as a pitcher with the Yankees, been converted to the outfield for New York for nine years, then been farmed out to the minors for two years. He had returned as a pitcher this year with

44

the Pirates but was destined to be peddled to the Phillies before the season ended. Antonelli had good control and one of the lowest earned run averages in the league; Lindell was on his way to leading the league in bases on balls, and he was allowing about five runs per nine innings. Antonelli was a weak hitter, having never hit his weight; Lindell was a very good hitter who in 1944 hit .300 with eighteen home runs and 103 RBI's, who in 1947 tied the batting record for a seven-game World Series by hitting .500, and who in this game got a hit and drove in a run in his only at-bat. Antonelli would pitch a complete game victory this day; Lindell was in the showers by the fourth inning.

Actually the Braves began their onslaught slowly. They did not score until the second inning, and they did not hit a home run until the third when Eddie Mathews hit a solo shot to put Milwaukee ahead by two. The Pirates got one back in the third, but in the fourth the Braves got rough. Jim Pendleton, subbing in rightfield because of Andy Pafko's injured ankle, led off with a

Mathews scores behind leaping catcher Joe Garagiola, May 14, 1953.

home run that left Forbes Field entirely. The Braves quickly scored two more runs and chased Lindell before he could get anyone else out. The Pirates summoned a low-overhead pitcher named Robert Hall from the bullpen.

Hall got the Pirates through the inning without further damage, but in the fifth he gave up a run, then sealed his own fate with an error leading to a three-run homer by Johnny Logan. Jim Waugh replaced Hall in the sixth; he gave up back- to-back home runs by Del Crandall and Pendleton, then stayed around long enough to give up a three-run blast by Pendleton in the seventh. Pendleton had entered the game with just one major league home run, but using a bat borrowed from fellow bench-warmer Bob Thorpe, Pendleton became the second rookie in league history to hit three home runs in a game (the first had been Eddie Mathews in 1952). In the process he also drove in five runs and scored five. Pendleton could have established further records if his long fly to center in the ninth had been pulled to left.

With the Braves leading 15-1, the Pirates scored twice in the last of the seventh. Apparently insulted, Milwaukee completed its barrage against new pitcher Roger Bowman in the eighth with a leadoff home run by Jack Dittmer, then a three- run blow by Mathews, his second round-tripper of the game. When the dust had settled, Antonelli and the Tribe had a 19-4 victory, achieved with twenty hits, eight walks, and two Pirate errors. The score might have been more lopsided, but the Braves left eight runners stranded.

The Braves sent Bob Buhl to the mound in the second game to oppose Paul La Palme. Johnny Logan staked Buhl to a 1-0 lead with a first-inning home run, but this time the Pirates fought back. They worked Buhl over for five runs on eight singles, four walks, and a home run by second baseman Johnny O'Brien, half of Pittsburgh's twin-brother doubleplay combination. When re- liever Don Liddle finally came to Buhl's rescue in the fifth, the Pirates were ahead, 5-4, despite another Mathews home run in the third. The Bucs still led by that score going into the seventh inning.

La Palme's fielding support (the Pirates also had the league's worst fielding average) failed him in the seventh. Pendleton singled, Sid Gordon singled, and Eddie O'Brien, the shortstop twin, booted Dittmer's grounder, allowing Pendleton to tie the score. Liddle and pinch hitter Crandall were retired, but Logan delivered a two-run triple, and Mathews singled him home. Joe Adcock climaxed the inning with a patented Adcock drive to the deepest part of centerfield. The ball landed at the base of the wall,

46

and Adcock lumbered home with his second inside-the-park homer of the year.

Sid Gordon administered the coup de grace in the eighth with a solo home run, making the final score 11-5. Gordon's homer gave the Braves twelve for the day, a new league record, and also brought the Braves' total bases for the two games to 71, seven more than the previous doubleheader record set by the Pirates in 1922. Forty-seven of those total bases were produced in the first game. Another record was established by Ed Mathews, whose three homers gave him 28 for the year in opponents' ballparks, bettering Ralph Kiner's old mark of 25. Mathews also extended his season home run total to 43, one fewer than Babe Ruth hit in an equal number of games in 1927, the year he hit 60.

Pirate manager Fred Haney summed up the day, calling it "the greatest demonstration of power I ever saw."

Milwaukee Journal Photo

Milwaukee Journal's Sam Levy, Manager Charlie Grimm, Walker Cooper, Sid Gordon, and Journal sports editor Russ Lynch at spring training, 1953

1953 Swan Songs

"No one is a pull hitter in the first year of marriage."

—Walker Cooper, 1945

Thirty-two ballplayers wore the tomahawk-fronted uniform of the Milwaukee Braves in the initial season. Every one, in the glossy eyes of the fans, was a star. Sure, some were better pitchers or better hitters than others, but each Brave was a celebrity. If you saw one on the street or received an autograph from one, his batting average or fielding percentage meant little; if he wore a Braves uniform, he was a hero. These were the Milwaukee Braves—the Originals.

More than a third of the original players were gone before the start of the 1954 schedule. After that they departed gradually, one or two at a time, over the next dozen years. The community felt the loss of each of them.

Some in the first year barely had time to say hello, much less establish loyalties. Pitcher Dick Donovan was with the team for the first week and a half but never got into a ballgame. Paul Burris appeared twice in a catcher's mask, batted once, and was gone. Billy Klaus appeared twice as a pinch hitter, the second time batting for Warren Spahn in St. Louis in the season's fifth game. He hit into a force play in the fifth inning, scored a run in Spahn's 9-4 loss, then vanished from the Milwaukee roster forever without ever playing at County Stadium. Pitcher Virgil Jester had a similar Milwaukee Braves career, pitching twice in relief, one inning each time, both times on the road. He bid farewell on April 23 at Wrigley Field, pitching the final inning in a 6-2 loss for Vern Bickford. Jester allowed a walk and two singles, the latter by Eddie Miksis scoring the final two runs of the day.

"The Originals": 1. Ed Mathews 2. Dick Donovan 3. Andy Pafko 4. Bob Buhl 5. Vern Bickford 6. Billy Bruton 7. Del Crandall
8. Don Liddle 9. Charlie Grimm 10. Dave Jolly 11. Sam Jethroe 12. George Crowe 13. Coach John Cooney 14. Murray Wall
15. Max Surkont 16. Johnny Logan 17. Joe Adcock 18. Sibby Sisti 19. Sid Gordon 20. Warren Spahn 21. Coach Bucky Walters
22. Virgil Jester

On Friday night, July 31, a hometown crowd of 29,802 turned out to fete Sid Gordon, pushing home attendance over the million mark. The fans also witnessed the last Braves' pitching performance by Dave Cole, whose record was 0-1 in ten games, all in relief. Cole pitched the ninth inning of a 5-1 loss to Robin Roberts and the Phillies, giving up a hit and a walk but no runs.

The Braves lost a Labor Day doubleheader to the Cubs in Chicago. In the nightcap, Vern Bickford pitched for the last time with the Braves as his club lost, 6-4. Bickford had been the workhorse of the National League in 1950 when he led in innings pitched, won nineteen games, and pitched a no-hitter against the Dodgers. In 1953, however, he worked just 58 innings, winning two games and losing five. In his final appearance he relieved loser Jim Wilson in the third inning, allowing no runs on no hits and one walk before yielding to a pinch hitter in the visitors' fifth. On May 6, 1960, Bickford died of cancer at the age of 39, the first of the Braves' Originals to meet his death.

On September 12 Charlie Dressen's Dodgers beat the Braves at County Stadium, 5-2, clinching the pennant with the victory. In that game Walker Cooper, the well-traveled 38-year-old backstop, played his final innings as a Brave, handling the entire game behind the plate. Cooper went hitless in three official trips but drew Carl Erskine's only base on balls and scored the Braves' first run after reaching on a Billy Cox error in the second inning.

In that same game rotund Max Surkont, the pride of Milwaukee's Polish community, made his valedictory appearance. Surkont had achieved nine victories by June 16, but his next two wins took over five weeks, and after July 24 he never won again for the Braves. In his last mound chore, he relieved Bob Buhl with two out in the sixth and retired the only four batters he faced, giving way to pinch hitter Harry Hanebrink in the seventh. The day after Christmas, 1953, the portly Pole was traded to the Pirates in the Danny O'Connell deal.

The next Original Brave to take his leave was 23-year-old Johnny Antonelli. On September 20 Charlie Grimm's team closed out its home schedule with a doubleheader against the Redlegs; the starting, and losing, pitcher in game one was Antonelli. He entered the game with a 12-11 record, the mediocrity of which betrays an earned run average barely over 3.00. For five innings against Cincinnati he led 1-0 on a run he scored himself after singling in the third. In the visitors' sixth, though, a two-run homer by Jim Greengrass gave them a 2-1 lead, and two more Redleg runs in the seventh brought Grimm out of the dugout. To a resounding chorus of boos, Grimm replaced Anto-

50

nelli with Dave Jolly, who promptly gave up a single and the fifth run chargeable to Antonelli. The next time the young southpaw pitched, he was in the employ of the New York Giants, whom he led to the 1954 pennant and the World Series championship.

[Antonelli, unique among Milwaukee Braves originals, performed a reprised swan song on September 4, 1961. After being repurchased from Cleveland on the Fourth of July that year, Antonelli won one game, losing none, in nine games with the Braves. He concluded his Milwaukee rebirth (and his career) in a two-inning relief job on Labor Day, working a scoreless seventh inning and allowing a run-scoring triple by Ron Santo in the last of the eighth in a 6-2 loss to the Cubs.]

On September 23 in St. Louis, a familiar figure returned to the starting lineup after a sixteen-day absence. Sid Gordon took his regular place in left field for the last time with Milwaukee. He went hitless in his first two tries, but in the sixth inning he singled with two on and one out to tie the game at 1-1. Billy Bruton pinch ran for Gordon, and he was finished as a Brave. Two batters later Del Crandall singled in the lead run, and Warren Spahn eventually won his 22nd game of the year.

In the penultimate game of the Braves' first Milwaukee campaign, on September 26 in Cincinnati's Crosley Field, little Don Liddle pitched his last innings as a Milwaukeean, relieving in the sixth inning after the Braves had scored four runs to tie the ballgame, 6-6. He shut the Redlegs out in the sixth and seventh, but in the eighth he was not so fortunate. With runners on second and third and two out, Gus Bell hit a long drive into deep left center. Bob Thorpe, the leftfielder, got his glove on the ball but could not hold it. It was scored as a double, and two runs scored. A subsequent walk and another double added two more runs, and the four-run inning propelled the Redlegs to a 10-7 victory and pinned a sixth loss, against seven wins, on Don Liddle. As consolation he was traded to the Giants in the Bobby Thomson deal, and the following season he earned a victory in the World Series.

Finally, on September 27 in Cincinnati, Warren Spahn concluded Milwaukee's maiden voyage in the National League by beating the Redlegs, 8-2. He was assisted in no small measure by two ballplayers making their last contributions as Braves. The first was outfielder Bob Thorpe, who doubled in two runs in the fourth inning and singled home another in the fifth. The other player was catcher Ebba St. Claire who, although hitless in four at-bats (he had homered the day before), caught a good game and helped Spahn record his 23rd victory, a career high.

51

1954

"I've never seen the likes of the spirit on this ballclub. It was just like my 1935 title team all over again."

—Charlie Grimm

Between the 1953 and 1954 seasons, the Milwaukee front office made a number of deals that they thought would elevate the Braves from contenders to pennant winners. Some were minor: they released catcher Walker Cooper, sold pitcher Vern Bickford to the fledgling Baltimore Orioles, bought first baseman-outfielder George "Catfish" Metkovich from the Cubs, and traded pitcher Dave Cole to the Cubs for shortstop Roy Smalley. These were low/no-impact moves, but two others were important.

On the day after Christmas, the Braves sent six players plus some cash to the Pittsburgh Pirates for infielder Danny O'Connell, a versatile if unspectacular fielder with a .293 batting average in a year and a half in the big leagues. O'Connell had played mostly third base in Pittsburgh, but Milwaukee wanted him to replace Jack Dittmer at second. In exchange the Braves gave up relatively little. They sent now-corpulent Max Surkont, popular but clearly over the hill, and 36-year-old Sid Gordon, still spry but on the decline, along with four minor-leaguers—former speedster Sam Jethroe, destined to bat one more time in the majors; Larry Lassalle, who never made the majors; pitcher Fred Waters, who would win two major league games; and pitcher Curt Raydon, who finally reached the majors four years later and lasted one season. It was a good trade for Milwaukee, despite the fact that O'Connell would be a disappointment and would pay dividends mainly by being traded away in 1957. But that is another story.

The other major trade, on February 1, 1954, was a deal that Braves' officials expected would result in a pennant. They were right, but unfortunately the pennant belonged to the New York Giants. The Braves obtained obscure catcher Sam Calderone along with the "Staten Island Scot," Bobby Thomson, the hero of the 1951 playoff and propelling force behind the "shot heard 'round the world," a line drive that could have been a home run only in the Polo Grounds but which earned Thomson baseball immortality. The Braves coveted Thomson's long-ball hitting as a substitute and then some for the departed Sid Gordon in leftfield. The slugging Glaswegian was 30 years old but had averaged 25 home runs and 94 RBI's for the previous seven seasons. His righthanded power figured to be a perfect complement to the lefthanded muscle of Eddie Mathews.

Of course Thomson did not come cheap. The Braves had to give up quality to get quality, and what they gave up was a brace of lefthanded pitchers, Don Liddle and Johnny Antonelli, plus throw-ins Ebba St. Claire and Billy Klaus. Liddle was to win nineteen games and lose just eight during the next two years with the Giants, but it was Antonelli who turned out to be the critical factor. He had been part of the Braves' regular rotation in 1953, finishing 12-12 but with the fifth-best earned run average in the league, 3.18. He had pitched in the majors at 18 and now, at 24, was maturing into a very capable starting pitcher—so capable that in 1954 he would win 21 games while losing only 7, pacing the National League in winning percentage and ERA (2.30) and leading the Giants to a World Series sweep.

And Bobby Thomson? He broke his ankle in spring training on March 13. (Lovers of irony will note that Thomson's accident occurred exactly one year after President Lou Perini announced he would move the Braves to Milwaukee—and in St. Petersburg, where in March, 1953, National League owners voted to approve the shift.) Thomson would not return to the lineup until August 22 and would not start in the outfield until August 24.

Even with Thomson unavailable, though, the Braves had reasons for optimism, not the least of which was highly-touted rookie Henry Aaron, who had begun in the minors as a cross-handed-hitting infielder but was now being groomed for Thomson's intended spot in leftfield. They also brought up six-foot eight-inch Gene Conley, a pro basketball player with the Boston Celtics during the winter, and baseball's Minor League Player of the Year in 1951 and 1953. In addition to roster changes, the Braves had increased their seating capacity at County Stadium to 43,340 with two grandstand extensions and had planted trees ("Perini's Woods") beyond the centerfield fence to provide a better hitting background.

*Braves' opening day lineup, sans pitcher, 1954: Bruton, O'Connell,
Mathews, Pafko, Aaron, Adcock, Logan, Crandall*

As it turned out, Thomson's disabling injury was only the
beginning of a season-long series of mishaps which would hinder
and ultimately defeat the Braves. In fact, the Braves were able to
start their intended lineup in just four games all season—the first
time being on September 4. A week after Thomson was hurt, new
team captain Del Crandall sprained his ankle, and although he
was able to play most of the time, he was bothered by the injury
for half the season. On opening day in Cincinnati, Andy Pafko,
after hitting three doubles, was beaned by Joe Nuxhall, had to be
hospitalized overnight, and was out of the lineup for ten days.
Five days after Pafko was beaned, Billy Bruton contracted a virus
severe enough to keep him out of action for eleven days. On
August 22 Eddie Mathews was hit on the left hand by a pitch
from Hal Jeffcoat of the Cubs; Mathews missed the next two
weeks, returned for four days, then was struck on the ankle by a
line drive and limped the rest of the season. On September 5
Henry Aaron slid into a base and broke his ankle. Finally on

September 11, Joe Adcock was struck on the right wrist by a Don Newcombe pitch and missed the rest of the year.

Partially because of the injuries and partially because of inconsistent pitching, the Braves had a horrible April, winning five, losing eight, and ending the month in seventh place. Bob Buhl started four games in April, including the opener in Cincinnati, and failed to win a game. (Buhl, in fact, was 0-7 at the All-Star break. He had pitched winter ball in Puerto Rico and had lost his fastball.) The Braves did win the home opener in a game reminiscent of 1953—Spahn threw a complete game, and Bruton scored the winning run in the eleventh inning. Three days later, though, Pafko and Bruton were both out, and the results were disastrous. Before Bruton returned on May 4, the Braves had lost eight of eleven.

The first half of May was not much of an improvement over April. Milwaukee began the month by losing to the Phillies on a Johnny Logan error with two out in the tenth inning. The next two days their games with the Brooklyn Dodgers were postponed by rain and cold, and as they sat idle, they slipped into last place in the National League. On May 4 Bruton returned and Spahn struck out twelve as the Braves escaped the cellar by beating the Pirates in a game delayed eleven minutes by a snow shower. The next night Gene Conley won his first major league game, and the following afternoon Lew Burdette blanked Pittsburgh as the Braves climbed to fifth place. During the next week and a half they alternately played well and poorly, losing two of three to the Cubs, winning a pair from the Dodgers on a Conley shutout and a Burdette one-hitter, but losing two straight to the perpetually pathetic Pirates. After splitting a doubleheader in New York's Polo Grounds, the Braves arrived in Philadelphia in sixth place with a record of 13-14.

Milwaukee took two straight from the Phillies behind lefties Chet Nichols and Warren Spahn, then moved on to Chicago and swept a five-game series from the Cubs, including doubleheader sweeps on May 22 and 23. The hitting star of the last three games was former Cub Andy Pafko, and his clutch hitting boosted the Braves into a first-place tie with Brooklyn. (Pafko had been obtained from the Dodgers two months before the Milwaukee franchise was born, in exchange for cash and a second baseman named Roy Hartsfield, who never again appeared in a major league game after the Pafko trade.) Next it was on to Cincinnati, where Spahn and Conley extended the winning streak.

When the Braves arrived at the Milwaukee Road train station on May 27, after a sixteen-game road trip, a boisterous crowd of more than 2000 was on hand to greet them. The Braves had left town on May 9 in seventh place; they returned in first, leading by a game and a half and enjoying a nine-game winning streak with a seventeen-game homestand ahead. In the first game of the home stay the local heroes rallied for two runs after two were out in the twelfth inning to rescue a 3-2 win for Burdette, extending the winning streak to ten.

The good times, however, ended abruptly the next night. Despite the largest crowd yet at County Stadium (40,001), the Braves were hammered 12-7 by the St. Louis Cardinals. The Cards beat them again the next day, and when a doubleheader with the Reds was rained out, May ended with the Braves protecting a slim one-game lead and the Dodgers coming to town.

The Dodgers won the series opener behind Russ "The Mad Monk" Meyer, 2-0, as Buhl lost his fourth game without a victory. The next night, in a rain-soaked, twice-delayed, five-inning contest that gave the 37,044 diehards a little of everything except good baseball, the visiting Bums scored five times in the last (fifth) inning to edge Milwaukee, 7-6, and nudge them gently but, for the season, permanently out of first place. Mathews clubbed a grand slam in the game, as he did four games later against the Pirates, as did Joe Adcock two days later against the Giants, but interestingly, the Braves lost all three of those games. After the Dodgers left town, Charlie Grimm's charges split a four-game series with the Pirates and lost four straight to the Giants. They finally gained some measure of respectability by taking three from the Phillies, including a shutout by Burdette and a no-hitter by Jim Wilson [see Time Capsule] before going on the road. The Braves had arrived home with a one and one-half game lead; they left tied for third, four and a half out.

In the next four weeks before the All-Star break, the Braves sank almost out of sight. They lost seventeen, ten by one run, while winning just thirteen, and the All-Star game found them with a record of 41-41, in fourth place, fifteen games out of first. The brilliant pitching of the previous season had become inconsistent, often ineffective. Of the five Braves' starters from 1953, Antonelli and Surkont were gone through trades, and at All-Star time, Spahn was 8-10, Burdette was 7-9, and Buhl was 0-7. It seemed somehow fitting when, in the National League's 11-9 All-Star loss, Spahn faced six batters and retired just one, and Conley was the losing pitcher.

Despite the Braves' lack of success on the field, however, fan support only increased. Following the All-Star game the Braves returned to County Stadium on July 14 for a four-day, five-game

56

series with the Dodgers. The series attracted 160,131 delirious fans, oblivious to the fact that their team was running a distant fourth in the pennant chase. A doubleheader on July 15 established a new stadium record crowd of 43,633, a record that lasted eight days until 45,056 paid to watch the Braves play (and beat) the Giants. That Giant series set a new three-game attendance mark of 127,103. Win or lose, the Braves continued to be the hottest ticket in town.

The Dodger series after the All-Star game, in which the Braves won three of five, featured two noteworthy events, one local, one national. Before the record crowd on July 15, the Braves swept a doubleheader, winning 2-0 and 9-8, but the victory in the nightcap was remarkable in that it was achieved with the greatest comeback any Milwaukee Braves team would ever make [see Time Capsule]. The other occasion, obscure now but quietly meaningful then, was the game on Saturday, July 17, when for the first time in major league history, a team (the Dodgers) fielded a

Hank Aaron, Charlie White, and Billy Bruton with their spring training hostess

57

lineup containing more black players (called Negroes then) than white players: Junior Gilliam, Jackie Robinson, Sandy Amoros, Roy Campanella, and Don Newcombe.

On July 22, in fifth place and fifteen and a half games back, the Braves began another winning streak. First they beat the Phillies behind Burdette and a Mathews home run. Then they swept three from the Giants: Buhl won for the second time, with the winning hit delivered in the ninth by still-lame pinch hitter Bobby Thomson; Spahn evened his record at 10-10 and Mathews homered for the fourth game in a row; and Dave Jolly won in relief, with Pafko supplying the fireworks. Next Conley, Burdette, and Chet Nichols took turns beating Pittsburgh, after which the Braves moved on to Brooklyn's Ebbets Field for four games.

The series opener on July 30 saw home runs by Joe Adcock and Danny O'Connell and eight and a third innings of relief pitching from Ernie Johnson as Milwaukee won, 9-3. The next afternoon the Braves exploded. The Dodgers scored seven runs, but they never had a chance. Andy Pafko hit a home run, Eddie Mathews smashed two, and Joe Adcock rewrote the record book with four home runs and a double as the Braves won their ninth straight, 15-7 [see Time Capsule]. The next day the Braves pummeled the Dodgers again, 14-6, getting nineteen hits including three home runs, but Adcock paid the price—he was struck on the head by a Clem Labine pitch, nearly triggering a melee. The near-fight was a renewal of hostilities between the two teams. Fortunately Adcock was unhurt; a serious injury might have led to open warfare.

The next day the Dodgers ended the Braves' streak at ten games, edging Milwaukee 2-1 in thirteen innings. The Braves then split two games in Philadelphia before traveling to the Polo Grounds to meet the league-leading Giants. They immediately began a new win streak, beating former teammate Johnny Anto-nelli while sweeping New York in three games behind their "big three," Conley, Burdette, and Spahn. The Braves added three wins in St. Louis, then returned home to sweep Chicago in a three-game set attended by a record 129,588. Their streak was ended at nine games by St. Louis, but the most recent surge gave the Braves 20 wins in 22 games. During that span, from July 22 through August 15, Milwaukee climbed from fifth place, fifteen and a half out, to third, three and a half games out.

On Thursday afternoon, August 19, a Ladies' Day crowd of 50,024, the largest crowd that would ever watch the Braves play in County Stadium, saw the Braves lose to the Cardinals, beginning a modest three-game losing streak. They halted that brief slide by beating the Cubs as Bobby Thomson hit a two-run homer in his first time in the Braves' lineup other than pinch-hitting. They also won their next three against the Phillies. On August 27 the Giants visited Milwaukee and drew a new record paid attendance, 46,944, as Sal Maglie outdueled Gene Conley. The next day Spahn beat the Giants with the help of a four-run, eighth-inning rally during which Spahn contributed a two-run single. On Sunday, August 29, the Dodgers began their final Milwaukee appearance of the season.

The series opened with a doubleheader. A crowd of 45,922 pushed the Braves beyond the league attendance record they had set in 1953. The on-field news was not so cheerful, however, as Brooklyn took both games, the first with eight runs in the eleventh to swamp the Braves, 12-4, the second by an 11-4 margin. The next night, though, the Braves started a new streak by coming from behind to beat the Dodgers on Thomson's three-run homer. Conley shut out the Dodgers, 2-0, in their final

The Braves' starters, 1954: Gene Conley, Lew Burdette, Bob Buhl, Warren Spahn, and Chet Nichols

59

Milwaukee game, giving him five victories and no defeats against the defending N.L. champs. After Spahn beat the Pirates, the Braves visited Crosley Field in Cincinnati. Grimm's club won four games from the Reds, but not without cost.

The Braves won the first match, 3-2, in twelve innings on Jack Dittmer's home run, but the big story was a fight involving Johnny Logan, the Braves' pugnacious shortstop, and Redlegs Jim Greengrass and Johnny Temple. Though outnumbered, and outsized by Greengrass, Logan emerged a clear victor. The next day the Braves triumphed again, but Conley strained his back and was out for a week, and in fact would win no more in 1954. The following day the Braves took a doubleheader, 11-8 and 9-7, but again the victory was marred as Henry Aaron, after getting five straight hits, broke his ankle in the second game.

Returning to County Stadium for a Labor Day doubleheader against Chicago, the Braves pounded the Cubs twice, 13-2 and 6-1, led by Mathews' eight straight hits, including his 35th home run. The twin victory gave the Braves four wins in two days, extended their winning streak to nine, and moved them into

Milwaukee Sentinel Photo

Heading north from spring training, 1954: Bruton, White, Aaron, Jolly, Mathews, Gordon, Nichols

60

second place, just four games back of New York. The crowd of 43,207 made the Milwaukee franchise the first National League club ever to surpass the two million attendance mark. After a day off, the Braves traveled to Pittsburgh, where Spahn won his eleventh consecutive game since the All-Star break, making his record 19-10 and extending the team's victory skein to ten, their third streak of that duration. It also improved the Braves' post-All-Star record to 41 wins and 13 losses and strengthened their tenuous hold on second place ahead of their next opponent, the Brooklyn Dodgers.

In need of a strong performance, the Braves managed just one hit off Billy Loes in a much-delayed, rain-shortened contest that National League President Warren Giles decided should be called at 12:50 in the morning after just four and one half innings. The one hit by Milwaukee was a solo homer by Joe Adcock, his ninth of the year in Ebbets Field, setting a new league mark for home runs in an opponent's park, but the record offered little solace to the team. The next day, September 11, the Braves' pennant chase was effectively halted when Don Newcombe discovered a way to stop Adcock—he hit him on the wrist with a fastball and ended his season. With light-hitting Jim Pendleton already in Aaron's place in leftfield, the Braves were now forced to replace their leading hitter, Adcock, with Catfish Metkovich. The loss of offensive punch was more than the Braves could afford, especially with Mathews and Thomson playing on gimpy legs.

The Braves won two out of three games in Philadelphia and then moved to New York for three games with the leaders. Trailing by four and a half with only thirteen remaining, the Braves clearly needed a sweep—instead they were swept. They had their three mound aces ready for the Giants, but Conley lost a tough 2-1 decision, then Spahn and Burdette each lost 6-2 in a doubleheader on September 16, and the race was over. The Giants went on to win the pennant and sweep the Cleveland Indians in a World Series remembered mainly for the pinch-hitting of Dusty Rhodes and an amazing over-the-shoulder catch by Willie Mays.

And the Braves? They closed out their season by splitting their last ten games, finishing in third place behind the Giants and Dodgers, eight games out of first. Spahn won two more games to finish 21-12; Mathews hit three more home runs to finish with 40; Burdette tossed his fourth shutout and fifteenth win; and the adoring Milwaukee fans continued to pack County Stadium, totaling 2,131,388 for the season. The cry of "Wait 'til next year" echoed throughout the city that let beer make it famous.

1954 Nemesis - Robin Roberts

"Roberts just throws strikes and lets you try to hit them."

—Sid Gordon

Robin Roberts had a good fastball, even a very good fastball, but not a great fastball. His curve ball was good, not great. What was great about Robin Roberts was that he could pitch tirelessly and accurately. When Philadelphia's "Whiz Kids" won the 1950 National League pennant, the indefatigable Roberts started three games in the last five days of the season, going into extra innings in the final game and beating the Dodgers in Ebbets Field, 4-1. In the decade of the 1950's he *averaged* 301 innings per year, leading the majors in innings pitched five straight years. At the same time, in the ten years from 1951 through 1960, he was never worse than third in the league in allowing the fewest walks per nine innings, leading four times and finishing second four times. He also averaged 20 wins a season throughout the '50's despite pitching for some awful Phillies teams. He was, in fact, the Phillies' first 20-game winner since World War I. He richly deserved his election to baseball's Hall of Fame in 1976.

Considering his statistics, it would seem logical that Roberts gave the Braves trouble—and he did. From mid-August of 1951 until mid-June of 1954 Roberts beat the Braves nine times without a defeat. In the game he finally lost, on June 12, he made just two mistakes—solo home runs by Johnny Logan and Del Crandall—and even then it took Jim Wilson's no-hitter to beat him, 2-0. Roberts then won his next three starts against Milwaukee, all complete games.

With Roberts it was not just that he won, though; it was the way he won. He dominated the hitters. In his seven starts against the Braves in 1954, he experienced only one bad outing to go with six complete games. On April 29 he threw a one-hit shutout in Milwaukee, giving up only a double to Del Crandall. On June 12 he lost to Wilson's no-hitter. On July 21 a ninth-inning, two-out home run by Ed Mathews kept Roberts from a three-hit shutout. In Philadelphia on August 4 he allowed a run on back-to-back doubles by O'Connell and Mathews in the first inning, then shut out the Braves on three hits the rest of the way. His only poor effort was on August 24 when he gave up four earned runs on nine hits in six innings. That disaster raised his 1954 earned run average against Milwaukee to 1.98.

No pitcher in the league was tougher for the Braves in 1954 than Robin Roberts.

Hank Aaron pops up a Robin Roberts pitch.

1954 Feat of Clay

"It was an accident." —Jackie Robinson

Many people think Milwaukee has two seasons—July and winter. The Wisconsin climate is not that bleak, of course, but spring in Beertown is unpredictable and often miserable. In 1954 spring was both, generally cold and wet, resulting in four postponements before the end of May and numerous games played in football weather. Nevertheless, owing to a large advance sale of tickets, Braves' attendance continued to soar. On Saturday night, May 29, the first County Stadium crowd over 40,000 showed up for a game with the St. Louis Cardinals. On Wednesday night, June 2, 37,044 faithful followers, most already holding tickets, ignored the impending rain and came to watch the Braves try to cling to a tenuous hold on first place (by .004) against the second-place Dodgers. The Milwaukee club had lost three straight, losing a game and a half lead as the entire league began to bunch up in the standings. The Chicago Cubs were in seventh place, two games below .500 and just four and one half games out. Only the Pirates, thirteen games behind, had thus far refused to join the race.

Lew Burdette was pitching for the home team, opposing Brooklyn's Don Newcombe, who was struggling since returning from two years of military service. Rain began just twenty minutes after the game started, and not a gentle rain, but the umpires were oblivious. The Dodgers scored in the first, the Braves tied it in the second on a bases-loaded walk by Johnny Logan, and Brooklyn regained the lead with a run in the third. After their turn at bat time was called. The rain was now torrential. Play was suspended for ninety-one minutes, and should have been halted for the evening, but when the torrent diminished to a hard drizzle, the game was resumed.

64

Henry Aaron, still an untrusted rookie batting seventh behind Jack Dittmer, led off with a double, then scored on a double by catcher Charlie White, filling in for Del Crandall. Burdette was then hit by a pitch for the second time in the game, this time by second Brooklyn pitcher Bob Milliken, a clear sign that the Dodgers had not forgotten Burdette's knockdown pitches thrown at Roy Campanella the past August, nor the one-hitter he had hurled against them exactly three weeks previous in Ebbets Field. After Bruton was retired, Logan came to bat with men on first and second.

Logan took a strike, then fouled off Milliken's next offering. Next came ball one, then another foul, ball two, another foul, and ball three. After ball three Logan stepped out of the batter's box, picked up the resin bag, rubbed it on his bat, and returned to the plate. Umpire Lee Ballanfant, apparently having lost track of the count, signalled Logan to first base. The confused Logan knew better than to argue and trotted to first. The Dodgers, meanwhile, went berserk, surrounding Ballanfant and screaming that it was ball three. After a prolonged rhubarb the Dodgers returned to their positions and to the dugout, but several towels were tossed from the dugout in protest. With the bases loaded and the Dodger bench jockeys at full voice, Eddie Mathews belted Milliken's pitch into the rightfield stands for a grand slam home run and a 6-2 lead.

The Dodgers, who had been angry and disgusted, were now livid. Their outburst became so heated that umpire Ballanfant cleared the Brooklyn bench and banished all but the players in the lineup. After order was restored and the Braves had been retired, leftfielder Jackie Robinson strode to the plate to lead off the fifth inning, but before he could, he reopened the argument and was ejected from the game. In anger Robinson threw his bat toward the dugout. It skidded across the top of the dugout and struck two spectators, Mr. and Mrs. Peter Wolinsky, and an usher, Harry Yelvington. Robinson tried to apologize, but the crowd heaped abuse on him, and he left the field with a protective police escort.

Dick Williams batted for Robinson and lofted a pop fly into foul territory. Catcher White should have caught the ball, but he misjudged it and it landed untouched. Williams then stroked a fly to Aaron in left, but in the rain Aaron dropped it, so Williams was safe at second. Hodges singled between Burdette's legs and Williams took third. Roy Campanella struck out. Carl Furillo hit a double-play ball to Dittmer, but the second baseman booted it, Williams scored, and runners were at first and second. Billy Cox

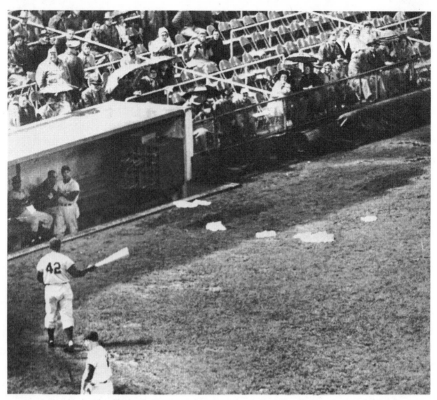

Frustrated Jackie Robinson about to throw his bat, June 2, 1954

singled to short left, Hodges held third, and the bases were loaded.

With the tying run now on first base, Wayne Belardi pinch hit for Milliken. Belardi appeared to strike out, but catcher White was unable to hold a foul tip on strike three—in fact, the ball lodged under White's mask. Belardi eventually worked Burdette for a walk, forcing in Hodges to make it 6-4. Johnny Podres ran for Belardi, and Burdette headed for the showers, replaced by Dave Jolly. Jolly got Junior Gilliam to ground to Logan, who forced Podres at second while Furillo scored to make it 6-5. Finally Pee Wee Reese capped the inning with a long double to rightcenter scoring Cox and Gilliam, and the Braves' lead had evaporated, the only thing that could on this night.

The rain continued to fall steadily, but by now it was clear the umpires, whether of their own volition or under orders, were not going to allow this game to be rescheduled. The Dodgers brought in their new pitcher, appropriately named Ben Wade. Dittmer greeted him with a single, and Aaron sacrificed. White had a chance to atone for his blunders, but he flied out harmlessly to Williams in left. Apparently in keeping with the conditions, Catfish Metkovich batted for Jolly and hit a soft fly to Snider in centerfield. With five innings complete to constitute an official ballgame, the umpire called time. It was now fifteen minutes before midnight and pouring; most of the fans had long since left; but still the game was not called off, merely delayed. Finally at 12:20 A.M., after a 35-minute wait, the game was terminated.

The Braves' front office had avoided the inconvenience and expense of 37,044 rainchecks, but the fans were subjected to a sorry exhibition, both on the field and off.

March 4, 1954: Jim Pendleton, Charlie White, Billy Bruton, Hank Aaron

Time Capsule - June 12, 1954

"I haven't pitched him much before because of the cold weather we've been having."

— Charlie Grimm

The athlete who overcomes adversity and succeeds against all odds through hard work and perseverance is one of the oldest cliches in sports. Nothing in fiction, though, could surpass the facts of Jim Wilson's life. A promising rookie pitcher with the Red Sox in 1945, Wilson was struck in the head by a vicious line drive off the bat of Detroit's Hank Greenberg. Doctors diagnosed a skull fracture and feared for his life, but he recovered and attempted a comeback. The next season he was disabled by severe recurring headaches from the blow. In 1947 he appeared ready to return, but a line drive struck and broke his leg. The following year he was on the roster of the St. Louis Browns, but a trailer accident in the pre-season crushed his hand. He went to the minor leagues, regained his health and prowess while jumping around from Toledo to Baltimore to Buffalo to Seattle, and after the 1950 season was purchased by the Boston Braves. After three undistinguished seasons he was relegated to the bench, pitching just eight and two-thirds innings in relief in the first two months of the 1954 season. Near the end of May the Braves sought waivers on him, but no one claimed him. Unable to waive him, they gave him a rare starting assignment on June 6 because of a doubleheader—he responded by shutting out the Pirates, 5-0. That job earned him another start six days later.

When Wilson left home for the ballpark on Saturday, June 12, his wife, who never went to games when he pitched, told him, "Pitch a no-hitter, and hit a homer." Neither seemed likely—he had never hit a home run in the big leagues, and his current

68

earned run average was above seven. Even winning looked doubtful—he was opposing Robin Roberts, whom the Braves had not beaten since August 14, 1951. Nevertheless he proved an obedient spouse, settling for a double at the plate but hurling the National League's first no-hit, no-run ballgame in two years as the Braves beat Roberts and the Philadelphia Phillies, 2-0.

Wilson gave no early sign that this would be a historic game. The game's first batter, Willie Jones, hit a hard bouncer into the hole toward left, but Eddie Mathews was able to spear it and throw him out. The next hitter, Richie Ashburn, poked one down the line in left that Henry Aaron caught in foul ground. Wilson then retired Earl Torgeson, and after Johnny Logan staked him to a 1-0 lead with a home run in the bottom of the first, Wilson retired slugger Del Ennis and then Granny Hamner to start the second. Smoky Burgess worked him for a base on balls, but Wilson got Johnny Wyrostek to end the inning.

Using mostly sliders and slow curves, Wilson continued to cut down Phillie hitters until Burgess managed another walk with one out in the fifth. The next hitter, Wyrostek, struck out on a hit-and-run, and Burgess was doubled up at second, Crandall to Logan. Through five innings Wilson still had not allowed a hit, and no runner had reached second base. Del Crandall padded Wilson's lead with a solo homer in the last of the fifth, and in the top of the sixth Wilson set down Bobby Morgan, Roberts, and Jones without a problem.

By the seventh inning the 28,218 fans in attendance were not only conscious of Wilson's masterpiece-in-progress but were transfixed by it. They seemed alternately to cheer wildly and to hold their breath. Every pitch took on immense importance. Even the routine seventh inning, with substitute centerfielder Danny Schell, Torgeson, and Ennis being dispatched without difficulty, made the crowd nervous. It offered nothing to match the eighth inning, though.

After Wilson disposed of Hamner to start the frame, the peripatetic Burgess, the Phils' only baserunner of the day and a .390 hitter entering the game, lofted a little popup outside of third. Mathews seemed to get a late start on the ball and failed to catch it. The doomsayers in the stands sensed impending disaster, but Burgess flied harmlessly to Aaron in left. Next came veteran outfielder Wyrostek who, before the crowd could resume normal breathing, bounced a high chopper over Wilson's head toward centerfield. To all appearances the no-hitter was lost, but Logan ranged far to his left, gloved the ball almost behind second, and threw off-balance to Joe Adcock at first in time to beat the

Lew Burdette, Jim Wilson, Charlie Grimm, and Warren Spahn, in
spring training, 1954

runner. The crowd leaped to their feet in tribute to Logan's saving play.

In the bottom of the eighth Billy Bruton singled and stole second, but Henry Aaron struck out to end the threat. No one cared, of course—the only matter of interest was Jim Wilson.

The first batter to face Wilson in the ninth was shortstop Bobby Morgan. He took a high fastball for ball one as the crowd groaned. The next pitch was inside for ball two. The fans cheered at Wilson's next offering, a fastball down the middle for strike one. The next pitch was a curve that caught the corner for strike two. On the 2-2 pitch, Morgan swung late and popped the ball to Adcock at first. There was one out, and the crowd stood and yelled.

Mel Clark, a reserve outfielder, batted for Roberts. Clark took a ball, then a strike, then ball two. Wilson seemed to be working too cautiously now, and he was falling behind the batters. The 2-1 pitch was high and inside; Clark ducked away from it. The ball,

70

however, struck his bat and caromed down the rightfield line, landing beyond first base but several feet foul. The crowd gasped, then exhaled in unison. On the next pitch Clark swung at a low-outside curve and missed. There were two outs.

The final impediment to Wilson's no-hitter was third baseman Willie "Puddin' Head" Jones, a respected clutch hitter. Still working carefully, Wilson missed inside with a curve for ball one. The next pitch was a curve that caught the corner for a strike. Next came ball two outside, then strike two on the outside corner, and ball three high and inside. On the 3-2 pitch Jones pulled a hanging curve down the leftfield line into the corner—but the ball landed foul by inches. The tension was palpable. Wilson's next pitch was a fastball that Jones fouled into the seats down the first-base side. Finally Wilson threw a slider, Jones tapped it weakly to O'Connell at second, O'Connell threw to Adcock, and Wilson's place in the record book was secure.

For a time Wilson became the biggest celebrity on the Milwaukee roster, thanks to one scintillating performance. In July he was picked for the National League All-Star team. On August 10 he would win his eighth game without a loss. That would be his last victory for the Braves, however. For the remainder of the season he would be used less frequently, and the following year he would be pitching in the American League.

Time Capsule - July 15, 1954

"I began to wonder if I'd ever win a game."

—Bob Buhl

Longtime Yankee catcher Yogi Berra, a member of baseball's Hall of Fame, is equally well-known for his colorful abuse of the English language. His most famous quotation, however, is nothing if not jejune—"The game ain't over 'til it's over." At County Stadium on Thursday night, July 15, 1954, in the second game of a doubleheader, the Milwaukee Braves proved the profundity of Berra's words. Losing 8-3 with two out in the ninth inning, the Braves rallied for an amazing 9-8 victory.

Two nights after the National League and Milwaukee's Gene Conley had lost the All-Star Game, the Braves were tied for fourth place, a distant fifteen and a half games behind the pace-setting Giants. They had lost the previous night to the Dodgers, 2-1, in twelve innings, despite great pitching by Lew Burdette. Tonight they were facing Brooklyn twice, entrusting their chances to their pitcher with the worst record (Bob Buhl, 0-7) and the one with the best record (Jim Wilson, 6-0, including a no-hitter and three shutouts). What promised to be one poorly-pitched game and one well-pitched game proved to be exactly that—but in reverse order of expectation.

Buhl began the opening game with nine starts, six relief jobs, and no wins to his credit. On this night, though, he reverted to the form he had displayed in his rookie season. He allowed just three scattered singles, although he pitched out of trouble throughout the game because of seven walks. His Dodger mound rival, Bob Milliken, pitched nearly as well, but a home run by Ed Mathews after Billy Bruton's leadoff single in the seventh condemned Milliken to defeat, 2-0. Buhl faltered in the eighth, walking Junior Gilliam and Pee Wee Reese to start the inning,

72

but he put down the meat of the Dodgers' order—Duke Snider, Gil Hodges, and Jackie Robinson—to protect his shutout victory.

In the second game Brooklyn blended three hits, a walk, and a throwing error by Andy Pafko to score three runs in th first off Wilson. The Braves got two back in their half of the inning on a walk to Bruton and Mathews' second two-run homer of the night, this one sliced to leftfield. After that Wilson and Billy Loes settled down to pitch scoreless ball until the fifth. Then a base on balls and three straight singles finished Wilson and brought on Ernie Johnson. Hodges greeted him with a single, Pafko threw the ball over Del Crandall's head, and the Dodgers were ahead 7-2.

In the last of the eighth the Braves knocked Loes out of the box—literally. With two men on and two out, Johnny Logan drilled one back at Loes, who deflected the ball into centerfield with his pitching hand. One run scored, and Loes was forced to leave with an injured little finger. Jim Hughes, the Dodger bullpen ace, came on and retired catcher Charlie White to abort the rally, and Brooklyn led 7-3 going to the ninth.

In the ninth Joey Jay, who had come on in the eighth as the third Milwaukee pitcher, gave up another run, and the Dodgers led 8-3. The crowd, or rather what was left of the record gathering of 43,633, began to pack up their belongings and guzzle their final beverages in anticipation of the ride home. Fewer than half the original number were still in the ballpark, the exodus having begun after the Brooklyn outburst in the fifth inning. Those who remained did so out of courtesy—nearly everyone assumed the game was out of reach, including the usually loyal radio announcers. The Braves were five runs down, with the pitcher leading off, against the National League's best reliever.

George "Catfish" Metkovich batted for pitcher Jay and managed a base on balls to begin the ninth. Bruton slashed a base hit, with Metkovich stopping at second. Danny O'Connell caught the Brooklyn infielders playing deep and tried to bunt for a hit, but he pushed the ball too hard and got thrown out at first as the runners advanced. Working carefully now, Hughes walked Mathews to load the bases, with clean-up hitter Henry Aaron up next. Rookie Aaron had earned the fourth spot in the order by hitting safely in ten consecutive games, raising his average to .289, but this time he fouled out and ended his evening hitless in nine tries. That left the bases loaded with two out. More fans started toward the exits, but Joe Adcock smacked a single, Metkovich and Bruton scored, and it was an 8-5 ballgame.

With the tying run now at the plate, Brooklyn manager Walt Alston yanked Hughes and brought in Erv Palica to squelch the rally. Andy Pafko, atoning for his two throwing errors, banged one off the third base bag down the leftfield line, and while Sandy Amoros ran it down, Mathews and Adcock came around and scored to make it an 8-7 game. By this time the remaining fans were incredulous and euphoric. Jim Pendleton went in to run for Pafko, representing the tying run. The next batter, Logan, lined the first pitch into leftfield for a single. Pendleton charged around third and headed for home, sliding in just ahead of a good throw by Amoros, and the game was tied. On the throw to the plate, Logan advanced to second.

With the winning run in scoring position, Charlie White was due to bat. White, the backup catcher, had entered the game in the sixth to give Crandall some rest. White was no great hitter, but Charlie Grimm's bench offered little help. Metkovich and Pendleton had already entered the game; even injured Bobby Thomson had been used as a pinch hitter for Ernie Johnson in the seventh, grounding out in his first appearance for the Braves after breaking his leg in spring training. White's batting average was a modest .250, but on this night he was Ty Cobb. After taking a ball, White bounced a seeing-eye single over second base, just out of reach of Pee Wee Reese. Gilliam ran it down in shallow center, but by that time Logan had slid (or "slud," as Dizzy Dean would have said) home with the 9-8 victory.

The win went to 18-year-old bonus baby Joey Jay, his first of the year and second without defeat in his brief career. The Braves' ninth-inning comeback would prove to be the greatest in their Milwaukee existence. It was also a lasting reminder to the County Stadium fans—"The game ain't over 'til it's over."   •

Time Capsule - July 31, 1954

"I think I'd hit 30 or 35 homers a season here if I played 77 games here [in Ebbets Field]."

—Joe Adcock

Not every boy in America grows up playing baseball. Joe Adcock grew up on a farm near Coushatta, Louisiana, and attended Louisiana State University on a basketball scholarship. His basketball coach, who was also the LSU baseball coach, introduced him to the national pastime—and the rest, as they say, is history.

If Adcock could have learned to pull the ball, he might have been the new Babe Ruth. Instead he led the league in long flies to deep center. Sometimes, of course, even deep center could not contain his prodigious blasts. In New York's Polo Grounds on April 29, 1953, he became the first player in the history of that mammoth stadium to hit a ball into the seats in center, 483 feet distant. In Brooklyn's Ebbets Field, where no such deep center existed, Adcock was a sight to behold. On July 31, 1954, he put on the greatest slugging demonstration that Brooklyn and the game of baseball had ever witnessed.

The Milwaukee Braves were hot, having won eight in a row, including a 9-3 win over the Dodgers the night before in which Adcock contributed a single, a double, and a home run. He was batting .442 for the year against Brooklyn pitchers, .467 in Ebbets Field. On the strength of their current winning streak, the Braves had moved from fifth place in the standings, fifteen and a half games behind the Giants, to third place, nine games out, and six behind second-place Brooklyn. On this sweltering Saturday afternoon, with the mercury approaching 100 degrees, Milwaukee was looking to gain some more ground.

Jim Wilson of the Braves was opposing Don Newcombe on the mound, but no pitcher was to experience success in this game. Wilson had won seven games without a loss, but he had failed to win in three of his last four starts. This afternoon Eddie Mathews staked him to a 1-0 first-inning lead with his 26th home run in the first inning, but Wilson gave it back on three hits in the home half.

In the second the Braves showed the kind of day it would be. Adcock, using a bat borrowed from teammate Charlie White because he had broken his own the night before, led off and slammed a Newcombe fastball into the seats in leftfield to regain the lead. Andy Pafko followed with a double, Johnny Logan scored Pafko with a single up the middle, and Newcombe was through for the day. Clem Labine replaced him and retired Del Crandall and Wilson, but Billy Bruton doubled into the gap in rightcenter and Logan came home for a 4-1 lead. After Labine got Danny O'Connell to fly out to retire the side, the Dodgers used a double, a hit batsman, and a single to load the bases and send Wilson on his way. Lew Burdette came on to strike out Rube Walker and get pinch-hitter Moose Moryn on a doubleplay ball, and the Braves still led by three.

Erv Palica (nee Pavliecivich) became the third Dodger pitcher, but any delusions of adequacy he may have harbored were dispelled when Mathews, the first man up in the third, blasted his 27th homer of the season into the seats in center. Palica got Aaron on a flyball to Carl Furillo in right, but Adcock crashed a double, his only non-homer of the day, and scored on Pafko's single to make it 6-1. Palica got the next two batters and, in a blaze of mound brilliance, retired Burdette, Bruton, and O'Connell in order in the fourth, the only inning of the day in which Milwaukee failed to get a hit.

The fifth inning, though, brought Palica back to earth. Mathews led off with a walk, Aaron singled to right, and Adcock slammed a three-run home run off the upper deck in leftcenter, his second four-bagger of the afternoon. Pafko popped out, but when Logan drew a base on balls, Palica was replaced by Pete Wojey, who escaped without further damage.

Don Hoak's sixth-inning home run off Burdette made the score 9-2 Braves. In the seventh, though, Milwaukee went back on offense. Aaron opened with a double to left off Wojey, then Adcock walloped his third homer of the day, and Pafko followed with another home run to make the score 12-2. The lead stood until the last of the eighth when the Dodgers showed their power and nearly made a game of it.

Brooklyn first baseman Gil Hodges opened the home eighth with his 28th home run of the season, putting him back ahead of Mathews. Sandy Amoros singled to center, Hoak grounded out, and Furillo drove Amoros home with a single. Walker then belted a home run over the scoreboard in right, making the score 12-6, and Burdette was excused for the day. Burdette, his sweat-drenched uniform a testament to six and one-third tough innings

Congratulations for slugger Joe Adcock from Del Rice

77

in the near-tropical heat, was relieved by Bob Buhl, but not for long. Buhl gave up singles to rival hurler Johnny Podres and second baseman Junior Gilliam and was quickly replaced by Dave Jolly. Jolly heightened the tension by walking Don Zimmer to load the bases, but he worked out of it by getting Shotgun Shuba to pop out and Hodges to ground out.

The moment of truth arrived in the ninth inning. The 12,263 paying customers, including a cluster of 600 fanatics from Milwaukee, were unanimous in wanting to see history made in the form of Adcock's fourth homer of the game. The big guy did not disappoint—after taking Podres' first pitch for a ball, he connected with a fastball that sailed over the wall in leftcenter field and landed deep in the record book. After that the Braves scored twice more and the Dodgers once, but it mattered not at all. The 15-7 final score was buried under the enormity of Adcock's achievement.

What Adcock had accomplished was incredible: in five times at bat, while receiving seven pitches, he had hit a double and four home runs, off four different pitchers, scored five runs, driven in seven runs, and accounted for eighteen total bases. The four home runs in one game placed him in a select category with men like Lou Gehrig and Chuck Klein; the eighteen total bases put him in a class by himself.

The immortal Babe's magic number of sixty home runs has been eclipsed, albeit with an asterisk; his unapproachable career total of 714 homers has been approached and surpassed (by Adcock's teammate). Yet even in the age of anabolic steroids and Nautilus machines, the baseball world has yet to see the equal of the awesome display of power put on by the ex-basketball player from Coushatta High School.

Time Capsule - September 22-24, 1954

"I thought two were out; that's why I ran to first."

—Bob Borkowski

The game between the Braves and the Redlegs began on Wednesday afternoon and ended on Friday. There was no rain delay. Milwaukee starter Ernie Johnson pitched eight innings and led 3-1 when reliever Warren Spahn took over; Spahn pitched the ninth inning, allowed no hits and no runs, and threw a wild pitch to win the game, but Dave Jolly got the victory. Catcher Del Crandall received credit for an unassisted doubleplay without catching the ball or tagging anyone. The game was played in Milwaukee County Stadium, but the visiting Cincinnati team stayed in a hotel in Chicago on both Wednesday and Thursday nights. Fans who watched the whole game had to buy two admissions. A few minutes after the game ended, Spahn pitched a complete game as the Braves beat the St. Louis Cardinals. It was bizarre.

Most of the game was perfectly normal, a pitchers' duel between Cincinnati rookie Corky Valentine and Ernie Johnson of the Braves. Well, it was not completely normal; Johnson was primarily a relief pitcher, but he started occasionally. He allowed just one run on five hits in eight innings, while striking out seven, but he left for a pinch-hitter losing 1-0. His adversary Valentine was brilliant through the first seven innings, allowing only a single by Jack Dittmer in the fourth and a base on balls to Danny O'Connell in the fifth. In the eighth, though, Johnny Logan singled, O'Connell singled, and Johnson's pinch-hitter, Charlie White, singled to drive Logan home with the tying run, O'Connell moving to third. Next batter Billy Bruton hit a grounder that second baseman Johnny Temple fielded. Temple had an easy

79

play at first or second but, concerned that O'Connell may try to score, faked toward third. Bruton was safe at first and the bases were loaded. Dittmer struck out, but Eddie Mathews bounced a hit up the middle to score two runs, giving Milwaukee a 3-1 lead.

Since reliever Johnson had started, it was only logical that ace starter Spahn, who had pitched a complete game victory two days before, would come in to relieve in the ninth. Spahn walked Gus Bell leading off, retired Ted Kluszewski, then walked Wally Post. Leftfielder Lloyd Merriman was due to bat next, but Bob "Bush" Borkowski was sent to pinch hit. At this point the game turned left into the Twilight Zone.

Spahn had shown indications that he had no control of his pitches by walking two of the first three batters he faced. Against Borkowski he proved he had no control. After getting two strikes on Borkowski, Spahn uncorked a wild pitch that Crandall could not knock down. Borkowski, though, had no more command of the strike zone than Spahn had of his pitches—he swung at the errant toss for strike three. Then, to prove he also had no grasp of the game situation, Borkowski ran toward first base.

If Borkowski's strikeout had been the third out, or if first base had been unoccupied, Borkowski could, under the rules of baseball, have tried to reach first base when Crandall failed to catch the pitch. In this case, Borkowski's actions were contrary to the rules. Nevertheless, when the baserunners saw the ball get past Crandall, they advanced. Crandall retrieved the ball and threw to Mathews at third, but Gus Bell beat the throw. Mathews, seeing Borkowski running to first, threw the ball there. The ball struck Borkowski and rolled into rightfield. Bell and Post both came around and scored, tying the game—or so it appeared.

Braves manager Charlie Grimm ran screaming from the dugout. He descended on umpire Hal Dixon and loudly pleaded his case. After a ten-minute recess, the umpires rendered their decision: Borkowski had been out on strikes for the second out, and when he ran to first illegally, it constituted interference. Lead runner Bell was therefore declared out, making three outs, and the game was over. The Braves had won, 3-1. On a strikeout the catcher receives credit for a putout, and since the interference was part of the same play, Crandall was credited with an unassisted doubleplay. Ernie Johnson was the winning pitcher, Valentine was the loser, and Redlegs' manager Birdie Tebbetts was left to argue after the fact.

Predictably, Tebbetts announced he was protesting the outcome of the game. Unpredictably, the protest was upheld the following afternoon by National League President Warren Giles.

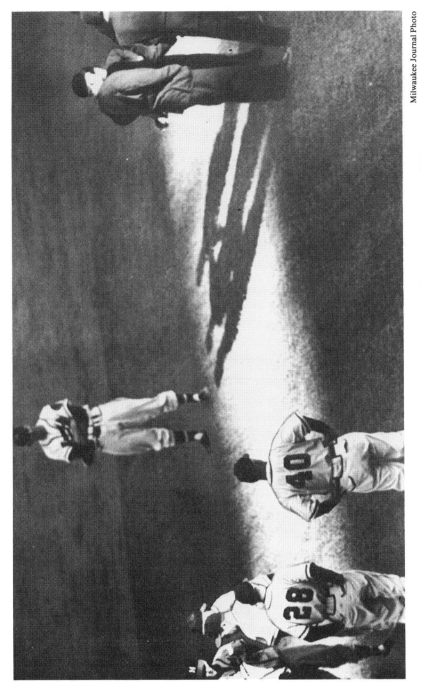

Milwaukee Journal Photo

The Braves confer while the umpires confer—prelude to a rare successful protest.

Citing Rule 7.09(e), Giles said the interference clause provided only that Borkowski be declared out. Because the confusion occurred after Bell reached third base, the game was to be replayed with Bell on third, Post on second, and Milwaukee leading, 3-1. The Redlegs were idle Thursday and Friday before finishing the season in two weekend games with the Cubs, so the game was ordered to be completed Friday afternoon preceding the Braves' ballgame against the St. Louis Cardinals. So confident were the Redlegs of their appeal that, although they traveled to Chicago as scheduled Wednesday, they had left much of their equipment in Milwaukee. Friday morning they returned to complete the game.

When the game resumed, Saturnino Escalera was sent in to run for Wally Post at second base, and with righthanded Johnny Temple due at the plate, Dave Jolly was brought in to administer the final out. One pitch might conceivably have ended the affair, but Temple thwarted that notion by lining Jolly's first pitch to center. Bell scored, and when Bruton fumbled the ball, Escalera scored to make it 3-3. Jolly retired Andy Seminick, but now Milwaukee needed to score again.

They wasted no time in doing so against new pitcher Frank Smith. Jim Pendleton legged an infield hit to deep short, Logan sacrificed him to second, O'Connell was walked intentionally, and Catfish Metkovich ended the struggle with a hit in the gap in leftcenter. Because the Reds had tied the game, Jolly replaced Johnson as the winning pitcher, and Smith replaced Valentine as the loser. After less than fifteen minutes of play, the Redlegs packed up and boarded their bus to Chicago.

In the regularly scheduled contest, Warren Spahn pitched a complete game and drove in the winning run with a double as Milwaukee beat the Cardinals and rookie Gordon Jones, 4-2. The 16,094 fans with tickets for the Cardinal game received a bonus by seeing the final inning of the Cincinnati game. The 11,585 who had paid to see the Redlegs' game were out of luck. League rules treated it like a suspended game, and rainchecks were not valid for its completion. The game had no impact on the standings—the Giants had already clinched the pennant, and this day's Dodger victory gave them second. Nevertheless, Friday's 16,094 fans witnessed the only instance in major league history when a team defeated two different ballclubs in the same ballpark on the same day.

1954 Swan Songs

"At no time, not even after the injury to my head, did I ever think of quitting baseball."

—Jim Wilson

The end of the Milwaukee Braves' second season marked the departure date for two of the Originals. Actually one of them, utility infielder Sebastian "Sibby" Sisti, merits only a footnote in the 1954 season, appearing in nine games only as a pinch runner and scoring twice. Sisti had been a longtime Brave, playing third base for Casey Stengel's Boston teams before World War II. In 1948, filling in at second base after Eddie Stanky broke his ankle, Sisti helped the Braves win the pennant.

Sisti's final appearance for Milwaukee occurred on June 6, 1954, in the second game of a doubleheader in Pittsburgh's Forbes Field. He ran for rookie Henry Aaron, who in turn had walked for Dave Jolly, in the seventh inning of a 6-4 loss to the Pirates in which all the Braves' runs scored on Eddie Mathews' grand slam. A week later Sisti was waived to become a coach and make room on the roster for Al Spangler.

Jim Wilson was a different story, having achieved baseball immortality by pitching the first no-hitter in County Stadium on June 12, 1954, nine years after narrowly escaping death from a Hank Greenberg line drive. He went on to win eight and lose two as a sometime starter in his second and final year with Milwaukee before being sold to the American League.

Wilson's last appearance in a Braves' uniform came on a muggy Saturday night in St. Louis, September 18, 1954. The veteran righthander lost his second straight game, although his first decision in a month, after winning his first eight. Wilson worked five and two-thirds innings, allowing seven hits and three

83

runs, all earned. He allowed a home run to the second Cardinal batter he faced, rookie Joe Cunningham. The Cardinals added a run in the fourth and another in the sixth, with runners at first and third when Charlie Gorin relieved Wilson. The score at the time, 3-0, became final as rookie hurler Gordon Jones threw a seven-hit shutout at the Braves.

Getting in shape with a rigorous game of shuffleboard, spring training, 1954—(watching) Chet Nichols, Sibby Sisti, Joey Jay (playing) Johnny Logan and Danny O'Connell

1955

"Milwaukee's major league appetites commenced too high on the hog."

—Shirley Povich, *Washington Post*

In 1955 the National League had no pennant race. The Braves won their opener, then lost their second game to fall a game behind—and they never caught up. Milwaukee won six of their first eight but trailed by three games. By May 10, four weeks after opening day, the Braves were in third place, ten games behind the Brooklyn Dodgers. They would get no closer to first place than eight games. The Braves moved into second place on July 7 and stayed there for the rest of the season, but during that time they trailed Brooklyn by anywhere from ten to seventeen games, finishing the season thirteen and a half games behind.

The reason there was no pennant race was not so much the Braves or the other lesser teams, but the Brooklyn Dodgers—they simply ran away and hid from the rest of the National League. The Dodgers won their first ten games, the best start in modern major league history; then after losing two of three, they won eleven straight to end anyone's hopes of catching them. The Dodgers smothered the Braves in Milwaukee, 10-2, on September 8 to clinch the pennant, the earliest that any National League team had ever done so. Fittingly, Brooklyn went on to win their first World Series, beating the cross-town Yankees in seven games behind the pitching heroics of Johnny Podres and the spectacular game-saving catch of Sandy Amoros.

The Brooklyn team that annihilated the competition was, on paper, not as strong as the 1953 Dodger club had been. The 1955 edition scored fewer runs, hit seven fewer home runs, stole eleven fewer bases, hit fourteen points less in team average, and won seven fewer games. Nevertheless, the 1955 team led the league in each of those categories. Carl Furillo, Gil Hodges, Roy Campanella, and Duke Snider all had excellent seasons for the Bums, hitting for both power and average. In addition, the Dodgers led in earned run average despite having just one outstanding starter, Don Newcombe. Their bullpen, with Clem Labine, Ed Roebuck, and rookie Don Bessent, was magnificent, and to add insult to injury, Newcombe also batted .359 and hit seven home runs. All in all, 1955 was a bad year for Dodger-haters.

The Braves' front office had chosen not to make any trades prior to the 1955 season, believing that their lineup of the previous year was capable of winning the pennant if they could stay healthy. Charlie Grimm went so far as to predict a pennant, so talent-laden was his team. As it turned out, he and the front office were mistaken, although once again injuries hindered the team. Eddie Mathews underwent an emergency appendectomy and was out of the starting lineup for fifteen days; Gene Conley missed more than two months with a shoulder injury; and Joe Adcock had his arm broken by a Jim Hearn pitch and missed the last two months. Yet even without these injuries, it seems unlikely the Braves could have overtaken Brooklyn. The Braves had three glaring weaknesses, all of which were well-known even to casual observers, none of which the Milwaukee management addressed.

First was relief pitching. The role of reliever had not yet fully evolved into the specialty it was to become, but even by the standards of the day the Braves' bullpen was inadequate. When Lew Burdette became a starter on July 26, 1953, the Braves were left without a late-inning stopper. Dave Jolly did a fine job in 1954, winning eleven games and saving ten, but in 1955 he had poor control and was ineffective, saving just one game. Ernie Johnson pitched well at times but not with consistency. The plain fact was that the Braves had the weakest relief pitching in the league. While the Dodgers led with 37 saves, the Braves ranked last with twelve. They also ranked last in shutouts with five and first in complete games with 61. Either their starters won, or the team lost.

The second weakness was just that—at second. The Braves had hoped the acquisition of Danny O'Connell in December of 1953 had fulfilled that need, but O'Connell was not the answer. As a hitter, he was an adequate fielder. He had batted a creditable .279 in 1954, but in 1955 he slipped badly, hitting only .225. Jack Dittmer was still around, but the esteem in which he was held can be gauged by the fact that highly-prized young slugger Henry

Danny O'Connell, Johnny Logan, and hero-worshippers

Aaron played 27 games at second base. Aaron had been an infielder in the minor leagues, but he was better suited to the outfield, free to utilize his speed and strong arm and safe from the flying spikes of runners intent on breaking up the doubleplay. O'Connell was left to fill the position, if not the need.

The Braves' other obvious weakness was in leftfield. As with O'Connell, the Bobby Thomson trade had failed to fulfill the expectations. Like O'Connell, Thomson was just adequate in the field, and his bat was a regular disappointment. He showed occasional flashes of his old power, but he hit only .257. Actually, against a few teams, notably the Dodgers and Phillies, Thomson hit quite well, but against others, especially the Pirates and Cardinals, he was pathetic.

Despite their recognizable weaknesses, the Braves made only a few significant roster changes in 1955. They called up two lefthand hitters coming off big minor league seasons: outfielder Chuck Tanner from Atlanta and first baseman George Crowe from Toledo. In April, on the 14th and 30th respectively, they sold no-hit pitcher Jim Wilson to the Baltimore Orioles and non-hit shortstop Roy Smalley to the Philadelphia Phillies. On June 4 they acquired veteran catcher Del Rice from the St. Louis Cardinals for minor leaguer Pete Whisenant. Rice, one of the league's slowest runners, became the personal catcher of Bob Buhl and provided needed rest for Del Crandall for the next four seasons.

The 1955 season was a big year for power hitting in the National League, led by Willie Mays with 51 home runs. The Braves hit a team-record 182 homers, led by Eddie Mathews with 41, his third consecutive year of 40 or more. The Dodgers hit 201 to lead as the National League set a new record for home runs in a season. On September 25, in the Braves' final game of the year, Wally Moon hit a homer in the last of the ninth to beat Milwaukee, 8-5; that home run was the league's 1263rd of the season, a major league record that stood until the expansion of the American League in 1961.

As might be expected in a record year for home runs, earned run averages soared. Only one pitcher had an ERA below 3.20 (Bob Friend, 2.83), and the Braves' team ERA was two-thirds of a run higher than the previous year. Only two National League pitchers won more than seventeen games; even Warren Spahn failed to win his customary twenty, for only the third time in his nine seasons. Braves' hurlers Buhl and Spahn ranked third and fourth, respectively, in earned run average, but Burdette, Conley, and Nichols all had ERA's over 4.00. Combined with the lack of a strong reliever, the ineffectiveness of the Milwaukee starters kept the team from seriously challenging the Dodgers.

The one-game pennant race began with elements of *deja vu*. For the third year in a row, Billy Bruton scored the winning run, Warren Spahn was the winning pitcher, and the Braves won their home opener, beating the Cincinnati Redlegs, 4-2 [see Time Capsule]. That was on April 12. On April 14 in St. Louis, the Braves squandered a 7-2 lead (no relief), allowed five Cardinal home runs, and finally lost on Bill Virdon's homer in the eleventh. Joe Adcock left eight baserunners stranded in the game. The loss dropped Milwaukee behind Brooklyn for the duration of the season.

On April 16 and 17 in Cincinnati, the Braves demonstrated the kind of season it was to be. They outscored the Reds in three games, 24-12, but won only two of the three. They breezed to easy victories, 9-5 behind Burdette and 10-1 behind Spahn, as they hit five home runs; but they lost 6-5 when reliever Jolly could not put the clamps on the Redlegs. Through their first five games the Braves hit ten home runs and scored 35 runs, but they also allowed fourteen homers and 27 runs. All season they proved they could score—they scored nine runs or more in eighteen games—but they also allowed nine or more runs on sixteen occasions.

For example on May 10 the Braves, struggling to stay "just" nine games behind the Dodgers, gave up eight runs in the eighth inning to the perennial last-place Pittsburgh Pirates and lost, 9-6. On June 2 in Brooklyn, Bob Buhl was locked in a pitchers' duel with Billy Loes through seven innings before the Dodgers exploded for ten runs in the eighth inning to win, 13-2. And on August 4 in County Stadium, with Mathews on the bench after cutting his finger while slicing a roast beef sandwich, the Braves took a 10-6 lead into the ninth inning against the Dodgers but lost, 11-10. The losing pitcher, as in the May 10 debacle, was Ernie Johnson.

The first month of the season was disastrous for the Braves—and the second month was no better. Of the first thirteen games, the Braves won eight. The five they lost were all by one run. With some breaks, or a top-notch reliever, they could conceivably have kept pace with the streaking Dodgers. They were scoring runs in bunches, thanks mainly to Bobby Thomson and Johnny Logan. Thomson blasted four home runs, including a grand slam against the Cubs on April 20, and he drove in seventeen runs in the first ten games to lead the league. Logan hit .364 with three homers in April and continued to hit surprisingly well all season, carrying a .307 average into the All-Star Game and batting .297 for the year, his highest in the big leagues. Sophomore outfielder Hank Aaron also hit well, both for average and power, but others in the lineup were struggling.

Joe Adcock was batting less than his weight in the first week of May before he started to hit. By the time he did, he had to take up the slack for Thomson, who injured his right shoulder in a loss to the Pirates on May 5 (during which Mathews hit into a triple play). Thomson missed nearly two weeks, and when he returned, it was at a level of mediocrity. His substitutes, Andy Pafko and Chuck Tanner, were no great shakes, but on May 18, Pafko was moved to third base, a position he had not played since his Brooklyn days, after Mathews underwent an emergency appendectomy.

Mathews had hit just .216, with no home runs, through the end of April, but from May 8 through 15 he slammed five home runs, and he raised his average nearly 40 points. On May 25, exactly one week after his surgery, he worked out with his teammates at

County Stadium. On May 30 he pinch-hit in a game in Cincinnati, then again in Brooklyn on June 1 and 2, smashing a home run in the latter appearance. On June 3, just sixteen days after his operation, he was back in the lineup. From June 4 through 6 he clubbed four home runs in four games. Between his return and the All-Star Game on July 12, he crashed fifteen homers, raised his average to .297, and earned a place in the starting lineup of the National League team. Additionally, of course, his rapid recovery from the appendix removal did nothing to diminish his tough-guy image.

The primary factor keeping the Braves in the first division during April and May was six-foot eight-inch Gene Conley. He carried a 7-1 record into June, including three wins over the Cubs and two over the Giants. After he hurled a three-hitter against the Cubs on May 22 for his sixth victory, manager Charlie Grimm called him "the best pitcher in the league" at the time, and he may not have been exaggerating. Conley's only loss had been 2-0

Equipment manager Tommy Ferguson, Gene Conley, Dave Jolly, and Del Crandall

to Carl Erskine of the Dodgers on May 2. In 1954 he had won fourteen games without winning any in September and had compiled the fifth-best ERA (2.97) in the league. In 1955 he was to win eleven before the All-Star Game (in which he struck out all three batters he faced, earning the victory), including ten complete games, but a shoulder injury on July 22 ended what should have been a great season. He would pitch only one more time (August 13) until the following May 25.

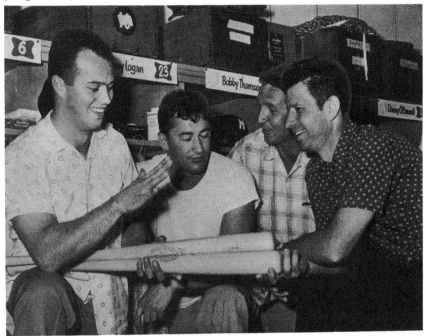

Eddie Mathews, Johnny Logan, Bobby Thomson, and Andy Pafko
in spring training, 1955

The inability of the Braves to win consistently in the early season is reflected in the record of meal-ticket Warren Spahn. At All-Star time he had won only seven games while losing nine, with an earned run average of 3.75—and that, of course, was without facing the Dodgers, against whom he rarely worked. Through the end of May he had pitched just two complete games, and his 6-0 shutout of the Pirates on June 22 was his first whitewash in more than a year (it was also the team's first of the season). He had even lost two games in relief. Many people were wondering if Spahn, at age 34, had not finally reached the ninth inning of his career.

When a team does not perform as well as expected, the inevitable rumors surface regarding the future employment of the manager. After the Dodgers scored ten runs in the eighth inning to crush the Braves on June 2, whisperings of Charlie Grimm's demise could be heard. Fortunately for him, the next night Billy Bruton hit a game-winning, tenth-inning home run; the next day the Braves walloped four homers and Spahn hurled a complete game; the day after that Mathews belted two homers in a 5-4 victory over the Phillies. The Braves did not make a miraculous turn-around, but Grimm's job remained secure for another year.

The Braves' 1955 campaign, despite their failures and foibles, was not really a bad one. Even in their early-season fumblings they never fell further than three games below .500. On May 5, after losing five straight, three to the Pirates, they did plunge for one day into fifth place, and again during a four-game losing streak from May 18 to 21 they bounced into fifth, but on June 18 they were back up to third, and when Bob Buhl beat the Cubs on July 7, the Braves were in permanent possession of second place. Just before the All-Star Game they won six straight, nearly seven, and again from July 24 to July 30 they won six in a row. The pitcher that broke that streak, and also Joe Adcock's arm, was Jim Hearn.

Coincidentally, Adcock suffered his season-ending injury exactly one year after he had destroyed the Dodgers in Ebbets Field with four home runs and a double. The injury not only contributed to the end of the Braves' streak but also deprived the team of their leading Dodger-killer in the four-game series with Brooklyn that began the next day. Without Adcock the Braves lost three of four games, two by one run, and when the Dodgers left Milwaukee on August 4, the Braves were fifteen and a half games out of first.

In the latter part of the season the Braves played solid but unremarkable baseball, with strong hitting from Aaron and Mathews and strong pitching by Spahn and Buhl. Aaron not only led the team in batting with a .314 average but also demonstrated unexpected power, finishing with 27 home runs, second on the club. Mathews hit nineteen homers after the All-Star break, totaling 41 for the season, and also surpassed the 100 mark in RBI's with 103. Buhl, who had been 1-4 on June 2 and 5-7 on the Fourth of July, raised his record to 13-8 by Labor Day, and Spahn, proving that he was by no means too old to pitch, won eight of his last ten decisions.

The Braves also received some good pitching performances from Lew Burdette, Chet Nichols, and Ray Crone, but none was

Teamwork—an 8-man rundown: (from top left) LF Tanner, 2B O'Connell, SS Logan, 3B Mathews, CF Bruton, runner Don Hoak, P Robinson, C Crandall, 1B Crowe

able to win regularly. Logan continued to hit and field effectively, Del Crandall began hitting home runs, and George Crowe did the same filling in for Adcock. Beginning on August 13 the Braves made their final overture toward catching the Dodgers. They won eleven of thirteen to move within ten games of the leaders, but a doubleheader loss to the Pirates on August 28 squelched any ideas of a miracle finish. It was only a formality when, on September 8, the Dodgers crushed Milwaukee, 10-2, at County Stadium, then adjourned to Mader's German restaurant to celebrate their pennant.

Home attendance dropped off immediately after the Dodgers made the pennant officially theirs, but the Braves' final home appearance, on September 18, drew enough loyalists to boost the season total to 2,005,836, the second year in a row over two million. It was a measure of the club's progress that, just three years removed from being a pitiful collection of failures in Boston, a second-place team was now a serious disappointment. Being competitive and talented and exciting would no longer suffice—only a pennant would satisfy the team and their fans.

1955 Nemesis - Herman Wehmeier

"Hermie has been playing baseball as long as he can remember."

—1952 Topps Baseball Card

Herman Wehmeier's career record reads like a good-news, bad-news joke. The good news is that he pitched in the major leagues long enough to record 200 decisions; the bad news is that he lost 108 of those games, and that of all the pitchers in the twentieth century who figured in that many decisions, not one had a worse career earned run average than Herman Wehmeier's (4.80). From 1949 until 1956 he did not have a winning season. Three times he led National League hurlers in bases on balls (in 1952 he averaged more than five walks per game). For his career he walked more batters than he struck out. In three different seasons he had the worst earned run average of any starting pitcher in the league, and in the only season during which he was primarily a relief pitcher, he produced the worst ERA of all—7.16. Needless to say, batters loved to face Herman Wehmeier.

After nearly a decade with the Cincinnati Redlegs, Wehmeier was traded to the Phillies in mid-1954, and in early 1955, he abandoned his whipping-boy role and became a Milwaukee nemesis. On April 29 he beat Warren Spahn, 13-4, in a rain-shortened contest in Philadelphia. He allowed just four hits, and three of the Braves' runs scored on a triple that was an Andy Pafko single until outfielder Stan Palys slipped on the wet grass and fell down.

On June 5 in Philadelphia, Wehmeier started the second game of a Sunday doubleheader and led 4-0 in the seventh inning, but the game was suspended because of Pennsylvania's 7:00 P.M. curfew on Sunday games. The game was completed the next day by reliever Jack Meyer, who lost the shutout but preserved

Wehmeier's victory. And on June 15 Wehmeier ran his streak of shutout innings against Milwaukee to sixteen, blanking them 4-0 on a six-hitter and beating Gene Conley, the Braves' leading pitcher, for the second straight time.

The Braves did catch up with Wehmeier later in the season, but the final laugh was his. After being traded to the St. Louis Cardinals on May 11, 1956, Wehmeier got the chance to be the ultimate spoiler. In the next to last game of the 1956 season, with Milwaukee tied for first and battling for its first pennant, Wehmeier outdueled Warren Spahn and spoiled the Braves' season, 2-1, in a dramatic twelve-inning game in Busch Stadium. Two years later Wehmeier was out of baseball, his career cut short at age 31 by an elbow injury.

Capacity crowd at County Stadium, September 24, 1956

Time Capsule - April 12, 1955

"And to think that I was ready to give it all up last spring."

—Chuck Tanner

Chuck Tanner is a classic example of an overnight success who took nine years to get there. He may have been created by Horatio Alger and painted by Norman Rockwell. His life story positively reeks of Americana—born on the Fourth of July, growing up in a working-class city in Pennsylvania during the Great Depression, wanting more than anything else to be a major league ballplayer. He began his baseball apprenticeship as a teenager with Owensboro in the Kitty League, then worked his way slowly up the bush league ladder: Eau Claire, Pawtucket, Denver, Atlanta, Milwaukee, Toledo. He endured low pay, sparse crowds, matchbox ballparks, bus rides between jerkwater towns. He suffered knee and leg injuries. He thought of quitting baseball, but his wife talked him out of it. He hit over .300 for seven straight years but never got called up. Finally he got his chance in the big leagues.

It was Opening Day, 1955, played at County Stadium for the first time in the Braves' brief history. The weather was cool and hazy with a threat of rain. As usual Warren Spahn had the honor of initiating the season, opposing Gerry Staley and the Cincinnati Redlegs. Spahn and Staley had done battle in the 1953 home opener, with Spahn prevailing in ten innings. In this game the Braves wasted no time in giving Spahn a lead. Billy Bruton led off with a single, and after two outs Bobby Thomson drove him in with a double to the fence in leftcenter.

With one out in the second, Cincinnati got base hits from Ed Bailey and Wally Post plus a sacrifice bunt by Staley, but Spahn got Johnny Temple to end the inning on a flyball to Henry Aaron.

The Braves accomplished nothing against Staley in the second and third, and in the fourth the Redlegs threatened again. Ray Jablonski singled and Spahn hit Bailey with a curve ball to put two men on, but Post, as he often did, grounded into a double-play to quell the uprising. The Braves put two men on in their half but failed to score; the Reds put one on but none across in the fifth. In the sixth and seventh neither team got a hit. Heading into the eighth Spahn and Staley remained locked in a 1-0 struggle.

In the eighth inning, though, the Redlegs reached Spahn. Second baseman Temple slapped a single just out of Logan's reach to lead off. Roy McMillan dutifully sacrificed the tying run to second. Gus Bell flied out. Ted Kluszewski, the major leagues' leading home run hitter the year before with 49, connected with a sidearm fastball and parked it in the rightfield bleachers for a two-run homer. Spahn then got Jablonski to end the inning but went to the dugout down 2-1.

Staley retired Crandall to open the home eighth; Spahn was scheduled to hit next. He was a fair hitter, with ten career home runs and a single earlier in the day, and except for one pitch to Kluszewski he was pitching a fine ballgame, but the situation clearly demanded a pinch-hitter. Charlie Grimm brought in a lefthand swinger against the righthanded Staley. Only the most fanatic Braves fans recognized the number or the name when the stadium announcer said, "Now batting for Spahn, number 18, Chuck Tanner." The applause that greeted the announcement was entirely out of habit. Had the crowd been allowed to vote, they probably would have elected to let Spahn bat.

But the fans scarcely had time to ask "Who's he?" before Tanner had imitated Kluszewski. He hit Staley's first offering into the seats beyond the fence in right to tie the game. The crowd was delirious. As Tanner loped around the bases, the fans stood and screamed and whistled and pounded each other on the back. The game was tied, 2-2.

The next batter, Bruton, also jumped on Staley's first pitch and drilled it into leftcenter for a base hit. The crowd repeated their outburst. And when Hank Aaron greeted Staley's next pitch with a long triple to the 394-foot sign in rightcenter, the stands erupted again. Staley was replaced by tiny lefthander Jackie Collum, who walked Ed Mathews. Collum made a quick exit, giving way to righthander Jerry Lane. Bobby Thomson drove Gus Bell almost to the warning track, and Aaron tagged and scored. With Joe Adcock at bat, Mathews was thrown out trying to steal second, but Milwaukee led 4-2 going to the ninth.

Joe Adcock, Bobby Thomson, Warren Spahn, and Del Crandall

Dave Jolly, the Braves' star reliever of '54, came on to save Spahn's victory. He struck out Jim Greengrass, got Bailey on a ground ball to Jack Dittmer at second, and caught Post looking at strike three to end the game. For the third straight year the Braves had won their home opener; for the third straight year they had won it in their last turn at bat; for the third straight year Bruton had scored the winning run; for the third straight year Spahn was the winning pitcher; for the second time in three years the losing pitcher was Staley.

After the game, though, all the talk was of the new kid, Chuck Tanner. This guy had to be destined for stardom. His first time at bat in the big leagues, the first pitch in the big leagues, and bam—a home run. Actually, 25 players before Tanner had hit a home run in their first time at bat in the majors. Five players had hit their first major league pitch out of the park (including, on April 23, 1952, pitcher Hoyt Wilhelm, who, in twenty-one seasons, would never hit another homer). One player, Eddie

"Pepper" Morgan in 1936, had performed the feat as Tanner did—as a pinch-hitter. No one knew any of this at the moment, of course, nor would they have cared—not the fans, and not Chuck Tanner. He knew only the ecstasy of instant stardom after long obscurity.

"Nothing," Tanner said after the game, "can top this thrill. Not even if I play in a World Series." He never would. The Braves sold him to Chicago in June of their first pennant-winning season, 1957. Tanner never played regularly in the majors except during that partial season with the last-place Cubs. He retired as a player in 1962 at age 33 after an undistinguished major league career shorter than his minor league term. For one brief moment in Milwaukee, though, he was the people's choice.

Clair J. Wilson Photo

Auto supplier to the Braves, Wally Rank, with 1957 fleet

Time Capsule - July 10, 1955

"You know that Spahn. Sometimes he's hot; sometimes he's cold."

—Flagpole Sitter William J. Sherwood

In the summer of 1955 America found itself engulfed by a Davy Crockett craze. At the same time an imaginative entrepreneurial stunt captured Milwaukee's attention. Under the auspices of the Teutonia Avenue Advancement Association, a man named William J. Sherwood spent the summer sitting atop a flagpole. Sherwood mounted the structure, a specially-constructed pole built on top of a two-story building at 2777 N. Teutonia Avenue, on June 23, vowing to remain aloft until the Milwaukee Braves won seven games in a row. A winning streak of that duration hardly seemed unlikely—the previous season Milwaukee's heroes had strung ten consecutive victories three times, and nine games once. This season, though, would be different. The imaginative stunt kept Sherwood on his perch until late September when he finally descended after the Braves no longer had a mathematical chance of achieving the desired streak. Twice during that three-month span the Braves won six straight. In the first instance, they went to the final inning before being beaten.

After dropping a doubleheader to the Cardinals on the Fourth of July, Milwaukee took a two-game series from the Cubs, swept a Friday night doubleheader from the Redlegs, and beat the Redlegs in a single game on Saturday for five in a row. Gene Conley, Bob Buhl, Warren Spahn, Lew Burdette, and Ray Crone each contributed a complete-game victory, allowing only ten runs during that stretch. On Sunday, the final day before the All-Star break, the Braves needed to sweep a twin-bill from Cincinnati to bring Sherwood back to earth.

101

In the opener the Braves took a 1-0 lead in the first inning, the Redlegs tied it in the second, then Conley doubled home a run in the last of the second to make it 2-1. Cincinnati scored twice in the fifth to take a 3-2 lead, and Ted Kluszewski hit his 29th home run, tops in the majors, to make it 4-2 Redlegs in the middle of the sixth.

Milwaukee rallied in the bottom of the sixth to take the lead for good. Eddie Mathews led off with a single, Hank Aaron was retired, Bobby Thomson singled, and Andy Pafko grounded out. Mild-mannered Pafko was so incensed at the call at first that he threw his hat down and was promptly thrown out of the game, the first time in his thirteen-year career he had been ejected. With two gone Joe Adcock walked to load the bases. Del Crandall, no speed merchant, beat out a bouncer to deep short scoring Mathews, and when Roy McMillan threw the ball away, Thomson came in with the tying run. Finally Conley grounded to third baseman Chuck Harmon, who booted the ball and allowed Adcock to score the lead run.

Bobby Thomson's two-run homer in the seventh added insurance to Conley's cause, putting the Braves up 7-4. The only other blow of the game was struck by Conley in the eighth. His hard grounder back to the mound took a wicked bounce and struck Reds' pitcher Art Fowler on the forehead. Fowler was helped from the field. As the saying goes, they examined his head but found nothing. Conley held the Reds in the ninth, and the Braves' streak was at six games.

The nightcap matched Braves' lefty Chet Nichols, 5-5 for the year, against lefty Jackie Collum. Nichols, whose father had been a big-league pitcher during Prohibition, winning one game in a six-season career, had been a promising 20-year-old rookie in 1951 when he led the National League with a 2.88 earned run average. After that he spent two years in the military, and since his Army days he had been a disappointment. As a hitter he rivalled the legendary Bob Buhl for futility. Nichols had batted just .137 hitting righthanded in his rookie term, so in 1954 he changed to the left side and hit .086. Now he was switch-hitting and proving equally inept from either direction.

Nichols was given a 1-0 lead in the second inning and held it until the fifth, when he was the victim of shoddy fielding, including his own. With one out Nichols hit his counterpart Collum with a pitch. Johnny Temple laid down a bunt, Nichols got a poor jump off the mound, and Temple legged it for a hit. Stan Palys followed with a double to score Collum, tying the game at 1-1. Kluszewski was given an intentional walk to load the bases. That decision looked good when Wally Post hit a slow grounder to Mathews, who charged and flipped the ball to catcher Del Rice for a force at the plate. Rice dropped the ball, though, allowing Temple to score. Gus Bell grounded to Adcock, who threw home and forced Palys. The inning should now have been over. The next batter, long-time American Leaguer Matt Batts, hit a blooper into short centerfield. The normally reliable Bruton failed to judge the ball in time, it landed in front of him, and three more runs scored. Nichols left the game after the end of the inning trailing 5-1, with four of the runs unearned.

Relief pitcher Phil Paine, recently returned from the minors, hurled shutout ball through the sixth and seventh, and in that inning his teammates rallied to tie the game. Aaron tripled, Thomson singled, Pafko singled, and Collum was removed, replaced by Joe Nuxhall.

Nuxhall had become the youngest player in major league history in 1944 when he pitched for Cincinnati at age 15. In his brief debut he had walked a batter, retired two, walked four more, thrown a wild pitch, and allowed two singles. The five runs he allowed in two-thirds of an inning contributed to his team's 18-0 loss that day and gave him a staggering earned run average of 67.50 for that season. In relief of Collum against the Braves he was only slightly more effective. He fanned both Adcock and Rice, but pinch-hitter Del Crandall walked to load the bases, Bruton delivered a two-run single, and Johnny Logan singled Crandall home to tie the game.

Lew Burdette came in to pitch the eighth, but he hit Bobby Adams and gave up a bunt single to McMillan. Warren Spahn came in to try to save the day. He got Ray Jablonski on a popup and struck out Temple. In the bottom of the inning the Braves also failed to score, and the game stayed 5-5.

Spahn retired Palys to open the ninth, but the situation deteriorated rapidly after that. Kluszewski singled, and Wally Post followed with a long home run over the leftfield fence. After Spahn disposed of the Redlegs, the Braves tried to come back after two down in the ninth. George Crowe singled batting for Spahn. Bruton doubled him home, but Joe Black, the former ace reliever for Brooklyn, got Logan to end the game. The winning streak was finished at six. The headline in *The Milwaukee Journal* the next day said it all: "Post Keeps Pole Sitter on Top of Post."

Time Capsule - July 12, 1955

"This homer—well, it's got to be listed the biggest thrill of all."

—Stan Musial

Short of a World Series, the biggest thrill the Braves could have offered their fans was the All-Star Game. On July 12, 1955, it arrived. Baseball's showcase, originated in 1933 to highlight Chicago's Century of Progress Exposition by matching the legendary ballplayers of the rival major leagues, had a storied past and an aura of excitement and glamor. The game evoked images of Babe Ruth blasting the first All-Star home run; of Carl Hubbell fanning, in order, Ruth, Gehrig, Foxx, Simmons, and Cronin; of Ted Williams' game-winning two-out, three-run homer in the last of the ninth. In a note of supreme irony and sadness, the start of Milwaukee's edition of the All-Star classic had to be delayed an hour to allow baseball people time to attend, in Chicago, the funeral of the inventor of the All-Star Game, *Chicago Tribune* Sports Editor Arch Ward.

Had the team remained in Boston, the Braves would have hosted the 1953 All-Star Game, but when the new Milwaukee team switched schedules with Pittsburgh in spring, 1953, the Braves also exchanged places in the All-Star rotation with Cincinnati. The Boston Braves had hosted the fourth All-Star festivities, back in 1936; the National League manager in that game was Charlie Grimm, then skipper of the Chicago Cubs. The Nationals beat the Americans that year for the first time, 4-3, led by pitchers Dizzy Dean and Carl Hubbell. Prophetically, perhaps, the game in Boston drew just 25,534 fans, the smallest crowd ever to witness an All-Star Game. Milwaukee's attendance nearly doubled that total with a 45,314 full house.

The game offered the baseball world a look at record-setting

104

Hawk Taylor, Charlie Grimm, and George Crowe

County Stadium, and it offered Wisconsin fans a chance to see some of their heroes recognized as among baseball's best. Catcher Del Crandall and third baseman Eddie Mathews were in the starting lineup for the National League; Henry Aaron and Johnny Logan contributed off the bench; pitcher Gene Conley earned the victory for his team. Conley's victory atoned for his loss in the 1954 classic in Cleveland. Local fans also saw local product Harvey Kuenn start at shortstop for the American League.

For National League partisans, the game could not have started out worse. Robin Roberts, starting his fifth All-Star Game for the National League, gave up a single to Kuenn on the second pitch of the game. Nellie Fox singled him to third, and a wild pitch by Roberts put the Americans ahead, 1-0. Ted Williams walked, and Yankee slugger Mickey Mantle slammed a towering home run into Perini's Woods beyond centerfield, scoring Fox and Williams ahead of him for a quick 4-0 advantage.

Roberts then got out of the inning, but Billy Pierce, the

105

American League starter, gave Roberts' teammates no chance to retaliate. Leadoff batter Red Schoendienst lined a single up the middle, but with Del Ennis at bat, catcher Yogi Berra let a pitch roll out of his glove in front of the plate, then gunned down Schoendienst when he tried to go to second. Pierce then struck out Ennis and Duke Snider to end the inning. Roberts held the American League scoreless in the second and third, but Pierce did the same to the Nationals, retiring the last eight men he faced.

Harvey Haddix replaced Roberts in the fourth and held the opposition scoreless for two innings, but Early Wynn did the same in place of Pierce. In the fifth the National League team had their first scoring threat when Ted Kluszewski doubled to lead off and Don Mueller singled him to third with one out. Ernie Banks and Smoky Burgess, however, both failed to bring Big Klu home, and it stayed 4-0.

In the top of the sixth the American Leaguers added to their lead against Haddix. After Berra singled with one out, 20-year-old Al Kaline, the league's leading hitter, slashed a vicious shot that caromed off Mathews' wrist into leftfield for a double. (Mathews was replaced after the inning, but X-rays revealed no fracture.) Berra held third but scored when Mickey Vernon grounded out to Kluszewski at first, putting the American League up 5-0. They nearly expanded the lead in the seventh, but Willie Mays leaped above the fence in center to rob Ted Williams of a two-run homer.

The National League finally scored in the last of the seventh. Mays led off with a single off Whitey Ford, Kluszewski and Ransom Jackson both flied to Mantle, Aaron walked, and Johnny Logan rewarded the home fans with a bloop single to score Mays. Stan Lopata, batting for Burgess, hit a bouncer to good-field, no-hit Chico Carrasquel who, naturally, bobbled the ball, picked it up, threw it away, and Aaron scored to make it a 5-2 game.

In the eighth National League manager Leo Durocher brought in fearsome Cubs' pitcher Sad Sam Jones, an erratic sidewinder who wavered between brilliant and awful. Exactly two months previous Jones had pitched eight hitless innings against the Pirates, then walked the bases loaded in the ninth, and finally struck out the side on eleven pitches to preserve the no-hitter. In his All-Star appearance Jones remained in character. He struck out Mantle and retired Berra but hit Kaline on the ankle, walked Vernon on four pitches, and walked Al Rosen on four pitches. Joe Nuxhall had to rescue him by striking out Whitey Ford to end the inning.

Ford retired Cardinals Schoendienst and Stan Musial to start the bottom of the eighth, but Mays singled to right, Kluszewski did likewise, Jackson drove Mays in with a single, and Ford was yanked. Frank Sullivan, the six-foot seven-inch righthander from Boston, relieved and gave up the fourth straight single, this one by Aaron. Kluszewski scored, Carrasquel failed to cut off Kaline's throw from rightfield, the ball ticked Jackson and flipped past Rosen, Sullivan forgot to back up the play at third, and Jackson scored the tying run. Sullivan finally got Logan to end the inning.

Pitchers Nuxhall and Sullivan took control of the game for the next two innings. Both teams put men on base in the ninth but neither could score and the game became history's second extra-inning All-Star classic. In the tenth Nuxhall walked the leadoff man, then struck out the side. Sullivan allowed a hit but fanned two and escaped without damage.

The American League nearly broke the deadlock in the eleventh. With Bobby Avila on third, Mantle on first, and two out, Berra chopped a grounder past the mound. The ball appeared destined for centerfield, but Schoendienst got his glove on it, pivoted and threw over his shoulder, and nipped Berra at first on a play Berra hotly disputed. Sullivan put the Nationals down in the bottom of the inning, and the game entered the twelfth.

To a huge ovation, Durocher brought in Milwaukee's Gene Conley to work the twelfth. Conley and St. Louis' Luis Arroyo were the only substitutes left for the National League, and since two of the next three hitters were righthanded and Arroyo was a southpaw, Conley was the logical choice—and as it turned out, the correct one. Conley struck out Kaline, Vernon, and Rosen in quick succession and walked off to another tall ovation.

Stan Musial was the first hitter in the last of the twelfth. A six-time batting champion in his twelfth All-Star Game, Musial was 0-for-3 for the day, but he made up for his previous failures in a hurry. He smacked Sullivan's first pitch deep into the rightfield bleachers to give his team, and Gene Conley, a 6-5 victory. Musial's home run narrowed the American League's edge in All-Star competition to 13-9 and gave Milwaukee fans a moment to remember.

1955 Feat of Clay

"I bragged about my strong bench last spring. Look at it now."

—Charlie Grimm

The man had power. Nobody in the league hit the ball farther than Joe Adcock. He hit four home runs and a double in one memorable game in Ebbets Field in 1954. He was the first man to hit a ball into the centerfield bleachers in the Polo Grounds, and the first to hit a ball over the leftfield grandstand roof in Ebbets Field. He loved to dig into the batter's box, square to home base, right elbow high and stiff, his body leaning almost over the plate, daring the pitcher to put one in the strike zone. He could really muscle a pitch. The problem was that he could not get out of the way of one.

Jackie Robinson was often "dusted," but with his lightning reflexes he usually avoided getting hit. Eddie Stanky was able to receive the ball on a fleshy part of his body and avoid injury despite being hit often. Joe Adcock, though, was simply a six-foot four-inch stationary target. His movements were ponderous, and he was prone to injury.

The day after Adcock hit four home runs in Brooklyn, Clem Labine of the Dodgers demonstrated the big guy's vulnerability by caroming a pitch off the left side of Adcock's head. His protective helmet saved him from serious injury. On September 11, six weeks later, Labine's teammate Don Newcombe finished Adcock's season prematurely by hitting him with a pitch and dislocating his left thumb, precluding Adcock's participation in the final sixteen games of the pennant race and effectively ending Milwaukee's chances of catching the first-place Giants.

On July 31, 1955, exactly one year after Adcock's home run outburst in Brooklyn, the Braves were playing the New York Giants at County Stadium. On the mound for the Giants was Jim

Hearn, a tall, powerful righthander never renowned for his control, opposing Warren Spahn. The Braves had won six games in a row and needed the victory to bring the flagpole sitter down. Hearn not only broke the streak but also Adcock's right forearm in the second inning with an inside fastball. Adcock ran to first and finished the inning as a baserunner, but after the inning he was sidelined for the final third of the season.

The broken arm would not be the last of Adcock's misfortunes. He also suffered a broken leg while sliding into second base on June 23, 1957, against the Phillies at County Stadium, disabling him for two and a half months. His entire career was really a series of mishaps. In a seventeen-year major league career, Adcock played in as many as 140 games only twice. He spent more than a quarter of his career recuperating. As with players like Mickey Mantle and Herb Score, students of the game can only speculate on the potential accomplishments of Joe Adcock if he had been healthy throughout his career.

1955 Swan Song

"Big George has hit well with every minor league team with which he has played."

— 1953 Milwaukee Braves Yearbook

George Crowe was a big, soft-spoken first baseman, a veteran of the Negro baseball leagues and one of the finest minor league ballplayers in the country, at Pawtucket, at Hartford, at Milwaukee (Brewers, American Association, 1951), and later at Toledo. When he finally got a chance to play for the Braves after Joe Adcock broke his arm on July 31, 1955, Crowe hit well, both for power and average, and played a respectable first base. He was traded to the Cincinnati Redlegs the day before the Braves' 1956 season opened, a trade that truly benefitted both teams, especially the following season: the Braves got Hurricane Hazle, and Crowe hit 31 homers for Cincinnati in 1957.

Crowe played his final game for Charlie Grimm's Braves on a Sunday afternoon in St. Louis, September 25, 1955, the team's last game of the year. The Braves lost, 8-5, on a three-run homer with two out in the ninth by Wally Moon, their second straight loss to the Cardinals, but it was no fault of George Crowe's. He singled, walked, and homered in four trips to the plate. His fourth-inning home run narrowed the St. Louis lead to 3-2 and gave Crowe three home runs for the three-game series and eight home runs in the final four weeks. He also registered two assists and eight putouts at first base in his farewell appearance.

Spring, 1955: Hank Aaron, Billy Bruton, Charlie White, Jim Pendleton, and George Crowe

1956

"We just couldn't do it. It was almost as if we weren't supposed to win it."

—Fred Haney, September 30, 1956

Even after the disappointing season the Braves endured in 1955, finishing thirteen and a half games distant from the Brooklyn Dodgers, the Milwaukee front office disdained any major trades. The only deal they made was on April 9, sending back-up first baseman George Crowe to Cincinnati in exchange for minor league outfielder Bob Hazle and the proverbial player to be named later, who on May 10 turned out to be pitcher Corky Valentine. The swap became a long-term success but an immediate failure. Crowe gave the Redlegs a power-hitting back-up first baseman and pinch-hitter; Hazle did not join the Braves until mid-1957, and Valentine never again appeared in the majors. To replace Crowe the Braves called up Frank Torre from their Toledo farm club. Their other changes were in the coaching ranks: Bucky Walters and John Cooney were released, replaced by Charlie Root and former Pittsburgh manager Fred Haney.

The National League pennant race in 1956 was a gem, the first real three-team scramble since the 1920's. The Brooklyn Dodgers were defending champions, returning from a runaway the previous year and their first World Series championship ever. They still boasted a veteran line-up of well-known stars, augmented by the acquisition of third baseman Ransom Jackson from the Cubs. The Dodgers had excellent fielding; they had a quartet of home run sluggers in Gil Hodges, Carl Furillo, Duke Snider, and Roy Campanella; they had the best bullpen in the league, with Clem Labine, Ed Roebuck, and Don Bessent; and they had a good corps of starting pitchers, led by big Don Newcombe. On May 16

112

the Dodgers made the most important trade of the year, acquiring the other starting pitcher they needed to repeat as champions—ancient Sal "The Barber" Maglie, the formerly-despised ex-New York Giant. Maglie was acquired from the Cleveland Indians and won thirteen games against five losses, many of his wins, including a no-hitter, coming in crucial ballgames. The Dodgers' only real weakness was age, but as the season proved, they were just young enough.

The Cincinnati Redlegs, meanwhile, muscled their way out of the second division and into contention. To say their pitching was mediocre is to praise it extravagantly. They had one starting pitcher, Brooks Lawrence, who had the season of his life, winning his first thirteen decisions and finishing 19-10, although his ERA was a pedestrian 3.99; otherwise their pitching staff was unremarkable. They did, however, have an exceptional defense, especially their doubleplay combination of Roy McMillan at shortstop and Johnny Temple at second base. The true story of the Reds in 1956, though, was brute power.

The Redlegs nearly had five players hit 30 or more homers each. Frank Robinson tied the rookie home run record with 38; Wally Post poled 36; Ted Kluszewski slammed 35, his lowest total in four years; Gus Bell missed the 30-mark by one; and catcher Ed Bailey chipped in with 28. Three other players hit at least ten—Ray Jablonski (15), Smoky Burgess (12), and ex-Brave George Crowe (10). Even the seldom-used Bob Thurman slammed three in one game against Milwaukee. The Cincinnati team total of 221 matched the all-time home run mark set in 1947 by the New York Giants. The Redlegs displayed no subtlety in their style of play—they simply swung for the fences.

The Braves, of course, were not without talented ballplayers of their own. Their fielding was solid, although Johnny Logan's percentage slipped at shortstop and Eddie Mathews led third basemen in errors. Logan and Danny O'Connell formed a formidable combination up the middle, Joe Adcock led league first-sackers in fielding and his substitute Frank Torre was even better, and catcher Del Crandall was clearly the league's best at his position. Henry Aaron had established himself as one of the best hitters in baseball and in fact led the league with a .328 average. Adcock had his best home run season, belting 38, and Mathews slammed just one fewer. Yet without doubt the Braves' strength was their marvelous pitching staff, led by their perennial Big Three—Warren Spahn, Lew Burdette, and Bob Buhl.

At age 35 Spahn showed no lessening of his ability to pitch. As the speed of his fastball gradually declined, he developed other pitches and improved his control. He pitched more innings than all other league pitchers except two, his earned run average was second lowest, behind teammate Burdette, and his twenty wins were surpassed only by MVP and Cy Young Award winner Don Newcombe. Spahn experienced his customary slow start, with a 7-7 record at the All-Star break and 10-9 as late as August 6, but he won ten of his last twelve decisions to notch his seventh twenty-game season. His ratio of walks to innings pitched was third best in the N.L., and his twenty complete games were exceeded only by Robin Roberts.

Also enjoying an excellent season, his best up to that time, was Lew Burdette, the fidgety, suspected spitballer who drove rival managers, especially Birdie Tebbetts, to distraction with his motions. Burdette won nineteen, lost ten, and led the league with six shutouts and a 2.70 earned run average. The third portion of the starting triumvirate, Bob Buhl, added eighteen victories, his highest total, against eight losses. Rounding out the starting rotation, Ray Crone and Gene Conley contributed eleven and eight wins respectively. The bullpen, with Ernie Johnson and Dave Jolly, provided unspectacular relief.

For the fourth consecutive year the Braves won their home opener, but for the first time Warren Spahn was neither the starter nor the winner. A crowd of 39,766 brave souls sat through occasional light rain and snow to watch Burdette blank the Cubs, 6-0. The Braves won four of their first six games before experiencing what may have been the longest rain delay ever—eight days. From Sunday, April 22 until Monday, April 30, Milwaukee was rained out of five games. When they finally did get to play, an intimate gathering of only 6090 fans paid to see the chilly afternoon contest with the Cardinals, the smallest crowd from the team's arrival in 1953 until September 25, 1961. The hardy folks who did turn out saw Spahn pitch six and two-thirds hitless innings but finally lose, 2-0.

Between May 3 and May 10 five more games were rained out, making ten postponed games in sixteen days. Because of the terrible weather, when Ray Crone pitched (and won) the second game of a doubleheader on May 13 in Cincinnati, he was pitching with twenty days' rest. The May 18 and May 23 games were also rained out, but despite the intermittent schedule, or perhaps because of it, the Braves played good baseball through the first month and a half of the season. On May 30 they split a Wrigley Field slugfest with the Cubs, losing 10-9 and winning 11-9, in the process setting a record with fifteen home runs by two teams in the doubleheader. In the first game the Braves also tied a record

Doubleplay tandem Danny O'Connell and Johnny Logan

with consecutive homers by Mathews, Aaron, and Thomson. The next day Charlie Grimm's club belted five more home runs, tying major league records of fourteen homers in three consecutive games and sixteen in four games, in a 15-8 victory. Burdette carried a 15-0 lead into the ninth inning but, incredibly, required relief assistance from 35-year-old rookie Red Murff. It was hardly a clean kill, but the win sent the Braves into June in first place, leading the second-place Cardinals, who had played ten more games than Milwaukee, by one game.

June, however, was a disaster. First the Braves lost three out of four to the perennial tailenders from Pittsburgh. Then they were shut out on three hits by the reconstituted Sal Maglie, recently arrived from his exile in Cleveland. At age 39 Maglie was considered obsolete. He had not won a game since the previous July. On July 30, 1955, the Braves had faced Maglie when he was with the Giants. Milwaukee scored four runs before Maglie could get anyone out, and the next day he cleared waivers and was sold to the Indians. He never won a game for them, but now, back in the National League, he blanked the Braves on two singles by Mathews and a bunt single by Bruton. It was an ominous return for Sal the Barber.

After getting just three hits off Maglie, the Braves got only two the next afternoon against Roger Craig, then five hits the following evening against Don Newcombe for their sixth loss in seven games, leaving them in fourth place. Buhl beat Brooklyn in the series finale, but the Milwaukee club lost two of three to New York and then two of three to the last-place Phillies, plunging into the second division.

On June 15 in Ebbets Field the Dodgers beat the Braves, 5-4, on a bases-loaded single by Rube Walker with two out in the ninth, and word began to circulate that Charlie Grimm was on his way out as manager. The Braves were now just three games above .500 and playing lousy baseball. The next afternoon, Saturday, June 16, the Braves lost again, 3-2, on two unearned runs and an eighth-inning home run by Duke Snider. A few hours later Charlie Grimm made the expected and customarily diplomatic announcement that "I've decided to let somebody else take a crack at the job."

That somebody was Fred Haney, who had managed the Pittsburgh Pirates to three straight last-place finishes before being dumped and hired as a coach by Milwaukee on October 25, 1955. Haney assumed the reins of a team in fifth place, having lost nine of its last thirteen games, but still only four games out of first. Before leaving, Grimm told his team that they "could still win the whole thing," and that "any team that wins ten or twelve in a row...can win it."

Grimm's optimistic words became prophetic when, under Haney's guidance, the Braves proceeded to win eleven straight games. Jolly Cholly, the best lefthanded banjo-playing manager baseball ever saw, also left another legacy to the Braves—in his final decision, a couple hours before being told to resign voluntarily, Grimm reinstated the slump-ridden Joe Adcock in the starting lineup in place of Frank Torre.

The next day, in Haney's debut as Milwaukee's pilot, Adcock smashed three home runs, one a tape-measure shot over Ebbets Field's leftfield grandstand, in leading the Braves to a double-header sweep of the Brooklyn club. Dodger-killer Bob Buhl earned the win in the opener, his fourth straight against the Bums; Ray Crone won the nightcap, 3-1; and the Braves were on their way.

Next they traveled to Pittsburgh, swept a four-game series from

116

Haney's former club, and regained first place. Then they swept four games from the Giants, extending their victory parade to ten. In the New York series the Milwaukee pitching staff allowed just five runs in four games, bringing to nine the succession of games in which they allowed no more than three runs. On June 25 they lengthened their winning streak to eleven by scoring three runs in the ninth to beat nemesis Stu Miller, 8-5.

On June 26 the bubble finally burst. Robin Roberts beat the Braves and Ray Crone, starting a modest but sobering three-game losing skein for the Braves. The brief string of failures was cut in Wrigley Field when rookie Wes Covington missed a "take" sign on a 3-0 pitch and instead slammed a three-run homer to win the game, 4-3. The Braves alternated winning and losing for a week, including a doubleheader split at home on the coldest Fourth of July Milwaukee had ever recorded, and at the All-Star break they were in second place, a game and a half behind Cincinnati.

Milwaukee Sentinel Photo

Andy Pafko on concertina, Bob Roselli on clarinet, and Charlie Grimm on banjo

117

After the National League stars defeated their American League counterparts, 7-3, in Washington, D.C., the Braves initiated a new winning streak. At County Stadium on July 12 Bob Buhl shut out the Dodgers, his fifth straight victory over them, aided by a Joe Adcock home run. The second game of the scheduled doubleheader was postponed by an electrical storm and cloudburst so severe that the parking lots flooded and over 40,000 were forced to wait out a 45-minute downpour inside the stadium. The following night the Braves and Dodgers were able to complete a doubleheader, with Milwaukee winning both games, 8-6 and 6-5. Adcock led the way again with a home run in each game and seven runs batted in for the night. The next afternoon Haney's henchmen made the series unanimous, coming from behind to win, 3-2, in ten innings after Adcock's two-run homer in the seventh had tied the game. The Brooklyn team left town in third place, four and one-half games behind the pace-setting Milwaukeeans.

After the Dodger series the Pirates visited County Stadium for three games. Milwaukee hurlers allowed just four runs in the series and the Braves swept, extending their latest streak to seven. Next came the New York Giants, who succeeded in ending the win streak but then yielded to the hot-hitting Braves in the next two games.

The Phillies closed out Milwaukee's home stand with four games. Buhl shut them out on two hits in the opener, 10-0. The Phils won a fifteen-inning test of endurance in the second contest, the longest game the Braves had played at County Stadium, both in innings and in time. The battle lasted five minutes under five hours, but including two rain delays, it stretched out for six hours and twenty minutes. The home club gave the visitors a big send-off by bombing them twice, 8-7 and 16-5, in a Sunday doubleheader in which the Braves rapped 27 hits, including seven home runs, with Mathews and Adcock both hitting one in each game. The shellacking took such a toll on the Phillie pitching staff that shortstop Granny Hamner pitched the last inning for his team (and retired the side in order).

Before traveling to New York on July 24 to take on the Giants, the Braves stopped off in Toronto for an exhibition contest with the International League All-Stars. At a dinner before the game, Braves' President Lou Perini put the monkey on his team's back by proclaiming, "This is the best ball team in America. If I were as certain of a good seat as I am of winning the pennant, I would be a happy man."

Perini's ballplayers did nothing in New York to disappoint

118

him, sweeping their three games, the last an 11-0 rout behind Gene Conley's shutout hurling. The victory was the Braves' fifth in a row, fifteenth in seventeen games following the All-Star Game, and their ninth of the season without a defeat in the Polo Grounds, although only 3671 Gotham fans paid to witness the occasion. With the victory the Braves reached what was to be their high-water mark for the season—a five and one-half game advantage over the Redlegs, and six over the champion Dodgers.

From New York the Braves moved to Philadelphia's Connie Mack Stadium to tangle with the only team in the league who boasted an advantage in the season series. The Phillies increased that advantage at once, dumping the Braves twice by identical 5-2 scores, with a rain-out in between.

On July 30 Milwaukee beat the Dodgers in Brooklyn, 8-6, with Buhl beating the Flatbush favorites for the sixth time in 1956. The next night, though, the Dodgers took their show on the road to a minor league ballpark in Jersey City where a "home" crowd of more than 26,000 paying customers watched the Dodgers edge the Braves, 3-2, on a ninth-inning hit by Jackie Robinson. Back in Ebbets Field the Dodgers took two more from Haney's club behind excellent pitching by rejuvenated Sal Maglie and enormous Don Newcombe, and once again the Braves were in a horse-race.

In Pittsburgh the Braves took three out of four, the only loss accruing to Spahn on two ninth-inning Pirate tallies. The first victory of the three also was the first major league victory for Bob Trowbridge, who had been injured by a line drive from Lee Walls in a game on July 15. Ironically, Trowbridge's win was earned in relief after Braves starter Bob Buhl received a chip fracture of his right index finger on a line drive from Lee Walls. Buhl's injury, while not season-ending, caused him to miss one start and hindered his effectiveness for the remainder of the year. Before the injury Buhl had won fourteen games; after it he won just four in eight weeks.

For the next month, until Labor Day, the Braves played solid baseball and maintained their first-place standing, but they also suffered some disappointing losses. On August 8 they lost a ten-inning duel with old nemesis Herman Wehmeier, now with the Cardinals, by a 3-2 score. In that game Henry Aaron's 25-game hitting streak ended. Lew Burdette went the distance without walking or striking out a single batter and finally lost in the tenth.

Milwaukee later lost a game to the Cardinals and Murry Dickson, who at age 40 hurled a complete game victory, and two games to 36-year-old Larry Jansen of the Redlegs. Jansen, former New York Giant and 23-game winner in New York's miraculous 1951 pennant year, had not had a winning season since and had spent the previous two years pitching in the Pacific Coast League for Seattle. Within twelve days of being rescued by Cincinnati from obscurity in the Great Northwest, though, Jansen had beaten the Braves twice, both complete games, 8-1 and 8-2. On August 18 the Redlegs unleashed their full offensive fury on the Braves, blasting a major league record-tying eight home runs in destroying the Braves, 13-4, in Crosley Field. And on August 30, Milwaukee lost the right to play one of its home games at County Stadium—it was moved to Pittsburgh!

The unusual occurrence came about because the Braves and Pirates, in their final Milwaukee appearance of the season, tied 1-1 in a game called in the ninth inning due to rain. Under league rules, the site of the game was transferred to Pittsburgh, where the two teams had another game scheduled for September 18. In order for the rule to be suspended, allowing the game to be played in Milwaukee, all seven opposing National League clubs needed to approve the exception. Braves' President Perini petitioned the league for such an exception, but predictably the Pirates insisted the game be replayed in Forbes Field, not County Stadium. The game was scheduled for September 19 in Pittsburgh but was rained out again. The next day the game was finally played, with the Braves losing, 2-1, in ten innings.

Haney's team entered September in first place, two and one-half games ahead of Brooklyn and three and one-half up on Cincinnati. In a Labor Day doubleheader on September 3, a record County Stadium crowd of 47,604 saw Burdette beat the Redlegs in the opener for his eighteenth victory and the team's sixth in a row. The nightcap, though, marked the beginning of a disastrous five-game losing streak, three to Cincinnati and two to the Chicago Cubs. Milwaukee broke the string with a doubleheader sweep in Wrigley Field on September 9, then split a two-game set in Brooklyn, with Buhl losing to Maglie but winning the next day in relief for his eighth win of the year against the Dodgers, tying a 48-year-old record. On September 15 the Braves lost to the Phillies and fell out of first, by percentage points, for the first time since July 13, at the same time losing the season series to Philadelphia, 12-10.

In New York on September 17, the Braves split a doubleheader, making their twin-bill record for the year eleven wins, nine splits, and only one loss. They won a game and lost a game in Pittsburgh, then returned home and took two out of three from

120

the Cubs, regaining first place by a half-game over Brooklyn. On September 25 they beat the Reds in Cincinnati, with Spahn earning his 20th victory for the seventh season in his career, maintaining a one-half game lead as Brooklyn's Maglie threw a no-hitter at the Phillies. The next day, while the Braves were idle, Robin Roberts beat the Dodgers in front of an embarrassing "crowd" of 7847 in Ebbets Field, so the Braves entered the season's final weekend in first place, one game ahead.

Haney and his team were confident as they traveled to St. Louis for the climactic three-game series. They had Buhl, Spahn, and Burdette ready to face the Cardinals. They needed to win two games to clinch a tie for the pennant; a sweep guaranteed a date with the Yankees. All of Wisconsin eagerly awaited Milwaukee's first pennant and faithfully listened to the radio broadcasts—but it was not to be.

In the series opener the Cardinals jumped on Buhl in the first inning, scoring three runs, one unearned thanks to Jack Dittmer's error, while Buhl retired no one except a runner caught stealing at second base. The Braves tied the game in the fifth, but St. Louis scored twice in the sixth, getting the game's decisive run on a throwing error by, of all people, Del Crandall, only the second error of the year by the league's leading catcher. A Braves' rally in the eighth fell one short, and they lost, 5-4 The Dodgers were rained out, so Milwaukee remained in first by a technicality.

In the most important game in the brief history of the Milwaukee franchise, on Saturday night, September 29, Warren Spahn pitched magnificently—but lost [see Time Capsule]. The Dodgers had swept the Pirates in an afternoon doubleheader, so Brooklyn led by a full game. The next day Burdette struggled to a 4-2 win, but it was too little, too late. At 2:31 P.M. Milwaukee time, the Dodgers beat the Pirates, 8-6, to win the National League pennant. In the autumn of 1956, there was no joy in Beerville.

121

1956 Feat of Clay

"He's not only a great pitcher, but he's a great competitor, too."

—Frank Torre, September 29, 1956

When an athlete is the best at what he does, fans tend to think of him as invincible. Warren Spahn won 202 games during the 1950's, more than any other pitcher in the majors, but he also lost some important ones. Sometimes the fault was his teammates'; sometimes it was his own; sometimes it was just bum luck. In the 1956 season, in a pennant race decided by just one victory, it would be easy to cite Spahn's heartbreaking 2-1, twelve-inning loss to the Cardinals on September 29 as the crucial defeat. In actuality, in a season in which he won twenty and lost only eleven, Spahn suffered a disproportionate number of tough losses.

On April 30, a week after his 35th birthday, and after a full week of rainouts, Spahn went against the Cardinals on a cold Monday afternoon at County Stadium. For six and two-thirds innings the high-kicking southpaw flirted with a no-hitter, allowing only a first-inning walk to Stan Musial, then retiring eighteen batters consecutively. With two out in the seventh, though, and the game still scoreless, Spahn was touched for a Ken Boyer single off Mathews' glove, a solid hit by Rip Repulski, and a soft liner by Wally Moon just over Logan's mitt. Spahn left in the eighth for a pinch-hitter, losing 1-0, and suffered the loss to Cardinal Tom Poholsky.

Lack of fielding support caused Spahn's downfall against Cincinnati on May 25. Pitching at home, Spahn breezed through six innings with a four-hitter and a 5-1 lead. In the seventh Eddie Mathews kicked a grounder, Billy Bruton dropped a long fly off Frank Robinson's bat, and the Redlegs helped themselves to

122

three unearned runs. Milwaukee still led going to the ninth, but Spahn yielded a run before Bruton completed the Braves' generosity with a throwing error to allow the fourth unearned (and winning) run to score. Charlie Grimm was so agitated by the blown lead that he sent Andy Pafko to pinch-hit for Mathews in the bottom of the ninth, the first time the slugger had given way to a pinch-hitter since Buzz Clarkson batted for him in June of his rookie season with Boston. Pafko failed, the Braves failed, and Spahn took the defeat.

Against the Pirates at County Stadium on June 1, Spahn carried a 1-0 lead (he drove in the run himself) into the eighth inning. He gave up a pinch single to Jack Shepard (hitting .209), retired two batters, then allowed a single to Dick Groat. Pinch-runner Elroy Face tried to advance to third and should have been an easy out, but Henry Aaron threw wide of Mathews. The inning should have been over—instead Lee Walls smashed Spahn's next pitch over the fence in left, and Spahn had another loss.

Nine days later, again in his home park, Spahn opposed the lowly New York Giants. For six innings he was working on a three-hitter, leading 3-0 (two RBI's were his) and trying for his 37th career shutout. In the seventh inning, though, the plans went awry. The visitors used five hits, a walk, and an error to score four times and take the lead and ultimately the game. What hurt most was the nature of New York's hits—a bloop single by Bill White; a soft flyball by Daryl Spencer that fell along the leftfield line, inches beyond Bobby Thomson's reach, for a double; and the puniest triple imaginable by Foster Castleman. Castleman ducked out of the way of an inside fastball, the ball struck his bat and caromed over first base, and before Aaron could retrieve the ball from foul territory, Castleman was laughing at third.

For being tantalizingly close to victory yet failing to win, Spahn could hardly surpass the game in Philadelphia on June 27. He was enjoying a 3-2 lead in the ninth, he had retired ten batters in a row, he had two outs, and he had registered two strikes on Willie Jones. Jones singled, though, and when Jim Greengrass doubled to tie the game, Lew Burdette was brought in to finish the inning. He did, but in the eleventh Stan Lopata led off with one of the longest home runs ever hit in Connie Mack Stadium, and Ernie Johnson and the Braves were saddled with a bitter defeat.

On August 3 in Pittsburgh, Spahn labored through seven innings of a 1-1 tie, then gave up a run in the eighth on a walk, a double, and a sacrifice fly. With two out and nobody on base in the Milwaukee ninth the cause appeared lost, but Wes Covington singled, Bruton singled, and Del Crandall drove them home with a long double off the leftfield wall, putting the Braves on top, 3-2. Spahn had only to record three outs, but he could not. He got the leadoff batter, but back-to-back singles brought in reliever Dave Jolly with an opportunity to save Spahn's eleventh win. Jolly walked pinch-hitter Bob Skinner on four pitches, retired Lee Walls on a popup for the second out, but then gave up a hit by Dick Groat that scored both runners, and Spahn had his ninth loss.

The great lefty's luck against the Pirates continued bad on August 28 back in Milwaukee. Thanks largely to a pair of Mathews home runs, Spahn was staked to an early lead and looked determined to maintain it. He had a one-hit shutout for five innings and a 3-0 advantage, soon to become 4-0 in the sixth. Then with two out in the Pittsburgh seventh, Bill Virdon beat out a drag bunt, Groat slapped a single, Dale Long cracked a three-run homer, Bruton let in a run with an error, and the game was tied. Spahn was replaced by Bob Trowbridge, who gave up a run in the eighth and absorbed the 5-4 loss.

Even the greatest lefthander in baseball history cannot win them all, but under slightly different circumstances, Spahn might easily have increased his twenty-victory total and in the process carried the Braves to their first pennant.

1956 Nemeses - Stu Miller and Stan Lopata

"There's the first pitcher I ever saw that changed speeds on his change-up."

—Dusty Rhodes, of Stu Miller

One of them was a big, stocky catcher and occasional first baseman; the other was a wiry pitcher so slight he was blown off the mound by a gust of wind during the 1961 All-Star Game in Candlestick Park. The catcher had the oddest batting stance in baseball, a squat so deep as to make him appear sedentary; the pitcher had a 60-mile-per-hour fastball and a collection of slow curves, knucklers, and lobs. Neither was a world-beater: the catcher played regularly in only one season of a thirteen-year career and hit .254 lifetime; the pitcher achieved a 5-9 record in 1956 with a 4.50 earned run average. Against the Braves, though, both looked like they were on the fast track to Cooperstown.

The pitcher was Stu Miller, a junk-ball artist who shuttled between the minors and the majors until he was 30 years old, stopping off in four big-league cities without notable success—except against Milwaukee. In 1953 with the Cardinals, while on sabbatical from Columbus of the American Association, he beat the Braves three times, including a shutout. Of Miller's first eighteen major league victories, eight were garnered against the Braves—he was 8-2 vs. Milwaukee, 10-15 vs. the rest of the National League.

On May 11, 1956, Miller was traded from the Cardinals to the Phillies. He had spent all of 1955 pitching for Omaha in the American Association, and with the Cardinals in 1956 he had appeared in only three games, winning none while losing one. Nevertheless, a few hours after his arrival in Philadelphia he started against Milwaukee—and pitched a six-hitter to beat Lew

Burdette, 3-1. It was no fluke. On June 11 Miller faced the Braves again and beat them again, 6-2, outpitching Gene Conley for his second complete game. Finally on July 21 in a brief relief appearance in a fifteen-inning game in Milwaukee, Miller earned his third win of the season at the Braves' expense—one more victory than he earned against the remainder of the league all season.

If Stu Miller was the immovable object where the Braves were concerned, then Phillies' catcher Stan Lopata was the irresistible force. The hulking Lopata had never played in 100 games in a year until 1956. He had displayed power, hitting 22 homers in a part-time role in 1955; he had also shown the ability to punish the Braves, hitting a two-run, ninth-inning home run to beat Warren Spahn, 2-0, on September 9, 1953. It was not until 1956, though, at age 30, that Lopata reached his prime, against Milwaukee and the rest of the league.

In 1956 the Phillies were the only team in the league to hold an edge over the Braves, and one of the major reasons was Stan Lopata. In Stu Miller's first game with the Phillies, his 3-1 win on May 15, Lopata provided the needed offense, getting two hits in three tries, driving in one run and scoring another. On two occasions, July 22 and August 23, Lopata homered twice in one game against the Braves. On July 21 he contributed two singles, a double, and two intentional walks in the fifteen-inning game that Stu Miller won in Milwaukee. Perhaps most devastating, however, were back-to-back games in Philadelphia in late June. On the 26th the Phillies snapped Fred Haney's eleven-game winning streak after assuming managerial chores. The score was 4-2, and in three separate innings Lopata led off with a base hit and scored. The next night the Phils tied Milwaukee in the ninth, then beat them 4-3 in the eleventh inning on a home run by Lopata that cleared the roof of the grandstand in left field, only the fifth ball ever to do so.

As an ironic touch, both Miller and Lopata finished their careers as Braves, Lopata in 1959 and 1960 in Milwaukee, Miller in 1968 after the team had absconded to Atlanta.

Time Capsule - May 26, 1956

"Sure, I felt bad about it, but what else could [Birdie Tebbetts] do?"

—Johnny Klippstein

On May 26, 1956, the baseball world mourned the passing of Aloysius Szymanski, better known as Al Simmons. Old Bucket Foot Al, once "The Duke of Mitchell Street" before Connie Mack purchased him from Otto Borchert of the Brewers, had been elected to the Hall of Fame during the Braves' first year in Milwaukee, a well-deserved honor for a man who hit .381 and .390, respectively, in 1930 and 1931, beating out fellows named Gehrig and Ruth. To distract Milwaukee fans from the sadness of the day, the Braves and Redlegs staged one of the most unusual exhibitions of Abner Doubleday's invention that County Stadium ever witnessed.

It was a game in which Cincinnati used six different outfielders and six different Reds hit second in the batting order. It was a game that ended with the Cincinnati shortstop playing second base, the second baseman playing leftfield, and an outfielder/third baseman playing first base for the only time in his career. It was a game in which a man pitching a no-hitter through seven innings was taken out for a pinch-hitter. It was a game in which Cincinnati manager Birdie Tebbetts lost an argument with the umpires and, because he lost, his team tied the game—which cost the Redlegs a no-hitter. It was a game in which three Cincinnati pitchers allowed no hits for nine and two-thirds innings—and lost.

It was a day that should have belonged to Cincinnati pitcher Johnny Klippstein. The seven-year veteran and former Cub had never achieved a winning record, but since adopting a slider, he was in the midst of what was to be his most successful season in an eighteen-year career. He had shown promise in the past; against the Dodgers in 1955 he had come within two outs of a no-hitter before Pee Wee Reese spoiled it. His control, though, was never sufficient to allow consistency in his work. On this day in Milwaukee he pitched seven innings, allowing no hits but walking seven batters and hitting one.

In the second inning Klippstein's first pitch hit the dirt in front of home plate. His second pitch hit Henry Aaron. Klippstein proved his wildness was genuine by walking the next two batters, Bobby Thomson and Billy Bruton. Rookie first baseman Frank Torre, subbing for slump-ridden Joe Adcock, lined a ball that Frank Robinson caught in leftfield, but Aaron tagged and scored. Klippstein avoided further problems by striking out Del Crandall and rival pitcher Ray Crone, but Aaron's run proved to be Klippstein's undoing.

From the third through the sixth Klippstein and Crone were in charge, not even permitting a serious scoring threat, but in the bottom of the seventh Klippstein realized he was working on a no-hitter. He began to fidget, go to the resin bag, and take much more time between pitches. He walked Thomson leading off. Bruton sacrificed Thomson to second, then Torre flied out to Robinson again. With first base open and the pitcher due up afterward, Tebbetts ordered an intentional pass to Crandall. Crone nearly ruined the strategy by drawing a walk to load the bases, but Klippstein fanned pinch-hitter Wes Covington, batting for Danny O'Connell, to end the inning.

In the Cincinnati eighth Klippstein was scheduled to bat third. If his turn came with two out and nobody on base, he would hit. Smoky Burgess singled, though, and Roy McMillan bunted him to second, putting the tying run in scoring position. Tebbetts, just five outs away from a 1-0 loss, had no choice but to send in a pinch-hitter for the weaking-hitting Klippstein. Despite the possible no-hitter, Joe Frazier batted in Klippstein's place and grounded out. Ed Bailey did the same, the inning was over, and Klippstein was finished, replaced by ace reliever Hershell Freeman. Freeman retired the Braves on three flyballs, and the Redlegs came to bat in the ninth, still trailing 1-0. If Cincinnati failed to score, the Braves would become the first team to win a game without getting a hit.

It almost happened, but not quite. Crone retired pinch-hitter Bob Thurman, batting for Freeman, and then retired Gus Bell for the second out. Ted Kluszewski kept the Reds alive, though, with a bloop single to short center. Jim Dyck went in to run for the lumbering Kluszewski. Wally Post slapped a grounder toward third, Mathews made the pickup and threw to first, but Post beat the throw for an apparent infield hit, with Dyck moving to second. Home plate umpire Frank Secory, though, overruled third base umpire Frank Dascoli and called the ball foul. The Redlegs argued but lost, so Dyck returned to first and Post returned to the batter's box. With two strikes, Post then doubled to the fence in leftcenter. The throw in from the outfield reached the cutoff man, Johnny Logan, who had Dyck dead at the plate, but the throw was off target and Dyck scored. Crone got Ray Jablonski on a flyball to end the inning.

In the last of the ninth Dyck took Kluszewski's place at first base and Joe Black, the ex-Dodger, replaced Freeman, still protecting the no-hitter. Black had no problem with the Braves, getting three infield outs, and the game moved to extra innings. The Reds put a man on base on a Torre error but failed to score in the tenth. Black disposed of Crandall and Crone, but with two out Jack Dittmer, the seldom-used second baseman who had entered the game in the eighth for O'Connell, banked a double off the fence near the rightfield foul pole, narrowly missing a home run. The hit was the Braves' first of the day and Dittmer's first of the season. Logan hit a line drive toward left, but McMillan leaped and caught it for the third out.

Cincinnati threatened in the eleventh with a single and a walk, but Crone worked out of the jam. In the bottom of the inning the Braves finally ended the strange contest. Black retired Mathews, but Aaron sliced a ball off the end of his bat into the rightfield corner. Post misplayed the ball, and Aaron legged it to third. Pinch-hitter Chuck Tanner was intentionally passed, as was Bruton, setting up a force at any base. Torre then lined the ball past outfielder Dyck playing first base, and Aaron scored for a 2-1 Milwaukee victory.

After the game even the standings were strange. Owing to Milwaukee's ten early-season rainouts, the Braves, 15-9, had the National League's best winning percentage, .625, yet trailed St. Louis, 20-13, by a half game.

Time Capsule - July 17, 1956

"It's a good thing I didn't catch him."

—Joe Adcock

Joe Adcock's inability to evade a pitched baseball bordered on legend, but on the night of July 17, 1956, the big first baseman outdid himself. He was struck twice in one time at bat by Ruben Gomez of the New York Giants, and he never even got to first base. All he had to show for his travail was a bruised right wrist, a lemon-sized lump on his left thigh, and a wallet lighter by $100.

The Braves entered the game at County Stadium with a two-game advantage over second-place Cincinnati in the National League race. They were enjoying a seven-game winning streak begun after the All-Star Game, while their guests, the Giants, had lost seven straight. Milwaukee's Ray Crone was opposing the always-tough Gomez on the mound, and the player most likely to supply the offensive punch was the red-hot Adcock, who had slammed eight home runs in the past ten games.

The Milwaukee club wasted no time in jumping on Gomez, scoring twice in the first inning on a Danny O'Connell double, a walk to Eddie Mathews, and a pair of run-scoring singles by Hank Aaron and Wes Covington. Crone allowed nothing to the visitors in the first two frames, and in the bottom of the second, Adcock led off. The first pitch from Gomez was in tight, not a beanball but probably a brushback. Adcock, in his customary rigid stance, was struck on the right wrist, near the spot broken fifty weeks before by Gomez' teammate, Jim Hearn. The wounded Adcock began walking toward first base, rubbing his wrist and glaring at Gomez.

Halfway to first Adcock yelled an expression of his anger at Gomez, who responded with an obscenity. Like a wounded

130

animal, Adcock pivoted and charged toward the mound. Gomez froze in surprise, but only for a moment. Faced with an imminent battery by an enraged athlete fifty pounds heavier than himself, the slender hurler took the baseball he was holding and fired a strike at the approaching Adcock from just twenty feet away. The ball slammed into Adcock's left leg but barely slowed him down.

The ballfield was immediately engulfed by ballplayers from both dugouts, but Gomez had no inclination to wait for reinforcements. He sprinted toward the visitors' dugout. As he crossed the third-base line, Braves' coach John Riddle attempted an open-field tackle but missed. New York manager Bill Rigney sprang from his dugout to fend off Riddle. On-deck batter Del Rice, Adcock's roommate, joined the chase and dove into the dugout in pursuit, knocking over the Giants' Jackie Brandt in the process and scraping up both of them. Adcock followed into the dugout but was restrained by a crew of New Yorkers. More players arrived, joined by several police officers. With order still not achieved, stadium organist Jane Jarvis began to play "The Star-Spangled Banner." The ballplayers, patriots all, returned to their proper places, and in a short time play was resumed, with Frank Torre on first base in Adcock's place and Marv Grissom on the mound replacing Gomez.

One more minor disturbance impeded the progress of the game. New York manager Rigney loudly insisted that the police officers be removed from inside and in front of the Giants' dugout. Umpire Bill Jackowski informed the police that baseball rules prohibited outsiders from being in the dugout. Major league rules superseded the law of the land, and the police left. After the game, however, a bevy of plainclothesmen returned to escort Gomez from the clubhouse to a taxi.

After the fracas had been quelled, the Braves scored again to lead 3-0, but the Giants tied the score in the fourth. With two out and Willie Mays on second, Crone unleashed a wild pitch. Mays scored all the way from second, and Crone, visibly upset, promptly gave up home runs on successive pitches to Bill White and Dusty Rhodes. The Giants scored single runs in the sixth and seventh, the latter on a pinch home run by Jackie Brandt off lefty Lou Sleater. In the last of that inning Hank Aaron put Milwaukee back on top with a three-run homer off Hoyt Wilhelm, but a pinch double by Don Mueller off Gene Conley in the eighth tied the score at six.

Neither team could score in the ninth or tenth; in the eleventh, though, New York went ahead. Brandt singled and moved to second on a sacrifice by Ed Bressoud. Red Schoendienst was thrown out on a grounder to Conley. With two out and first base open, Braves' manager Fred Haney chose not to walk Mays intentionally. Mays immediately slammed a long double to the fence in leftcenter, scoring Brandt with the lead run. Hank Thompson followed with a hit to drive in Mays with an insurance run.

In the bottom of the eleventh the Braves tried to rally against former teammate Johnny Antonelli. Del Crandall singled with one out. Pinch-hitter Andy Pafko forced Crandall at second. Danny O'Connell walked to put the tying run on base, but Logan's line smash toward left was speared by third baseman Daryl Spencer for the final out. The latest winning streak was ended at seven.

In the visitors' locker room after the game, some New York players were critical of teammate Gomez for failing to hold his ground against the attacking Adcock. Gomez, however, clearly felt he had made the correct choice by thinking with his feet. In his Puerto Rican accent he explained, "I deedn't want to get my reebs broke, so I run." The following day Gomez was informed by National League President Warren Giles that he had been fined $250 and suspended for three days. The suspension was moot since Gomez would not have pitched on those days anyway. For his part, Adcock was fined $100 with no suspension.

Adcock was to face Gomez several more times during 1956 with no recurrence of their hostilities. The mayhem that he had tried to commit against Gomez went uncommitted. But while his vengeance was forgotten, his message apparently was received. Adcock was not hit by a pitch again during the remainder of the season.

Time Capsule - July 19, 1956

"Joe can hit the ball as far as anyone in baseball on a given day."

—Eddie Mathews

When Joe Adcock was bad, he was very bad—when he was good, he was dangerous! Through April and May of 1956 he was bad. He was hitting far below his weight when Charlie Grimm benched him on May 20, replacing him with rookie defenseman Frank Torre. On May 31 Grimm gave Adcock another chance— and the big guy smashed two home runs against the Cubs. Within a few days his cold bat put him back on the bench. He sat more than he played until June 16, Grimm's last day as manager, when he pinch-hit a home run, earning his starting job back. The next day in a doubleheader he hit three home runs, one of them a tape measure blast over the grandstand in Ebbets Field. Then he cooled off again until July 6.

On that Friday evening Big Joe belted a homer off Cubs' bonus baby Don Kaiser, an event of no apparent significance at that moment but which, in retrospect, signalled the start of an onslaught. The next afternoon he went homerless, but on the following day Adcock clubbed a pair of four-baggers against Kaiser's teammate Bob Rush. The All-Star Game and a rainout followed, but when competition resumed, so did Adcock, with a vengeance. Against Brooklyn on July 12 he hit a homer off Roger Craig in a 2-0 victory, then hit one in each game of a twin-bill with the Dodgers the next day.

In the first game he poked a two-run shot to cap a six-run first inning off Don Newcombe. In the nightcap he walloped a grand slam off Carl Erskine to lead the Braves to a 6-5 comeback win. The next day Adcock smashed a two-run shot off Sal Maglie in a 3-2, ten-inning Milwaukee victory, his fifth straight game hitting

133

a home run, giving him seven homers in seven games. The following afternoon he was shut out in the opener of a double-header, but in the second game he regained his home run touch against Pittsburgh's Gonzalo Naranjo.

For the next three games Adcock failed to hit one out of the park, although the middle game of the trio was the Ruben Gomez incident in which Adcock never got a chance to swing at a pitch. On July 19, though, the powerful first baseman climaxed his power binge with the most productive game of his career. He had hit more home runs in a game (4) and tallied more total bases (18), but he had never before driven in as many as eight runs in one game.

The powerful swing of Joe Adcock

It was the final game (announcer Earl Gillespie probably called it the rubber game) of a three-game series at the Stadium with the New York Giants, a series that had begun with Gomez tattooing Adcock and the cellar-dwelling New Yorkers snapping the Braves' seven-game winning streak. Warren Spahn was on the mound for the home club, opposing the nefarious Jim Hearn, the big righthander who had broken Adcock's arm with a pitch 353 days before. The Braves pounded Hearn immediately. Leadoff man Danny O'Connell walked, Billy Bruton singled, Ed Mathews singled home O'Connell, and Hank Aaron walked to load the bases for Adcock.

With a light drizzle falling, Adcock took Hearn's first pitch for a strike. On the next pitch he connected and drove the ball far beyond the fence in leftcenter, his fourth grand slam of his career and his second within a week. The Braves led 5-0, there were still no outs, and Hearn was replaced by rookie southpaw Joe Margoneri. While the pitching change was being made, the drizzle turned to a downpour and time was called. For an hour and thirty-seven minutes Adcock and his teammates waited for the rain to stop and preserve his grand slam and their grand start. Finally the cloudburst abated, play resumed, and Margoneri put the Braves down without further damage. He did so again in the second and third while Spahn also went unscored upon.

In the fourth the Giants got a run back when Jackie Brandt singled home Willie Mays, but Milwaukee scored three in the home fourth on base hits by O'Connell and Bruton, a Mathews double, and an RBI single by Adcock. New York bunched three hits in the sixth for another score, but again the Braves responded with an explosion, this time against fourth Giant pitcher Dick Littlefield, the peripatetic lefty working for his eighth team in seven years.

As in the opening inning, O'Connell started the trouble by drawing a base on balls. Bruton bunted for a hit, and Mathews, trying to sacrifice, bunted too well and was also safe to load the bases. Aaron bounced a grounder up the middle that Ed Bressoud flagged down but could not throw to beat Aaron to first. O'Connell scored and the bases should have remained full, but Mathews inexplicably broke for third. Seeing him approaching, Bruton had no choice but to try for home, but he was a dead duck. With Milwaukee leading 9-2, the baserunning blunder had no impact on the outcome of the game. Adcock, though, made the *faux pas* significant by belting a Littlefield pitch into the bleachers for his second four-bagger of the afternoon. Had Mathews not chased Bruton off third, Adcock would have entered the record book as the first National Leaguer to hit two grand slams in the same game, a record held by three American Leaguers, the last being former Milwaukee Brewer Rudy York.

Adcock's blast gave him four hits in four at-bats for the day: a single, a double, and two home runs, two runs scored and eight driven in. Manager Fred Haney showed his disdain for individual records by pulling Adcock out after the sixth inning and substituting Torre, depriving Adcock of any chance to equal Jim Bottomley's major league record of twelve RBI's in one game, set in 1924. Thereafter each team scored one more run, Milwaukee's coming in the last of the eighth on an RBI single—by Adcock's sub, Frank Torre. Spahn retired the last nine men he faced to earn an easy 13-3 win, his ninth of the season.

Adcock's latest offensive burst gave him nine home runs in his last eleven games, and ten home runs in his last thirteen games, while raising his average to .310. The most surprising feature of this home run binge may have been that all of it occurred in County Stadium, a ballpark in which Adcock had never had much success because, he said, the background did not allow him to see the ball well.

The hot streak was no fluke, though. Three days after his eight-RBI performance, he hit two more homers in a doubleheader, also in County Stadium. He finished the season with 38 home runs, by far his highest total, and his ratio of home runs to times at bat was the best in the league.

Time Capsule - September 13, 1956

"This is the greatest thrill I've ever had in baseball."

—Warren Spahn

The Braves entered the doubleheader in Philadelphia's Connie Mack Stadium needing to win. The five and a half game lead they had enjoyed seven weeks earlier had been dissipated and now stood at one game over the defending champion Dodgers. On this night the Phillies, the only team in the league the Braves did not lead in the season series, were tough, as usual, but Fred Haney's team made all the clutch plays and won both games. Rookie lefthander Taylor Phillips and veteran southpaw Warren Spahn were both brilliant; Henry Aaron drove in the winning run in each game; and Bobby Thomson saved each game by throwing out a runner at the plate. The Braves looked like pennant winners.

Rookie Bob Trowbridge started the opener for Milwaukee and put himself in the hole by walking the leadoff batter, Richie Ashburn, then advancing him to second with a wild pitch. Stan Lopata drove him home with a single, and Philadelphia led 1-0 in the first. They added a run in the fourth on a sacrifice fly by Czechoslovakian-born Elmer Valo, so when Trowbridge left for a pinch-hitter in the sixth, he was losing 2-0.

For the first six innings the Braves only put one runner on base, and that was on Danny O'Connell's weakly-hit single. Jack Meyer, an infrequent starter, was in the midst of pitching what would be the finest game of his career (his career was ended prematurely by a back injury in 1960, and he died before reaching 35). In the seventh, though, O'Connell singled again, Aaron doubled him home, and Eddie Mathews singled to tie the game.

137

After the Braves tied it, neither team could generate much offense. The Phillies put two men on in the seventh, but Taylor Phillips, Trowbridge's replacement in the sixth, got dangerous Stan Lopata to ground into a doubleplay. Phillips continued to pitch out of trouble in the ninth, when the home team got two hits, and in the tenth, when two Phillies walked. Meyer became invulnerable after his seventh-inning lapse, and the game stayed tied at two through eleven innings.

In the bottom of the twelfth Ted Kazanski led off with a hard smash on the ground toward third base. Mathews fielded the ball but threw badly toward first and the runner was safe. Willie Jones tried to sacrifice but bunted too hard and forced Kazanski at second. Lopata beat out a bouncer to Logan at deep short, advancing Jones. Then Del Ennis, the Phillies' perennial RBI leader, lined the apparent game-winning hit to leftcenter. Bobby Thomson charged the ball, scooped it up cleanly, and rifled a throw to catcher Del Crandall in time to tag the sliding Jones. Phillips got Marv Blaylock on a popup to end the inning.

In the thirteenth O'Connell was grazed on the shoulder by an inside pitch, and he scored the lead run moments later when Aaron blasted a triple off the scoreboard in rightcenter. The Braves failed to bring Aaron across, but Phillips completed his eighth straight inning of shutout relief to sew up a 3-2 victory. Meyer, despite a thirteen-inning seven-hitter, took the loss.

The second game matched the National League's two mound masters: Spahn, trying for his 200th career victory, and Robin Roberts, winner of 177 games and the league's top winner for four years running. On August 24 Spahn had bested Roberts on a five-hitter in a 6-1 win, and on September 1 he had hurled a two-hitter at the Cardinals. Since then, however, he had struggled, getting knocked out in the second inning in each of his two latest starts.

Once again the second inning was traumatic for Spahn. Two banjo-hitters, Jim Greengrass and Andy Seminick, whose combined 1956 batting averages were exceeded by Ted Williams alone in 1941, hit back-to-back home runs to put Philadelphia ahead, 2-0. Roberts held Spahn's mates scoreless until the fifth, so in that inning Spahn himself doubled off the scoreboard to drive home Bruton and Crandall and tie the score. After that Roberts and Spahn held their opponents at bay until the last of the ninth.

As in the twelfth inning of the first game, an error put the Braves in imminent danger of losing. This time Johnny Logan mishandled a bouncer by Ashburn to put the winning run on base. Kazanski bunted him to second. Willie Jones received an intentional pass. Spahn retired nemesis Lopata, but, as in the opener, Ennis lined a single to leftfield for the apparent game-winning hit. Again Thomson charged the ball, fielded it, and fired to the plate. Once again Crandall put the tag on the sliding runner, and once again the runner was out. The Phillies argued vehemently but lost. Manager Mayo Smith was ejected, and the Braves had new life.

Neither team scored in the tenth. Spahn's third hit of the game and Logan's second gave them a chance, but O'Connell bounced a doubleplay ball to Roberts to kill the rally. Spahn walked a man but got former teammate Roy Smalley to ground into a twin-killing to end the inning.

Hank Aaron led off the eleventh inning with a line shot into the seats in centerfield to put Spahn ahead 3-2. Milwaukee put two more men on base but failed to pad the margin because of sloppy baserunning, which seemed insignificant when Spahn fanned pinch-hitter Granny Hamner and retired Ashburn. With two out, though, Ted Kazanski, a non-slugger with fewer than half as many career home runs as Spahn, lined a Spahn pitch into the seats in left to tie the game at three. Willie Jones then popped out.

Ben Flowers replaced Roberts, who had departed for a pinch-hitter, and after he retired Crandall, Spahn drew his second walk of the game. Logan also walked, and Flowers was yanked. Curt Simmons replaced him but did no better—he walked O'Connell to load the bases. Aaron hit a long flyball to score Spahn with the lead run, and Mathews grounded out.

In the Phillies' last turn at bat, Spahn gave up a leadoff base hit to Lopata, but Mathews turned Ennis' hot smash into a doubleplay. Finally, Greengrass popped up to Adcock, and Spahn had a 4-3, twelve-inning win—his long-awaited 200th victory.

The double victory increased the Milwaukee lead over idle Brooklyn to two games. The two game-saving throws by Thomson persuaded Fred Haney to rescind the $100 fine he had levied against the Flying Scot for trying to steal home without authorization the day before in Brooklyn. Clearly, though, the moment belonged to the Braves' star southpaw and his historic victory.

Time Capsule - September 29, 1956

"The whole country is going to be sore at us for spoiling it for the Braves. Everybody wanted them to win."

—Cardinal Outfielder Hank Sauer

St. Louis-born T.S.Eliot, the Nobel Prize-winning poet, wrote that "April is the cruellest month." Had Eliot been in his home town at venerable Busch Stadium on Saturday, September 29, 1956, watching the local ballclub play the Milwaukee Braves, he might have rewritten that line. The Braves had begun September in first place, two and one-half games ahead of the Dodgers. They had arrived in St. Louis on September 28 one game in front with three games remaining. They had their top three pitchers ready to wrap up their first pennant. The anticipation of their first World Series had driven Milwaukee fans near delirium. For this series every radio in Wisconsin was tuned to the ballgame or was in the repair shop.

In the series opener on Friday night, the Cardinals had driven Bob Buhl off the mound in the first inning and gone on to a 5-4 victory. The loss had cut the Braves' lead to a half-game over the Dodgers, who had been rained out. On Saturday afternoon Brooklyn swept two games from the Pirates, putting Milwaukee in a must-win situation. The man assigned the task of earning the biggest victory in the history of the franchise was, fittingly, Warren Spahn.

Spahn was completing what was for him a typical season, which is to say outstanding. He had begun slowly, sporting a modest 7-7 record at the All-Star break and only 10-9 as late as August 6. Since that time, though, he had been magnificent, winning ten of eleven decisions, twice saving games in relief the day after hurling complete games, registering his 200th career

140

triumph, and earning his 20th victory for the seventh season.

Spahn's counterpart, Herm Wehmeier, had a history of giving the Braves trouble, but he showed no early sign of it this night. The second batter of the game, Billy Bruton, smacked Wehmeier's first pitch to him onto the roof in rightfield to put Spahn ahead, 1-0. In the third Logan and Bruton started the inning with hits off Wehmeier, but Logan rounded the bag too far and was picked off before he could get back. That carelessness proved costly when Hank Aaron hit a grounder that would have advanced Logan to third and Eddie Mathews lofted a fly that would have sent Logan home with another run. Instead Milwaukee's total remained at one.

In the meantime, Spahn was untouchable. Through the first five innings the old southpaw did not allow a hit, the only Cardinal baserunner coming in the third when Bobby Del Greco drew a base on balls. In the sixth Spahn extended his no-hitter by retiring Del Greco and Wehmeier, but second baseman Don Blasingame broke the string by placing a double in the gap in rightcenter. Al Dark, Spahn's teammate from the 1948 Boston pennant team, followed with a double off the wall in left to drive Blasingame home with the tying run. After those two aberrations, Spahn retired Stan Musial to end the inning. He then put the Cardinals down in order in the seventh and again in the eighth. Wehmeier, though, was being just as stingy with the Milwaukee club, and the teams stayed tied 1-1 going to the ninth.

In the ninth, however, it became increasingly clear that this ballgame belonged not so much to Wehmeier or Spahn but to Frank "Trader" Lane, the cigar-chomping General Manager of the Cardinals. Lane, who had always treated ballplayers as if they were so many bubblegum cards to be swapped, had engineered a series of deals back in late spring which now, in the waning stages of the most important game the Milwaukee Braves had ever played, were having a collective effect on the pennant race—not for St. Louis, but for Milwaukee.

On May 11 Lane had peddled pitchers Ben Flowers, Stu Miller, and Harvey Haddix to the Phillies for pitchers Herman Wehmeier and Murry Dickson. On May 17 Lane dealt outfielder Bill Virdon for two Pittsburgh Pirates, pitcher Dick Littlefield and outfielder Bobby Del Greco. On June 14 Lane packaged Littlefield with second baseman Red Schoendienst, catcher Bill Sarni, and outfielder Jackie Brandt and shipped them to the New York Giants in exchange for catcher Ray Katt, former Braves pitcher Don Liddle, first baseman Whitey Lockman, and shortstop Alvin Dark. The eight players obtained by St. Louis had no significant effect on the Cardinals' season; they still lost more games than they won. However, three of Lane's acquisitions took on significance in this game with the Braves. Dark, of course, doubled in the sixth to drive in the tying run; Wehmeier kept his team in the game despite Spahn's brilliant hurling; and in the ninth, Del Greco became a genius in cleats in centerfield.

Mathews led off in the Milwaukee ninth and for the first time in the series hit the ball hard—very hard. He hit the ball nearly 420 feet. It looked and sounded like a home run at impact, but Del Greco raced back to the deepest part of the field and caught the ball on the run at the wall in dead center. Joe Adcock followed with a base hit. Bobby Thomson watched a called third strike. With two out, Jack Dittmer took a hefty swing at heroism and lined the ball toward the wall in rightcenter. The drive look like a certain extra-base hit, but Del Greco, sprinting out of obscurity, lunged and speared the ball in the webbing of his glove just inches in front of the wall.Once again Spahn's teammates had failed to get him a run. Undaunted, Spahn set the Cardinals down in order for the seventh time in nine innings.

The Braves failed to score again in the tenth. The Cardinals got the third hit off Spahn, a single by Ken Boyer, but nothing close to a run. In the top of the eleventh Aaron legged his third infield hit and Mathews walked, but Adcock and Thomson each hit into a fielder's choice to kill the threat. In the last of the eleventh Spahn breezed through another three-up, three-down inning.

The denouement occurred in the twelfth. Dittmer led off the Milwaukee half with a base on balls. Felix Mantilla went in to run for him. Crandall dutifully sacrificed, bringing up Spahn with the lead run in scoring position. Haney needed a pinch-hitter, preferably a lefthanded hitter. Wes Covington should have been available for the job, but he had felt ill before the game and had returned to the hotel. Rookie defensive specialist Frank Torre was on the bench, but Spahn was probably his equal with a bat. Haney let the veteran hurler hit for himself, and he made good contact, but Del Greco hauled in his medium-length fly. Logan was the last chance. He sent a long fly to the warning track in center, but once again Del Greco made the catch.

In the bottom of the twelfth the dream died. Logan made a nice play on Dark's grounder and threw him out, but Stan Musial, hitless in four at-bats, hit Spahn's slow curve off the wall in rightcenter for a double. Boyer received an intentional pass to set up a doubleplay. Still battling, Spahn threw Rip Repulski a sinker and got the hard grounder he wanted for the twin-killing. It was not meant to be. The ball bounced crazily, struck Mathews

142

on the knee, and rolled in foul territory down the leftfield line while Musial trotted home with the deciding score. The crowd of 25,587, who had loudly cheered the visiting Braves all night, gasped and sat stunned.

As the courageous southpaw walked from the mound, tears visible on both cheeks, an enterprising photographer approached to record the moment. Spahn threw his glove at the interloper and trudged to the dugout.

Milwaukee Journal Photo

Feisty Fred Haney almost, but not quite, led the Braves to the pennant in 1956.

1956 Swan Songs

"I'm not going to Wichita. If I'm not sold to another major league club, I'll quit."

— Jim Pendleton, June 15, 1956

Two of the Braves' Originals left the club after the 1956 season, neither a star, but both sharing important moments in the early years. The first, versatile Jim Pendleton, had been a semi-regular outfielder in 1953, a .299 hitter in 251 times at bat. He could run and he could hit. Pendleton was never considered a slugger, hitting just eight homers as a Brave, but on one memorable Sunday afternoon in Pittsburgh, August 30, 1953, "Sunny Jim" smacked three home runs in one game as Milwaukee buried Pittsburgh, 19-4.

Pendleton's final appearance with the Braves was uneventful, as were his final two stints with the team in 1955 and 1956 (he was 0 for 21 during those years). Pendleton pinch-hit in the seventh inning of a crucial game in Milwaukee on September 22, 1956. He was called out on strikes with runners on first and second and one out. He then stayed in the game and played second base, failing at bat amid a three-run eighth-inning rally as the Braves suffered a critical 5-4, ten-inning loss to the Cubs. The defeat in the sixth-last game of the season cost the Braves a chance to slip into first place; eight days later they lost the pennant by one game.

The man for whom Pendleton batted that day was second baseman Jack Dittmer, the Braves' regular second sacker in their first Milwaukee season, who also left the team after the 1956 campaign. Dittmer never received much playing time after the trade for Danny O'Connell, although Dittmer's 1953 batting statistics far excelled those of O'Connell while he played in Milwaukee.

The final appearance by Dittmer in a Milwaukee uniform occurred in the Braves' toughest loss—the twelve-inning defeat in St.Louis on September 29, 1956, which cost the Braves the pennant [see Time Capsule]. Dittmer played the first eleven innings at second base, leaving for a pinch-runner in the top of the twelfth. He nearly became one of the greatest heroes of the Milwaukee years when, with two out in the ninth and a runner on base, he smashed an apparent extra-base hit toward the wall in rightfield. Bobby Del Greco's miraculous catch, however, snatched Dittmer from the jaws of Milwaukee baseball immortality. Dittmer had one more chance, leading off the twelfth with a base on balls against Herman Wehmeier, then yielding to the swifter-running Felix Mantilla. Mantilla died at second, though, and Dittmer never again took the field for the Braves.

Jack Dittmer fires to first base.

145

1957

"When somebody always came through to keep us up there, I was convinced that here was a club that wasn't going to be beaten by anything."

—Fred Haney

It was not easy, but they made it. After four years of high hopes, moral victories, great promise, bitter disappointments, and an agonizing near-miss, the Braves reached the World Series in Fred Haney's first full season as their manager. With a talent-laden club and a recent history of first-division finishes, Milwaukee's first pennant hardly qualified as a surprise. Most baseball prognosticators, journalists, and local fans anticipated the event; nevertheless, the accomplishment produced euphoria along the western shore of Lake Michigan. Wisconsin'e largest city was given cause for celebration to rival V-E Day and the repeal of Prohibition.

The Braves had approached their fifth season in Milwaukee with the same nucleus of players with whom they had begun in Wisconsin. On Lincoln's Birthday they sold second baseman Jack Dittmer to the Detroit Tigers, and two weeks before opening day they traded Jim Pendleton to the Pittsburgh Pirates for infielder Dick Cole. They also released veterans Chet Nichols and Lou Sleater. Their other acquisitions were catcher Carl Sawatski, from Toronto, and lefthanded pitcher Juan Pizarro, called up from Wichita. The rest of the team was held over from 1956—with the same strengths, but also the same weaknesses.

The most urgent needs Haney had for 1957 were long-standing ones: a second baseman who could both hit and play the position, a leftfielder who could hit for a respectable average and drive in runs, and a relief pitcher who could come in and protect a lead in the eighth or ninth inning. Bobby Thomson and Danny O'Con-

146

nell had failed to fulfill the expectations with which they had been obtained in 1954, and Dave Jolly and Ernie Johnson were only occasionally effective out of the bullpen. As the season developed, the team's needs turned out to be even more severe than expected, for in 1957 the Braves were besieged by injuries, yet never overcome by them. Amazingly, every need was filled as it arose.

The major injuries of the season were suffered by Joe Adcock and Billy Bruton. Adcock, the big but brittle slugging first baseman, broke a bone in his right leg while sliding into second on June 23 at County Stadium. The injury kept him out of the lineup until mid-September and made a full-timer out of defensive specialist Frank Torre. Bruton's injury was worse—strained ligaments in his knee, suffered in a collision with Felix Mantilla on July 11, sidelined the fleet centerfielder until May 24 of the following year. Bruton's incapacity forced a series of lineup changes that sometimes became comical.

Other injuries less serious but of substantial duration forced adjustments by Haney. Lew Burdette was rendered essentially useless from mid-May until mid-June by a strained ligament in his pitching arm. Mantilla missed nineteen games after his collision with Bruton damaged his knee. Johnny Logan missed over three weeks in August and September because of an infected shinbone, and Bob Buhl was disabled for the same span by a sore shoulder, preventing a sure 20-game season for him. Even manager Haney missed five games while hospitalized with an attack of gastritis, returning the day Adcock broke his leg.

The combination of injuries and poor performance caused numerous roster changes during the season, some minor some major. On June 8 Chuck Tanner was deemed expendable and was sold to the Chicago Cubs. Had he lasted another five weeks or so, he might have gotten the chance to play regularly, but by the time the chance came, he was a regular in Wrigley Field.

During the week following Tanner's departure, though, the Braves' crucial deal of the year—perhaps the decade—was hatched. Milwaukee General Manager John Quinn traveled east to try to bolster the Braves' lineup through a trade, either for the Giants' second baseman Red Schoendienst or the Pirates' outfielder Frank Thomas. Milwaukee had coveted Schoendienst for some time, since his days in St. Louis. Cardinal General Manager Frank Lane had offered him to the Braves, but he wanted Bob Buhl and Joe Adcock in return. The Giants reportedly were willing to take Buhl and Danny O'Connell, a somewhat more reasonable price but still too high. As the June 15 trade deadline approached, the deal seemed to have fallen through, but at the end Quinn was able to pry Schoendienst loose in exchange for pitcher Ray Crone, O'Connell, and Bobby Thomson. Thomson was hitting so poorly that his trade value was almost nil, and O'Connell was superfluous once Schoendienst was obtained, so the trade essentially was Crone for the Redhead. Quinn should at least have been fingerprinted.

All Schoendienst did for the Braves was bat .310 (75 points higher than O'Connell was hitting at trade time), hit safely in 23 consecutive games spanning most of July (second-longest streak in Milwaukee's history), go to bat 425 times and strike out just seven times (rookie Johnny DeMerit fanned more in 34 at-bats), and achieve the highest fielding average among league second sackers. Meanwhile back in the Polo Grounds, O'Connell hit .266 with the Giants, Thomson hit .242, and Crone won four games while losing eight.

As important as Schoendienst was for Milwaukee, he was by no means the only meaningful addition. On June 19 outfielder Wes Covington was recalled from the Wichita farm team after being sent down on May 17. In just 96 games he blasted 21 home runs and drove in 65 runs to more than offset the loss of Bruton. A week after Covington was recalled, relief pitcher Don McMahon was brought up from Wichita, and his impact was immediate and electric. In his first six appearances as a Brave, the fireballing fireman hurled ten innings while allowing five hits and one walk, striking out nine and giving up no runs. Of course his earned run average could not remain at zero forever; by season's end it had ballooned to 1.54 in 32 appearances covering 47 innings. If the '57 Braves had an unsung hero, it was Don McMahon.

On July 6, with Adcock convalescing, the Braves again beat the bushes and flushed out Vernal "Nippy" Jones, a first baseman whom they purchased from Sacramento of the Pacific Coast League. Finally, with outfielders still in short supply, the Braves again raided their Wichita farm club on July 28 and came up with Bob Hazle, quickly dubbed "Hurricane" Hazle by the sportswriters. He proved to be one of the shortest-lived heroes on record, but in the final two months of the season he batted .403 and gave Milwaukee fans some moments to remember.

Fill-ins and substitutes were important, but the bit players and walk-ons did not earn the Braves a place in the 1957 World Series. Milwaukee's first pennant can be explained in two words—pitching and power, in that order. As it had since 1953, pitching meant the Big Three—Spahn, Burdette, and Buhl. As was the custom, Spahn led the way with 21 victories, the highest

Red Schoendienst, acquired in mid-1957, led the Braves to the pennant.

total in the league and his eighth season winning twenty or more. He also led the National League in complete games with eighteen, tied for second-most shutouts, tied for second-lowest earned run average, and had the third-best winning percentage. It was a typical Spahn season, achieved with the customary mediocre start—he was 10-8 on August 5—and a customary steamroller finish—he won nine straight in 33 days from August 6 through September 7.

Burdette followed the same pattern, starting slowly because of an injured pitching arm, then winning eight of his last ten decisions to finish 17-9. On the contrary, Buhl won sixteen games by August 14 but succumbed to arm trouble after that and finished at 18-7, a step behind Spahn with a 2.74 ERA. Among the Big Three, they accounted for 99 games started, 56 wins, and 46 complete games.

To augment their pitching prowess, Haney's club hit more home runs than any Braves team ever had, a major league high

199. The four-baggers were distributed throughout the lineup, but their largest concentration fell on two hitters— perennial slugger Eddie Mathews, although his 32 homers marked his lowest total since his rookie year in Boston, and emerging slugger Henry Aaron, the free-swinging 1956 batting champ. Aaron had been best-known as a high-average line-drive hitter, but in 1957 he started with a game-winning blast in the home opener and never let up, finishing with major league highs of 44 home runs, 132 runs batted in, and 369 total bases. So complete was Aaron's home run metamorphosis that on July 5, when he slammed his seventh home run in eight games, he moved two games ahead of Babe Ruth's pace from his record year of 1927. It was a brief chase, however; Aaron was not destined to break a Ruth home run record until seventeen years and a franchise shift later.

Along with the pitching and power the Braves possessed, they also received a fine managerial performance by Fred Haney. He did not have the luxury of simply selecting a lineup during spring training and then sending them out in clean uniforms every day. The team's spate of injuries required judicious use of young pitchers like Bob Trowbridge and Juan Pizarro. Even more troublesome was the outfield corps.

Following the injury to Bruton in July, Haney's selection of starters was often based not on who was best at a position or who was hot but on who was ambulatory. For instance on July 18, in a game in which his team regained first place after a 16-day absence, Haney penciled in a starting lineup that included 36-year-old Andy Pafko in rightfield, subbing for Aaron, now the centerfielder in place of the injured Bruton, but who was himself disabled after stepping on a drain pipe in Philadelphia the night before; Frank Torre, replacing the injured Adcock; Wes Covington, summoned from Wichita after Thomson was traded; and Johnny DeMerit, a 21-year-old "bonus baby" making his first big-league start, in Aaron's new spot in center. Late in the game Del Crandall (on the bench in favor of Buhl's personal catcher, Del Rice) pinch-hit for DeMerit, necessitating Schoendienst's move to centerfield, his first time in the outfield since 1949, while Dick Cole filled in at second base. Two days later Crandall started in rightfield for the first time, and the day after that, recently-acquired first baseman Nippy Jones took his turn as a rightfielder, his first time in ten years. During these times, a fan could not tell the lineups even with a scorecard. Nevertheless, the Braves continued to win.

They had started winning on opening day. Spahn threw a four-hitter at the Cubs in Wrigley Field to win, 4-1. Two days later Burdette hurled a six-hit shutout, Aaron slammed a home run, and Milwaukee beat Cincinnati, 1-0, to win their fifth straight home opener before 41,506 partisans. On April 22 the Braves won their fifth consecutive game of the year by beating the Cubs, 9-4, with help from the nefarious Bobby Del Greco, who dropped an easy flyball to allow three runs to score. Before April was over the Braves had won nine of ten games, their best start since coming to Milwaukee, and it was May 16 before they relinquished their hold on first place.

On May 27 the Braves lost their third straight ballgame, 11-6, in ten innings against Cincinnati to fall three and one-half games out of first, the lowest level they would reach all season. That loss was punctuated by a brawl, the principals of which were Johnny Logan and the Reds' Hal Jeffcoat, who fought to a draw after a tag play at third base. On June 1 in a loss to the Cardinals at County Stadium the Braves again fell three and a half games back, this time in fourth place. For the first time the Milwaukee fans booed manager Fred Haney as his team lost its tenth game of the homestand (while winning seven). In all likelihood they were more angry with absentee owner Lou Perini than with Haney; Perini refused to allow Braves games to be televised, even road games, even those shown nationally. Considering the fans' record-breaking support at home, they at least felt entitled to watch their heroes in an occasional away game.

Back on the road, Haney's team began to play better. On June 10 they evened their Jersey City record at one apiece (having lost there on July 31, 1956) as Dodger-killer Bob Buhl beat the Bums with a four-hitter. Three days later Buhl's teammates fought their way back into first place in an 8-5 win in Ebbets Field. The Dodgers' 20-year-old hurler Don Drysdale initiated a melee by hitting pugnacious Johnny Logan in the back with a fastball. Before the fracas was over, Mathews had knocked Drysdale down, and Logan and Drysdale had both been ejected. After the dust cleared, though, the Braves stood back atop the National League standings after a four-week hiatus.

For the next month Haney's ballclub ducked in and out of the lead, not straying far either way. At All-Star time on July 9 they were in second place, two and one-half out. After the break they took three of four from Pittsburgh, then moved on to Brooklyn. If the season had a turning point, it occurred in the two-game series in Ebbets Field on July 14 and 15.

The Dodgers won the opener, 3-2, beating Buhl on a two-run homer in the ninth by Gil Hodges. The next night Bob Trowbridge started for Milwaukee, opposing Brooklyn's Drysdale.

151

Trowbridge only lasted two and two-thirds innings, giving up five runs, but he did well by comparison. The Dodgers took a commanding 11-4 bulge into the last of the eighth, then proceeded to tattoo Taylor Phillips for nine runs in the inning, on five hits, four walks, and a hit batsman. The resulting 20-4 shellacking marked Milwaukee's worst defeat and either embarrassed or galvanized them into playing baseball, for after leaving Brooklyn, the Braves traveled to Philadelphia and swept three games from the league-leading Phillies, reclaiming first place in the process. They stayed in first for two weeks, lost the lead briefly to St. Louis, and finally on August 6 took over the top spot for good.

Beginning on August 4 the Braves put together a ten-game winning streak, their longest of the year, to propel them from a half-game behind St. Louis to an eight and one-half game lead on August 15. During the streak the Braves' Big Four pitchers (the Big Three plus Gene Conley) won every game: Buhl and Spahn each won three, including Buhl's first win ever against Cincinnati, and Burdette and Conley each won two. The real story,

Milwaukee Journal Photo

Manager Haney had a list of reasons to be pleased with Gene Conley and his teammates in 1957.

however, was the hitting; the Braves scored 91 runs in the ten games. Aaron, Mathews, and Covington each smashed four home runs during the stretch, including grand slams by the last two men. Even Lew Burdette, who had never before hit a home run, slugged two in one game against the Redlegs. And the hottest hitters of all may have been Red Schoendienst and newly-discovered outfielder Hurricane Hazle. Despite batting leadoff, Schoendienst drove in ten runs in one homestand. Hazle, who started his first big-league game on July 31, was an instant sensation, getting four hits in one game and three hits three times in just his first nine starts. At the conclusion of their winning streak, the Braves' had won 17 of their last 19, and 24 of 29 games following their 20-4 debacle in Brooklyn.

From mid-August to Labor Day, Haney's troops performed well enough to maintain their eight and one-half game lead over the Cardinals despite losing Buhl and Logan to injuries. Spahn and Burdette continued to win, McMahon continued to squelch opponents' rallies, Hazle continued to hit at a near-.500 clip, and the ballclub continued to battle. On August 31 they used five home runs to crush the Redlegs, 14-4, in a game spiced by another bench-clearing fight. The disagreement started when Wes Covington slid into Johnny Temple at second base, and the two tussled. The only solid punch of the night was landed by Braves coach John Riddle, who broke the nose of a drunken fan who had stumbled onto the field, tried to put a bear hug on Frank Torre, and taken a wild swing at Taylor Phillips. Two days later in a Labor Day doubleheader, Milwaukee batters channeled their hostilities into their bats, burying the Cubs, 23-10, in the opener. The next day Spahn shut the Cubs out, 8-0, his 41st career shutout and eighth straight victory, to further cement Milwaukee's eight and one-half game advantage.

The very next day, however, in an unpleasant flash of *deja vu*, the lead began crumbling. Herman Wehmeier beat the Braves in twelve innings, cutting a game off the lead. The defeat started Haney's club on their worst slide of the season—eight losses in eleven games. When Spahn lost to the Phillies on September 15, 3-2 in ten innings, the Milwaukee lead shrank to two and one-half games ahead of the Cardinals. Aaron was in a slump, Spahn had lost two in a row, and nerves were on edge in Beertown. Their once-safe lead had nearly disappeared in less than two weeks, and two more weeks remained.

On September 16, though, the Braves began another winning streak that carried them to the pennant. First Buhl made a triumphant return from shoulder trouble, beating the Phillies 5-1

153

for his first victory in over a month, his first complete game since August 9. Then Trowbridge beat the Giants 3-1, helped by great fielding from Mathews and the first home run by Joe Adcock since breaking his leg. Burdette hurled his team past the Giants again, 8-2, as attendance passed the two million mark again on September 18. In Wrigley Field on September 20, Spahn became a 20-game winner for the eighth time. The following afternoon Buhl beat the Cubs with another complete game. Then in the season's final road game, the Braves overcame a four-run Cub first inning, tied the game in the ninth on a Mathews home run, and won with a Hazle homer in the tenth, 9-7. The victory, their sixth in a row, sent the Braves back to County Stadium with a five-game lead over St. Louis. The Cardinals were arriving in Milwaukee the next night for a three-game series, needing to win all three.

The Braves prolonged the suspense for a little while, but only until the eleventh inning of the first game of the Cardinal series. Henry Aaron's dramatic home run clinched the first Milwaukee pennant [see Time Capsule], and happiness was being a Milwaukee Braves fan. The Braves had only to finish out the schedule, give the fans a few more thrills, and get ready to meet the Yankees. The night after the pennant-clinching, Spahn won his 21st game, backed by Aaron's grand slam off Sad Sam Jones. Buhl lost to the Cardinals the next day, 4-1, to finish 18-7, his best record yet. In the campaign-ending weekend series with Cincinnati, Burdette hurled a complete game for his seventeenth win, and Spahn lost trying for his 22nd. The villain was Johnny Klippstein, who sixteen months earlier had combined with two teammates to hold Milwaukee hitless for nine and two-thirds innings. This time he went the distance himself, allowing only a bloop single by Hazle with two out in the eighth in posting a 6-0 win.

The season finale gave 45,000 loyal backers a few last thrills in the regular season. The home team carried a 2-0 lead into the ninth, but the Redlegs fought back with three runs to take the lead. In their last at-bat, the local idols strung base hits by Adcock, pinch-hitter Ray Shearer (the only major league hit he would ever get), Schoendienst (his 200th of the season), and the winner by Felix Mantilla. The victory was the team's eighteenth in 22 games with Cincinnati and gave the Braves a 95-59 final record, eight games ahead of the second-place St. Louis Cardinals. The final day crowd boosted the season total attendance to 2,215,404, a new National League record. Three days later the Braves were in Yankee Stadium taking on Casey Stengel's world

154

champions.

A measure of the Braves' success in 1957 is reflected in their post-season awards. Fred Haney was chosen Manager of the Year by the Associated Press. Warren Spahn received the Cy Young Memorial Award as the best pitcher in the major leagues. Aaron, Mathews, Schoendienst, Burdette, and Spahn were all selected to the major league all-star team by both the Associated Press and the Baseball Writers of America. Finally, Henry Aaron was voted the National League's Most Valuable Player by the Baseball Writers of America, with Schoendienst finishing third in the balloting and Spahn finishing fifth. It was that kind of season.

Milwaukee Journal Photo

The record-setting swing of Henry Aaron

1957 Feat of Clay

"If there's cartilage [damage] in Bruton's knee, then there could be trouble."

—Fred Haney

Henry Aaron began his professional baseball career as the hard-est-hitting shortstop in the Northern League with Eau Claire in 1952. The next season he was a slugging second baseman for Jacksonville of the Sally League. In 1954 Bobby Thomson obligingly cracked an ankle in spring training, making room for Aaron to become a promising leftfielder with Milwaukee. The year after that Aaron played rightfield for the National League All-Star team. On the evening of July 11, 1957, in Pittsburgh's Forbes Field, Aaron was transmogrified into a centerfielder, although the move did not take effect until the following night. The catalyst for this latest change of venue was a fielding blunder, involving two of Aaron's teammates, that would have embar-rassed ballplayers in a tavern softball league.

The actors in this tragicomedy of the absurd were Billy Bruton and Felix Mantilla. Bruton, of course, was the capable veteran centerfielder; Mantilla was a sophomore utility player who could perform at nearly every position, sometimes well. "Felix the Cat" had joined the Braves from Sacramento the day before Charlie Grimm's resignation and had played for the first time in a 7-2 Milwaukee victory over Pittsburgh in the sixth game of Haney's inaugural eleven-game winning streak. Mantilla had formed a doubleplay tandem with Aaron at Jacksonville, Mantilla at short, Aaron at second base.

Mantilla was the starting shortstop in this game because manager Haney had grown tired of the prolonged slump of regular Johnny Logan, struggling at .259. Now, two days after the

156

All-Star Game, the Braves' skipper had benched Logan in favor of the young Puerto Rican, a questionable judgment considering the replacement's .224 average. Nevertheless, baseball managing is an occupation ruled by hunches.

In the bottom of the first inning, Pittsburgh leadoff batter Bill Virdon blooped a weak fly into short centerfield. Bruton sprinted toward the infield in pursuit; Haney's Hunch turned and ran toward the outfield, watching the ball over his shoulder. The two fielders intersected violently, nearly face-to-face, in short centerfield. Both fell to the ground, spaced about fifteen feet apart, and lay for several minutes. Mantilla had had the wind knocked out of him and had suffered a bruised chest; later it was also discovered he had injured his knee. Bruton, who was helped to his feet and into the dugout shortly after Mantilla walked off, received a cut lip requiring eight stitches, a loosened tooth, and what appeared to be a bruised knee. Virdon received a cheap double and subsequently scored on a Dee Fondy single.

Andy Pafko replaced Bruton in the outfield, and the slump-ridden Logan replaced his own replacement. Three innings later Logan crashed a two-run homer to cap a four-run rally and put the game out of reach, later adding a run-scoring single in the eighth. In the ninth the Pirates donated two more runs on four errors, and Milwaukee had a 7-2 victory for Bob Trowbridge and had gained a game on the first-place Cardinals.

Mantilla's knee injury turned out to be somewhat more serious than first thought, keeping him out of the lineup for nineteen games. Bruton's injury turned out to be far more serious than its preliminary diagnosis—he had damaged ligaments in his right knee and would not return until May 24, 1958. And the next night Henry Aaron became a centerfielder for the first time, and for the rest of the season.

Time Capsule - July 26, 1957

"It's been a long time between homers up here. I haven't hit one since 1952 when I was with the Phillies."

—Nippy Jones

Necessity is the acknowledged mother of invention, but one of her lesser-known sons is substitution. After the Braves lost Joe Adcock, Billy Bruton, and Felix Mantilla to injuries in a span of less than three weeks, their lineups became increasingly creative: rightfielder Henry Aaron became a centerfielder, and catcher Del Crandall became a rightfielder. The Braves also sought assistance from minor league players such as Wes Covington and Bobby Malkmus. On July 26 at County Stadium, they received a game-winning home run from an entirely unexpected source—a former paraplegic who had spent the previous five seasons out of the major leagues. Of such contributions are pennant-winning seasons made.

The game began normally enough. Lew Burdette was seeking his ninth win of the year, trying to protect his team's slim half-game lead over the second-place St. Louis Cardinals, opposed by Ruben Gomez and the New York Giants. Burdette was pitching good baseball except for his old bugaboo, the gopher ball. He gave up home runs to Hank Sauer in the second, rival moundsman Gomez in the third, and Ed Bressoud in the seventh. Gomez, meanwhile, allowed little besides Ed Mathews' solo home run in the fourth. Entering the bottom half of the eighth, Burdette was on the short end of a 3-1 ballgame.

Gomez retired Johnny Logan to begin the home eighth. Andy Pafko singled for the Braves' sixth hit of the evening. Carl Sawatski was sent to bat for Burdette but popped up weakly for the second out. Red Schoendienst, hitless in three tries, then extended his hitting streak to 23 games with a double in the left-centerfield gap, scoring Pafko. Frank Torre followed with a smash through the box to bring in Schoendienst and tie the game. Johnny DeMerit ran for Torre, representing the lead run. After Mathews walked, Gomez was given the hook and replaced by Al Worthington, who induced Aaron to pop out in the infield and end the inning.

First basemen Frank Torre and Nippy Jones

Burdette and Torre were replaced respectively by Gene Conley and Nippy Jones, the latter a recent acquisition from the boondocks of the Pacific Coast League. Conley had lost to the Phillies two days before because he could not find the plate, but in relief of Burdette he was perfect, facing and retiring nine batters with no ball leaving the infield. The fact that he needed to pitch three innings was due to his teammates' inability to cash in on an opportunity in the last of the tenth against nemesis Stu Miller.

Jones opened the tenth by bouncing out to third baseman Ray Jablonski. Schoendienst singled and was sacrificed to second by Conley. A hit and a walk loaded the bases and brought up Wes Covington with a chance to be the hero. As it turned out, Covington received two chances to be the hero, but he failed both times. The first chance came when one of Miller's off-speed junk pitches got away from him and zeroed in on Covington's right leg. If the outfielder's reflexes had been slower or his thought

159

processes had been quicker, the ball would have struck him harmlessly and forced in the winning run. An Eddie Stanky or Solly Hemus would have instinctively blocked the pitch with his body and won the game; Covington instinctively avoided the pitch. Shortly thereafter he compounded the mistake by standing with his Louisville Slugger on his shoulder while strike three wafted past.

With Conley unhittable, the Braves entered the last of the eleventh for another attempt at tie-breaking. Catcher Del Crandall surprised Miller and the assembled 33,743 faithful by laying down a perfect bunt for a base hit. Shortstop Logan followed with a bunt of his own to advance the winning run into scoring position. Pafko received the obligatory intentional walk to set up a force or a doubleplay. The next batter was substitute first baseman Jones.

Vernal "Nippy" Jones had been the St. Louis Cardinals' regular first baseman in 1948 and 1949, with Stan Musial moving to the outfield to make room for him. He hit .300 in 1949, but a herniated disk that year required post-season surgery, and the surgery left him paralyzed from the waist down. He spent most of that winter in a wheelchair, fearing he would never play baseball, or perhaps walk, again. Through rehabilitation he regained use of his legs and showed up for spring training, but he was assigned to the minor leagues and stayed there for the better part of five seasons, mostly with Sacramento.

The Braves purchased him from Sacramento on July 6 as a fill-in for Torre, subbing for injured Joe Adcock. Entering the game with the Giants, Jones had just one hit to show for eleven trips to the plate as a Brave. He had reported early for the game and taken extra batting practice, though, hopeful of helping the team that had rescued him from obscurity in the minors. Now in the last of the eleventh, he had his chance.

His teammates had instructed Jones to hit flatfooted against Miller's super-slow offerings, rather than stride forward as usual. Jones first took a strike and then took the advice. He made solid contact with a Miller change-up and pulled it down the line. The ball landed just inside the foul pole, just beyond the leftfield fence, scoring Crandall and Pafko ahead of Jones and making Conley a 6-3 winner, as well as keeping Milwaukee a half-game in front of St. Louis.

The game-winning home run was Jones' first real contribution to the Braves' finest season. It would not be his biggest contribution, but it was his most spectacular. It was also the event that made Braves fans stop asking, " Nippy who?"

160

Time Capsule - July 31, 1957

"I will not tolerate antics such as you have engaged in."

—Telegram, N.L. President Warren Giles to Bobby Bragan

Bobby Bragan called it his major league debut as a clown. Umpire Frank Dascoli warned Bragan to get off the field or he would forfeit the game. Umpire Frank Secory told Bragan to "cut out the bush league stuff." League President Warren Giles fined Bragan $100 and admonished him in a telegram: "Your repeated farcical acts on the field indicate it is not your nature to take the game on the field seriously." On a warm evening at County Stadium on July 31, 1957, 24,522 Braves fans were given a sneak preview of their team's manager six years hence. They also witnessed a baseball game, although it was overshadowed by the evening's extracurricular shenanigans.

Bob Buhl was seeking his thirteenth victory of the season and his team's fourth straight, opposed by Bob Purkey and the Pittsburgh Pirates. The Braves were in first place, a half-game ahead of the Cardinals; the Pirates were in seventh place, a game and a half from oblivion. Red Schoendienst had staked Buhl to a modest lead with a solo home run in the third. With the Braves comimg to bat in the home fifth, they still led 1-0.

Shortstop Johnny Logan quickly doubled the advantage by leading off with another home run off Purkey. The Pirate righthander then retired Del Rice, but Buhl nubbed a slow roller and legged it for a base hit. Schoendienst followed with a double, Buhl advancing to third. Bragan stood on the steps of the third base dugout and yelled to Purkey to throw to second base, claiming Buhl had failed to touch second on his way to third. Purkey tossed the ball to second; umpire Stan Landes signalled "safe." Bragan ostentatiously held his nose, showing his opinion

161

of the call. Landes walked toward Bragan and thumbed him out of the game. The ejection was not unique for the Pittsburgh manager—he had been banished three other times earlier in the season by the same crew of umpires.

What was original was Bragan's reaction to being kicked out. He sent his one-eyed pitcher, Whammy Douglas, into the stands to purchase a soft drink from a vendor. He also sent the bat-boy to buy him a hot dog. The hot dog was slow in arriving, but Bragan took his carton of orange juice, equipped with two straws, and strolled onto the diamond, sipping. He offered to share his beverage with the umpires, who showed no amusement at his antics. The men in blue ordered him off the field. Umpire Secory told Bragan he was acting "bush," so Bragan threatened to throw the citrus drink in his face. Eventually Bragan made his way to the dugout and ultimately to the visitors' clubhouse.

Bragan's buffoonery did not sprout overnight. In his tenure as a minor league pilot in Fort Worth and Hollywood, he had developed a reputation for clownishness. He once sent in eight consecutive pinch-hitters just to harrass the umpires. He had a bat-boy coach third base one time, and in his favorite stunt, he lay down on top of home plate and refused to move. The word often used to describe Bragan was *brash*, but to many people in baseball, notably Frank Dascoli's crew of umpires, the operative word was *jerk*.

After Bragan's removal, the Braves had runners on second and third and one out. Perhaps distracted by the managerial foolishness, Milwaukee failed to score as Nippy Jones and Eddie Mathews both failed to do anything productive. The next inning, though, the Braves expanded their 2-0 lead. Hank Aaron and Wes Covington started the inning with base hits. Aaron then took a big lead off second and was picked off, but Pirate catcher Hardy Peterson threw the ball away and Aaron scored. Rookie Bob Hazle, starting his first game with Milwaukee, slammed a double into the gap in leftcenter, driving in Covington. After Logan was retired, Del Rice singled, but Hazle got a poor start off second and was thrown out at the plate. Buhl hit a bloop single and Schoendienst walked, but Jones again failed to drive anyone home. In the inning, despite a walk, an error, and five hits, one of them a double, Milwaukee scored just two runs.

Noteworthy in the sixth was Buhl's base hit, his second in two innings, surely a career highlight for him. Buhl's inability to hit defied statistical probability. In 1954 he batted 31 times and achieved just one hit. A natural right-hand batter, he later tried switch-hitting, with little improvement. In 1962, briefly with the

162

Braves but mostly with the Cubs, Buhl set a new standard for batting impotence—in 70 times at bat, he went hitless. His batting career had to serve as living testimony years later when the American League considered, and adopted, the designated hitter rule.

Also worthy of note in the sixth inning was Bob Hazle's double, his first hit as a Brave and the start of one of the most phenomenal streaks in baseball history. In the final two months of the season he hit .403, earning and fulfilling the nickname "Hurricane" Hazle. He had been an unwanted minor leaguer because of a chipped ankle bone and a wrenched knee, but a chiropractor friend saved his career. He had been a throw-in on April 9, 1956, when the Braves traded George Crowe to the Redlegs for pitcher Corky Valentine—more than a year later, he was a sensation.

Buhl protected his 4-0 lead until the ninth, then weakened and allowed Pittsburgh to score two runs. A nice play by Mathews on Frank Thomas' line drive produced an important out, though, and Buhl fanned former teammate Jim Pendleton to end the game. Fans leaving the Stadium were pleased that their heroes had held onto their slim league lead. They were also pleased that the jester in a Pirate uniform was the Pittsburgh manager, not the Milwaukee manager. Little did they suspect.

In Chicago two days later, Bobby Bragan was fired as manager of the Pittsburgh Pirates, replaced by coach Danny Murtaugh, a former Milwaukee Brewer second baseman. In Bragan's absence, the Pirates won more games than they lost during the remainder of 1957. In 1958 they finished second in the National League. In 1960 Pittsburgh won the World Series.

Milwaukee Journal Photo

Hurricane Hazle came through after Bruton was injured.

163

1957 Nemeses - Lindy and Von McDaniel

"[Von McDaniel] jammed our bats down our throats. What else can I say?"

—Fred Haney, July 2, 1957

The older one was age 21, a veteran in his third major-league season; the younger one, just 18, had been in high school when the season began. Their given names were Lyndall and Max, but their baseball names were Lindy and Von McDaniel. Both had signed $50,000 bonus contracts with the St. Louis Cardinals right out of Arnett High School near Hollis, Oklahoma. For much of the 1957 season, Cardinal fans thought they were seeing a new-generation version of Dizzy and Daffy Dean—a pair of big, strapping southern farmboys pitching up a storm for the big-league ballclub in St. Louie.

Lindy had joined the Cardinals for the final month of the 1955 season but had pitched sparingly that year. He earned his first professional decision on April 21, 1956, beating the Braves with a strong five-inning stint in relief while Red Murff, in his major league debut at age 34, failed to protect a 5-2 Milwaukee lead. Lindy lost his only start against the Braves that year in the second game of a doubleheader on the coldest Fourth of July Milwaukee had ever recorded. His other decision against the Braves that season was a big one—he beat them in relief on September 28 in the opener of the pennant-decisive series in St. Louis.

In 1957 the Braves and Cardinals battled for the National League flag, finishing 11-11 in head-to-head competition, making St. Louis the only club over whom the Braves did not enjoy an advantage. In games in which one of the McDaniels pitched, however, the Cardinals boasted a 6-2 winning margin. Lindy beat the Braves three times, his best effort a complete game victory over Juan Pizarro on May 31 in Milwaukee. Von only beat the Braves once, but the fashion in which he did so was sensational.

On July 2 in St. Louis, Von made his first appearance against the Braves, opposing Warren Spahn, who was double the youngster's age. Spahn had won 211 games in his career, the first when Von was in second grade; the junior McDaniel had pitched in three major league games, winning them all, compiling an earned run average of 1.48 in the process. The Braves had the highest-scoring team in the majors and topped the National League standings, but on this night McDaniel embarrassed them. For six innings he not only led 3-0 but did not allow a Milwaukee player on base. The Braves finally reached him for two runs in the seventh, and Hoyt Wilhelm relieved in the eighth, but the Braves left town that night in second place, and the youthful McDaniel remained undefeated.

The future was not kind to Von McDaniel. He developed arm trouble later in the season and never won a game after 1957, pitching just two innings the following year before abandoning his baseball career. Brother Lindy also suffered in 1958, his ERA ballooning to near six runs per game and sending him to Omaha for his first and only minor league experience. He later returned and worked exclusively as a reliever until long after the Braves had fled Milwaukee, finishing with more games pitched than anyone except Hoyt Wilhelm.

Time Capsule - September 2, 1957

"That's what reserves can do for you." —Fred Haney

Chicago's Wrigley Field is a hitter's paradise, an ivy-covered launch pad for horsehide-covered missiles. When the prevailing wind is blowing toward the outfield, every batter in the lineup is a home run threat. In 1930 Hack Wilson walloped 56 home runs, still the National League record; the same year he drove in 190 runs, still the major league record. By no small coincidence did Wilson play half his games that year in Wrigley Field. When the Braves tied a record on May 30 and 31, 1956, by hitting fourteen home runs in three consecutive games, they achieved that feat in Wrigley Field. In that May 30 doubleheader, the Braves and Cubs combined for a record total fifteen home runs. In that three-game series, the Braves scored 35 runs, the Cubs 27— that is Wrigley Field. When the Braves won the opener of a Labor Day double-header in 1957 by a score of 23-10, they were playing in—do you have to ask?

Like every team, the Braves had their ups and downs in scoring runs. They had scored more than anyone else in the league, but not in any consistent pattern. Three days previous in Cincinnati they had ripped the Reds, 9-5, hitting four home runs. The next day in a contest interrupted by a brawl, the Braves belted five home runs and crushed the Redlegs, 14-4. In the series finale the following afternoon, in the same ballpark, Milwaukee managed just five hits off Brooks Lawrence and lost, 6-0. After scoring 23 runs in two games, they scored none. The following day, Labor Day, they scored 23 in one game in Wrigley Field.

Lew Burdette was the Braves' starting pitcher. Two days earlier he had lasted just a third of an inning against Cincinnati despite being presented with a five-run cushion in the first inning. In this game with Chicago his teammates went a step further, scoring six

166

times before Burdette ever took the mound. The Cubs got one back against Burdette, so the Braves scored two more in the second. The Cubs matched those two, so Milwaukee scored five in the third, the last three on Wes Covington's home run. That gave Burdette a 13-3 margin to work with, but it still was not enough. Assisted by a Felix Mantilla error, Chicago scored four times in the third to chase Burdette and bring Ernie Johnson to the rescue.

Faced with a lead of only 13-7, the Braves' offense went back to work and scored two more runs in the fourth on a single by Henry Aaron. Throughout the game, in fact, the Braves continued to score runs whether they needed them or not. They scored in every inning except the fifth; in that frame they failed to score because Mantilla was tagged out at the plate when Del Crandall missed the ball on an attempted squeeze. And only in the seventh did they score a solitary run; otherwise their runs occurred in groups of at least two. Their team totals for the game were impressive: 26 hits, 43 total bases, and 23 runs scored. Along with the barrage of base hits, they drew five bases on balls and had a hit batsman, and Chicago kicked in three errors. The Braves really had a chance to score far more than they did—they left ten runners on base.

Picking a Milwaukee batting star for this game would be impossible. Every player in the Braves' lineup got at least two hits except Burdette, and his relief man, Johnson, got two. Four players achieved three hits: Mathews, Aaron, Covington, and Mantilla. Frank Torre and Bob Hazle each banged out four hits. Aaron and Covington each drove in six runs, while Mathews and Aaron both scored four times. Perhaps most surprising, Torre, one of the slowest-moving members of his species, scored six runs, tying the major league mark held by Mel Ott and Johnny Pesky. Torre went to bat seven times and reached base on every try: he slammed a triple and three singles, walked once, was safe on an error, and was hit by a pitch by rookie Bob Anderson, the second Chicago hurler. The one time he did not score, he was on first base when Mathews made the third out.

The Braves showed no favoritism in roughing up the Chicago pitchers. Starter Bob Rush achieved just one out in the first inning while the Milwaukee hitters raked him for six runs. His replacement, Anderson, got through the rest of that inning unscathed but was worked over for seven runs in the next two innings, the last three on Covington's homer. Tom Poholsky was the only Cub hurler to escape without allowing a run, but he faced just two batters, and one of those got a base hit. Turk Lown was

167

the most generous, giving up twelve hits and eight runs in his five-inning turn. Elmer Singleton worked the final inning and yielded a triple by Torre and Mathews' 29th home run of the season.

After scoring a week's worth of runs in one game, the Braves had to return for a second game. Predictably, their hitting fury had been spent in the opener, and they had to struggle for runs in the nightcap. Chicago second baseman Jerry Kindall took pity and provided two unearned runs in the third inning by muffing a grounder. Then after Cub pitcher Dave Hillman gave way to a pinch-hitter in the sixth, Cubs' manager Bob Scheffing did his bit for the Milwaukee cause by bringing back Bob Rush, who had failed to complete an inning in the opener. Rush was a little more effective this time, but only a little. He gave up a two-run triple to Covington in the eighth. The Chicago largesse was more than adequate. Bob Trowbridge hurled a three-hitter for his first big-league shutout and a 4-0 victory.

While the Braves were sweeping the Cubs, the second-place Cardinals were being swept by the Redlegs in Crosley Field. Milwaukee's league lead was increased to eight and one-half games. Their pennant flight had entered its glide pattern.

Milwaukee Journal Photo

Delirious Braves mob hero Henry Aaron after his pennant-winning home run.

168

Time Capsule - September 23, 1957

"I think that was the most important home run I ever hit."

—Henry Aaron

On September 23, 1957, the bridesmaid finally became a bride. On a chilly evening at County Stadium, after four unsuccessful pennant races, after the previous year's bitter disappointment on the final weekend of the season, after a siege of crippling injuries offset by unexpected heroics from surprising heroes, after eleven tension-packed innings, after two were out, Henry Aaron stroked the ball over the centerfield fence and lifted his team up the final step to the National League pennant. It was not the most important event in the lives of the assembled 40,926 idolaters, or the countless thousands of spellbound radio listeners—it just seemed like it. At twenty-six minutes before midnight, Aaron's home run made official what Braves' fans had known for some time—the Braves were the best in the National League.

Three and a half hours earlier Lew Burdette had taken the mound against the St. Louis Cardinals, the team he had beaten at Busch Stadium in the final game of 1956 when it was too little, too late. The second-place Cardinals were not extinct but were certainly on the endangered list. They trailed Burdette's team by five games with only six remaining. Burdette was opposing Vinegar Bend Mizell, trying to extend the Braves' current winning streak to seven and clinch the league flag for his club with his seventeenth win of the season.

Burdette's teammates threatened to end the suspense in the second inning. Aaron led off with a single to left. Joe Adcock got a hit off the glove of second baseman Don Blasingame. With the Cardinals expecting a bunt from Andy Pafko, the veteran from Boyceville faked the infielders back with a half-swing, then bunted the next pitch for a base hit that Mizell could not pick up.

With the bases loaded, Wes Covington lifted a fly to Wally Moon in center, deep enough to score a run, but Moon dropped the ball. Aaron scored, the bases remained full, and Larry Jackson relieved Mizell. What might have been a decisive inning turned sour after Vinegar Bend's departure when Crandall and Burdette grounded into forceouts at the plate and Red Schoendienst lined to shortstop. The lead was only 1-0.

The fidgety Burdette protected his slender advantage until the Cardinal sixth when, after one out, Moon singled. Stan Musial, who had scored the run that cost Milwaukee the pennant the year before, doubled. Irv Noren was walked intentionally to load the bases. Burdette got dangerous Del Ennis to pop out to the infield, bringing up Al Dark. Dark, whom the Braves had traded in 1949 for, among others, Sid Gordon, whom the Braves had traded in late 1953, with others, for Danny O'Connell, whom the Braves had traded on June 15, with others, for Red Schoendienst, bounced a single past Burdette to drive home two runs and put the Cardinals in front, 2-1.

Milwaukee tied the game after the seventh-inning stretch. Schoendienst began with a single, Johnny Logan sacrificed, and Eddie Mathews doubled down the rightfield line, scoring Schoendienst. Aaron was purposely passed, but Joe Adcock aborted the rally by grounding into a doubleplay.

Both teams had scoring chances in the eighth. After a Moon walk and a Musial single, the Cards had men on first and third with nobody out. Noren bounced a ball toward Logan, playing in close to prevent the run. The ball bounced crazily, reminiscent of Rip Repulski's bad-hop double off Mathews the year before in St. Louis, but Logan reacted quickly, gloved it, and eclipsed the sliding Moon at the plate. Burdette then disposed of Ennis and Dark to close out the half-inning. The Braves also put two men on base with two out, but Jackson escaped by getting Schoendienst on a foul popup.

Neither club could break the deadlock in the ninth. Jackson departed for a pinch-hitter, so Billy Muffett replaced him on the mound. Muffett was a 27-year-old rookie by way of Helena, Monroe, Shreveport, Macon, Omaha, and Houston who was enjoying some of his greatest success now that he had reached the big leagues. He continued that success by shutting out Milwaukee in the last inning of regulation play.

Burdette held the Cardinals one more time in the top of the tenth. In the latter half of that inning it appeared he would be rewarded with a victory. The Braves loaded the bases with just one out, and Burdette was the next scheduled hitter. With righthander Muffett pitching, Haney went to his bench and selected lefty Frank Torre to bat for his pitcher. A medium-length fly ball, a slow ground ball, a walk, a hit— any one of them meant victory for Burdette and pennant for Torre's team. Instead big Frank slapped a sharp grounder, the throw came home for a force, the catcher's throw to first easily beat the glue-footed runner, and the game went to the eleventh.

Gene Conley was summoned from the bullpen to combat the Cardinals. Conley had become something of a forgotten man of late, having lost his last four decisions and having failed to win a game since August 11, when he beat the Cardinals at Busch Stadium. He quickly justified his selection by Haney for this important relief job, however, by breezing through a three-up, three-down inning. Once again the Braves' fate belonged to the offense.

Schoendienst led off against Muffett with an easy fly to Moon in center, but Logan lined a single up the middle to give the shivering fans some hope. The temperature had dipped to 44 degrees by now, but of course no one was leaving before the verdict. Mathews lofted another routine fly to Moon, and the groan from the crowd was audible. A rumble of anticipation seemed to accompany Aaron's approach to the batter's box. The slender young outfielder with the powerful wrists was the league leader in home runs and runs batted in; if anyone could end the game with one swipe of the bat, certainly Aaron could—and did. He pounced on Muffett's first pitch and lined it toward the centerfield fence. Moon leaped but could not come down with it. The ball landed six feet beyond the wire and took a high bounce into the hands of a leaping spectator. The fan, Hubert Davis, carried off the season's prime souvenir; gleeful Braves players ran onto the field and carried off Aaron, the man of the hour, on their shoulders.

While the Milwaukee ballclub was claiming its first pennant, the New York Yankees were clinching their eighth American League flag in nine years without even playing. The Yanks were idle, but Kansas City beat runner-up Chicago, 6-5, to close out the White Sox season and set up a New York- Milwaukee date in Yankee Stadium on October 2.

1957 Swan Song

"The real value of a guy like Jolly is in saving games for you rather than starting them."

—Charlie Grimm

Dave Jolly's name belied his personality. He was in fact a serious, taciturn man known to his teammates by the ironic nickname of "Gabby." He labored in the Milwaukee bullpen for five seasons, reaching peak effectiveness in 1954 when he won eleven games, lost six, saved ten, and compiled an earned run average of 2.43. On July 17, 1954, in Milwaukee, Jolly made the only start of his big-league career, pitching ten innings against the Dodgers and allowing just four hits and one run, although the Braves went on to lose in the eleventh, 2-1, with Lew Burdette suffering the loss.

Jolly pitched for the Braves for the last time on September 14, 1957, at County Stadium. The Dodgers swamped the Braves for the second day in a row, 7-1, cutting the Milwaukee lead to four games. The starter and loser was Lew Burdette. Jolly, nearly a forgotten man on the roster, entered the game with a 6-1 deficit and pitched the eighth and ninth innings, allowing a walk, two hits, and one run while striking out one batter. The run was produced by Gil Hodges' home run in the eighth.

Jolly did not make an appearance in the World Series. A week after the Series he was sold to the New York Giants, but he never again pitched in the big leagues. He pitched in the minors through the 1961 season, then retired. On May 27, 1963, Jolly died of a brain tumor at the age of 38.

Time Capsule - October 6, 1957

"One good thing about having it happen this way—it proves we've got nothing but old pros on this ballclub."

—Warren Spahn

Warren Spahn was a fierce competitor. He did not need extra incentive to pitch well, but in the fourth game of the 1957 World Series, the incentive was considerable. He was looking for his first Series win as a Milwaukee Brave, although he had beaten the Cleveland Indians once in 1948 with Boston. He was seeking to square his record against the Yankees after losing the Series opener to Whitey Ford. More important, he was attempting to bring his team, trailing two games to one, back to even in the best-of-seven struggle for baseball supremacy. Perhaps nearly as important, though, Spahn had a score to settle with the Old Perfessor, Yankees' manager and genius-in-residence, Casey Stengel.

In 1942 Spahn had made his major league debut with the Boston Braves, then managed by Stengel. The Boston club never finished in the first division in six years under Stengel's guidance, a testament to Casey's managerial prowess at the time. Further evidence is provided by Stengel's conclusion that Spahn would not make it in the majors—Stengel ordered Spahn to throw at Pee Wee Reese, but the pitcher refused, so Stengel took that to mean Spahn had no guts. Spahn then went off to World War II, Stengel was demoted to the minors, and fifteen years later their paths crossed on October 2 in Yankee Stadium, and now on October 6 in County Stadium.

Stengel's team wasted no time scoring against the high-kicking lefthander. Gil McDougald singled home Mickey Mantle in the first inning to give sixteen-game winner Tom Sturdivant a lead to protect. He defended the lead until the Braves exploded in the fourth. Johnny Logan drew a base on balls to lead off and moved to third on Eddie Mathews' double off the rightfield wall. Sturdivant then tried to fool Hank Aaron with a one-ball, one-strike change-up. Aaron whacked the slow pitch into the bleachers in left to put his team ahead. The New York pitcher retired Wes Covington, but Frank Torre, starting in place of Joe Adcock, knocked a ball into the grandstand extension near the rightfield line to make it 4-1 Milwaukee.

From the first inning until the eighth, Spahn was in complete command. After allowing two hits and a walk in the opening frame, the Braves' southpaw allowed just two singles and no walks for the next six innings. In the eighth New York threatened again when third baseman Andy Carey doubled and pinch-hitter Jerry Lumpe, batting for relief man Bobby Shantz, singled to put men on first and third with one out. Spahn took control again, though, inducing Tony Kubek to ground into an inning-ending doubleplay.

Schoendienst doubled leading off the home eighth, but Logan and Mathews failed to move him around. Aaron walked with two out. Fourth Yankee hurler Tommy Byrne then caught Covington looking at strike three. The failure to score seemed meaningless, of course, with Spahn mowing down the Yanks and only three outs to go. Many in the crowd prepared for a fast ninth inning and a hasty exit from the stadium.

Spahn quickly retired Hank Bauer and Mickey Mantle, and the game was all but over—or so it seemed. Yogi Berra poked a single to keep New York alive. Spahn tried too hard not to walk McDougald and put the ball where he could hit it for a base hit. Suddenly the crowd got nervous, and so did Fred Haney. The Braves' skipper walked out to the mound to settle Spahn down, to tell him to keep it in the park. The advice went unheeded. First baseman Elston Howard got a low-inside screwball and golfed it over the fence in left. The game was tied, 4-4, and the crowd was in shock. Spahn was stalking around the pitcher's mound, visibly upset. He finally retired Carey, but it was a new ballgame.

Joe Adcock batted for Torre in the last of the ninth but grounded out. Byrne also disposed of Pafko and Crandall without incident, so the game went to extra innings. Spahn started the Yankee tenth just as uneventfully, retiring Gerry Coleman and mound rival Byrne. As in the ninth, though, trouble began with two down. Kubek bounced a ball toward center that Schoendienst gloved but could not throw in time. Then Bauer, who had a ten-game World Series hitting streak going back a year and three

174

days to Ebbets Field, slammed a 400-foot triple off the centerfield fence, a ball that Aaron could not reach but a healthy Billy Bruton might have caught. Spahn cut down Mantle to end the inning, but the game that had looked like a sure win now looked dismal.

Spahn was due to bat first in the last of the tenth. Haney called on Nippy Jones to bat for him, which offered the fans little comfort. When a Byrne pitch bounced inside and in the dirt, Jones jumped back, claiming the ball had struck his foot. Plate umpire Augie Donatelli rejected the idea and called it a ball. Jones, in a move that was to immortalize him for Braves fans, called for an examination of the baseball. When Donatelli discovered a smudge of shoe polish on the horsehide, he overruled himself and sent Jones skipping to first base. Felix Mantilla was sent in as a pinch-runner, thus ending the brief but heroic World Series career of Nippy Jones. Apparently perturbed by this turn of events, Stengel yanked Byrne and brought in Bob Grim, his ace relief man.

Braves' brass Joe Cairnes, John Quinn, and Lou Perini watch the Series at Yankee Stadium.

The situation called for a sacrifice bunt, and Schoendienst obliged, successfully, putting the tying run in scoring position. Stengel called time and, for reasons only an inspired baseball tactician could fathom, sent Enos Slaughter to play leftfield, mover Kubek to center, and removed Mantle. The next batter, Logan, took the first two pitches, both outside the strike zone, then hit a shot just inside the third base line into the corner. Mantilla scored easily with the tying run, and the stands erupted.

Next up was Mathews, having a terrible Series at bat. The Braves' third-sacker had one hit to show for eleven tries, a pathetic .091 average. First base was open, and a walk would set up a force or a doubleplay. Stengel, however, as he so often did, scorned the conventional wisdom and chose to pitch to the slumping slugger. He was quickly rebuked. Mathews, using a bat borrowed from Joe Adcock because his own had a knob at the bottom that had caused a blister on his right hand, worked the count to two balls and two strikes, then connected with a waist-high fastball. The sound on impact told the crowd the game was over. The ball landed in front of the rightfield bleachers, Logan loped home, Mathews followed, and the scene that had accompanied Aaron's pennant-winning blast two weeks earlier was re-enacted.

This Mathews swing evened the Series at two games each.

World Series, 1957

"You can say for me that we'll show up for the World Series."

—Fred Haney, September 23, 1957

Even for the champions of the National League, a visit to Yankee Stadium to play Casey Stengel's defending world champions was an intimidating experience. "The House That Ruth Built" was jammed beyond capacity with 69,476 baseball aficionados, more than half-again the size of a County Stadium sellout, yet relatively sedate by comparison (a New Yorker would say "sophisticated"). On October 2, 1957, the Yankees opened the Series with their ace southpaw, Whitey Ford, opposing the visitors' ace southpaw, Warren Spahn. Both were veterans of World Series play, Spahn having won one and lost one in 1948 against the Cleveland Indians, Ford having won four and lost two in four separate fall classics. The game shaped up as a pitchers' duel, and as it happened there were no surprises.

Each pitcher held the opponent scoreless through the first four innings. In the last of the fifth New York finally reached Spahn when Hank Bauer doubled home Gerry Coleman. In the next inning the Yanks padded the lead with another run on two hits and a walk, finishing Spahn. Ernie Johnson relieved, giving up a third run on a squeeze bunt by Coleman. Milwaukee score once in the seventh on a Wes Covington double and a bleeder through the infield by Red Schoendienst, but after that Ford stiffened and mowed the Braves down the rest of the way for a 3-1 Yankee triumph.

The following afternoon the Braves not only gained respectability but evened the Series behind the seven-hit pitching of Lew Burdette. The fidgety righthander had begun his major league career as a Yankee, making two brief appearances with them in

177

1950 before being traded to the Braves in late 1951, along with $50,000, for Johnny Sain. For a year the deal looked good for New York, but after the Braves left Boston, it became obvious that Milwaukee had received the bargain.

As good as Burdette was this day, he had to share the honors with often-maligned outfielder Wes Covington. With the score tied 1-1 in the bottom of the second and two men on base, diminutive Yankee pitcher Bobby Shantz lined a drive toward the fence in leftfield, near the foul line, that appeared destined for extra bases. Covington raced toward the corner and made a backhand catch on the dead run, preventing two runs from scoring and keeping Burdette in the game. After the two teams matched home runs in the third inning, Logan getting Milwaukee's first in the Series, the Braves took the lead for good in the fourth. Adcock and Pafko singled, and Covington, after twice failing to sacrifice, drove Adcock home with a base hit that proved to be the winning run. The throw from the outfield eluded third baseman Tony Kubek, Pafko scored, and Burdette had a 4-2 lead to protect. He had to pitch out of trouble in the sixth and the ninth, but he did so successfully and earned Milwaukee's first World Series victory.

The 1957 World Series, from Veterans' Hill

When the Yankees arrived in Milwaukee for game three, they immediately and scornfully described the unrestrained enthusiasm of the Braves' fans as "bush" —the ultimate in baseball put-downs, equating the locals with minor leaguers. The remark was widely reprinted and provided Wisconsin fans with a rallying-cry. (Of course, to suave individuals like Yogi Berra, renowned for his bon mots, and Mickey Mantle, a native of cosmopolitan Spavinaw, Oklahoma, a city like Milwaukee had to be a rube town.) Nevertheless, in the third game of the Series, on Saturday, October 5, the boys from the Big Apple could afford to gloat and cast aspersions—they annihilated the Braves, 12-3.

Bob Buhl started for Milwaukee but failed to complete the first inning. He allowed two hits, including a home run, walked two men, and threw away a pickoff attempt at second base, giving up three runs before the crowd had located their seats. The Braves got a run back in the second inning and knocked Bob Turley out of the game, but Stengel brought in Don Larsen, and the game was as good as over. Larsen, who had created baseball legend in his previous World Series appearance by pitching a perfect game against the Dodgers on October 8, 1956, extended his streak of perfection to 34 batters before Johnny Logan singled in the fifth inning, by which time New York led 7-1.

Milwaukee scored twice in the fifth, but at the start of the seventh inning the stadium lights were turned on, and the Yankees, apparently thinking it was some sort of signal or omen, scored five more times to put the game beyond the limits of prayer. The Braves tied a record in the game by leaving fourteen runners on base; Larsen was far from perfect, but he was easily good enough.

The Yankees' biggest hero of the day, though, was Milwaukee-born Tony Kubek, whose father had played for the Brewers at Borchert Field. Kubek outproduced the Braves' entire team, smashing two home runs and a single, driving in four runs and scoring three. His round-tripper on Bob Buhl's third pitch of the day put New York on the scoreboard first; his three-run blast off Bob Trowbridge in the seventh closed out the scoring for the day for both teams.

Once again the Braves faced a must-win situation in game four. Had they lost they would have faced a three-games-to-one deficit and would have needed to win three straight, the last two at Yankee Stadium. Instead, in the most exciting game of the Series, they rallied in the tenth for a heart-stopping victory [see Time Capsule] to even the Series.

Even after tying the Series at two games each, the Braves

needed to win in game five to avoid the necessity of a two-game sweep in New York. Lew Burdette, the winner in game two, was again called upon, and he responded with the best-pitched game of the Series. He scattered seven hits, all singles, never allowing two in the same inning; he walked no one, and he struck out five. He allowed only two Yankees to reach second base and none to go beyond it. The only scoring threat for New York was a long drive in the fourth inning that looked like it could clear the fence in left. As in game two, however, Wes Covington saved the day, crashing into the fence and holding onto the ball to rob Gil McDougald and save Burdette.

Burdette's New York counterpart, Whitey Ford, also pitched his second strong game of the Series. The only run Ford allowed came in the sixth inning. With two out and nobody on base, Eddie Mathews bounced a high chopper toward second baseman Gerry Coleman. Coleman, shunning the short hop, took one step backward to field the ball. Mathews hustled down the line and narrowly beat the throw to first. Aaron followed with a bloop single into rightcenter, and Adcock lined a hit to right. Mathews sprinted home with the winning margin in Burdette's 1-0 masterpiece.

Back at home for game six on October 9, the Yankees refused to die. Bob Buhl was the Milwaukee starter, but he had only a little more success than in his previous attempt. While the Braves were batting in the third, Cuban revolutionaries dispersed a torrent of propaganda leaflets onto the field from the upper deck. In the bottom of the third, the Yankees started their own uprising against Buhl. After two outs, 41-year-old Enos Slaughter drew a base on balls, one of four Buhl issued, and Yogi Berra followed with a home run down the line in rightfield. It was Berra's tenth World Series home run—only the Babe had hit more. A single by McDougald and a walk to Jerry Lumpe then convinced Haney that Buhl was a bad idea and Ernie Johnson was preferable. Johnson got out of the inning.

The Braves tied the score with solo home runs by Frank Torre in the fifth and Hank Aaron in the seventh. In the home seventh, though, Hank Bauer hooked a line drive off the leftfield foul pole for a cheap but devastating game-winning home run against Johnson. Bob Turley finished strong for a four-hit, eight-strikeout victory, and the Series went to its seventh game.

The deciding game of the Series should have been Warren Spahn's to win or lose, but the veteran lefty was still feeling the effects of the flu he had developed two days earlier. Conley, Trowbridge, or Pizarro could have received the important assignment, but Haney elected to use Burdette with just two days' rest. Burdette proceeded to make his manager look like a genius—he won his third game of the Series, pitched his second shutout, extended his string of scoreless innings to 24, and led his team to a 5-0 victory and the world championship.

The Braves jumped on Don Larsen in the third inning for all the runs they needed. With one out Bob Hazle singled, his first Series hit, and Logan was safe on a throwing error by Kubek. Eddie Mathews sent both runners home with a double into the rightfield corner. Shantz replaced Larsen and gave up a run-scoring single by Aaron, a hit by Covington, and a fielder's choice by Torre that scored Aaron to make it 4-0. Del Crandall's home run in the eighth produced the final tally.

In the ninth New York almost got to Burdette. McDougald singled with one out, Coleman singled with two out, and pitcher Tommy Byrne, a good enough hitter that Stengel let him bat, singled off Felix Mantilla's glove to load the bases. Moose Skowron hit a hard smash down the line toward third, but Mathews lunged, backhanded the ball, and stepped on the base for the final out.

City Council President Martin Schreiber and Mayor Frank Zeidler celebrate the Series win.

From the moment Mathews stepped on third until far into the early hours the next morning, Milwaukee was pandemonium! The product that made Milwaukee famous flowed freely, and people hugged and kissed. In the midst of the downtown street celebration, one hand-lettered, hand-held sign, photographed by a newsman, said it all—"Bushville Wins!"

Downtown Milwaukee erupts in celebration.

1957 World Champs: (row 1) Hazle, Paine, ball boy Blossfield, bat boy Wick, DeMerit, Phillips (row 2) PR dir. Davidson, trav. sec. Lewis, Logan, Coach Root, Coach Keely, Coach Riddle, Haney, Coach Ryan, Pafko, Mantilla, Prop. Man. Taylor (row 3) Trainer Feron, Buhl, McMahon, Bruton, Trowbridge, Burdette, Torre, Mathews, Sawatski, Pizarro, Adcock, Bat Pr. Pitcher Lang (row 4) Roach, Schoendienst, Spahn, Jones, Taylor, Rice, Covington, Crandall, Aaron, Hanebrink, Johnson, Jolly, Conley

1958

"This time we did what people expected of us, despite our injuries."

—Fred Haney

The seed that the Braves planted with their migration from Boston germinated in the fertile mind of Walter O'Malley and finally blossomed in April of 1958. O'Malley had known for years that a baseball club could not prosper amid the urban decay of Brooklyn. He had investigated building a new stadium in Brooklyn but had been rebuffed by city officials. He had taken his Bums to play each team once in Jersey City in 1956 and again in 1957, testing the waters outside Flatbush and offering a hint of his inevitable flight. Finally he persuaded New York Giants owner Horace Stoneham to join him on the west coast, in San Francisco, making the shift feasible by justifying the long trip west for visiting clubs.

In California Stoneham's Giants set up shop in the City by the Bay in a minor league park, Seals Stadium, seating a cozy 23,000 fans, appropriate since they needed to huddle together for warmth. O'Malley's Dodgers, in sunny southern California, went to the other extreme, adopting the Los Angeles Memorial Coliseum, a mammoth structure built for college football and seating more than 93,000. Both parks were, of course, temporary homes. The day before the 1958 All-Star Game, the San Francisco Board of Supervisors approved contracts for a new $15 million ballpark at Candlestick Point for their new team.

That deal was paltry compared to O'Malley's transaction with the City of the Angels, though. In one of the shrewdest schemes since Peter Minuit bilked the Indians out of Manhattan Island for $24 worth of trinkets, the Dodger impresario conned L.A. city fathers into exchanging 300 acres of undeveloped real estate near

184

downtown Los Angeles, known as Chavez Ravine, for Wrigley Field, a minor league ballpark in a semi-industrial area of Los Angeles. O'Malley even finagled the city and county into forking out $4.75 million for grading the land and constructing roads. The deal generated passionate opposition, but in a referendum on June 3 called Proposition B, voters reaffirmed the transaction. The construction of Dodger Stadium soon followed.

The move west created changes in scheduling for the Braves, such as five game series and fewer train rides. The shift also meant fans had to stay up past midnight to follow their team's exploits via the radio broadcasts. On the field, however, the Braves planned few adjustments. They were the champions, experts predicted they would repeat as champions, and the Braves themselves expected to remain champions.

Personnel changes were few. Nippy Jones had been assigned to Wichita five days after the World Series, never to reappear in the big leagues. The following day former ace reliever Dave Jolly was sold to the New York Giants, also never to play in the majors again. Coaches John Riddle, Charlie Root, and Connie Ryan were released in late October, 1957, replaced later by John Fitzpatrick, Whitlow Wyatt, and Billy Herman. Coach Bob Keely resigned in March due to ill health, replaced by George Susce. The significant player acquisitions came from the Chicago Cubs: infielder Casey Wise, for cash plus three minor leaguers; and veteran pitcher Bob Rush plus two throw-ins, Don Kaiser and Ed Haas, in exchange for catcher Sammy Taylor and pitcher Taylor Phillips. Rush had been Chicago's top starting pitcher for eight years, and he won ten games for Milwaukee as a part-time starter.

Not surprisingly, the Braves did repeat as National League champions. Their run production was down substantially from 1957, with fewer home runs and a slightly lower team batting average. Their fielding percentage remained the same, still second-best in the league, but their doubleplay total plunged, attributable to injuries in the infield. The story of the 1958 Braves, though, was definitely their superior pitching. Their team earned run average was easily the league's best, and the Milwaukee pitching staff's complete games and shutouts far outstripped their rivals. Spahn and Burdette excelled all other teams' starting pitchers; Bob Rush filled in ably for the injured Bob Buhl and Gene Conley, both of whom developed arm trouble; Juan Pizarro, Joey Jay, and rookie Carl Willey were often brilliant as replacement starters; and Don McMahon provided strong relief hurling.

185

If the Braves' repeat performance as flag winners was not surprising, the way in which, and the ballplayers with whom, they accomplished the encore proved unexpected. Manager Haney continually faced juggled lineups because of injuries, as he had the year before. The anticipated return of Billy Bruton in centerfield, following knee surgery in 1957, was delayed until late May. The presence of Wes Covington in leftfield was delayed until May 2, and interrupted periodically throughout the season, by a knee injury suffered while sliding in an exhibition game in Austin, Texas, a week before opening day. Red Schoendienst missed a third of the year, and was hindered when he could play, by a variety of ailments, the most serious of which was diagnosed after the season as tuberculosis. Substitute second baseman Mel Roach, finally fulfilling the promise he had shown five years earlier when he was Milwaukee's second bonus player, shattered a knee on August 3 and missed the balance of the season. Other lesser injuries also hampered the team's regulars, again forcing Haney to improvise: infielders Joe Adcock, Felix Mantilla, Mel Roach, and Harry Hanebrink all became occasional outfielders.

The lineup that Haney was able to put on the field had one remarkable, consistent quality—they were slow. Players such as Del Rice and Frank Torre were practically stationary, but most of the others also lacked speed afoot, owing to injuries, advancing age, or native ability. Haney's team set a record for the fewest times caught stealing—just eight times all year. They also were dead last in stolen bases, though, with 26. Their game was to get on base, wait for a home run, and count on their marvelous pitching staff to keep the opponent in check—and the strategy worked.

Another surprising feature of the 1958 season was the performance of future Hall of Famers Aaron and Spahn. Both had very good years, not surprisingly, but Aaron, usually immune to prolonged slumps, started the season poorly and Spahn, traditionally a slow starter, won his first six decisions and eight of his first nine. Aaron struggled through May hitting in the .230's and failed to hit his sixth homer of the season until the last day of May. Spahn, meanwhile, did not fail to last nine innings unti May 19 (and then he pitched eight and two-thirds). In the first game he lost he had a perfect game for six and one-third innings. He was 8-1 until the Cubs beat him with five home runs at Wrigley Field on June 10. Spahn finished the year with a league-leading 22 wins, his ninth twenty-plus season.

One other surprise occurred on opening day at County Stadium—the Braves lost, 4-3, in fourteen innings to the Pittsburgh

186

Frank Torre charges a bunt.

Pirates. So unusual was the opening loss that it generated a riddle in Milwaukee: Q. "Why can't the Braves sell beer at County Stadium this year?" A. "They lost the opener." Spahn pitched nine good innings and Mathews smashed a pair of home runs, but Gene Conley gave up a run in the fifth extra frame to disappoint 43,339 partisans. The Braves quickly made amends by winning their next three games, behind Burdette, Buhl, and a shutout by Spahn.

On April 29 Spahn hurled his team into first place for the first time by beating the Cubs in Wrigley Field. The next three days, though, the Cubs defeated the Braves. The third game in the string saw Milwaukee leading, 7-0, in the middle of the sixth, yet Chicago rallied to win, 8-7, with a Moose Moryn homer in the last of the ninth. The losing pitcher was Dick Littlefield, a lefthander purchased from the Cubs on March 30, making his first appearance as a Brave. The itinerant Littlefield was with his tenth, and last, team in nine years, and this game would be the last in which he would earn a decision. The loss dropped Milwaukee to fifth place with an 8-7 record, but just two games out of first. The next day the Braves beat the Cubs in the series finale, beginning a seven-game winning streak that carried them into first place.

After Chicago the Braves traveled to Busch Stadium to play the Cardinals. Arriving in St. Louis, Bob "Hurricane" Hazle was hitting far below .200, with only two runs batted in. In a 12-8 victory on May 6, Hazle finally began hitting, driving home three runs. The following night he came to bat after his teammates had scored five runs off Herman Wehmeier in the first inning, with just one out. Larry Jackson was brought in to relieve. Jackson's first pitch was a fastball that struck Hazle on the right ear. Hazle collapsed in pain and had to be removed on a stretcher. He suffered a concussion but no fracture. He returned in a few days but managed just one hit in his next eight at-bats. On May 24, seventeen days after being beaned, Hazle, batting .179, was sold to Detroit. By the end of 1958 his big-league career was over.

Hazle became expendable not only because he was hitting next to nothing but also because of the return of Bill Bruton on the day he was sold, as well as the prominent return of Wes Covington. Returning on May 2, Covington slammed a two-run homer in his second plate appearance. In his first six games he drove in ten runs, and he smashed four home runs in his first eight games. His knee was still not healed, but Haney could not afford to keep him on the bench. Bruton's return was less spectacular but no less welcome, allowing Aaron to revert to rightfield, a positional change that nearly coincided with his batting resurgence.

The Braves closed out May in Pittsburgh's Forbes Field, pounding the Pirates for eighteen hits in an 8-3 win that pushed Milwaukee back into first place, eleven percentage points ahead of the San Francisco Giants. The lopsided victory was Spahn's eighth of the year against a single loss. The Braves' offensive barrage was highlighted in the first inning by home runs by Aaron, Mathews, and Covington on successive pitches by Ronnie

188

Kline, each home run landing in the same area of the lower grandstand in rightfield. The Braves became the 26th team in National League history to achieve three consecutive home runs.

On the day when the voters of Los Angeles were approving the transfer of Chavez Ravine to the Dodgers, just as the polls were closing, the Braves were playing their initial West Coast ballgame 300 miles to the north in Seals Stadium. The team from Wisconsin arrived in California in second place, a game behind the San Franciscans. After three dramatic games, each decided by one run in the last inning, the Braves left town in first place by percentage points.

Milwaukee took the opener, 7-6, with five home runs, including two each by Covington and Aaron. Aaron's second came in the ninth inning and gave Don McMahon his fifth win of the year without a loss. The next night the Braves fought back from a 7-1 deficit to win, 10-9, in eleven innings [see Time Capsule]. The Giants finally earned a measure of revenge by taking the series finale, 5-4, in twelve innings after the visitors had tied the game in the eighth.

After the exhilaration of an exciting series in brisk, windy San Francisco, Haney's troops marched into the doldrums of hot, smoggy Los Angeles for three games with the displaced Brooklyn-ites in their monstrosity of a stadium. Walt Alston's once-proud champions had fallen on hard times in Smogville and were in the National League cellar. They had always given the Braves trouble, though, and this series did nothing to change the pattern. The Dodgers swept the three games, giving them five straight for the season against the Milwaukee team and seven in a row going back to September 12, 1957, in Milwaukee. The Dodgers won the first two Coliseum games with home runs over the screen in left, beating McMahon and Burdette. The third game was a nineteen-hit, 12-4 blowout in which Conley yielded four runs in the first before leaving with one out. The L.A. team led 7-0 after two innings and never looked back.

Back in the Midwest, the Braves lost to the Cubs, 9-6, at Wrigley Field, Spahn's second loss of the year and the team's fifth loss in a row. The next day, June 11, Joe Adcock's grand slam in the first inning propelled the Milwaukee club to a 10-7 victory over Chicago that boosted them back into the league lead, a lead they held for over a month. The win over the Cubs was marred, however, by a recurrence of Covington's knee injury, keeping him out of action until the Fourth of July.

After the Cub series, Haney's team moved to St. Louis for three contests with the Cardinals. In the first game Joey Jay threw a four-hit shutout curtailed by rain after six innings, giving his team a 2-0 win. The next day the Cardinals and the elements collaborated and exacted their revenge, a 2-1 St. Louis triumph in a game also shortened to six innings by rain. To make the defeat even more excruciating for Spahn, the Braves had loaded the bases with one out in the seventh, with Spahn himself the next batter, when the rains came and washed away the budding rally. The Braves concluded their long road trip the next day by erasing a 2-1 deficit in the ninth for a 4-2 win, Logan tying the game with a squeeze bunt and Hairbreadth Harry Hanebrink, a .164 hitter, winning it with a two-run blast.

In the three-week homestand that took them up to the All-Star break, the Braves struggled and won just nine of twenty games. They split two with the Cubs, then lost two of three to the Cardinals. In the opener of the St. Louis series they won on a grand slam by Aaron in the eighth off Billy Muffett, a flashback of the pennant-clinching game of the previous September. In the series finale 41-year-old Cardinal retread Sal Maglie beat 22-year-old Joey Jay. The next night, June 23, Carl Willey, in his first major league starting assignment, shut out the second-place Giants, 7-0. Willey had begun the season with the Braves, appearing briefly in relief; been sent back on May 15 to Wichita, where he pitched a no-hitter on May 23; been recalled to the parent club on June 14; and now blanked the powerful Giants in his starting debut. Five days later Willey halted a three-game Milwaukee skid by hurling a complete-game victory against the Dodgers, the Braves' first win of the season in eight tries against Los Angeles. The next day Bob Rush also beat the Dodgers, helped by Aaron's second grand slam in ten days.

On June 30 Spahn beat the Redlegs for his tenth win. The next night Burdette blanked Cincinnati, 1-0, but on July 2 Brooks Lawrence beat Jay, 1-0. The Phillies then swept three games at County Stadium, the last two in a Fourth of July doubleheader. On July 5 the Pirates beat Burdette for the first time in over four years, the Braves' fifth loss in a row. That night, despite his team being in first place, an effigy of Fred Haney was found hanging from a construction crane at a demolition site in downtown Milwaukee, with a sign: "Down with Haney." The next afternoon, in the last pre-All-Star ballgame, Jay shut out Pittsburgh, 2-0, while striking out nine and walking none. In five starts Jay had won twice by that score and lost 2-1, 3-1, and 1-0.

The four Milwaukee participants in the All-Star classic in Baltimore on July 8—Aaron, Crandall, Logan, and Spahn—failed to distinguish themselves in the 4-3 National League loss.

190

Even a World Series champion can't please everyone.

The next night in the Los Angeles Coliseum, the entire Braves team failed to distinguish themselves, getting crushed 10-3 by the tailenders from Tinseltown. The following night, though, Burdette used his arm and his bat to singlehandedly overwhelm the Bums [see Time Capsule], and the day after that, Aaron, Covington, and Mathews did the damage as Jay won his third game and stopped the Dodgers, 7-4. Covington stayed hot throughout July, averaging better than one home run per ten at-bats, and Jay earned honors as National League Player of the Month for July, winning five games, two of them shutouts, and losing two well-pitched games.

Haney's ballclub continued to struggle because of injuries, and after they had lost three out of four, Johnny Logan explained the reason in a pre-game radio interview: " We are a tiresome team," the eloquent shortstop explained, and Ring Lardner could not have said it better.

191

Frank Torre, Mel Roach, Lew Burdette, and Del Crandall

On Wednesday night, July 30, at County Stadium, two significant events occurred: Warren Spahn threw a complete-game, 4-3
victory that put the Braves in first place to stay; and more
remarkably, Spahn beat the Dodgers. The great lefthander had
started just once against them in five years, lasting only until the
end of the second inning on June 5, 1956. He had not beaten the
former denizens of Ebbets Field since his Boston days, on
September 25, 1951. He still had not, in fact, beaten them on
their home turf since the pennant-winning year of 1948, August
21 to be exact. To sweeten the occasion still further, the game
marked Milwaukee's first victorious effort against fireballing
Sandy Koufax after four losses in three years. And of the three
runs Spahn allowed, only one was earned.

Spahn's vanquishing of the Dodgers began a six-game winning
streak for the Braves that included a four-game sweep of the
runner-up Giants. On Friday, August 1, the Frisco team came to
town one game out of first; they left Sunday night five games

back, and the pennant race, for all practical purposes, was over. The next night they crawled one game closer, but three days after that they were seven behind, and they never approached closer than five games after that.

The month of August belonged to the Braves' pitching staff, especially three men: Spahn, who won four games; Willey, who won five; and Burdette, who won seven. Burdette reiterated teammate Jay by earning recognition as August's National League Player of the Month. Juan Pizarro also contributed two complete-game victories, and Jay tossed an eight-inning one-hitter, punctuated by eight walks, against Cincinnati. Perhaps the Milwaukee mound mastery was best demonstrated in a four-game weekend series with the Phillies at County Stadium from August 15 through 17. The Braves used four pitchers in four games: Willey shut out the Phils, 1-0; Spahn beat them, 2-1; and in a doubleheader, Pizarro and Burdette closed down their guests, 5-1 and 4-1 respectively.

Rookie Carlton Willey hurled four shutouts.

Following the Philadelphia series, the Braves visited California for the final time in 1958, starting at the L.A. Coliseum on August 19. The Dodgers ripped the Wisconsinites four times in five games, failing only when Burdette shut them out, 4-0, on August 21. The Braves regained most of what they had lost, however, by taking four out of five games in San Francisco, dropping the Giants into third place behind Pittsburgh. When the Braves then took two of three from the Pirates, no serious challenger remained.

The month of September was really just a matter of finishing out the schedule and getting ready to meet the Yankees again. The strength of the Braves' pitching staff made the pennant a foregone conclusion. Spahn and Burdette continued to win, but no less impressive was rookie Carl Willey. After blanking the Pirates, 2-0, on the last day of August, his fourth shutout since being called up from Wichita, Willey pitched nine shutout innings against Pittsburgh five days later only to lose 1-0 in the tenth inning. The record shows he led the league with four shutouts, but counting his 1-0 loss in ten innings, he pitched five shutouts in his first fifteen big-league starts.

On September 21 in Cincinnati, the foregone conclusion became reality—the Braves clinched the National League pennant with a 6-5 win over the Redlegs. A four-run outburst in the fifth inning, initiated by a Spahn double, plus Hank Aaron's two-run homer in the top of the seventh gave the Braves' star southpaw a seemingly safe 6-0 cushion. When Spahn faltered in the last of the seventh, giving up five runs, relief ace Don McMahon came in, extinguished the threat, and saved Spahn's 21st victory and his team's second straight league championship. Talk of a dynasty was not long in coming.

1958 Nemesis - Don Drysdale

"The trick against Drysdale is to hit him before he hits you."

—Orlando Cepeda

He stood six foot five, but on the pitching mound he towered nearly eight feet tall. When he whipped a sidearm fastball it came in to a righthand batter via third base, directly at the hitter's ribs. He was plenty fast enough, just wild enough, and more than mean enough to make batters bail out. Braves' hitters hated and feared Don Drysdale. They got into a brawl with him before he was old enough to vote, after he drilled a pitch into Johnny Logan's back. Witnesses to the fight claim Eddie Mathews landed several punches on Drysdale that day. If so, it was one of the few times the Braves were able to hit him hard.

After posting a 17-9 record in 1957 in his first full season with the Dodgers, Drysdale endured a terrible year in 1958—against everyone except the Braves. His season earned run average was a hefty 4.17; against the Braves it was about half that much. Against the other six National League teams, Drysdale won 7 and lost 13; against the Braves he won five without a loss. He was the first pitcher to beat Milwaukee five times in a year since Billy Loes in 1953. In addition to his pitching, he also killed the Braves with his bat.

In Milwaukee on May 21 Drysdale allowed just one run in six and a third innings and got relief help from Clem Labine in beating Bob Rush, 2-1. On June 26 at County Stadium he hurled a complete game and also hit a home run, his first of the year, in winning 4-1. Once more in Milwaukee on July 29 Drysdale beat the Braves, 4-2, carrying a shutout into the final inning before requiring relief from Johnny Klippstein.

His successes in Milwaukee were mere warmups, though, for what happened later in Los Angeles. In August he threw two complete-game victories against the Braves in one series. On the 19th he won 4-1 with a five-hitter, walking none, only a third-inning Bruton home run marring his performance. In that game Drysdale also hit a home run. Then on the 23rd, in Milwaukee's final Coliseum appearance of the campaign, the indomitable righthander fired a four-hitter and drove in four runs with two homers in a 10-1 slaughter, giving him five home runs against the Braves and seven for the season, tying Don Newcombe's league record.

As in 1953 and 1955, the Dodgers were the only team to enjoy an advantage over the Braves in 1958, winning fourteen and losing eight despite a seventh-place finish. Of those fourteen wins, half were in games Drysdale started. In 1958 the Braves lost as many times to Drysdale as they did to the Cincinnati Redlegs.

Milwaukee Journal Photo

Looking like ushers, Schoendienst and Adcock show off their traveling blazers.

1958 Feat of Clay

"They had room at the Los Angeles Coliseum for 93,000 people and two outfielders."

— Sportscaster Lindsey Nelson

The Los Angeles Memorial Coliseum was built in 1923 to accommodate college football games, back when college football was not played by professionals (and for that matter, neither was professional football). Thirty-five years later Walter O'Malley fled Brooklyn and moved his Dodgers into the Coliseum to play baseball while his permanent shrine-with-bases was being constructed in Chavez Ravine. The baseball field that was inserted into the huge oval stadium was a caricature of a ballpark. According to venerable sportswriter Red Smith, every game played in the Coliseum took on "a quality of suspense unequaled this side of Edgar Allan Poe." The Dodgers played miserably there in 1958, but the Braves played even worse.

Most notorious and recognizable of the Coliseum's idiosyncrasies, of course, was the absurdly close leftfield fence, just 250 feet from the plate. To limit the number of home runs, a 42-foot high screen was erected, suspended from two towers connected by a suspension cable. Surmounting the screen were lengths of yellow-painted metal pipe. Any ball passing over the pipe was a home run.

To counterbalance the Little League distance in left, and not coincidentally because Duke Snider was the Dodgers' only lefthand hitter, the rightfield fence was set back almost out of sight—390 feet at the foul pole, dropping away quickly to 440 feet. Not surprisingly, after hitting 40 or more home runs five years running, Snider hit only fifteen in his first year in Los Angeles. If Babe Ruth had played in the Coliseum instead of in

"The House That Ruth Built," he might have remained a pitcher throughout his career. To round out the ballpark's anomalies, it had the worst infield above Class A ball—hard, rough, sprinkled with sand, and frequently bespangled with dew.

What the Coliseum did offer was an enormous seating capacity. An early-season exhibition with the Yankees to benefit catcher Roy Campanella, crippled in an off-season auto crash, attracted 93,103 fans, some of whom could see the playing field with the naked eye. Opening day drew a record throng of 78,672. The expectation was that Los Angeles would shatter all existing attendance records in its first season, although they failed to do so. In addition to having problems seeing the field, many fans had trouble enduring the oven-like heat of the wind-free sunken stadium. During a game with the Giants on April 20, two dozen spectators suffered heatstroke as the temperature soared to the century mark.

Adding insult to heat prostration for L.A. fans, the Dodgers frequently lost in front of the home crowd, often decisively. In the sweltering heat on April 20, for example, San Francisco pounded the Dodgers, 12-2, with Danny O'Connell, of all people, hitting two homers. O'Connell had played three years and two months with the Braves and never hit a home run in County Stadium; in the Coliseum he blooped two over the leftfield screen in one game.

The Dodgers did not lose all the time at the Coliseum, though—sometimes the Braves came to visit. Milwaukee was the last National League team to play there, appearing initially on June 6, but it was too soon. The Braves blew a 3-1 eighth-inning lead and lost 4-3 on Don Zimmer's home run over "The Screen" in the ninth off Don McMahon, the first home run given up by the Milwaukee relief ace since joining the Braves the previous June. To prove the loss was no fluke, Haney's guys lost to the last-place Dodgers again the following night, 5-2, as Pee Wee Reese hit two home runs over the yellow pipe atop the screen, bumping Milwaukee out of first place. The Braves then concluded their maiden voyage on the S.S. Coliseum with a 12-4 drubbing in which the Dodgers belted four pitchers for nineteen hits—but no homers.

The day after the All-Star Game the Braves, again leading the league, returned to Los Angeles for another try at the Coliseum, but again the Dodgers were there so the Braves lost, this time a 10-3 shellacking. In the second game of the series, though, Goliath smote David, which is to say the top team in the league beat Walt Alston's cellar-dwellers, 8-4, as Lew Burdette did everything but rake the infield between innings [see Time Capsule]. To close out the series Joey Jay and Don McMahon pooled their pitching talents, Wes Covington went four for four, and Ed Mathews became the third batter in three months to hit a home run to rightfield as Milwaukee prevailed, 7-4.

The Braves' third and final Los Angeles odyssey of 1958, beginning on August 19, was an unmitigated disaster. Fortunately for them they were leading the league by eight games when they arrived. In the five-game series Milwaukee scored just nine runs. They began by losing a doubleheader, 4-1 and 7-2, with Carl Willey a victim of "screenos" in the opener. The third game was a tough 2-1 loss for Warren Spahn; ironically the only lefthand hitter in the Dodgers' lineup, Norm Larker, drove in the deciding run with a triple. On August 21 Burdette turned slugger again, went two for three with a home run, and shut out the home team to boot in a 4-0 facesaver. The final game of the year in the Dodgers' chamber of horrors, however, was downright embarrassing. Don Drysdale led a 10-1 assault on Milwaukee's sensibilities by blasting a pair of home runs and driving in four, earning his second victory of the series.

The Dodgers barely escaped the basement and wound up in seventh place, their worst finish since World War II; the Braves won the pennant by a comfortable eight-game margin. When they played each other, though, they must have switched uniforms. The Braves won only 8 of 22 games with Los Angeles and in the Coliseum managed to win just three while losing eight.

Time Capsule - May 27, 1958

"I still say that I hit righthanders better than lefthanders."

—Joe Adcock

Choose the correct answer to the following statement: " The game is never over until..."

a) the last man is out.
b) it's over.
c) the fat lady sings.
d) all of the above.

Anyone who chose *a* as the correct response is an incurable optimist. Anyone who chose *b* as the answer is a fan of either Gertrude Stein or Yogi Berra. Anyone who chose *c* is a mixer of metaphors and/or a pro basketball fan. Anyone who chose *d* has taken a course or read a book on how to prepare for the College Board exams.

On a Tuesday night, May 27, 1958, Joe Adcock gave 21,940 Milwaukee baseball agnostics a reminder of the truth in the above statements. The Coushatta Strongman took a game that looked like an ordinary loss—one game in a long season, not a crucial game, not an exciting game, not a game (yawn) in any way remarkable—and made it unforgettable. He was able to achieve this feat because his manager shunned the percentages, the book, and just played a hunch. Such is the mystique of baseball.

The Braves' starting pitcher was Warren Spahn, looking for his seventh straight victory of the year and the 49th of his career against the Cardinals. Four nights earlier Spahn had suffered his only defeat of the campaign against the Giants at County Stadium, pitching six and one-third perfect innings before faltering in the late innings, allowing two homers in the eighth and one in the ninth. On this night against the Cardinals, Spahn began

200

with three perfect innings, finally gave up a hit in the fourth, and yielded his first score when he got a pitch up and in to Curt Flood for a solo home run in the fifth. In the seventh the old southpaw allowed two singles, an intentional walk, and an unintentional walk to Don Blasingame to force in a run. He worked out of further difficulty, but he went to the last of the ninth trailing 2-0 and facing imminent defeat.

The reason Spahn's team was losing was a tall, lanky, toothpick-chomping fireballer with the biggest curve and some of the worst control in the league. Sad Sam Jones was a brilliant but erratic righthander who had twice led the National League in bases on balls and had lost twenty games in 1955; however, he had also hurled a no-hitter against the Pirates in 1955 and in 1958 was in the process of leading the league in strikeouts as well as walks while compiling the lowest earned run average among all the starting pitchers in the league. Jones had allowed Milwaukee just four walks and two harmless singles by Logan and Spahn, and no Braves runner had ventured past second base.

Eddie Mathews offered faint hope to the home fans by bouncing a single past first baseman Stan Musial to start the last of the ninth. Perhaps angry at allowing a base-runner, Jones then hit Wes Covington on the foot with an 0-2 pitch. Felix Mantilla ran for Covington, and the Braves were threatening. Playing for a tie, Haney had Frank Torre bunt to move the runners into scoring position, but Torre bunted too hard and forced Mantilla at second. Eddie Haas ran for Torre. Johnny Logan, who had been one for 26 before singling in the seventh, hit a hard grounder that forced Haas at second; Mathews scored as Logan barely beat the relay to first. Cardinals' manager Fred Hutchinson stormed out of the dugout and berated first base umpire Deacon Delmore, insisting Logan had been out, but as usual the call stood. A run was in, Logan was at first with two out, and Billy Bruton was due up.

Bruton was starting only his third game since his collision with Mantilla on July 11, 1957. He was a lefthanded batter, but he was no home run threat. Haney could have had Logan try to steal second to set up the tying run in case Bruton got a base hit, but Logan was not fast, not a good base-stealer—his biggest stolen base total was in 1957 with five. The Braves were not a running ballclub, and they had no good baserunner available to substitute for Logan. Haney's best chance of bringing home the tying run was a long hit; Bruton was not the answer.

On the bench in the Milwaukee dugout, Haney had two available lefthanded hitters to face the righthand curves of Sam

Jones. Harry Hanebrink was a once-promising infielder who, since 1953, had performed mostly in the minors and now in the majors was batting below .200. The other choice was Carl Sawatski, a boxy third-string catcher out of Shickshinny, Pennsylvania, who had more strength than power and who, as a pinch-hitter in the 1957 World Series, had struck out in both his appearances. Neither choice looked promising.

Of course there was also Joe Adcock. The big slugger had fallen on hard times of late, platooning at first base with Torre, batting mostly against lefties. Against a righthanded curveball and side-arm-fastball specialist like Jones, though, baseball custom called for a lefty hitter. Certainly Haney, who had played infield against Babe Ruth and managed against Al Simmons, was experienced enough to know that. Besides that, Adcock was in a slump, with just two hits in his last thirteen at-bats. Haney scanned his bench and made his choice.

"You're the man," Haney told Adcock. "Knock one out of the park."

Adcock took the first pitch, a curve, outside for ball one. Jones' next offering was a high fastball on the inside corner. Adcock took a prodigious swing; the sound signalled that the game was over. The ball landed far back in the bleachers to the left of Perini's Woods, nearly 450 feet away. The crowd went wild as Logan, then Adcock, crossed the plate. During the celebration some overzealous bleacher inhabitant managed to snatch the World Series championship flag from the pole beyond center-field, but no one was in a mood to notice or mourn the loss. The victory, Spahn's 231st, propelled the Braves to within a game of pace-setting San Francisco.

Time Capsule - June 4, 1958

"The same kind of pitch I missed by nine million miles on the first swing."

—Warren Spahn

On June 3, 1958, the Milwaukee ballclub began its first West Coast excursion with a three-game series in San Francisco's Seals Stadium, a hastily-converted minor league park seating 23,000 Bay Area residents. The confrontation matched the top teams in the National League, with the Giants leading by one game. The Braves' California debut produced three games that typified the Giants' first year in their new home: lots of scoring, sloppy fielding, but plenty of excitement.

The Braves won their first game west of the Rockies, 7-6, with five home runs, including two each by Wes Covington and Henry Aaron, the winner being Aaron's solo blast in the ninth. The Giants took the series finale, 5-4, on Orlando Cepeda's winning base hit in the twelfth inning off Gene Conley, after a two-run eighth-inning rally by Milwaukee had forced extra innings. The most intriguing and exciting game of the series, though, was the middle game, an afternoon affair on Wednesday, June 4. The contest lasted eleven innings, more than three and a half hours, and utilized every able-bodied player on the Braves' roster.

What looked on paper like it might be a pitchers' battle quickly deteriorated into a slugfest. Newly-acquired Bob Rush, Milwaukee's second-best hurler in the early season, was opposing Mike McCormick, San Francisco's 19-year-old lefthander, but Rush was not around long. Felix Mantilla led off the game with a home run, but the Giants roughed up Rush for four runs on six hits before the second inning was over. Bob Trowbridge offered temporary relief, but the Giants belted him for three runs in the third and took a 7-1 lead.

While Joey Jay, Humberto Robinson, and Don McMahon held the fort, the Braves whittled away at the six-run deficit. Del Crandall cracked a solo home run in the top of the fifth to get one back. The score was 7-2 in the seventh when McCormick lost control, walked Del Rice after two were out, walked Mantilla, and was given the hook, replaced by Al Worthington. Aaron greeted the veteran relief man with a base hit, and Rice chugged home to make it 7-3. The Braves added a cheap run in the eighth when leftfielder Bob Speake and shortstop Daryl Spencer let Johnny Logan's popup fall for a double, Logan's 1000th career hit, after two outs, and Andy Pafko singled to make it 7-4. Rice was then called out on strikes to end the inning. His displeasure at the called third strike led to his ejection, and Haney's protest of Rice's removal led to his own eviction. The Braves thus entered the last of the eighth with a three-run deficit, a third-string catcher (Carl Sawatski), and no manager.

McMahon shut down the Giants in the last of the eighth, and Worthington dispatched Mantilla for the first out in the visitors' ninth. As the fans prepared to leave, Aaron singled to provide a spark of hope for his team. Eddie Mathews smashed a long flyball to left, but defensive replacement Don Taussig ran it down and made the grab for the second out. Joe Adcock slammed a double to keep Milwaukee alive, and Giants' manager Bill Rigney had seen enough. With lefthanded batter Wes Covington scheduled to hit next, Rigney summoned southpaw Pete Burnside from the bullpen to record the final out. First base was open, but Rigney chose not to walk Covington, who had hit two home runs the night before, and face Logan. Covington promptly walloped a long three-run homer to tie the game at 7-7. The blow sent the crowd into shock and Burnside into a different league—an hour after the game he was sold to Phoenix, and when he reappeared in the big leagues it was with Detroit in the American League.

Don McMahon again held the Giants hitless in the last of the ninth. Pafko led off the tenth with a single but was forced at second on a grounder by Harry Hanebrink, batting for McMahon. Sawatski drew a base on balls, but relief man/nemesis Stu Miller retired Mantilla for the second out. Aaron bounced to Ray Jablonski at third, but Jabbo booted it to load the bases. Mathews then singled home Hanebrink and Sawatski. The Braves led, 9-7.

Needing three outs, the Braves called on Ernie Johnson to work the tenth inning. Johnson quickly disposed of Whitey Lockman and Willie Kirkland. Now it was San Francisco's turn to dodge the bullet with two out. Hank Sauer, the hulking 39-year-old slugger who could neither run nor field but could still

204

Milwaukee Journal Photo

When healthy and inspired, Wes Covington hit home runs with the best.

hit home runs, hit a home run batting for ex-Brave Danny O'Connell. Then Bob Schmidt, a rookie catcher, batted for Taussig and duplicated Sauer's feat, to nearly the same spot in the leftfield seats. The lead was gone. Willie Mays beat out a bunt and stole second base; the situation was desperate. Johnson escaped, though, striking out Jablonski to send the ballgame to the eleventh inning.

Covington reached first on a walk to start the inning for Milwaukee. At that point Billy Herman, subbing for the evicted Haney as manager of the Braves, made a curious decision—he sent in Billy Bruton to run for Covington. The decision was curious for two reasons: first, it meant that, should the Braves fail to score, they would lose the services of their leading hitter for the remainder of the game; second, it meant that a pitcher would bat fourth in the inning. Logan sacrificed Bruton to second, Pafko flied out for out number two, and the batter was Ernie Johnson, a weak hitter even among pitchers. Had Bruton not gone in as a runner, he would have been able to bat for Johnson. Now Herman's choices were few: let Johnson bat, let Warren Spahn bat, or let Gene Conley bat. The only other player in uniform was Red Schoendienst, ailing with pleurisy. Spahn was scheduled to pitch the next day, so if either Spahn or Conley pinch-hit for Johnson, Conley would have to pitch the rest of the game. Herman chose Spahn to bat for Johnson.

Spahn, of course, was no slouch at the plate. He had hit nineteen home runs in his career and often contributed to Braves' victories with his bat. Pinch-hitting, though, was a different matter. He had tried it ten times with just one success—a single on the second-last day of the 1953 season, batting for Bob Buhl in a losing effort in Cincinnati. This time he faced junkman Stu Miller, whose first pitch had Spahn swinging much too early and missing by a yard. The next pitch was strike two. On the 0-2 pitch, however, Miller got careless and put the ball in the strike zone, medium-speed. Spahn slapped the pitch into rightcenter for a base hit, scoring Bruton easily with the lead run.

The last of the eleventh belonged to Gene Conley. The lanky righthander fanned Orlando Cepeda, retired Daryl Spencer on a nice shoe-top catch by Henry Aaron in right, and fanned pinch-hitter Johnny Antonelli (the Giants were also divest of qualified batters), batting for Miller, to earn Ernie Johnson his second win of the season and move the Braves a full game ahead of the Giants. Spahn would go on to record many more hits in his career, over a hundred more, including sixteen more home runs, but he would never again get one as a pinch-hitter, let alone a game-winner.

Time Capsule - July 10, 1958

"Since when did Spahn hit two homers in one game?"

—Lew Burdette

Lew Burdette was no slugger. In six full seasons with the Braves, five of those in Milwaukee, he had hit exactly two home runs—both in one game off Joe Nuxhall in Cincinnati's Crosley Field on August 13, 1957. Unlike his roommate and partner in zaniness, Warren Spahn, Burdette had never been used, nor for that matter considered, as a pinch-hitter, although occasionally as a pinch-runner. In the Alice in Wonderland world of the Los Angeles Memorial Coliseum, however, Burdette was as likely a long-ball threat as Willie Mays, or Danny O'Connell. Two days after the 1958 All-Star Game, he proved it.

Haney's Braves were leading the league by a half-game but certainly not because of their hitting. In their previous eight games, the defending World Series champs had scored a total of ten runs—twice being shut out, and three times scoring a single run. The only two games they had won in that stretch were on shutouts by Burdette and Joey Jay. To make the picture even more ominous, Milwaukee had never won in Los Angeles, losing its first four games there by a combined score of 31-12, and the pitcher Burdette was opposing, Johnny Podres, boasted seven wins in the Coliseum without a loss. It looked extremely rocky for the Beerville nine that day.

Burdette's teammates put Podres in jeopardy right from the start, but he wriggled out of trouble. Second baseman Mel Roach, subbing for ailing Red Schoendienst, singled with one out in the first. Eddie Mathews belted a double, moving Roach to third, and Hank Aaron was passed intentionally to load the bases for Joe Adcock. The powerful Adcock, though, was over-anxious; he overswung and fouled out on the first pitch. Del Crandall then hit an infield popup to finish the threat. The Braves repeated the threat in the third. Roach again singled after one out, and Mathews added another base hit. Aaron killed the rally, though, grounding into a fast doubleplay. After three innings the game remained scoreless.

After Adcock failed to reach base to start the visitors' fourth, Crandall beat out an infield hit. Johnny Logan slashed a double, sending Crandall to third, and Andy Pafko was purposely passed, loading the bases and bringing up Burdette. The Braves' hurler quickly fell behind Podres in the count, but on a 1-2 curve ball, Burdette swung and made fairly good contact—not great contact, not enough to carry it out of any major league baseball park—but this was not a major league baseball park, it was the L.A. Coliseum. The high, lazy flyball drifted toward the monstrous screen in leftfield, cleared the yellow pipe at the top like a high-jumper straddling the bar (this was before the "Fosbury Flop" was invented), and dropped almost straight down on the opposite side.

Burdette's blooper became the 89th home run hit in O'Malley's temporary funhouse, and regular Dodger-watchers insisted it was the cheapest of the bunch. Nevertheless, it brought home four runs and gave Burdette a leg up (again, before Fosbury) on the first Milwaukee victory in Tinseltown. The puny four-bagger so unnerved Podres that he grooved his next pitch and Felix Mantilla smacked it into the stands to the right of thr screen for a 5-0 lead, finishing Podres.

The Dodgers got a run back in the last of the fourth. After Norm Larker singled, Duke Snider smashed a hard grounder toward Adcock for a potential doubleplay. The ball took an errant bounce off the hard, rough infield surface and struck Adcock above the right eye, dropping the first baseman in a heap. Snider received credit for a hit; Adcock received a cut above the eye and a bump on the forehead, causing him to be replaced by Frank Torre after the inning. Carl Furillo hit into a doubleplay, but John Roseboro singled home Larker to make it a 5-1 game.

In the next inning Los Angeles scored again. Second baseman Charlie Neal hit a short fly to rightcenter; Aaron and Mantilla each thought the other would catch it, so neither did. Neal reached second on the play and scored when Pee Wee Reese looped a single to almost the same spot. In the seventh the Dodgers pulled within two runs as Gil Hodges grounded into a doubleplay, Logan to Roach to Torre, scoring Ransom Jackson, who had doubled and moved to third on Logan's throwing error.

208

With the game getting close, it was time again for Burdette to take charge. With two out and nobody on base in the top of the eighth, Burdette stepped in to face Ed Roebuck, the fourth Dodger pitcher. The count went to two-and-two before Burdette connected with a pitch and knocked it into the seats in left, not over but beyond the screen. This was no cheap "screeno," carrying well over 300 feet, although in County Stadium the leftfielder would have received a putout. The Braves' lead was 6-3.

Lew Burdette starred in the '57 Series but could not repeat in '58.

The Dodgers scored a run in the eighth through no fault of Burdette's. Logan fielded Larker's ground ball and fired it into the box seats, sending the runner to second. Larker tagged and advanced to third on Snider's fly to Aaron in right. Furillo then grounded out, scoring Larker to make it 6-4 for Milwaukee.

In the ninth Burdette had a chance to enter the record book, but first his teammates put the game safely out of reach. Roach drew a walk to lead off. Mathews tried to sacrifice, Roebuck threw the ball into rightfield, and Roach reached home while Mathews sprinted to third. After Aaron popped out, Torre executed a perfect suicide squeeze, so perfect that Mathews scored and Torre reached first safely. The lead was now a comfortable 8-4. Crandall singled, Logan was retired, and Pafko was hit by a pitch, loading the bases once more for Burdette.

No ballplayer in National League history had hit two grand slams in the same game; unfortunately neither did Burdette. With slugging immortality staring him in the face, Lanky Lew blinked—three times. Roebuck struck him out on three pitches. Burdette, though, did earn his seventh season win by shutting out the Dodgers in the last of the ninth, earning the first Braves' victory in the Coliseum.

If the game had been played in Ebbets Field in Brooklyn, Burdette would not have become the only active league pitcher to have hit a grand slam. He would not have tied Don Newcombe's record of twice hitting two homers in a game. And in Brooklyn he certainly would not have posed for postgame pictures with actress Lauren Bacall.

Time Capsule - October 5, 1958

"That game was all Spahn." —Hank Bauer

It was a classic match-up: the best lefthander in the National League versus the best lefthander in the American League. Warren Spahn and Whitey Ford had faced off twice before, at Yankee Stadium in the opening game of the 1957 World Series, and at County Stadium in the opening game of the 1958 World Series. Ford had triumphed in the former, 3-1; Spahn had won the rematch, 4-3, in ten innings. On Sunday afternoon, October 5, 1958, at Yankee Stadium, the two quintessential southpaws met to break the tie.

The game was the fourth of the Series, the Braves having won the first two in Milwaukee, the Yanks having won the third in New York. Ford was trying to pitch his first complete game since August 8. He had been bothered by a sore arm since that time, although he had finished the regular season with a 14-7 record and a 2.01 earned run average, by far the lowest in either league. In the Series opener he had lasted seven innings before giving way to myopic flamethrower Ryne Duren. Spahn, on the other hand, a 22-game winner in league competition, had worked a ten-inning complete game in the post-season curtain-raiser.

For the first five innings the pitchers looked as tough on the mound as they did on paper. Spahn walked Norm Siebern to lead off the Yankee first inning, although both Spahn and his catcher Del Crandall were upset that the 2-2 pitch had not been called strike three. Siebern never reacher second base, though, as Spahn retired Gil McDougald, Mickey Mantle, and Hank Bauer in order. In the third Spahn committed the cardinal sin by getting too cute on a 3-2 pitch to mound rival Ford and walking him with one out, but Ford died at first base.

In the last of the fourth the Yankees produced their only

211

scoring threat of the day. Batting righthanded, Mantle caught hold of a screwball and slammed it over 400 feet into leftcenter, a drive that would have been a home run in the Braves' ballpark. In spacious Yankee Stadium the blast put Mantle on third with nobody out. Spahn toughened, though, and dispatched Bauer, Moose Skowron, and Yogi Berra without a ball leaving the infield. Berra came close, lining a shot toward rightfield, but Red Schoendienst leaped high, knocked the ball down, and fired to first a split-second ahead of the diving Berra. Schoendienst's effort was the play of the game.

The Braves did not score in the fifth, but they witnessed a precursor of future scores. Crandall hit a short fly into leftfield. Norm Siebern, starting in left because Elston Howard had injured himself in Game Two by running into the fence while chasing Burdette's home run, got a late start on the ball and failed to catch it. Then he watched helplessly as the ball bounced past him. Mantle was backing up the play, so Crandall was held to a single and did not score. "I didn't have much chance on it," Siebern said of the play after the game, but many observers disagreed.

In the sixth the Braves finally got on the scoreboard, with Siebern's help. Schoendienst hit a flyball into leftcenter that should have been an easy out, but Siebern hesitated, then ran toward it, and at the last moment shied away, seemingly waiting for Mantle to make the catch. The ball rolled past them to the fence. Schoendienst received credit for a triple and scored moments later when Johnny Logan's grounder scooted between the legs of shortstop Tony Kubek. "I lost the ball against the lights," Siebern told reporters of Schoendienst's hit. "It was my ball. I simply lost it."

Spahn blanked the Yanks in the sixth, then received another donation in the Braves' seventh inning. Crandall led off with a base on balls, the only one Ford issued. Covington flied out. Andy Pafko lined a double into rightcenter, just out of Mantle's reach. Then Spahn lofted a pop fly into short leftfield. Siebern once again got a late start and caught the ball on the first bounce, with Crandall scoring. "I might have caught it," Siebern said in the postgame interview, "but I didn't start quick enough." Schoendienst bounced into a doubleplay to end the rally.

The Yankees got their final baserunner of the day in the last of the seventh. With one out Moose Skowron lined a ball up the middle. Spahn deflected the ball with his glove, but Skowron was on first before anyone could retrieve it. Skowron progressed no further, though. Spahn got Berra to foul out on a low, outside pitch, then disposed of pinch-hitter Elston Howard on a called

212

third strike.

Milwaukee added a final insurance run in the eighth. The first batter, Logan, slammed a long fly toward the leftfield fence. Siebern retreated but had no idea where the ball was. At the last moment he could do nothing but cover his head to prevent decapitation. The ball landed short of the fence and bounded high in the air and into the stands for a ground rule double. Siebern's only explanation: "I lost it in the sun. I never saw the ball after it left the bat." Eddie Mathews followed with a double off the concrete wall in rightcenter, Logan scored, and it was 3-0. Mathews' blast chased Whitey Ford. Relief man Johnny Kucks loaded the bases but retired Pafko to escape further damage.

Spahn easily set down New York in the eighth. He cancelled 42-year-old pinch-hitter Enos Slaughter on a called third strike, the fifth Yankee called out on strikes, then retired pinch-hitter Jerry Lumpe and the unfortunate Siebern. After 42-year-old Murry Dickson stopped the Braves in the ninth, the much-younger Spahn (37), still throwing a deft mixture of fastballs and screwballs, retired McDougald, Bauer, and Mantle to complete a two-hit, no-run masterpiece. Bauer's failure ended his record seventeen-game World Series hitting streak. Spahn's victory put the Yankees down 3-1 in the Series, a deficit no team had overcome since Pie Traynor and the Pittsburgh Pirates fought back to overtake Walter Johnson and the Washington Senators in 1925.

After the game the attention of the sportswriters focused on two ballplayers: Norm Siebern and Warren Spahn. New York manager Casey Stengel tried to deflect criticism from Siebern, saying, "I'll tell you one thing. I'm not asking waivers on him." He did not, but neither did he allow Siebern ever again to appear in a World Series game in a Yankee uniform. And Spahn—he was asked bluntly if it was the best game he had ever pitched. "Yes," the great lefthander answered, "I'd have to say it was."

1958 Swan Songs

"Johnson does more work in the bullpen than is obvious to the fans or writers."

—Pitching Coach Bucky Walters

On September 28, the last day of the 1958 season, manager Fred Haney cleared the bench and utilized a number of ballplayers who seldom got much chance to play—men like Joe Koppe, Bob Roselli, and Hawk Taylor. Also appearing that day were two Braves' Originals in their final year with the Milwaukee club—pitcher Ernie Johnson and outfielder-infielder Harry Hanebrink.

Johnson entered the ballgame in the seventh inning, the third Milwaukee hurler of the meaningless game. The Braves trailed the visiting Cincinnati Redlegs at the time, 2-0. Haney was using the finale to get a last look at the pitchers he was considering to start Game Three of the upcoming World Series, and one of the possibilities was Johnson, recently brought back from the Wichita farm team. Johnson worked a scoreless seventh inning, but in the eighth he gave up the final two runs of the season on three hits. He left for a pinch-hitter in the bottom of the eighth. He was added to the World Series roster as a replacement for Joey Jay, out with an injured finger, but he did not pitch against the Yankees.

Hanebrink finished the game as a replacement for Eddie Mathews at third base, batting once but failing to get a hit. His Milwaukee career was extended, though. In World Series Game Three at Yankee Stadium, won 4-0 by New York, Hanebrink batted for losing pitcher Bob Rush in the seventh inning and popped out. He then finished his tenure as a Brave by pinch-hitting for Juan Pizarro in the eighth inning of Game Five, also at Yankee Stadium, also won by New York (7-0), and again he

214

popped out, this time in foul ground.

The following March 31, Hanebrink was traded to Philadelphia along with Gene Conley and Joe Koppe.

Johnson, Willey, Conley, Robinson jog in Yankee Stadium

215

World Series, 1958

"We scored 17 runs in the first two games and 25 for the Series. That's it in a nutshell."

—Warren Spahn

A graph of the fortunes of the Milwaukee Braves baseball franchise would peak during the 1958 World Series—not at the end of it, but during the Series. Fred Haney and company had won the World Series the previous year, had repeated as National League champions, and took a nearly insurmountable lead in the first four games in the 1958 Series—and then died.

On October 1 at County Stadium the Braves began their defense of the world baseball championship. Manager Haney immediately raised some eyebrows by choosing as his starting pitcher someone other than Lew Burdette, the fabled Yankee-killer of 1957. Burdette had won twenty games for the first time in 1958, but Haney elected to start the old reliable, Warren Spahn. Haney was soon vindicated when Spahn hurled a ten-inning complete game to beat New York, 4-3. Spahn even contributed two base hits and drove in one of the runs.

Bill Skowron hooked a line drive around the leftfield foul pole for a cheap home run in the fourth to put the Yankees ahead. The Braves scored two runs in the bottom of the inning to give Spahn a 2-1 advantage. In the next inning Haney's pitcher walked his counterpart, Whitey Ford, then served up a fat 2-0 pitch to Hank Bauer that landed in the leftfield bleachers to put New York back on top. After Bauer's smash Spahn stiffened, allowing no more runs in the final five innings. The Braves scored a run in the eighth to tie the game, then produced the winning run in the tenth on singles by Joe Adcock, Del Crandall, and Bill Bruton. The 4-3 win came at the expense of Ryne Duren, the Yankee bullpen ace

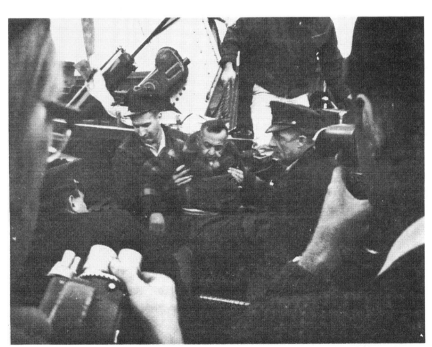

Highlight (pun intentional) of Game 1: 60-year-old Brooklynite Anthony Albano scaled a 115-foot light tower and watched 10 innings, but descent required assistance.

217

out of Cazenovia, Wisconsin.

Game Two, also in Milwaukee, offered Burdette his fourth opportunity to plague the team that had traded him away in 1951. Burdette took the opportunity to beat Casey Stengel's team for the fourth straight time, with his fourth straight seven-hitter. The fidgety righthander allowed just three hits and two runs, one of them unearned, through the first eight innings before New York counted three meaningless tallies in the ninth, long after the outcome had been decided.

The story of Game Two, though, was the Braves' offense. They scored early and often and did not relent until the game was beyond question, all in the 42-minute first inning. Bruton smashed a leadoff home run off starter Bob Turley. The Braves added a double by Red Schoendienst, and after Eddie Mathews was called out on strikes, Hank Aaron walked, Wes Covington singled home Schoendienst, and Turley was hastily replaced by Duke Maas. A walk to Del Crandall loaded the bases, Johnny Logan singled home two more runs, and Burdette climaxed the inning with a long three-run home run, his first homer in County Stadium. Burdette's drive was only the fifth World Series home run ever hit by a pitcher, the last having been hit by former Braves coach Bucky Walters with Cincinnati in 1940. Milwaukee's seven-run explosion was the largest opening inning ever in a World Series game, leading to a 13-5 victory. No team had ever scored more runs against the Yankees in post-season competition.

The Series shifted to New York on October 4 for Game Three. Desperately needing a win, Stengel called on Don Larsen, of perfect game fame, as his starter. Larsen had been bothered by an elbow injury throughout the latter part of the season and had not pitched a complete game since July 18, but Stengel's instincts proved reliable. Larsen worked seven shutout innings before leaving for a pinch-hitter, earning his victory with the help of two hitless innings by relief man Ryne Duren. All the Yankees' runs were produced by Hank Bauer on a two-run single in the fifth and a two-run homer in the seventh, giving them a 4-0 triumph.

Bob Rush started for the Braves and allowed only three hits in six innings. His undoing, though, was his lack of control; he walked five batters, including three in the fifth before Bauer's broken-bat single drove home the only two runs Rush gave up. Reliever Don McMahon threw the gopher ball to Bauer in the seventh, and the Braves were saddled with a defeat. They had a chance to score in the sixth with a single, a walk, and a single, but bad baserunning by Schoendienst and Aaron took them out of the

218

inning and kept them scoreless.

Game Four belonged to Warren Spahn, who outdueled Whitey Ford to put Milwaukee up three games to one [see Time Capsule]. The Yankees fought back in Game Five, though, to keep their slim chances alive. In a game disrupted by pro-Castro banner-carriers and numerous witless exhibitionists on the field, Bob Turley, bombed in the first inning just four days earlier in Milwaukee, was in total command with a five-hit, ten-strikeout shutout. The losing pitcher was the erstwhile pillar of invincibility, Lew Burdette. He pitched well through the fifth, yielding only a flimsy solo home run off the leftfield foul pole by Gil McDougald in the third inning. In the sixth, however, four singles and a walk finished Burdette. By the time the dust settled the Yankees had a six-run inning en route to a 7-0 victory. The two teams returned to Milwaukee with the Braves leading the Series, three games to two.

Needing only one victory in two home games, the Braves seemed secure, all the more so because Spahn was working the sixth game. Returning after two days' rest, the high-kicking lefty was his usual brilliant self, limiting the Yanks to two runs in nine innings, one of them tainted. Bauer poked a home run into the seats in the first inning, but the other New York run in regulation time was made possible because Billy Bruton could not pick up Elston Howard's single in the sixth. Bruton's fumble allowed Mickey Mantle to take third; he then scored on Yogi Berra's flyball.

Had Bruton made the routine pickup, Spahn would have earned the victory with his arm and his bat. Aaron singled home Schoendienst with the tying run in the first, and in the second inning Spahn singled to drive in Wes Covington with what might have been the winning run. After Spahn's hit, Schoendienst walked to load the bases with one out, setting up the worst mental error of the Series. Starter Whitey Ford was replaced by Art Ditmar. Johnny Logan hit Ditmar's first pitch in the air in short leftfield. Elston Howard made the catch without difficulty. Incredibly, though, third base coach Billy Herman sent Andy Pafko to try to score from third. Pafko's 37-year-old legs made the attempt a suicide mission—he was dead at the plate, and so was the Braves' potential big inning.

Ryne Duren entered the game for New York in the sixth, and Milwaukee's hitters went numb. Before Duren the Braves had scoring chances but failed to capitalize; after Duren's arrival their chances disappeared. After nine innings the teams were still tied, 2-2. In the tenth Spahn's magic went the way of his teammates'

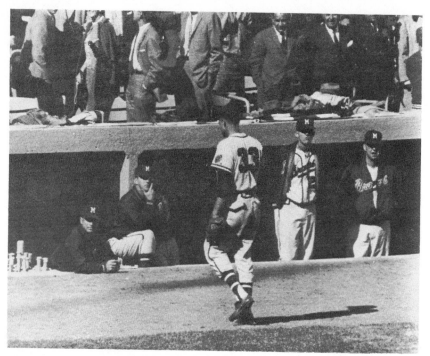

Unlucky Lew Burdette trudges to the dugout after a valiant but losing effort.

support. McDougald belted a leadoff home run to put the Yanks ahead, 3-2. After two outs the Yankees used three hits to score another run. In the bottom of the tenth the Braves fought back within one run and had men on first and third with two out, but Bob Turley came in and got pinch-hitter Frank Torre to hit a game-ending popup. Duren and the Yanks won, 4-3, robbing Spahn of a hero's role comparable to Burdette's the previous year. The old guy deserved better.

The seventh and deciding game was played on Thursday afternoon, October 9. Haney chose Burdette for the crucial start; Stengel chose Larsen. The Braves scored in the first to lead 1-0; the Yanks scored twice in the second, both runs unearned thanks to Torre's two errors, both on bad underhand tosses to Burdette covering first. Ironically, Torre had led National League first basemen in fielding in 1958.

Del Crandall's home run in the sixth tied the score at 2-2. However, with two out in the top of the eighth, nobody on base,

220

and Burdette seemingly in control, the Braves' world collapsed. Yogi Berra lined a double off the rightfield wall, narrowly missing a home run. Elston Howard broke the tie with a single up the middle. Andy Carey lined a base hit off Mathews' glove, his only hit of the Series. Finally Moose Skowron, who in 1958 had his worst year ever in the major leagues, timed a Burdette change-up and blasted it over the fence in leftcenter for a three-run homer, a 6-2 New York lead, and a long winter for Milwaukee.

In the last two innings the only excitement Braves followers experienced was watching a drunken fan in a brown suit sprint onto the field and execute a hook-slide into second base. The home team put two men on base in the ninth but failed to score again. The star for Stengel's team was, once again, Bob Turley, who allowed only Crandall's home run in six and two-thirds innings of relief. Burdette, like Spahn the day before, finished a loser, a victim of egregious non-support.

Milwaukee's disappointing finish to a fine season can be explained in two words—poor hitting. Mathews and Logan had particularly poor Series, but as a team the Braves hit only .250, with three home runs in seven games. They scored more runs in Game Two than in the six other games combined.

Milwaukee Journal Photo

Somber fans wade through expressway construction after Braves lose the Series finale.

1959

"I guess it just wasn't meant to be. This just wasn't our year."

—Red Schoendienst

The Milwaukee Braves should have won their third straight National League pennant in 1959. Before the season few doubted that they would. They had a star-studded veteran lineup, flawed in one or two spots but clearly the strongest in the league overall. They had a proven pitching staff with youngsters fighting for a chance to show their talents. They had experienced consecutive World Series and fought the vaunted New York Yankees to a standoff. On paper the Braves had their best team ever in 1959. In the distant retrospect of more than a quarter century they still look like champions on paper, but they somehow failed to win the pennant.

An apologist for this team would cite the list of injuries Haney's club had to endure. Scarcely a month after the 1958 World Series defeat by the Yankees, the perplexing ailment of Red Schoendienst was diagnosed as tuberculosis, removing him from all but three token appearances in 1959. Mel Roach started the season late, finished early, and was hobbled in between by the knee injury suffered on Daryl Spencer's body-block the previous August 3. Del Rice broke his leg trying to tag the sliding Willie Mays on June 1 and was lost for the season. Wes Covington was still plagued by knee trouble periodically, then ended his season on August 20 with an ankle injury. Joe Adcock seemed to have at least one injured limb throughout the year. Eddie Mathews missed a week and a half in late May with a bum hip. Bob Buhl was out from mid-June to mid-July with arm trouble. The list goes on, mostly with nagging, minor hurts. Injuries have always been a factor in sports, though—these were nothing out of the ordinary, certainly no worse than in the previous two seasons.

Sliding Willie Mays breaks leg of Del Rice.

The two principal reasons why the Braves should have repeated as league champs were healthy all season—Warren Spahn and Lew Burdette. They worked 292 and 290 innings respectively, ranking one-two in the league in innings pitched, neither missing a turn all year. The two fun-loving roommates not only performed frequently, however; they also performed with distinction, each earning a league-leading 21 victories to accompany 15 losses, and ranking one-two in complete games with 21 and 20 respectively. Each also hurled four shutouts, tying for league honors.

The similarity between their records, though, is deceiving, as their earned run averages prove—Spahn's was 2.96, fourth-best in the league, while his partner's was 4.07, his worst ever. What's more, if Spahn had adhered to his former custom of not pitching against the Dodgers, his record would have appeared far more impressive. He lost to Los Angeles five straight times, including twice in relief, extending his career against the former Flatbushians to 14 wins, 30 losses. Burdette, on the other hand, beat the

223

Dodgers twice without a loss and would have had a third win given proper relief help in the ninth inning of the season finale.

To complement their dynamic mound duo, the Braves received unprecedented offensive support from their slugging tandem of Aaron and Mathews. Each started fast and sustained the production, with minor fluctuations, throughout the season. Mathews slammed a home run on opening day in Pittsburgh; Aaron stroked a single and two doubles. Mathews clubbed seven homers in the Braves' first eleven games; Aaron hit .508 for the month of April. Mathews totaled sixteen home runs by the end of May; Aaron was still batting above .400 on June 15. At the time of the year's first All-Star Game (yes, in 1959 major league baseball's masterminds decided that two of anything is better than one) on July 7 Mathews had 25 home runs; Aaron had 21. Mathews finished the season with a career-high .306 batting average and 46 home runs, tops in either league and his highest total since his first year in Milwaukee; Aaron finished with a .355 average and 400 total bases, the largest total since 1948. Together

Milwaukee Journal Photo

Henry Aaron was 1959's hottest hitter.

Mathews and Aaron accounted for 752 total bases, a figure unsurpassed by two teammates since 1930, the watershed year in which the lively ball enabled National League batters to establish a number of enduring records: Hack Wilson smashed 56 home runs and drove in 190 runs, and Bill Terry tied the record for base hits with 254 and became the last .400 hitter the league would see.

In addition to Mathews and Aaron, Haney received good production from other hitters. Adcock contributed 25 home runs and hit .292; Crandall clouted 21 homers and his highest RBI total ever; Logan rebounded from his lowest average to his second-best, .291; and Bruton hit a career-high .289. The Braves led the majors in home runs and boasted the best ratio of runs scored to runs allowed of any team in either league. Defensively Milwaukee posted the second best fielding percentage in the big leagues, and Crandall and Adcock led league fielders at their respective positions.

Aside from the Big Two on the mound, Haney received fifteen wins from Bob Buhl, with a 2.86 earned run average, third-best in the league. Bullpen ace Don McMahon fashioned a 2.57 ERA in 60 appearances and saved a league-high fifteen games, although that statistical measure was officially a decade in the future. Hitting, fielding, pitching—the Braves lacked none of it.

What they did lack, according to some observers, was a capable manager. Fred Haney was the skipper who had led the MIlwaukeeans to consecutive pennants, nearly three straight, and a World Series victory, but many people blamed him for the Braves' failure to establish a dynasty. Haney had been hired to replace the easy-going Charlie Grimm, to bring discipline and firm guidance to a free-spirited, headstrong group of players. Under Haney, though, the Braves were not terribly different from the way they had been under Grimm. Some players were openly critical, publicly dissatisfied with their manager, the more so of course after he retired following the season. Johnny Logan was one player, according to reporters covering the team, who did not see eye-to-eye with the Braves' field general. "We should have won by ten games without any question," Logan said after Haney's resignation.

Joey Jay offered an even stronger indictment of his ex-manager. "Fred Haney didn't manage the club," Jay said. "He sat in one corner of the dugout, gulping down pills and saying to Crandall, 'What should we do, Del?' " It should be noted that in mid-July Haney had demoted Jay to the bullpen, saying he was lazy and out of shape.

Haney was criticized primarily for two facets of his managing—relying too heavily on Spahn and Burdette rather than using his young pitchers more, and being too conservative, too reliant on "percentage" baseball. His teams did not use the hit-and-run or steal many bases, always finishing at or near the bottom in steals; with the powerful lineup the Braves had, though, his teams rarely needed a stolen base. While many fans believed that with better managing the Braves would have won four straight pennants, Haney's predecessor and his three successors pale by comparison.

For whatever reason the Braves failed to pull away from the pack and ultimately lost a heartbreaking playoff series to the Dodgers, National League fans witnessed an exciting three-way pennant race, even closer than the 1956 race. All three teams—the Dodgers, the Braves, and the Giants—began the final day of the 154-game schedule with a chance to win the pennant. As defending champions, the Braves were no surprise. Somewhat surprising, however, were the San Francisco Giants. Bill Rigney's club had been a distant sixth-place finisher in 1956 and 1957, then had climbed to third behind the Pirates in 1958. The next step, from respectability to genuine contention, was accomplished mainly through the addition of three players: first baseman Willie McCovey, brought up from Phoenix on July 30, and two starting pitchers, Jack Sanford and Sam Jones, obtained in off-season trades. McCovey batted .354 and hit thirteen home runs in just two months; Sanford and Jones combined with Johnny Antonelli and Mike McCormick to give the Giants the best four-man pitching rotation in the league.

If San Francisco was somewhat of a surprise, Los Angeles was a shock. From a seventh-place finish in 1958, after being last most of the season, the Dodgers came back to win the pennant. Several of their veterans simply had better years than the year before—Gil Hodges, Duke Snider, Junior Gilliam, Don Drysdale—but as was the case with the Giants, several additions to the roster, three of them pitchers, helped immensely. Roger Craig, returned from the minors, won eleven games and pitched sensationally. Danny McDevitt, in his first full season in the majors, won ten games. Larry Sherry, summoned from St. Paul in mid-year, won seven games and saved three. The story of the year at the L.A. Coliseum, though, was Wally Moon, obtained in a trade after one bad year with the Cardinals. A lefthanded batter, Moon mastered the art of swinging late and popping cheap home runs over the nearby screen in leftfield. These "Moonshots" helped keep the Dodgers in contention early in the season before their pitching staff stabilized and made Walt Alston's team genuine contenders.

226

In contrast to the California clubs, the Braves made no significant additions to their roster. The major change was a deletion—Gene Conley was traded to the Phillies. After years of incredible promise and potential and flashes of brilliance interrupted frequently by sore arms, the Braves' front office finally gave up on the tall disappointment and swapped him, along with Harry Hanebrink and Joe Koppe, for catcher-first baseman-nemesis Stan Lopata and second baseman-pitcher-twin Johnny O'Brien. Conley, of course, won twelve games for the last-place Phillies; only five starting pitchers in the league compiled lower earned run averages than Conley's 3.00. The only roster change that had an impact on the standings was the Conley trade—it may well have cost the Braves the pennant.

The players obtained at the expense of Conley proved essentially worthless. Lopata, once a feared slugger, was used sparingly, never got an extra-base hit, and hit less than half his weight. O'Brien hit above his weight but below Lopata's and was dismissed, his major league career over, on July 21. The ballplayers

Milwaukee Journal Photo

Twin-killing, Logan to Adcock

227

brought up from the minors contributed nothing. Chuck Cottier was a good-field, no-hit second baseman. Jim Pisoni was a non-playing outfielder. Joe Morgan had a career with remarkable similarities to that of Warren Spahn: each threw lefthanded, each played minor league ball with Hartford and Evansville, then went into military service; Spahn had a lifetime slugging percentage of .287, Morgan's was .283; Spahn's lifetime batting average was .194, Morgan's was .193. The main difference between the two is that Spahn was a pitcher, while Morgan was an infielder. Needless to say, Morgan's contribution to the Braves was below measure.

During the season the Braves obtained several other players in a futile attempt to fill their needs. Curiously, all but one were of an age more appropriate to coaching than to playing. Two days into the season they traded slender 28-year-old Panamanian pitcher Humberto Robinson to Cleveland for slender 41-year-old first baseman Mickey Vernon, the pride of Marcus Hook, Pennsylvania. Vernon appeared primarily as a pinch-hitter and emergency outfielder, performing unspectacularly. On July 21 the Braves bought 35-year-old second baseman Bobby Avila, a former American League batting champ, from the Red Sox. Avila won two games for Spahn with ninth-inning home runs but gave back at least that many with his fielding. On August 20 the Milwaukee front office purchased gimpy-legged 36-year-old infielder Ray Boone from Kansas City. Finally on September 12 the Braves obtained from the Yankees the services of 43-year-old Enos Slaughter, born before the United States entered World War I, for the final two weeks of his illustrious career. The non-ancient player the Braves added during the season was Lee Maye, a 24-year-old outfielder who performed commendably after being called up from Louisville on July 17. Maye hit .300 and filled in capably for Wes Covington.

Sparked by the hitting of Mathews and Aaron and the pitching of Spahn and Burdette, the Braves began the season with every indication that they would repeat as National League pennant winners. They won their first four games, seven of their first nine, and finished April in first place, percentage points ahead of the surprising Dodgers. They struggled for the next week and a half, then won nine of ten games to take a four and one-half game lead on May 19, their high-water mark for the season.

The fact that the Braves tied the Dodgers for the pennant belies the fact that for two-thirds of the season, from May 17 through September 5, Haney's charges lost more games than they won. They managed to hold first place, with the exception of one day, from May 13 to the Fourth of July. After the first All-Star Game on July 7, though, they quickly dropped to third place, spending the greater part of July and August looking up at both the Giants and the Dodgers. As late as September 5 the Braves trailed San Francisco by four and one-half games. Then the pitching staff took control and the Braves reeled off seven straight wins and thirteen of sixteen, moving back into first place entering the final week of the season. Consecutive losses to the Pirates and Phillies dropped the Braves a game behind Los Angeles, but Spahn and Buhl beat the Phillies on the final weekend to create a tie and set up the third playoff in National League history.

The start of the season had offered no indication of such a tense finish. Behind the pitching of Warren Spahn, the Braves won both the opener in Pittsburgh, 8-0, and the home opener four days later, 4-3. The latter victory was not actually earned by Spahn; leading 3-1 with two out in the ninth and two strikes on the batter, he gave up a tying triple to Wally Post. Milwaukee

Milwaukee Journal Photo

Governor Gaylord Nelson throws out first ball at 1959 opener, watched by Warren Giles, Fred Haney, Lou Perini, and Phillies manager Eddie Sawyer.

won in the tenth inning, the victory going to reliever Don McMahon. An enthusiastic crowd of 42,081 watched the successful curtain-raiser, the last crowd of that size for quite some time. In fact the next crowd to total 25,000 occurred on May 10, fifteen home dates later. Attendance figures at County Stadium remained among the highest in the league, but the fervor of Milwaukee fans had clearly diminished. On April 30 a Stadium low night game total of 12,086 was established. A month into the season, attendance was down by about 6000 fans per game. By June 4 total attendance was lagging 168,000 behind the previous year; by mid-September it was down a quarter-million. The season total of 1,749,112 marked a decline of more than 220,000 and set a new season low, 77,000 below the 1953 total despite eight more dates. The thrill was not gone, but it was going.

The month of June was characterized by inconsistency for the Braves. It began with a four-game series at home against second-place San Francisco. The Giants bombed Joey Jay in the opener and scored eleven runs in the game in which Del Rice broke his leg. The next night Bob Rush struck out eight, walked nobody, and shut the visitors out, 4-0. Next Buhl and McMahon collaborated for a 7-4 win, but in the finale, Burdette failed to last five innings as the Giants walloped the Braves again, 11-5, punctuated by an Orlando Cepeda blast that completely cleared the leftfield bleachers, a Stadium first. The entire month followed that up-down pattern with the exception of one six-game stretch, June 20-26, during which Braves pitchers threw six straight complete games, winning five of them.

July also began with a lose-one, win-one motif, but then it deteriorated. Beginning on July 14 the Braves endured a seven-game losing streak, their longest since June of 1953. Those seven games—a three-game series in Chicago, three games in St. Louis, and one at home against the Redlegs—saw Milwaukee pitchers yield 50 runs while Braves hitters could produce just 24. The loss string was ended on a ninth-inning, two-run home run by Bobby Avila in his first appearance as a Brave. The next day, though, Avila's error allowed Willie Jones of Cincinnati to hit a game-winning grand slam against the unfortunate Joey Jay.

Following Avila's take-one, give-one set which dropped the Braves four and one-half games out of first, the Milwaukee pitching staff took over and brought the team back into the fight, sweeping a five-game series from Pittsburgh in spectacular fashion. On July 24 Juan Pizarro struck out twelve Pirates in an 8-0 triumph. Next Lew Burdette shut them out, 3-0, as Henry Aaron made his major league debut as a third baseman. In a Sunday

1959 starting pitchers: Bob Rush, Joey Jay, Carl Willey, Lew Burdette, Warren Spahn, and Bob Buhl.

afternoon doubleheader, Warren Spahn fired his 47th career shutout, 4-0, and Bob Buhl, with relief assistance, beat the Bucs, 2-1, the only Pirate run unearned. Joey Jay closed out the series with a 5-2 complete game victory. The Cubs stopped the winning streak at five, but Haney's crew won the next four in a row to arrive at the second All-Star break just one game behind the pacesetting Giants.

Following All-Star Revisited the Braves hit the road, beginning on the West Coast, and promptly lost eight of thirteen games to fall back into third place, where they remained with only momentary interruptions until September 12. On that day they won their seventh straight game on a two-run eighth-inning home run by Eddie Mathews, giving Burdette his 20th win and boosting his team into a tie for second, just one game back. A week earlier the Giants had appeared headed for the pennant, but now it was a three-horse race again.

In the final two weeks of the season the Braves played good, not great, baseball. Spahn lost a tough game in the team's final appearance in Crosley Field. Milwaukee split a pair in Los Angeles, losing a disputed ten-inning contest, then split a pair in San Francisco, Burdette hurling a shutout in the first, Spahn getting bombed in the second. With eight games remaining the Braves flew east, trailing the Giants by two games, for ballgames in Philadelphia and Pittsburgh. They won both games with the Phillies, then regained first place for the first time in seven weeks by beating the Pirates twice. In the final road game, in Pittsburgh on September 23, the Pirates scored in the last of the ninth to dump the Braves back into a tie with the Dodgers going into the final weekend series at County Stadium against the Phillies. Shades of 1956, only a game worse!

On a rainy Friday night, the Phillies belted Burdette and the Braves, 6-3, before a crowd of 24,912, scarcely more than half of capacity. The defeat pushed Haney's club a game below the Dodgers with two left. The next day, though, with an assist from the Chicago Cubs, who knocked off Los Angeles, the Braves and Warren Spahn beat the Phillies and Robin Roberts, 3-2, to knot the standings, with San Francisco just a game back. Heading into the final day the Giants needed to sweep a doubleheader from the Cardinals while the Braves and Dodgers both lost to create an unprecedented three-way tie. As it transpired, the Giants were swept and the Dodgers won. The Braves, though, also won behind Bob Buhl and Don McMahon and five unearned runs to send the season into a best two-of-three playoff between the Dodgers and Braves, commencing in Milwaukee the next day. (In retrospect, the biggest Wisconsin sports story of the day took place 125 miles north in Green Bay. This was the day Vince Lombardi made his bow as Packer head coach—his new team shocked Babe Ruth's old outfield predecessor, George Halas, and his highly-favored Chicago Bears, 9-6.)

Time Capsule - September 29, 1959

"Did we get the guy at first?"

> —Johnny Logan, first words after regaining consciousness

So this was it—the biggest game of the year, in the biggest baseball stadium in the world. After nearly six months of baseball, the National League pennant race came down to one contest, with another to follow if Milwaukee won.

In the playoff opener in Milwaukee the day before, the Braves had generated almost no offense, losing a rain-delayed 3-2 yawner to Larry Sherry and his Dodger teammates. Faced now with the formidable task of winning two straight in the Los Angeles Coliseum, the Braves counted on 21-game winner Lew Burdette to bring them back to even. Burdette's rival was hard-throwing Don Drysdale, a nemesis of long standing and a 17-game winner.

The Braves got to Drysdale in the first inning. With one out Eddie Mathews drew a walk, then moved to third on a Hank Aaron double. Frank Torre singled home both runners, and Burdette had a quick 2-0 lead. The Dodgers got one back in the bottom of the first when Charlie Neal tripled and Wally Moon drove him in with a base hit. The Braves regained their two-run advantage in the second on singles by Logan and Burdette and a throwing error by Duke Snider. Neal led off the Dodger fourth with a home run, but Mathews matched Neal's blast with one against Drysdale in the next half-inning to make it 4-2 Milwaukee. The score stayed at that level until the eighth inning, but the game's pivotal play occurred in the home half of the seventh.

Norm Larker, the Dodger leftfielder, was on first base when John Roseboro hit a sharp grounder toward Frank Torre. The Braves' first baseman scooped the ball up and threw to Johnny Logan covering second to force the rapidly-approaching Larker.

233

Logan fired the ball back to Torre, releasing the throw a split-second before the charging Dodger barreled into him. Larker's shoulder, lowered for a collision like that of a fullback running over a linebacker, caught the unprotected shortstop squarely in the chest. The relay to first beat Roseboro to complete the doubleplay, but Logan never saw it— he was rolling on the ground in agony. He lost consciousness for several minutes and had to be carried to the clubhouse on a stretcher. Along with him, as it turned out, went the Braves' pennant chances.

With Logan disabled, Felix Mantilla moved from the second base position to take Logan's spot. With the pennant hanging in the balance, manager Haney chose Red Schoendienst to play second base. The Redhead had appeared in just four late-season games and batted just twice since returning from his bout with tuberculosis. Nevertheless, Haney selected him over the able-bodied Bobby Avila, who had been the regular second baseman during the final two months of the season but who had contribut-

Milwaukee Journal Photo

Felix Mantilla pivots and fires to first base.

234

ed heavily to the loss in the playoff opener by failing to flag down two grounders.

The effect of Logan's loss is, of course, incalculable; several facts present themselves, however. Logan was concluding what was probably his second-best season in, at that time, a nine-year career. More important, he had hit nearly .500 for the year against Dodger pitching, including two hits in three tries before Larker leveled him. As for opportunities to help with his bat, Logan would have been the leadoff batter in the eighth inning (instead Schoendienst, batting in his slot, made the first out). Had he gotten on base, he would have scored when Del Crandall, batting next, tripled. In the ninth the Braves loaded the bases with two out; the scheduled hitter was Schoendienst, in Logan's spot. Haney sent in Mickey Vernon to pinch-hit—Vernon looked at a called third strike to end the inning. Finally in the eleventh the Braves loaded the bases with three walks against hurler Stan Williams, but with two out, pinch-hitter Joe Adcock, batting for Schoendienst's substitute Chuck Cottier, in Logan's batting spot, grounded into a forceout.

The other place Logan's absence was felt was in the field, although that void should never have mattered. After scoring in the eighth to take a 5-2 lead, and even after failing to capitalize on their bases-loaded chance in the ninth, the Braves had given Burdette a three-run cushion going to the last of the ninth. Burdette looked like a sure winner with three outs to go, having allowed just seven hits and no baserunner past first since Neal's home run in the fourth.

Wally Moon singled past Burdette, though, his third hit of the game, and Duke Snider did likewise. When Gil Hodges slapped the third straight single, loading the bases with none out, Haney had seen enough. The 21-game winner gave way to relief specialist Don McMahon. The Milwaukee bullpen ace had saved fifteen games, tops in the league, but he had worked in 59 games, including the previous two, and his bread-and-butter fastball was a piece of cake for Norm Larker, who slammed a base hit to drive in two runs. McMahon was hastily replaced by Warren Spahn.

Spahn had been 21-12 as a starter in 1959 but 0-3 in relief, giving him a career relief mark of 2-13. In those primitive days before team statisticians and computer printouts, it seems unlikely Haney knew of Spahn's bullpen proclivities—he knew only that he needed a reliable pitcher, preferably a southpaw, to face Roseboro. Instead Alston sent in pinch-hitter Carl Furillo, who banged a sacrifice fly to tie the game. Shortstop Maury Wills followed with a single, and after righthand hitter Chuck Essegian

235

was announced for pitcher Clem Labine, Spahn joined roommate Burdette in the clubhouse. Joey Jay was brought in, so Alston sent Ron Fairly to bat in Essegian's place. Fairly bounced into a force at second for the second out. On the play Joe Pignatano, running for Larker, advanced to third. Junior Gilliam belted an apparent game-winner into the rightfield corner, but Henry Aaron made a sensational fence-crashing catch to send the game to extra innings.

Stan Williams, the sixth Los Angeles pitcher, held the Braves hitless and, despite three walks in the eleventh, scoreless for the next three innings. Jay shut out the Dodgers in the tenth and, with help from Bob Rush, the eleventh. In the twelfth, though, after retiring Moon and Williams easily, Rush walked Hodges. Pignatano singled past Mathews to put runners on first and second. Finally, at 7:06 P.M. Milwaukee time, the Braves' dynasty ended, not with a bang but a whimper. Furillo bounced a high chopper toward shortstop, where Johnny Logan belonged. Mantilla fielded the ball but threw off-balance to first. The ball skipped in the dirt and over Torre's glove, hit Dodger coach Greg Mulleavy, and rolled toward the dugout. Hodges had stopped at third, but as the ball rolled in foul territory, he loped home with the pennant—Dodgers 6, Braves 5.

The agonizing defeat might have been easier to accept if the prospectus for 1960 had been brighter. Instead an examination of the list of 22 Braves who had played in the deciding game revealed an advancing problem—age. Ten of the ballplayers were over thirty. The three oldest—Enos Slaughter at 43, Mickey Vernon at 41, and Andy Pafko at 38— were expendable part-timers. Some of the key performers were also showing tread wear, though: Spahn was 38, Schoendienst was 36, Avila was 35, Rush was 33, Logan and Burdette were 32 each, and Adcock was 31. On the bench was Bob Buhl, also 31. It was beginning to look like the future was behind them.

1959 Nemesis - Larry Sherry

"The kid just never knew he wasn't supposed to be an athlete."

—Norm Sherry, Larry's older brother

Larry Sherry might have been created by Horatio Alger or some Hollywood scriptwriter. He was born with two clubbed feet and wore foot braces and orthopedic shoes during his childhood. When he entered high school in Los Angeles he stood five foot one inch and weighed scarcely 100 pounds. He wanted more than anything to be a ballplayer, though, and four years later, a foot taller and nearly twice as heavy, he signed a professional contract with the Dodgers. Six years after that he led Walt Alston's team to a World Series championship.

Even as a pigeon-toed minor league pitcher Sherry was no world-beater. In seven seasons with teams in places like Santa Barbara, Great Falls, Newport News, and Pueblo, only once did Sherry win more games than he lost—he was 6-5 with Bakersfield in 1954—and even then his ERA was a hefty 5.15. In 1959, having worked his way up to St. Paul, one step below the big leagues, he had a 6-7 record at the beginning of July when, unaccountably, he was summoned by the Dodgers.

Working both in relief and as a spot starter, Sherry pitched surprisingly well, improving greatly as he went on, especially out of the bullpen. His only complete game was a shutout of the Pirates on September 11, but as a reliever he was almost unhittable. In fourteen relief appearances totaling 36 and one-third innings, he won two games, lost none, and compiled an amazing 0.74 earned run average. Against the Braves on August 18, Sherry beat Warren Spahn, both of them in short relief, in the Dodgers' final scheduled appearance of the year at County Stadium. During the crucial final week of the season, Sherry pitched excellent relief against the Cubs. He saved his virtuoso performances, though, for the post-season.

In the opening playoff game in Milwaukee on September 28, Sherry relieved Danny McDevitt in the second inning with the score tied, 1-1, two men on base, one out, and a ball-two count on pitcher Carl Willey. An error by Maury Wills and a fielder's choice made the score 2-1, but Sherry allowed nothing further. In seven and two-thirds innings he gave up just four harmless singles, and no Milwaukee runner reached second base after the fifth inning. Sherry's mates scored twice to give him a 3-2 victory and send the Braves to Los Angeles needing two straight wins, which of course they failed to achieve.

In a note of tragic irony, during Sherry's sterling performance against the Braves, John "Red" Corriden died of a heart attack in Indianapolis while watching the game on TV. Corriden, a former big-league infielder and manager of the Chicago White Sox in 1950, had scouted Sherry and recommended to the Dodgers that they hire him.

After the Dodgers disposed of the Braves in the second playoff game, Sherry reached the pinnacle of his success in the World Series against the White Sox. He appeared in relief in four games, winning two and saving two, achieving a 0.71 ERA in twelve and two-thirds innings. The Dodgers won the Series, four games to two, winning whenever Sherry appeared and losing when he did not.

Time Capsule - May 26, 1959

"Just another loss, and that's no good."

—Harvey Haddix

It was the best baseball game ever pitched. Nothing before or since has come close. Harvey Haddix pitched twelve perfect innings against the Braves on Tuesday night, May 26, 1959, at County Stadium, but he lost. He retired 36 batters in a row, striking out eight. In twelve innings he need only 104 pitches. Until the twelfth he was never behind a hitter in the ball-strike count all night. In the thirteenth inning, against the fourth batter, Haddix threw what he called his only bad pitch of the night, a hanging slider. And he lost.

The Pittsburgh Pirates had arrived in Milwaukee that afternoon for a three-game series with the Braves. Haddix checked into the hotel and went to bed, suffering from symptoms of a cold and possibly the flu. He would have remained there except he was the scheduled pitcher that evening. He struggled out of bed and arrived at the ballpark to find weather less appropriate to baseball than to a performance of Macbeth—threatening skies, gusty winds, and intermittent flashes of distant lightning. The inclement weather helped hold the crowd down, although attendance was already on the wane, running 100,000 below the previous year. Despite the attendance of 19,194, in years to come at least ten times that number would claim to have witnessed this game.

Aside from his health, Haddix confronted another problem in the game—he was facing the most powerful lineup in baseball. Eddie Mathews had fourteen home runs, the most in the National League, in just a month and a half; Hank Aaron was hitting .453, highest in either league; and Joe Adcock, Wes Covington, and Del Crandall were all proven home run hitters. The Braves were two-time National League champs, currently in first place, three games ahead of San Francisco.

Against this array of sluggers, Haddix' chances seemed meager. He had once been among the leading pitchers in the league, hurling six shutouts and winning twenty games in 1953, his first full season in the majors. In 1959, though, he was working for his fourth team in four years, coming off a mediocre 8-7 season with Cincinnati, and entering the game against the Braves with a 3-2 record. Haddix was now 33 years old and beginning to lose the zip on his fastball.

The supporting cast for Haddix was hardly a match for the Braves' lineup. Second baseman Bill Mazeroski and centerfielder Bill Virdon were excellent fielders, adequate hitters; catcher Smoky Burgess and leftfielder Bob Skinner were good hitters, barely adequate fielders. Three of Pittsburgh's best, however, were absent. Shortstop Dick Groat was on the bench, replaced by Dick "Ducky" Schofield, who had never hit above .200. Rightfielder Roberto Clemente, brilliant but often injured, had gone on the disabled list the day before, replaced by erratic Roman Mejias. First baseman Dick Stuart, later nicknamed "Dr. Strangeglove" for his fielding misadventures, was the Pirates' only real home run threat, but tonight he had given way to Glenn "Rocky" Nelson, a three-time MVP in the International League but a six-time failure in the majors.

The task of opposing Haddix and his motley group of teammates fell to Lew Burdette, the leading winner in the National League with a 7-2 mark. He immediately served notice that he would be a formidable foe, retiring the Pirates in order in the first. Haddix, of course, did the same in the bottom half of the inning.

Rocky Nelson led off the Pittsburgh second with the game's first base hit, a single to right but, he was erased as Skinner bounced into a fast doubleplay, Adcock to Logan to Adcock. Burdette then dispatched Mazeroski to end the inning. Haddix struck out Adcock and retired Covington and Crandall on ground balls, and the game stayed scoreless.

In the third inning the Pirates produced their severest scoring threat of the night. Don Hoak, the third baseman obtained from the Redlegs along with Haddix, singled to left to start the trouble. Mejias grounded into a force play at second. Haddix lined a pitch through the box, striking Burdette on the leg. The ball rolled past the mound toward second, and as it did, the worst decision of the night was made. Mejias streaked around second without slowing down and without looking to the third base coach for a sign.

240

Johnny Logan scrambled in, gloved the ball, wheeled toward third, and threw Mejias out by ten feet. Mejias' error in judgment was spotlighted when the next batter, Schofield, singled to right, with Haddix taking third. Virdon flied out to end the inning. Mejias' squandered run was to be sorely missed.

Logan hit a hard smash toward leftcenter in the home third, but Schofield speared it before it left the infield. Other than that, Braves hitters remained powerless, going down in order inning after inning. Burdette remained nearly as tough, allowing harmless singles in the fourth and fifth, but no runs. By the last of the fifth the crowd was palpably aware of the incipient perfect game; Haddix knew he was working on a no-hitter but thought he might have walked a batter.

Both teams were three-up, three-down in the sixth. In the Pittsburgh seventh Skinner cracked a long drive toward right that appeared to be a tie-breaker, but the south wind held the ball in the playing field for a loud out. In the home seventh a steady drizzle drove many of the spectators under cover, but Haddix ignored it, retiring Johnny O'Brien and Henry Aaron on ground balls and striking out Eddie Mathews.

Both pitchers were untouchable in the eighth. In the ninth, though, Virdon singled with one out, and after Burgess flied out, Nelson rapped his second hit of the night, sending Virdon to third. Needing a hit to give Haddix a chance at winning his no-hitter, Skinner pulled a hard grounder just inside the first-base line. Unfortunately for the Pirates, Adcock was directly in line with the ball and made the play unassisted. Haddix entered the last of the ninth with a perfect game but without a chance to win.

Haddix had been down this road before. On August 5, 1953, as a St. Louis Cardinal rookie, he had entered the ninth against the Phillies with a no-hitter, only to lose it to a leadoff single by Richie Ashburn. (This was just four days after Ashburn spoiled Warren Spahn's otherwise perfect game with an infield hit.) If the thought was on his mind, Haddix gave no evidence—he struck out Andy Pafko, then got Logan on an easy fly to left. With two out and Burdette due to bat, Fred Haney had to decide whether to pinch-hit for his pitcher. He elected not to, and Burdette struck out.

With the strikeout of Burdette, Haddix achieved instant immortality. His was the eighth perfect game in baseball history, the first in the National League since 1880. Perfection not withstanding, he had achieved only a tie.

In the tenth inning each pitcher received a scare from a pinch-hitter. Dick Stuart, batting for Mejias, drove Pafko to the warning track in center, but the wind held the ball up. In the bottom of the inning Del Rice (Haddix' catcher in his near no-hitter with St. Louis) hit for O'Brien and duplicated Stuart's feat, with the same result. The next batter, Mathews, also drove one deep to center, but again it was caught. Haddix was now visibly tired, but he induced Aaron to ground to Schofield for the third out.

The Pirates put a runner on base to start the eleventh when Schofield singled off Burdette's hand, but a failed sacrifice and a doubleplay ended the threat. Haddix breezed through three more outs, becoming the owner of the longest no-hitter on record. Mazeroski singled after two were out in the twelfth but never reached second. Pafko, Logan, and Burdette were easy outs in the Braves' twelfth. The Pirates got another hit in the thirteenth on Schofield's two-out single, his third of the night and his team's twelfth, but Burdette retired Virdon. In the Pittsburgh dugout manager Danny Murtaugh suggested to Haddix that he call it a

Adcock does a double take as Aaron takes a shortcut to the dugout.

Aaron realizes something is wrong.

night, but the little lefthander would not hear of it.

Felix Mantilla, who had replaced O'Brien in the eleventh, led off against Haddix in the thirteenth. Haddix got two quick strikes on him, then thought he had thrown strike three. Plate umpire Vinnie Smith disagreed, and on the next pitch, Mantilla bounced to Hoak at third. The play was so easy that Hoak took his time, then threw in the dirt. Nelson could not scoop the low throw, so the Braves had their first baserunner. The perfect game was gone, but the no-hitter remained intact. On the next pitch, Mathews successfully bunted the winning run to second base. Aaron was purposely passed to set up a force play. The stage was set.

After taking ball one, Joe Adcock jumped on a hanging slider and parked it beyond the fence in rightcenter. The crowd erupted, Adcock's teammates streamed from the dugout, and Mantilla scampered home with the winning run. Aaron, thinking the ball had stayed in the park and seeing Mantilla cross the plate, tagged second, then cut across the diamond and jogged to the dugout.

Adcock, having seen the "home run" signal from the umpire, continued on to third before realizing something was wrong. By the time the Braves had sorted things out and returned Aaron to the field, many fans had left, thinking the Braves had won 3-0.

In fact, head umpire Frank Dascoli ruled Adcock out for passing Aaron; however, he also ruled that because Aaron had left the baseline voluntarily, without trying to evade a tag, his run would count, making the final score 2-0. It was not until the next morning that league president Warren Giles ruled that, because Adcock only received credit for a double, Aaron could only reach third; thus the final score was 1-0.

Regardless of rulings after the fact, the fact remains unmistakable. Harvey Haddix pitched the greatest game in the history of baseball—and Lew Burdette beat him.

Milwaukee Journal Photo

Harvey Haddix was perfect but not good enough.

Time Capsule - May 29, 1959

"That Adcock almost fouled me up."

—Henry Aaron

When something unusual was done by one of the Milwaukee Braves—something weird, something dramatic, something larger than life—more often than not it was done by Joe Adcock. The big first baseman had a flair for originality. The first player to hit a home run into the centerfield seats in the Polo Grounds, the first to hit a ball over the leftfield grandstand in Ebbets Field, the first to be hit twice by a pitcher on the same at-bat, the first to hit four homers and a double in one game—those were all Joe Adcock. The feat he accomplished on May 29, 1959, does not rank with his Herculean exploits, but its surprising nature certainly stamped it with the Adcock trademark.

A Friday night crowd of 20,334 had turned out at County Stadium to watch Carl Willey oppose ex-teammate Gene Conley, now laboring with the last-place Phillies. Conley had won two games while losing one, and one of the victories was a 6-0 whitewash of the Braves in Philadelphia five days earlier. In that appearance Conley had even succeeded in holding Henry Aaron, the major leagues' hottest hitter at .462, hitless in four tries. The Braves were seeking revenge against their former pitcher and looking to increase their lead over second-place San Francisco.

Willey had won his last two decisions, both complete games, but this was not to be his night. Thanks to an error by Johnny Logan, the Phils scored two unearned runs in the first inning. The Braves scored four times in the second to put Willey in the lead, but he could not keep it. A Richie Ashburn single and an Ed Bouchee home run tied the score with one out in the third, sending Willey to an early shower and bringing in Juan Pizarro.

245

The four-run Milwaukee outburst in the second inning nearly finished Conley, but perhaps figuring he had no one better to bring in, Phillies' manager Eddie Sawyer let Conley continue. Wes Covington had begun the onslaught with a single, and Adcock followed with a line-drive home run to tie the game, 2-2. Del Crandall lined a single. Logan sent Ashburn to the fence in center to haul down his smash. Johnny O'Brien, obtained in trade for Conley, also singled. Conley retired Willey but walked Billy Bruton to load the bases. Eddie Mathews capped the rally with a sharp single to drive home Crandall and O'Brien.

After Willey's departure, Pizarro kept the Braves in the game with four and two-thirds innings of strong relief, striking out seven batters while walking none. The only run he gave up came in the seventh when Chico Fernandez doubled and Bouchee singled him in. The Braves got the run back in the home seventh, though. After pinch-hitter Frank Torre flied out for Pizarro, Bruton singled, stole second, and scored on Aaron's base hit, his second of the game, making it 5-5.

In the eighth inning Milwaukee's premier reliever, Don McMahon, took over, shutting out the visitors on no hits in the last two innings and giving his team a chance to win the ballgame with a ninth-inning score against Conley. The fact that the tall hurler was still on the mound for the ninth was somewhat surprising, considering he had been roughed up for twelve hits and five runs. Nevertheless, he retired Mathews to start the ninth and got two quick strikes on Aaron. At that point Conley made what proved to be a fatal mistake—he tried to slip strike three past the man with the quickest wrists in baseball. Aaron lashed the ball deep to rightcenter, high off the fence near the 394-foot sign, and loped into third with a stand-up triple.

With the winning run ninety feet from the plate and only one out, manager Sawyer elected to walk the next two batters, Covington and Adcock, to get to Crandall in a forceout or doubleplay situation. Crandall was known to hit into many twin-killings, and the two hitters ahead of him were long-flyball hitters who could score Aaron from third. While Conley mechanically carried out the tradition of the intentional walk to Covington, Adcock knelt in the on-deck circle, watching intently.

Adcock noted two peculiarities while Covington was being passed to first: Conley's pitches were not very far outside, and second baseman Sparky Anderson (in his only big-league season) was stationed between Conley and second base lest one of catcher Carl Sawatski's tosses elude Conley. When Adcock stepped into the batter's box for his free pass to first, he used the information he had gathered while waiting his turn.

Conley's first pitch to Adcock was a waist-high, half-speed toss a foot beyond the outside edge of the plate. Being careful not to step outside the batter's box, Adcock extended his arms and bat fully and weakly made contact. The ball dribbled past Conley to the left of the mound. The flat-footed Phillies were entirely unprepared to field the ball. Anderson finally grasped the situation and scrambled to make the pickup and throw home. By the time he did, though, Aaron had sprinted home with the winning run. Adcock's teammates burst en masse from the first-base dugout, laughing and grinning, while the fans celebrated.

The strongman from Coushatta, Louisiana, is remembered for his powerful drives, but on this night his 80-foot roller, not even scored as a base hit, drove in the run that sent the Braves three games ahead of the Giants.

Milwaukee Journal Photo .

Bobby Avila receives congratulations for game-winning home run,
July 22, 1959.

1959 Feat of Clay

"We've got a problem at second base."

—Owner Lou Perini

Whoever formulated the geometric axiom that "The whole is equal to the sum of its parts" never observed the collection of second basemen the Milwaukee Braves employed in 1959. In all there were eight of them, each possessing athletic ability beyond the level of the ordinary citizen. One was a former batting champion; another had missed that accomplishment by just two points. A couple were good fielders, one had been a highly-sought bonus player, several were talented at more than one position. Added together in 1959, they were almost worthless. They made former Braves' second-sacker Danny O'Connell look like Hall of Famer Charlie Gehringer.

The Braves had solved this problem in June, 1957, by acquiring Red Schoendienst from the Giants. For half a year Schoendienst was great; for the next year he was all right. On November 18, 1958, though, he was diagnosed as having tuberculosis—and immediately the problem was back. If at that time General Manager John Quinn, soon to depart to join the Philadelphia Phillies, could have traded, say, Frank Torre and Wes Covington for a second baseman, say Tony Taylor of the Cubs, the Braves would have won a third straight pennant. Instead the Braves substituted numbers for quality and failed utterly.

With Schoendienst unavailable the logical replacement was Felix Mantilla, who had substituted at second before. Mantilla started on opening day, but within a week it was obvious his fielding was barely adequate and his hitting was less than that. Mantilla was benched, and Chuck Cottier was inserted in the slot.

Cottier was a 23-year-old rookie, an excellent fielder who had

248

hit moderately well at Atlanta in the Sally League. On April 21 he got his chance in the big leagues, fielded like a veteran, and rapped two hits in three tries. He looked like the answer, but in 21 subsequent times at bat he managed one hit. Exit Collier, enter Joe Morgan.

Morgan was also a rookie, up from Atlanta by way of Wichita. Unfortunately he was a shortstop, not a second baseman. The Braves tried to switch him to the other side of the bag, but the experiment failed. On April 25 in Cincinnati Morgan went three-for-five and drove in a run, but he also made two errors leading to two runs. That made a net loss of one, and the one was Morgan.

Next the Braves tried Johnny O'Brien, the former Pittsburgh Pirate twin sibling obtained in the Gene Conley deal. O'Brien fielded acceptably most of the time, although his fielding foibles did contribute heavily to losses on May 28 and July 2; however, he hit less than .200, and by July 21 he was permanently out of the majors.

O'Brien's ineptness with the bat created an opportunity for Casey Wise, a former Chicago Cub who had starred in the Pacific Coast League in 1956 but who reached his peak in the majors with the Braves in 1958, hitting .197. Unable to reach even that modest level again, Wise spent most of the season in the minors. In his brief tryout he did manage to cost them a game, though, by failing to field a grounder in the tenth inning on June 18, allowing the Giants two runs in a 4-3 San Francisco win. Then on July 4, as a pinch-runner, his foul-up on the basepath killed a rally in a 2-1 loss; the next day Wise was on his way to Louisville.

Second baseman number six was Mel Roach, the former bonus baby who had performed so well in 1958 until tearing up his knee on August 3. Roach finally returned to starting action on June 30, 1959, amid high hopes that he would bring sanity to the right side of the infield. Still hobbled, Roach played sparingly, hitting an anemic .097. Clearly no one the Braves had could fill the position.

On July 21 General Manager Birdie Tebbetts finally was able to purchase Bobby Avila from the Boston Red Sox. In the early 1950's Avila had been the best second baseman in the American League—better than adequate in the field, a solid .300 hitter at the plate, hitting .341 in 1954 to lead Cleveland to the pennant. In his Milwaukee debut on July 22, Avila hit a two-run, ninth-inning homer to give Spahn a 5-4 victory over the Redlegs. The next day, though, Avila's error allowed Puddin' Head Jones to hit a game-winning grand slam. Nevertheless Avila was the Braves' starting second baseman for most of the final third of the season, hitting .233.

The Braves' final entrant in the second base derby was the man whose absence had initiated the scramble—Red Schoendienst. The old redhead began working out with the team in July and finally made a few token appearances in September, including one in the season finale in Los Angeles. The fact that he played in that game speaks volumes about the situation at second.

In the first playoff game, in Milwaukee, Avila played the whole game at second base. In the first inning his inability to field a bouncing ball set up the Dodgers' first run; in the third inning a similar failure by Avila set up the Dodgers' second run. Both were scored as infield hits, but both were playable. The two runs led to a 3-2 Los Angeles victory.

Understandably chagrined by Avila's fielding, Haney benched him for the second playoff game in favor of Mantilla. When Johnny Logan got hurt in the seventh inning, Mantilla had to move to shortstop, and Haney needed a second baseman. In a crucial, must-win situation, Haney chose Schoendienst, 0 for 2 for the season, over Avila. Schoendienst batted once, unsuccessfully, then yielded for a pinch-hitter in the ninth. Needing another second baseman in the last of the ninth, Haney selected Chuck Cottier, recently returned from Louisville. Finally, after using a pinch-hitter for Cottier in the eleventh, Haney required one more second baseman, and Avila was the last one. His services were required for only two-thirds of an inning—transplanted second baseman Mantilla threw the ball away, a run scored, and the season was over.

Time Capsule - September 15, 1959

"Everybody knew they had a bad setup here but they all agreed to play. Now they've got to take the consequences."

—Umpire Frank Dascoli

Before every ballgame the umpires and the rival managers or captains meet at home plate, going over the ground rules and presenting the lineups. This perfunctory exercise predates even the playing of "The Star-Spangled Banner" before a game, or the seventh-inning stretch. It is one of baseball's peculiarities, an enduring and endearing reminder of an age in America when the water was clean and sex was dirty. This home plate meeting consists of little more than an exchange of pleasantries—how often do the ground rules have any bearing on the outcome of a ballgame? On September 15, 1959, they did.

With only eleven games left in the season, the Braves were in a dogfight with the Giants and Dodgers. San Francisco held the lead, a game ahead of Milwaukee and two ahead of Los Angeles. Fred Haney's defending league champs were visiting the Los Angeles Coliseum for the final time of the regular season, having beaten the Bums the night before, 4-1, behind Bob Buhl, with a great save by Don McMahon. The fireballing relief ace had entered the game in the ninth inning with the bases loaded and nobody out and had snuffed out the rally. In today's series finale Joey Jay, with a 5-10 record, was on the mound opposing Dodger Roger Craig.

The Braves climbed on Craig in the top of the first. Eddie Mathews singled, and after two outs Joe Adcock hit a mile-high pop fly to short leftfield, which in the Coliseum was covered with seats. The ball cleared the notorious screen and dropped almost straight down six feet beyond it, likely the shortest Adcock home run ever, barely half the length of some of his fabled drives.

251

Jay held the home club scoreless through the first three innings, but in the fourth they pummeled him with a barrage of base hits and five runs before Juan Pizarro came to the rescue. In the top of the fifth Johnny Podres replaced L.A. pitcher Craig, for whom Sandy Amoros had pinch-hit in the fourth after the big righthander had allowed seven hits, though just two runs, in the first four innings. The first batter to face Podres was Adcock.

With one home run to his credit already, Adcock greeted Podres with what looked like homer number two, a high drive toward the right extremity of the leftfield screen. The ball struck the steel tower supporting the screen and disappeared. Umpire Vinnie Smith made a circular motion with his arm, and Adcock trotted around the bases. After a brief conference, however, the umpires ordered Adcock back to second base on a ground rule double.

Haney and his associates argued vociferously that it was a home run—the ball had cleared the fence and did not return to the playing field. The umpires, though, decided that the ball was lodged in a gap between the screen and a reinforcing mesh attached to it. The two parts should have been together, but they had separated far enough to allow the ball to perch there. Local ground rules provided that a ball wedged in the screen would constitute a ground rule double, and so it was ruled. Subsequently a fan managed to shake the screen enough to dislodge the ball—it fell into the stands, not back onto the playing field—but that fact failed to sway the arbiters in blue. Haney immediately announced that his team was playing the game under protest.

The protest, of course, was doomed from the start. None had been upheld since the Redlegs' appeal of a decision was successful in Milwaukee on September 22, 1954, resulting in the Braves playing two different teams on the same day. In addition, the call involved a judgment by the umpires, not subject to appeal—only a rule interpretation may be protested. Nonetheless Haney protested on the basis that a home run in baseball is defined as a fair ball that leaves the playing field. Because the ball cleared the screen and did not return to the field, the Braves reasoned that Adcock was entitled to a home run. Instead he was returned to second base and did not score.

The Braves did get a run back in the top of the sixth to make the score 5-3. Ray Boone singled for Pizarro, Bruton advanced him with a hit, and Aaron scored Boone with a single. The Dodgers matched that tally in their half of the inning when rookie Maury Wills tripled and scored on Podres' sacrifice fly to Aaron. In the eighth Milwaukee moved close after Podres walked the bases loaded. Larry Sherry replaced him, then gave up a two-run double to Aaron. Adcock was purposely passed to fill the bases with one out, but Mickey Vernon, hitting for Andy Pafko, struck out, and Johnny Logan flied out to strand three runners.

Don McMahon stopped Los Angeles in the eighth. In the Braves' ninth Del Crandall hit a long drive that lacked inches of being a home run; he wound up on second base. Felix Mantilla singled him home to tie the game at six and send Sherry to the showers, replaced by Fred Kipp, who retired the side.

After McMahon again blanked Alston's crew, Aaron singled in the tenth, moved to third on Adcock's single, and scored the lead run on Logan's flyball. The Braves loaded the bases again, but Chuck Churn, the fifth L.A. pitcher, got Johnny DeMerit, the former Port Washington bonus player, to pop out in his first at-bat of the season. McMahon now had a 7-6 lead. The three men left on base, however, raised the Braves' total for the game to seventeen, one short of the league record.

In the bottom of the tenth the Dodgers made Milwaukee pay dearly for challenging that record. McMahon retired leadoff batter John Roseboro, but Wills slapped his fifth straight base hit to start trouble. Three years in the future Wills would set a new standard for base-stealing, but he had entered this game with a puny .238 batting average. The Dodger pitcher, Churn, was due up next, but Chuck Essegian (destined to be a hero in the upcoming World Series with two pinch homers) batted for him and singled Wills around to third with the tying run. Joe Pignatano went in to run for Essegian. Junior Gilliam drove Wills across with a sacrifice fly to make the score 7-7 with two out. Charlie Neal singled to move Pignatano into position for the winning score.

McMahon was now visibly tired. His velocity was down and his pitches were up. He obviously had lost his stuff when he walked Moon to load the bases. Haney stayed with him, though, judging that an arm-weary McMahon was still superior to a well-rested Bob Giggie or Bob Trowbridge. Haney's judgment could not have been worse—McMahon threw three balls in a row to Ron Fairly, finally put one over the plate, but then missed with a fastball for ball four, forcing Pignatano across with the deciding run.

Predictably the Braves' protest of the game was disallowed. The defeat shoved Milwaukee into a second-place tie with the Dodgers, two games behind the Giants with ten games to play. In a 154-game season that ended in a tie, Adcock's "stolen" home run stands as a crucial event.

Hard-sliding Andy Pafko was a Milwaukee favorite.

1959 Swan Song

"Andy Pafko got more than a gallon of milk from a patient Brown Swiss cow in two minutes to win a milking contest on the Capitol Square."

—News Item, June 8, 1956

The Braves had more talented ballplayers than Andy Pafko, but they may not have had any more popular. In 1953 he received a Cadillac for being voted "The Best of the Braves" by the adoring fans. The pride of Boyceville, Wisconsin, joined the Milwaukee team for their initial season and stayed seven years, the first two as a starting outfielder, the last five as a substitute. He batted .297 and .286 as a regular and contributed 31 home runs in those two years, but what most fans remember about Pafko is the belly-flop catches he made in the outfield. His style of fielding was both distinctive and effective.

"Handy Andy" played in two World Series for the Braves and nearly added a third. His final game as a Brave was also Fred Haney's final day: September 29, 1959, the day the Dodgers beat Milwaukee in the National League playoff in Los Angeles [see Time Capsule]. Pafko did not start the ballgame, but he flied out for Lee Maye in the fifth inning against reliever Johnny Podres. Pafko then played leftfield in the fifth and sixth innings before giving way to 43-year-old pinch-hitter Enos Slaughter in the top of the seventh. He left the game with the Braves leading 4-2, but a three-run Dodger rally in the ninth kept Pafko out of the World Series in his farewell season.

255

1960

"I don't think it will take much help for the Braves to win the number of games necessary for the pennant next season."

—Charlie Dressen, October 24, 1959

The Braves' near-miss in 1959 had signified a decline in several areas. Their failure to win the pennant after two consecutive league championships was obvious—a more subtle decline was indicated by their won-lost percentage of .551, not only a big drop from their 1957 peak of .617 but actually their lowest since arriving in Milwaukee. Attendance again diminished substantially, falling nearly a quarter-million from the previous year. Perhaps most meaningful of all, though, on October 4, 1959, five days after losing the playoff to the Dodgers, manager Fred Haney resigned.

During Haney's tenure as Braves field boss, his team won more games than any other team in the major leagues, including Stengel's Yankees. Even so, he was often second-guessed and criticized for being too conservative, and some of his players did not appreciate him. Johnny Logan, for example, blasted him in the press shortly after his resignation. "We should have won by ten games without any question," the scrappy shortstop said. "When they announced Haney was out you can bet very few of the players were sorry."

Popular or not, under pressure or not, Haney made the obligatory statement about quitting to spend more time with his family, then stepped down. He was replaced on October 23, 1959, by former Dodger manager Chuck Dressen, more recently the manager of the Washington Senators and most recently a coach with the Dodgers. Dressen, like Haney a man of small stature but much cockier than his predecessor, immediately began predicting

256

a great future for his new team.

A day or two later Dressen, after some reflection, opined that perhaps the Braves did need some help at second base, and another relief pitcher would be useful too. He added, though, that he did not believe the team was too old or too slow, as some had charged. Dressen indicated that he would have the ballclub run more than they had under Haney, to avoid doubleplays and steal bases.

Partially because the management saw no urgent need, and partially because no team wanted to trade with Milwaukee, the Braves reached opening day, 1960, with essentially the same team that finished 1959—for that matter, the same basic team they had put on the field since 1953. A week before Dressen signed on, the Braves had traded benchwarmer Casey Wise plus minor leaguers Mike Roarke and Don Kaiser to the Detroit Tigers for catcher Charlie Lau and minor league pitcher Don Lee. In doing so, they swapped a little-used infielder and two men who had never played for them in exchange for a catcher who would play in fewer than fifty games in two years and a pitcher who would never pitch for them. That was the extent of the off-season trading.

During the 1960 season the Braves made several changes in their roster, none of them earth-shaking. In May they called up Ron Piche, a French Canadian relief pitcher, from Louisville. Piche appeared in relief 37 times and on the whole pitched moderately well. Others with less impact included outfielder Al Spangler; versatile Al Dark, obtained from the Phillies on June 22 for Joe Morgan plus cash; and minor league hurlers Don Nottebart and George Brunet.

On the debit side, Bob Rush was sold to the White Sox on June 11; seldom-used Ray Boone was sent to the Red Sox; and little-known pitcher Ken MacKenzie and former semi-regular first baseman Frank Torre were released at the end of June. A Braves fan who had been out of the country for, say, six years could have returned and recognized most of the Milwaukee ballplayers on the field.

The biggest deal of the year for the Braves was one that was never made. During the preseason, and especially during the first two months of the season, General Manager John McHale ran up an enormous phone bill trying to pry loose a player to help the ballclub. A quality second baseman, someone like Tony Taylor of the Cubs (traded to the Phillies on May 13), or a power-hitting leftfielder, someone like Wally Post of the Phillies (traded to the Redlegs on June 15) would have helped immeasurably. Even a

257

higher priority was a relief pitcher, someone like the Cubs' Don Elston, whom McHale spent months trying to obtain. Just before the June 15 trading deadline the Braves and Phillies nearly consummated a deal that would have brought Milwaukee three key players: starting pitcher Jim Owens, relief pitcher Dick Farrell, and outfielder Post. In exchange the Braves would have sent the Phillies four players, including Joey Jay and Mel Roach. At the last minute the Phillies balked, and the trade was scrapped.

For a while at the beginning of the season, Dressen's fears about the second base position appeared unfounded. Red Schoendienst, age 37 but recovered from his bout with tuberculosis, hit .288 in spring training and fielded like the old pro he was. For the first two weeks of the season he batted above .400, made the plays at second, and looked ready to lead his team to the pennant, just as he had done when he was three years younger. Gradually, though, his hitting fell off. By the end of April he was batting .333; a little more than a month into the season he had slipped below .300; at the end of May he was hitting .250; by mid-June his average had sunk to .225. On June 25 in Milwaukee he hit his only home run of the year, his last as a Brave, and by July he was a full-time benchwarmer. Chuck Cottier tried replacing him again, with the same result as before—he fielded spectacularly, and with the bat, failed spectacularly, going hitless in 26 at-bats in late July but finishing strong to bat .227.

The other glaring weakness in the lineup, leftfield, remained weak. Wes Covington reported to the team grossly out of shape, much to the consternation of Dressen, and did not enter the lineup until May 4. When he did play he was a disappointment, hitting .249 with just ten home runs. Dressen tried numerous other outfielders in his place—local rookie Mike Krsnich, Lee Maye, Mel Roach, Eddie Haas, Felix Mantilla, Al Spangler, Al Dark, Len Gabrielson—all in vain. Leftfield troubled the Braves throughout the year.

When Dressen was hired to manage the Braves, he made it clear he would have his players steal more bases and hit-and-run more. He did. In 1960 they stole 69 bases, the most by a Braves team since the Boston version in 1951. Under Charlie Grimm the Braves had been among the leading teams in stolen bases, but that fact is misleading—Billy Bruton stole more bases than all of his teammates combined. During Haney's administration, the Braves stole fewer bases than any other team in the National League (in fact, the only team in either league that stole less often was the Washington Senators, managed for part of that time by

Wes Covington grimaces, not an infrequent experience for the much-injured slugger.

Charlie Dressen). Under Dressen's guidance, though, Bruton stole 22, his highest total since 1955; Aaron stole sixteen, his largest total since he left Eau Claire in the Northern League; and even Eddie Mathews stole seven, his second-highest figure as a professional.

Despite the change in philosophy, the Braves continued to be essentially a power team, leading the league in home runs by a wide margin, thirty more than their nearest competitor. Aaron and Mathews led the team with 40 and 39 homers respectively and ranked one-two in the league in RBI's with 126 and 124. Aaron also led in total bases with 334, while Bruton amd Mathews were the league's top two in runs scored with 112 and 108 respectively. Additional power was supplied by Joe Adcock with 25 homers, Del Crandall with 19, Bruton with 12, and Covington with 10. As a team Milwaukee ranked first in slugging percentage and second behind Pittsburgh in batting average and runs scored.

The Braves pitching staff again consisted of Spahn, Burdette, Buhl, and some other guys. Spahn won his customary 21 games to tie for the league lead. Burdette was not far behind with 19, and Buhl added 16 victories. No other pitcher, though, won more than nine. The team earned run average soared to 3.76, higher than four other teams, and after seven straight years of having at least two pitchers in the top five in earned run average, the Braves placed none in the top seven. Buhl led the team with 3.09, but Burdette's was 3.36, Spahn's was 3.50, and ace reliever Don McMahon's ERA was a horrendous 5.94, more suited to slow-pitch softball.

Dressen's pitching corps sorely lacked a fourth starter. Carl Willey, the Sporting News Rookie of the Year in 1958, had his second bad year in a row, winning six and losing seven, with a 4.35 ERA and just two complete games. Joey Jay again showed hints of future stardom but lacked consistency and lost eight games along with his nine wins. Juan Pizarro won six games for the third year in a row and again failed to fulfill his great promise, losing seven with a fat 4.55 earned run average. The departure of Gene Conley and Bob Rush in consecutive years had left the pitching machine short one gear, and the bullpen's weakness had made the shortage a fatal one.

Despite all the problems, the Braves might still have been able to win the pennant but for their ineptness on the road. For the second year in a row, and the second time in their Milwaukee existence, they lost more games on the road than they won. In County Stadium Dressen's club was excellent, winning 51 games, the most in the brief history of their franchise. In San Francisco's new Candlestick Park, however, the Braves were blown away seven times in eleven games. In two of the league's older parks, Pittsburgh's Forbes Field and St. Louis' Busch Stadium, the Braves were even worse, losing eight of eleven in each.

Another factor in the non-pennant was the Braves' terrible start, their second-worst in eight Milwaukee seasons. At the end of May, 1960, Dressen's team had a 16-16 record, noteworthy for two reasons: the only other time they had entered June without a winning record had been in 1955, when they were 21-22; and they had played just 32 games in more than a month and a half. As it had in 1956, the weather devastated the Braves' spring, causing twelve postponements in one month's time, seven in two weeks, and not just in Milwaukee but nearly coast to coast. They were rained out in San Francisco and Pittsburgh, St. Louis and Cincinnati; they were rained and/or frozen out in Chicago four days in a row; and they were rained out and even fogged out at

260

County Stadium. Every postponement occurred before the end of May.

Actually at the beginning of the season all the omens were positive. The Braves won on opening day at County Stadium in good weather before a crowd just a couple busloads under 40,000. Spahn pitched well and hit a home run, McMahon won in relief, Adcock hit the game-winning two-run homer in the eighth, and Burdette saved the victory for McMahon in the ninth.

Two days later Milwaukee lost the road opener in Philadelphia after blowing a 3-0 lead, but even in defeat they looked intimidating. Aaron slammed a home run and Adcock belted his second, a gargantuan blast that traveled more than 500 feet and cleared the scoreboard in Connie Mack Stadium, the first drive ever by a righthand batter to do so. In the next game in Philadelphia, Burdette breezed to a complete game victory backed by eighteen hits, including four by Schoendienst, three by rookie outfielder Al Spangler, and another home run by Aaron. Bob Buhl closed out the Phillie series with a complete game, supported by Mathews' 300th career home run and a three-run double by substitute first baseman Ray Boone. Milwaukee's favorite ballclub was on its way.

Very quickly, though, fans became aware that all was not well with the Braves. Returning home on April 20, they carried a 4-2 lead into the ninth inning and ended up losing 10-5. It was an occurrence that seemed to become habitual in May. During that month the Milwaukee team lost eleven games to the weather and an equal number to opposing ballclubs—and seven of those defeats were games in which the Braves led or were tied in the late innings but lost for lack of relief pitching. After three years of bullpen work, Don McMahon had apparently switched roles with the batting practice pitcher. Ron Piche was summoned from the minors but fared no better. Three times in four games between May 25 and May 29 the Braves lost on ninth-inning home runs, and two days later they closed out May by losing to the Phillies on a six-run eighth inning, dropping them to fourth place, six and one-half games out of first.

After a terrible May, June brought a marked improvement. The Braves began the month with four straight victories by their starting pitchers: a ten-hitter by Buhl, a poor performance by Spahn saved by strong hitting from his teammates, a good eight-inning job by Willey, and a complete game by Burdette marred only by one unearned run. For nearly the next two weeks the team alternated between losing and winning. Then beginning on June 16 they won nine of ten games and climbed to second

261

place, two and one-half games behind the Pittsburgh Pirates.

As quickly as they got well, though, the Braves reverted to their malaise. Beginning on June 30 their pitching failed and they lost four straight, allowing 33 runs in four games. Rookies Don Nottebart and George Brunet were worked over in two of the games, but aces Burdette and Spahn were victimized in the other two. On July 10, as both leagues adjourned for the three-day, two-game All-Star break, Dressen's ballclub held second place but trailed Pittsburgh by a healthy five-game margin.

The crevasse separating the Braves from the league lead contrasted starkly with the league players' assessment of the ballclub's talent—they elected four Milwaukeeans to the eight-man starting National League All-Star lineup. First baseman Joe Adcock, third baseman Eddie Mathews, catcher Del Crandall, and rightfielder Henry Aaron all were deemed best at their positions by their peers. In addition, pitcher Bob Buhl was selected to the NL pitching staff by manager Walt Alston. The

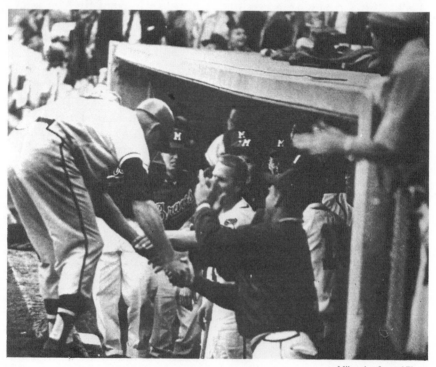

Milwaukee Journal Photo

Joe Adcock receives congratulations for another home run.

Nationals won both classics, 5-3 in Kansas City and 6-0 in New York, helped by contributions from all the Braves except Aaron, who went hitless.

After the intermission the Braves fought back with a vengeance, winning six in a row to pull within a half-game of the Pirates. Two losses put them back two steps, but a 3-0 shutout of the Cubs by Juan Pizarro, including a save by Piche, nudged them back within a game and a half, setting the stage for a Sunday doubleheader at Wrigley Field on July 24.

On that date, after struggling through more than three months, a total of 88 games, Dressen's Braves finally achieved first place. While the Pirates were being bounced by the Giants in San Francisco, the Braves were sweeping a pair from the last-place Cubs. In the opener Spahn yielded a couple of two-run homers but persevered for a 7-5 complete game victory, helped mightily by Jerry Kindall's three-run error. In the nightcap Buhl fired a four-hit shutout, just good enough to win, 1-0. The run that put Milwaukee atop the standings was produced in the ninth inning by three of the club's lesser lights. Mel Roach, who played only against lefties, doubled off the vines in leftcenter. Al Spangler went in to run for him and promptly stole third base. Al Dark, a medium-sized man whose weight exceeded Chuck Cottier's batting average, pinch-hit for the punchless second sacker and singled home Spangler with the contest's only score—first place at last!

The euphoria was, alas, short-lived. The following day, while the Braves were traveling to San Francisco, the Pirates won to regain first place by a half-game. It was a lead they would not relinquish. The Braves beat the Giants in their series opener, but after that they lost eleven of fifteen games, plummeting to fourth place, seven games out of first, on August 11. They would not challenge Pittsburgh again, getting no closer than five and one-half games before the Pirates clinched the pennant in Milwaukee on September 25.

The disastrous month of August that squelched Milwaukee's pennant hopes was caused by a combination of failures: sloppy fielding, inadequate relief pitching, and the inability of Braves batters to come through in the clutch. Some of the finest clutch hitting the Braves received in the last part of the season, in fact, came from the starting pitchers. On July 30 in Los Angeles, Burdette cracked a home run in the eleventh inning to win the game, 8-7. On August 26 in San Francisco, the deciding run in a 3-2 victory came on a Spahn home run. Most surprisingly, on September 10 against the Dodgers at County Stadium, Carl

Willey slammed the only homer he would ever hit as a Brave and knocked in the winning run.

Of the many causes of the August swoon, the performance by the starting pitchers was probably the least. Although the team only won sixteen games and lost fifteen, the starters actually pitched commendably in nineteen games. Included in that number were five complete-game shutouts: Buhl's second 1-0 win in four weeks; Spahn's 50th career whitewash, a 10-0 romp over St. Louis; and three consecutive scoreless masterpieces by the Duke of Fidget, Lew Burdette, including the veteran righthander's first no-hitter [see Time Capsule] and his 25th career shutout.

For the first time in five years, September was nothing more than a showcase for individual performances, and a sparsely attended one at that. Braves hitters assaulted enemy hurlers for nine runs or more eight different times in September, but witnesses were few. On September 8 at County Stadium Spahn pitched a complete game against the Giants for his eighteenth victory; he clouted his third home run of the year; Aaron smashed a home run; Mathews blasted a pair of homers and drove in five; the management offered a Cranberry Night promotion, climaxed by fireworks. Even so, only 12,950 fans attended, a thousand below the number of presold tickets. On September 20, mercifully, a cozy gathering of an even 10,000 watched the Cincinnati Redlegs bludgeon Dressen's team, 9-0, on his 62nd birthday. Sadly, though, just 6117 diehards showed up on Friday night, September 16, to witness Warren Spahn's finest performance in sixteen incredible years—a no-hitter to match that of his roommate Burdette [see Time Capsule].

After his no-hit game Spahn also won his next start, allowing no walks and only one run in earning his 21st win of the season. His last two starts of the year, though, both against Pittsburgh, were defeats. The contrast in Spahn's record versus Pittsburgh probably shows as well as any single comparison the difference between 1959 and 1960. During the prior season Spahn started six times against the Pirates, winning five without a loss, including two shutouts. In the first five starts he allowed a total of three earned runs in 42 and two-thirds innings. In 1960 the situation was entirely opposite. In six starts plus two relief appearances, he hurled no complete games, lost five games while winning only one (and that in relief), and four times failed to finish the fourth inning. Spahn's season record against the rest of the National League was 20-5, but 1960 was the Year of the Pirate.

The perennial National League doormats, who had been 7-15 against Milwaukee the year before, beat the Braves thirteen

264

times, lost only nine, and used the improvement to hoist themselves to the pennant. To cap their season, they beat the heavily-favored Yankees four games to three, winning the Series on Bill Mazeroski's celebrated bottom-of-the-ninth home run. For the Braves, it was "Look out below!"

Heading for N.Y. to meet the Yanks in the Series—Schoendienst, Mathews, et al. By 1960 post-season play was just a memory.

1960 Feat of Clay

"He's the greatest manager in baseball, but I don't think a lot of the Braves agree with me."

—Don Zimmer

There was a lot to dislike about Charlie Dressen. He was a small man, at most five-foot six-inches, who compensated with an overbearing, loquacious manner. He seemed to believe that any sentence he spoke was incomplete unless it contained the pronoun *I*. He was an unschooled man who knew everything and told you so. He was cocky, arrogant, abrasive, and controversial—but even his critics conceded that he knew baseball.

Whatever baseball savvy Dressen possessed, his hiring by the Braves on October 23, 1959, to replace Fred Haney, may have been the Braves' biggest mistake of 1960. They compounded the error by breaking team policy (established in 1956 when Haney replaced Charlie Grimm) and signing him to a two-year contract. After winning National League pennants managing the Brooklyn Dodgers in 1952 and 1953, Dressen had demanded a multi-year pact; instead owner Walter O'Malley signed Walt Alston to the first of a long series of one-year contracts, and Dressen went to the minors to manage. Lou Perini failed to learn from O'Malley's example.

As a ballplayer Dressen had been an intense competitor with mediocre skills, compiling a .272 lifetime batting average while playing third base, mostly with the Cincinnati Reds, from 1925 to 1933. Before that he had briefly played quarterback for the Decatur Staleys, forerunner of George Halas' Chicago Bears. A year after retiring as a third baseman, he began managing the Reds, finishing in the second division four straight years, two of them in last place. After laboring in the minors for fourteen years he resurfaced with the Dodgers in 1951. Only Bobby Thomson's famous "shot heard 'round the world" prevented Dressen's Dodgers from winning three straight pennants. He later returned to the majors, so to speak, as skipper of the Washington Senators in 1955, 1956, and a month of 1957, achieving his greatest success there in 1956 when the team finished seventh.

To say that the Braves did not take to Dressen would be charitable. They had a deserved reputation as a free-spirited, fun-loving, undisciplined ballclub; Dressen had achieved notoriety as a strict disciplinarian. "They brought me here to make rules," he said, "and I'm going to make them." He took pride in running a taut ship—he enforced a rigid curfew with frequent room checks. To a ballclub of veterans accustomed to Grimm and Haney, Dressen was Simon Legree.

Dressen's tactics—a heavy reliance on the bunt, the stolen base, the hit-and-run—were not universally popular but seemed effective until late July, 1960. His running game ran Milwaukee into first place on July 24, if only for a day, but after that his team's success and his personal popularity (no, never that—tolerability, perhaps) gradually declined together. Dressen became the target for boos as no one at County Stadium had been before.

Through all the criticism and second-guessing, and in spite of his basically honest and forthright manner, Dressen never seemed to accept the fact that any negative aspect of the team's performance was his fault. His excuses were nothing if not imaginative. After a tough ten-inning loss to Pittsburgh on July 5, a game in which the Braves blew a 2-0 lead in the ninth, Dressen had a unique explanation: "We lost the game because Spangler's grandfather died." His line of reasoning was this: Spangler was absent because he was attending a funeral, so Mantilla had to play outfield, so Mantilla was not available to pinch-run in the ninth, so Haas failed to score from second to win the game. What this train of logic overlooks is: Dressen left Carl Willey in too long on the mound; Dressen put Al Dark at an unfamiliar position, second base, allowing an important base hit; Dressen failed to use an available substitute (e.g., Burdette) to run for Haas. Dressen's explanation was more interesting, though, and he was able to come up with those day after day.

By the time Perini caught on to the scope of his team's problem, all but four weeks of a second season under Dressen had transpired. Birdie Tebbetts replaced Dressen as manager after the ballgame on Saturday, September 2, 1961.

1960 Nemesis - Glen Hobbie

"Wild as I am, I have to get the ball over the plate."

—Glen Hobbie

The Chicago Cubs had been looking up at the first division so long their necks were stiff. They had not won more games than they lost since 1946. The guys from the City of the Big Shoulders had never beaten their Milwaukee neighbors in the season series. In 1958 and 1959 they came close, though, thanks in large part to Glen Hobbie.

He was a big, blond righthander with a mean fastball and a vague notion of where that fastball was going. In his first two years in the league, his two best years, his only two winning years, he had averaged one walk per two innings. Against everyone in the league except the Braves in 1958 and '59, he won nineteen games and lost eighteen; against Milwaukee, the team with the best record in the majors, he won seven and lost one.

In 1960 Charlie Dressen's Braves exacted some revenge from their young tormentor, but it was not gained easily. On May 22 Juan Pizarro pitched brilliantly for the Braves, but it still took two fielding misplays by the Cubs and one careless pitch by Hobbie, resulting in a two-run home run by Joe Adcock, to give Milwaukee a victory. The next time out, Hobbie evened the score.

At County Stadium on the night of Tuesday, June 14, Hobbie flirted with a no-hitter. As usual he struggled to find the plate, walking three batters and hitting Del Crandall on the elbow, but he remained unhittable until Crandall struck back in the eighth, blasting Hobbie's first pitch over 400 feet for a home run. Afraid to take chances on walking any more batters, Hobbie grooved a fastball to Eddie Mathews with one out in the ninth. The Braves'

268

slugger ripped it into the rightfield bleachers to make the score 3-2, Cubs. Hobbie then got Henry Aaron on a called strike three and Joe Adcock on a fly to deep center to end the ballgame.

Hobbie faced the Braves four more times during that season, twice pitching strong complete games and twice getting knocked out in the fifth inning. All four games, though, were won by Milwaukee. Warren Spahn bested Hobbie three straight times, backed by solid hitting by the Braves. The final time, on September 15 at County Stadium, Lew Burdette fired a two-hitter and walked nobody to win 3-1. Thanks to his five defeats by the Braves, Hobbie led all National League hurlers with twenty losses for the 1960 season.

Charlie Dressen celebrates with Warren Spahn, Don McMahon, Lew Burdette, and Joe Adcock.

269

Time Capsule - August 15, 1960

"It happened so fast I don't know who swung first."

—Eddie Mathews

Most baseball fights have all the physical violence of a ballet. Usually somebody pushes somebody, five people intervene, fifty guys mill around for a few minutes, and the ballgame continues. Real violence is normally left to athletes in hockey and spectators in soccer. Notable exceptions stand out, though. On August 4, 1960, Reds' second baseman Alfred Manuel Pesano, the former Yankee who played (and fought) under the name of Billy Martin, broke the cheekbone of Cubs' pitcher Jim Brewer in a one-punch preliminary bout at Wrigley Field. Eleven days later in Cincinnati, Martin's teammate Frank Robinson challenged the Braves' Eddie Mathews, victor over Don Drysdale three years earlier, for the heavyweight championship of the National League. Robinson suffered a first-round TKO and one of the worst beatings in the history of the sport yet, bloody and battered, persevered to enjoy the night's last laugh.

The Braves entered the twinight doubleheader with the Redlegs in third place, six and one-half games behind the league-leading Pirates and a half-game behind the St. Louis Cardinals. Dressen's club had won three straight at home against the Giants before arriving in Cincinnati to take on Fred Hutchinson's sixth-place crew. The mound chores in the opener fell to Juan Pizarro, opposed by 20-year-old Cincinnati rookie Jim Maloney, seeking his first major league victory since being called up from Nashville.

Cincinnati had taken a 1-0 lead in the first when Martin doubled, advanced on a Vada Pinson flyout, and scored on a sacrifice fly by Robinson. The Braves tied the score in the second

270

on singles by Mel Roach and Joe Adcock and a forceout by Johnny Logan. The Redlegs then jumped on Pizarro for three runs in the third when the erratic lefthander walked three batters in a row and Wally Post cleared the bags with a double. Milwaukee got a run back in the fifth on a walk and two singles, with Mathews driving in the run. Wes Covington homered with the bases empty in the sixth, and Post matched it with a solo shot in the bottom of the inning, so the Reds led 5-3.

After the seventh-inning stretch, Robinson sliced a short fly down the rightfield line out of reach of first baseman Adcock and second baseman Roach. Roach tumbled into the box seats trying to make the catch, bruising his wrist and knee and making himself unavailable for the second game. Robinson rounded first and sprinted toward second. With the ball still loose, Robinson decided to try for a triple. Adcock retrieved the ball, fired to Mathews at third, and Robinson was a dead duck. As was his custom, Robinson slid hard into third, his hand striking Mathews' head as the third baseman applied a hard tag to the runner's nose.

Immediately two things happened—the two combatants exchanged angry words spiced with epithets, and blood began to flow from Robinson's nose. Mathews apparently spoke first, accusing Robinson of deliberately holding his arm out to strike him as he slid by. Robinson quickly responded with a heated complaint about the location and ferocity of the tag. Mathews' next response was a right cross to Robinson's eye, followed by a rhetorical question: "How about that tag?"

Before teammates or coaches could interfere, Mathews had knocked Robinson to the ground, striking him several times in the face. By now other ballplayers had reached the scene but no one attempted to rescue the supine Cincinnati slugger until Redleg coach Reggie Otero grabbed Mathews; then others joined in quelling the battle. The exchange of punches had been quick and one-sided. As manager Dressen described it later, "That Robinson was knocked down and he stayed down. He didn't want to get up. Why, he was bleeding all over."

With order restored, umpire Al Barlick ejected Mathews for his aggressive behavior. Robinson was not ejected, but the distinction was academic—the bruised Cincinnatian had to leave the game to have his facial injuries ministered to. He was bleeding from the nose and mouth, his right cheek was cut, his right eye was badly swollen, and his right thumb was bruised from striking Mathews' head. Mathews had a slight cut inside his lower lip and a painfully bruised right hand from using it as an implement of destruction. Subsequent X-rays of the hand revealed no fracture, but the injury bothered Mathews for several days.

Following the main event, any further action would have been anticlimactic. For the Braves, no further action ensued. They lost the opener, 5-3. In the nightcap Mathews returned from his brief exile; amazingly, so did Robinson, somewhat the worse for wear. His right eye was puffed nearly shut, and twice he had to call time and use a towel to stop his nose from bleeding. To add to Robinson's woes, Carl Willey hit him on the wrist with a pitch in the first inning of game two. Like Joe Louis rising from the canvas and winning, though, Robinson fought back with his bat and his glove.

With the nightcap still scoreless in the last of the sixth and Willey sailing along on a two-hitter, Robinson led off by blooping a double behind first base, much like his hit in game one that had led to his bout with Mathews. Gordy Coleman sacrificed Robinson to third. Spectators anticipated a renewal of the Mathews-Robinson feud; instead the two gladiators used the occasion to mend their differences, Mathews saying he was sorry and Robinson telling him to forget it. The next batter, Ed Bailey, hit a bad-bounce single over Chuck Cottier's head, scoring Robinson with the only run Bob Purkey would need.

In the last of the seventh Robinson put the game out of reach by tagging a Willey pitch for a two-run home run, but he still was not finished for the night. In the top of the eighth Robinson completed his revenge by making a running stab and diving headlong into the first row of seats to rob Mathews of an extra-base hit. The miraculous catch, along with four Cincinnati doubleplays, helped Purkey protect an eleven-hit, 4-0 shutout and give the Redlegs a sweep.

The following day National League President Warren Giles exonerated Mathews, saying the Mathews-Robinson affair was a "normal fight." Some of the Redlegs saw a double standard in light of Martin's previous $500 fine and five-day suspension for his knockout of Brewer, but the league found Mathews blameless and issued no fine or suspension. The Braves' management could have punished their third baseman, but they were hardly inclined to do so. Thirty years earlier Dressen had himself been a feisty third baseman. His words to Mathews after the game were: "Nice punching, kid."

Time Capsule - August 18, 1960

"Actually, it was one of my easiest games, except for the extra strain."

—Lew Burdette

Thirty-three-year old Lew Burdette was no stranger to no-hitters. Harvey Haddix had thrown one against him fifteen months earlier, and lost. Burdette had twice come close himself, hurling one-hitters against Brooklyn in 1954 and against Philadelphia in 1957 (losing the latter, 1-0). On a hot summer night at County Stadium in 1960, Burdette allowed the Phillies no runs, no hits, and no bases on balls. He faced the minimum 27 batters—only a hit batsman depriving him of the eighth perfect game in major league history, and that runner was erased by a double play.

The Braves were in second place, seven and a half games behind Pittsburgh and headed nowhere, when Burdette achieved every pitcher's dream. A disappointing crowd of 16,338 fans turned out to witness the performance. The oft-accused spitballer was opposed by former teammate Gene Conley, struggling with a 7-9 record for the cellar-dwelling Phillies. The Philadelphia team had historically been troublesome for Burdette, defeating him eighteen times while losing the same number until this season, when the Braves' righthander had beaten them in three of four decisions.

The closest the Phillies got to a base hit came in the top of the second inning. Cleanup batter Pancho Herrera surprised the Milwaukee infield with a bunt down the first-base line. Burdette scrambled after the ball, gloved it, and scooped it to Joe Adcock a split-second ahead of the lumbering Herrera. In the third inning the visitors had another near-miss when second baseman Mel Roach charged Ruben Amaro's slow grounder and fired an off-balance, underhand throw to retire the Phils' shortstop by a half-step.

In the bottom of the third the Braves recorded three consecutive singles yet failed to score. With one out Burdette singled, then went to second on Bruton's high bounder to deep short. Burdette overran the base, however, and was tagged out. When Herrera carelessly threw the ball away in returning it to Conley, Bruton advanced to second. The next batter, Del Crandall, bounced a high chopper to Lee Walls behind third base. Crandall beat the throw but Bruton, trying to score from second, was thrown out at the plate to end the inning.

With his slider and sinker working and his control flawless, Burdette kept the Phillie hitters pounding the ball into the dirt. With one out in the fifth, though, Lanky Lew let loose his only stray pitch of the evening. With a one-ball, one-strike count on Tony Gonzalez, Burdette fired a high, inside slider that clipped the rookie outfielder on the shoulder. The next man up, Walls,

Lew Burdette made his no-hitter look easy.

274

chopped a ball toward third. Eddie Mathews charged it, fielded it, and rifled a throw to Adcock to retire Walls. Gonzalez, thinking like a rookie, rounded second and headed for third. Adcock threw to Johnny Logan covering third; Logan tagged the sliding runner to complete a doubleplay and close out the only 'threat' of the night.

As tough as Burdette was, Conley stayed even with him, allowing base hits in nearly every inning but keeping Milwaukee runners from reaching home plate. In the sixth Crandall and Aaron both singled, but Conley got Wes Covington to hit into an inning-ending forceout at second. Entering the home half of the eighth the game remained scoreless as Burdette strode to the batter's box to the accompaniment of raucous cheers from the Braves' partisans.

On a high fastball Burdette ripped a line shot into the leftfield corner for a double, the ninth hit off Conley. The next batter, Bruton, slashed a line drive inside the rightfield line for a double, scoring Burdette. Conley disposed of the Braves' power hitters—Crandall, Mathews, and Aaron—without Bruton scoring, but Burdette now had a one-run margin to protect with just three more outs necessary.

In the ninth the Phillies had the bottom of the batting order to face Burdette—first-year catcher Jim Coker, shortstop Amaro, and Conley. Coker worked the count to three-and-two, only the second time all night Burdette had gone to a full count. Burdette then fooled the rookie with a sinker. Coker topped the ball back to the mound, Burdette tossed to Adcock, and there was one out. Philadelphia manager Gene Mauch went to his bench and summoned another rookie, outfielder Ken Walters, to pinch hit for Amaro. On a 1-1 pitch Walters hit a hard grounder right at Mathews. The throw to first was in plenty of time for the second out.

With the pitcher due up, Mauch again went to his bench. Conley, never a good hitter, was in the midst of his worst season ever at the plate, so Bobby Gene Smith was called to hit for him. Smith had little power but was a dangerous singles-hitting pinch hitter (he batted .314 as a pinch hitter in 1960). Burdette's first offering to him was a slider; Smith swung and missed. The next pitch was a low fastball that Smith foul-tipped off the foot of home plate umpire Bill Jackowski for strike two. As Jackowski tried to walk away the sting and the crowd buzzed expectantly, Burdette remained a picture of activity on the mound: rubbing down the baseball, going to the rosin bag, kicking dirt out of his cleats, adjusting the bill of his cap—a study in functionally superfluous yet purposeful and ultimately significant motion. When at last the umpire was ready, Burdette threw the pinch hitter a slider several inches outside the plate. Smith leaned forward, extended his arms, and lofted an easy fly toward Aaron in rightfield. Even before the ball nestled into the pocket of Aaron's mitt, the Braves' players and fans were rejoicing.

So effective was Burdette on this night that even the assists and putouts tell a story. Milwaukee infielders accounted for nineteen assists, led by Logan with eight, as Phillie hitters consistently swung over Burdette's sinker. Three batters struck out. Only one got under the ball enough to hit a popup, and four hit flyballs to the outfield: three to Bruton and the game's final out to Aaron. Leftfielder Wes Covington and his late-inning replacement Al Spangler could have remained in the dugout. Burdette required just 91 pitches to hurl the finest game of his career.

Spahn could not let Burdette's no-hitter go unanswered.

Time Capsule - September 16, 1960

"All right, just nobody say I've got a no-hitter going."

—Warren Spahn

At age 39 Warren Spahn had accomplished nearly everything a pitcher can accomplish. For most hurlers a 20-victory season highlights a career; Spahn had already reached that standard ten times and was closing in on eleven. For most pitchers an All-Star game selection represents the thrill of a lifetime; Spahn was a perennial All-Star participant with a victory in the 1953 classic to his credit. Every ballplayer dreams of competing in a World Series; Spahn had distinguished himself in three Series in the span of a decade. He had won 286 games in fifteen major league seasons, he had hurled fifty shutouts, and he had won the 1957 Cy Young Award as baseball's best pitcher. He had not, however, achieved a no-hitter—until Friday night, September 16, 1960.

Driving to the ballpark, Spahn's main concern that evening had been the weather. An all-day rain had placed the game, and Spahn's immediate opportunity for his 20th win, in jeopardy. Fortunately for him the Braves' front office was reluctant to postpone the game because it would necessitate a doubleheader on Sunday. The Braves still had a chance, however remote, to catch the first-place Pirates in the final two weeks. A doubleheader could only diminish the club's already slim chances. Rain or no rain, the Braves' management was determined to play the game as scheduled.

Because of the rain, because the Braves were all but eliminated from the pennant race, and because the high school football season was underway, a record-low night crowd of 6117 diehards showed up to watch the old southpaw try for win number twenty. In fact the sparse gathering was just 27 people larger than the

277

smallest single-game attendance total in the history of the franchise, established more than four years earlier for a Monday afternoon makeup game without a presale. The turnout this evening was unfortunate—the thousands who stayed away missed one of the finest pitching performances in league history.

Spahn entered the game with a 19-9 season mark, in stark contrast to his Phillie counterpart, John Buzhardt, sporting a 4-15 record, the worst among National League starting pitchers. Spahn's statistic was all the more impressive considering his slow start. Plagued by a sore knee and bad weather, the veteran lefthander did not earn his second victory until the season was a month old. As late as June 22 he had only four wins, and his record at the All-Star break was a modest 8-6. Beginning on August 7, though, he won six in a row and eight of ten over a five-week stretch. The unfortunate Buzhardt, meanwhile, entered the game with eleven straight losses.

Through the first three innings neither pitcher allowed a run; Spahn struck out six of the first nine hitters and did not allow a baserunner. After two were out in the fourth, outfielder Ken Walters worked Spahn for a walk, but he died at first as Spahn retired Pancho Herrera. Then in the bottom of the fourth Spahn's teammates gave him some breathing room. Hank Aaron singled, leftfielder Alvin Dark tripled over the centerfielder's head, and Joe Adcock scored Dark with a sacrifice fly to put Milwaukee ahead, 2-0.

With one out in the visitors' fifth, the Phillies put their last runner on base as catcher Cal Neeman drew the second base on balls issued by Spahn. Like Walters in the fourth, Neeman never progressed past first base. Then in the home fifth Spahn helped his own cause by drilling a single, advancing on Bill Bruton's single, and scoring on a base hit by Eddie Mathews to make it 3-0. Spahn continued to render Philadelphia helpless, and in the last of the seventh Bruton singled, stole second, and scored on a Del Crandall single to put Spahn up by 4-0.

Through seven innings Spahn had allowed no hits and had struck out eleven. (His best strikeout performance had been on June 14, 1952, when he fanned eighteen Chicago Cubs in a fifteen-inning game to tie the single-game major league record.) In the eighth he retired Neeman leading off, then whiffed pinch-hitters Tony Taylor and Lee Walls.

Buzhardt got the Braves out in the last of the eighth, then gave way to pinch-hitter Bobby Gene Smith leading off the ninth. Smith had made the final out in Lew Burdette's no-hitter 29 days earlier, and he was no more successful this time—Spahn made him his third straight strikeout victim and the inning's first out.

Next came Bobby Del Greco, who as a Cardinal in 1956 had robbed Spahn and the Braves of a possible pennant in the next-to-last game of the year with two incredible catches. He was manager Gene Mauch's fourth straight pinch-hitter, and Spahn made him the fourth straight strikeout.

The last man between Spahn and his no-hitter was second baseman Bobby Malkmus, Spahn's former teammate, currently a .212 hitter. Malkmus lined the first pitch back at the mound, the hardest-hit ball of the night by the Phillies. Spahn's reflexes allowed him to get his glove up, but only in time to deflect the ball, not field it. As Malkmus streaked down the first-base line, shortstop Johnny Logan scrambled in front of second base and gloved the ball. He hurried an off-balance throw toward first baseman Joe Adcock, but the ball was wide and in the dirt. Adcock extended his full length and scooped the ball backhanded out of the moist dirt a split-second before Malkmus' foot hit the base. A moment later Spahn and Crandall engulfed the big first baseman and smothered him in congratulatory hugs.

Relying mostly on a revived fastball, the aging southpaw had earned his first no-hitter and 51st shutout and set a personal high of fifteen strikeouts in a nine-inning game. His only unfulfilled goal was his 300th victory, but with just twelve games remaining, that milestone was left for another season.

1960 Swan Songs

"I remember what happened in 1957 after Bill got hurt. I switched to center and my average slipped about 25 points. Besides, it might hurt my chances of making the All-Star team. I'm no Willie Mays."

—Henry Aaron, told of Bruton's trade

The first Little League player to make it to the major leagues joined the Braves as a "bonus baby" in 1953, meaning that he had to remain with the team rather than learn his craft in the minors. Joey Jay's career was undoubtedly altered by his forced entry to the majors at age 18. Despite pitching in seven different seasons with Milwaukee, Jay did not fulfill his potential until being traded to Cincinnati at age 25, leading the Reds to a pennant. His best year with the Braves was 1958, when he won seven games, including three shutouts, and had a 2.14 earned run average.

Jay's last game with the Braves was on September 27, 1960, in Philadelphia's Connie Mack Stadium. As was often the case, he pitched well but was victimized by his teammates. Leading 3-1 with two out in the seventh inning, Jay lost when second base fielding specialist Chuck Cottier let a grounder go between his legs and four unearned runs subsequently scored, giving the Phillies a 5-3 victory and saddling Jay with his eighth defeat against nine wins.

The other Original who bowed out of Milwaukee in 1960 was Billy Bruton, the Braves' first hero. The speedy outfielder had been the star of the first two victories by Charlie Grimm's club in April of 1953, first in Cincinnati and then at home. His running catches, stolen bases, and clutch hitting endeared him to Milwaukee fans, who had already watched him play with the Brewers in 1952 before the Braves arrived. Bruton missed half of the 1957

280

season, the World Series, and the start of 1958 with a severe knee injury suffered in a collision with Felix Mantilla [see Feat of Clay], but he returned to form after that and probably had his finest year in 1960, leading the league in triples and runs scored.

Bruton's last game for the Braves was the 1960 season finale in Pittsburgh, a game the Braves lost, 9-5. With the standings already decided, manager Charlie Dressen let Lew Burdette pitch the entire game in quest of his 20th win, despite a fifteen-hit attack by the Pirates. Bruton played the entire game in center-field, led off, got one single in five times at bat, scored one run, and made an uncharacteristic error in the field. He was traded in the off-season, and his loss in the outfield plagued the Braves for several years.

Billy Bruton's basestealing brought excitement and led the league three times.

1961

"We can hardly say that we were entirely satisfied with the performance of the Braves under Dressen."

—General Manager John McHale

Nineteen sixty-one was a historic year for major league baseball, especially the American League. Reacting to threats by Branch Rickey to form a third major league, the Continental League, baseball's high-muck-a-mucks hurriedly decided to expand—American League teams were born in 1961 in Los Angeles and Washington, D.C., the latter replacing the previous team in that city, now transplanted as the Minnesota Twins. National League expansion was scheduled for the following year. Assisted by the addition of a score of pitchers who would otherwise have been in the minor leagues or unemployed, Roger Maris seized the opportunity to hit 61 home runs, surpassing Babe Ruth's enduring standard. Maris' total was an increase of 22 over his 1960 output. He was not alone—Mickey Mantle hit 54 homers, an increase of 14; Jim Gentile blasted 46, an increase of 25; Harmon Killebrew clouted 46, up from 31; Rocky Colavito slammed 45, up 10; Norm Cash smashed 41, an increase of 23; and so on.

Charlie Dressen's second season in Milwaukee was a year of change for the Braves. Unfortunately, in the National League standings the change meant decline, a drop to fourth place, the Braves' poorest finish since their arrival in Beertown. Two trades, one pre-season and one mid-season, dealt away members of the club that inaugurated County Stadium on April 14, 1953, leaving just a half-dozen of the "Originals." The old, familiar lineup that Wisconsin baseball fans had come to know as well as they knew their own relatives was gradually, steadily, giving way to a collection of outsiders and transients.

282

Less than twenty-four hours after Bill Mazeroski's home run decided the 1960 World Series, the Braves gave second baseman Red Schoendienst his unconditional release. The Redhead had been a Milwaukee hero, and many of the Braves felt that Dressen blamed Schoendienst for the team's failure to win the pennant in 1960, a charge Dressen vehemently denied. Nevertheless, on December 3, 1960, the Braves' front office added insult to injury by purchasing second baseman Billy Martin from the Redlegs. Martin, though five years Schoendienst's junior, was no more capable, and probably less capable, of helping the club than Schoendienst. The acquisition of Martin was interpreted as an insult by Schoendienst and by many of the Braves' players, further distancing them from Dressen.

On October 31, 1960, the San Francisco Giants traded infielder Andre Rodgers to the Braves for Alvin Dark, whom the Giants installed as their manager. Milwaukee then traded Rodgers to the Cubs on April 1, 1961, for two pitchers, Moe Drabowsky and Seth Morehead, neither of whom made a noticeable contribution to the Milwaukee cause nor lasted the season with the Braves.

The 1961 fortunes of Dressen and his club were, for all practical purposes, sealed in December, 1960, in three trades, two of which were consummated and one of which was not. During the first week of December the general managers of three teams—the Braves, the Cardinals, and the Phillies— nearly inked a pact that would have sent first baseman Joe Cunningham and pitcher Bob Gibson (an unproven former Harlem Globetrotter) from St. Louis to Philadelphia; sent outfielder Billy Bruton from Milwaukee to St. Louis; sent outfielder Wes Covington from Milwaukee to Philadelphia; and sent relief pitcher Dick Farrell from Philadelphia to Milwaukee. Why Bing Devine of the Cardinals would have considered such a deal is hard to understand, but he was spared eternal embarrassment when the Braves' John McHale backed out of the deal.

What the Braves chose instead was a trade with the Detroit Tigers. Milwaukee peddled Bruton, second baseman Chuck Cottier, and minor league prospects Dick Brown, a catcher, and Terry Fox, a pitcher. The Braves' management wanted more than anything else to solve their nagging second base problem, and they did—the Tigers sent Milwaukee Frank Bolling in exchange for the Braves' foursome. Bolling lived up to his billing, slamming fifteen home runs, leading the league in fielding, and earning a selection to the All-Star team, but the cost to the Braves was high. They gave up a starting outfielder; a talented backup catcher, which they soon needed; and a capable relief pitcher, whom they desperately needed.

Having obtained a solid second baseman, McHale and Dressen and company decided to round out the infield with a capable shortstop. Judging Johnny Logan to be over the hill at 34, the Braves acquired Cincinnati veteran Roy McMillan, like Bolling renowned more for his glove than for his bat. On December 15, 1960, in a three-team swap, Milwaukee sent promising pitchers Joey Jay and Juan Pizarro to the Redlegs and White Sox, respectively. The Reds sent pitcher Cal McLish to the White Sox and McMillan to the Braves. The Chisox completed the transaction by dispatching third baseman Gene Freese to Cincinnati. Of course the impact of any trade is difficult to gauge objectively, but three observations about this one are indisputable: Jay won 21 games in 1961 and led Cincinnati to its first pennant since before the attack on Pearl Harbor; Pizarro immediately became the ace of the Chicago staff, with a 14-7 record and a 3.05 ERA; and McMillan, a notorious banjo-hitter, batted .220, his career low and the lowest of any regular player in the league.

Roy McMillan executes a squeeze bunt, Sept. 9, 1961.

Only one rookie, pitcher Don Nottebart, survived the exhibition schedule and opened the season with the Braves. Very early, though, Dressen recognized that the club he possessed was not pennant caliber. As a result, he made numerous roster changes throughout the year. Reliever Ken MacKenzie was tested, then quickly discarded. On May 9 Mel Roach, superfluous at second base and inadequate in leftfield, was traded to the Cubs for veteran Frank Thomas, who immediately solved the Braves' problem in left. His arrival made Covington expendable. The big outfielder, once so highly prized by the Braves that they turned down numerous trade offers for him, cleared waivers and landed with the White Sox, Athletics, and Phillies in quick succession.

One unforeseeable deficiency arose because of an injury. Del Crandall, the league's best catcher, became incapacitated by a shoulder injury on April 20, appearing thereafter only as a pinch-hitter. To fill the enormous vacancy, Dressen called up Joe Torre from Louisville on May 20. The rookie backstop debuted with a single, double, and home run in a doubleheader, also throwing out three would-be base-stealers. Torre, younger brother of the Braves' former star defensive first baseman, played remarkably well all season, but Crandall's absence still hurt. To provide Torre with backup help, the Braves bought veteran Sammy White, who had sat out 1960 voluntarily, on June 15, at the same time optioning former substitute Charlie Lau.

Also on June 15, a few hours before the trading deadline, the Braves severed another tie with their Milwaukee tradition by dealing popular shortstop Johnny Logan to the Pirates for outfielder Gino Cimoli. Logan had won the hearts of local fans with his pugnacious, blue-collar approach to the game, but he had slumped to .245 in 1960 and could not field like McMillan. He had batted just nineteen times in the first two months of the season, so his absence made little difference, and the addition of Cimoli gave the Braves one more chance at solving their outfield woes.

Dressen's pitching staff also required assistance. The front office scoured the farm system for available talent but found little help. In early June they tried 33-year-old rookie Federico "Chi Chi" Olivo (whose brother Diomedes had made his rookie appearance with the Pirates in 1960 at age 41); Olivo allowed a home run to Jerry Lynch, the first batter he faced, and walked three before being replaced after retiring one batter. Later the Braves called up 20-year-old Tony Cloninger, who won seven games despite a horrible earned run average, and 22-year-old Bob Hendley, a promising lefty who won five with a much better

285

ERA. On July 4 the club even repurchased Johnny Antonelli, the old Braves hurler from the Truman years (both terms), from Cleveland. As it happened, he had one victory remaining in his good left arm.

The Braves made three other attempts at strengthening their team. On June 9 they purchased Bob Boyd from Kansas City to bolster their almost non-existent pinch-hitting corps, with modest success. On August 17 they brought up an outfielder named Barbra Chrisley, known mercifully as Neil, for the same reason, with less success. On July 11 they called up centerfielder Mack Jones to try to fill the vacancy left by Bruton's departure. Jones broke in spectacularly, tying a record held by Casey Stengel and Willie McCovey with four hits in his first game. Five weeks later, though, Mack the Knife was again shagging flyballs in Louisville after fielding sporadically and hitting a feeble .231 with no homers.

Despite the parade of roster changes, the 1961 edition of the Milwaukee Braves was basically not much different from previous ones. The team's offensive weapons remained the same—the bats of Aaron, Mathews, and Adcock. Milwaukee led the league in home runs for the third straight year, although the distribution was slightly different. This time Adcock set the pace with 35 homers; Aaron and Mathews dipped somewhat, to 34 and 32 respectively, and newcomer Frank Thomas, a late enrollee, contributed 25. Aaron led in average at .327, with Mathews matching his career high at .306. In run production Aaron also set the pace, driving in 120 to Adcock's 108 and Mathews' 91. Mathews led the league by drawing 93 bases on balls, while Aaron surpassed all other batters with 358 total bases and 39 doubles.

After two unsettled years at the second base position and some up-and-down seasons for Logan at shortstop, the addition of McMillan and Bolling stabilized the Braves' infield and gave them the best fielding team in the majors. Both Bolling and McMillan led at their positions, as did Adcock at his, and Mathews finished as runner-up at third base. Only in the outfield with Frank Thomas, and Mel Roach and Mack Jones when they played, were the Braves notably weak afield.

Hitting and defense are important, but as every baseball fan knows, pitching wins ballgames. In the Braves' first seven seasons in Milwaukee their pitching was the best or nearly the best each year, but in 1960 the number of complete games declined and the team earned run average soared. In 1961 the complete game total of 57 again led the league, but the team earned run average rose still further to 3.89, only fourth best among National League

286

Milwaukee Journal Photo

Hank Aaron, Frank Bolling, Frank Thomas, and Gino Cimoli

clubs. An especially telling statistic concerning the pitching staff was the total number of games saved (an unofficial statistic until 1969). Milwaukee relief pitchers saved only sixteen games in 1961, a total exceeded by every team except the last-place Phillies. Don McMahon earned half of that total and performed well in 53 outings, compiling a 2.84 ERA, but no other reliever pitched reliably, especially in long relief.

Further evidence of the Braves' diminished pitching prowess can be found in their shutout total—eight, second lowest total in the league. Spahn tied for the league lead with four, Burdette hurled three, Buhl tossed one shutout, and that was it. At one time Charlie Grimm or Fred Haney could employ a strong five-man rotation, but Dressen had the Big Three and little else—and even that trio was tarnished. In 1961 Buhl lost more games than he won (9-10), and his earned run average was a hefty 4.11—the worst of his career. Essentially that meant Dressen had two reliable starters. Carl Willey had been disappointing since his rookie campaign; Jay and Pizarro were gone; the next wave of youngsters were not yet ready. And of the Big Two, even Burdette, despite an 18-11 mark and the league's lowest ratio of walks per nine innings, allowed four runs every nine innings. The only unflagging mound performance belonged to the ancient warrior, four-decades-old Warren Spahn.

The most surprising feature of Spahn's 1961 season was his second no-hitter—not the fact that he achieved it, but the fact that he achieved it in April, five days after his 40th birthday. The great southpaw was not customarily great until after the All-Star break, when the pennant race was truly underway. In Spahn's first nine years in Milwaukee, only twice (11-3 in 1953 and 10-5 in 1958) did he win more than 60% of his pre-All-Star decisions, but he did so *every* season after the All-Star break. In 1961 he stumbled along at 8-11 until the Classic, then won thirteen of fifteen down the stretch, including six straight in August (earning him Player of the Month honors), five of six in September and ten in a row at one stretch. He ended with 21 wins, his sixth 20-plus season in a row, a league-leading 3.02 earned run average, and an impressive 21 complete games, six more than the league's next best total by Sandy Koufax.

Two long-standing traditions of Spahn's were reversed in 1961—he stopped breezing past the Redlegs, and he began beating the Dodgers. After amassing a 57-21 advantage over Cincinnati in his first fifteen seasons, Spahnie lost to them five times while winning just once, and even in victory he allowed the pennant winners eleven hits. Two of the losses were to former teammate Joey Jay.

Against Los Angeles, though, Spahn succeeded as never before, pitching brilliantly four of the five times he opposed them. On May 3 in Milwaukee he nearly hurled his second no-hitter in a row, losing the no-hitter and shutout on a misplay by Mel Roach in leftfield. On May 17 in L.A. Spahn took a 1-1 tie into the eleventh before losing when would-be reliever Seth Morehead walked in the winning Dodger run. On a cold May 26 night in Milwaukee the amazing lefthander overwhelmed the Angelenos, 10-2. Finally on September 2 the Milwaukee ace shut out the southern Californians at County Stadium, 4-0, his first whitewash of the Dodgers since August 20, 1949.

Despite Spahn's excellence and the strong showing of his old roommate Burdette, for Dressen's pitching staff it was strictly a case of "Spahn and Burdette and try to forget." Actually that should read "ex-roommate Burdette"—Dressen had changed road-trip bunk assignments more than once. The last time came after a series of extra-curricular escapades, including a Los Angeles helicopter ride by the fun-loving Spahn-Burdette tandem and a newspaper fire on the team bus following an 11-4 walloping by the Phillies in the nightcap of a doubleheader split on May 30. Dressen publicly blasted the players for their high jinks, although at the moment of the blaze the Braves were just four and one-half games out of first, the closest they had been since May 23 (when Dressen was absent with a fever) and closer than they would ever be again under Dressen's guidance.

In addition to lambasting the team in the media, Dressen instituted strict enforcement of the ballplayers' midnight curfew, the revocation of the players' $10 per diem for meals, the serving of sandwiches rather than full meals on team charter flights, and the designation of new pairs of roommates. Coach George Myatt, assigned the task of scrutinizing hotel lobbies and rooms for curfew violators, was given the prison monicker "screw" by the indignant players. Needless to say, the Braves did not exactly play their hearts out for Charlie Dressen during his final few months as Milwaukee pilot.

Milwaukee Journal Photo

Charlie Dressen was never a Milwaukee favorite.

As the team's performance on the field declined, the Milwaukee fans' idolatrous support also waned. The Braves' mere appearance no longer was cause for wild jubilation. The club's downward shift in the standings, along with the establishment of a ban on carry-ins of the beverage that made Milwaukee famous, reduced the season's attendance total to 1,101,441, half the peak total of 1957. Record-low single game figures were established: lowest Sunday total, September 24, 7262; lowest for a night game, September 25, 4689; lowest for any game, September 26 (the day Cincinnati clinched the pennant), 4277; and as an early indication that all was not well, the smallest opening day gathering, 33,327 on a frigid April 11.

What the two-thirds capacity crowd saw in the opener offered an accurate foreshadowing of the Braves' season. Eddie Mathews slugged a home run, Spahn pitched a fine ballgame, but the Braves lost, 2-1, in ten innings on a home run by Daryl Spencer. Milwaukee's heroes lost many one-run games in 1961, 33 to be

Milwaukee Journal Photo

The aftermath of Eddie Mathews punching out Reds' Jim O'Toole,
July 2, 1961

exact, while winning 30, symptomatic of an ailing bullpen. Often they lost on gopher balls—at one point Spahn, Burdette, and Buhl seemed to be vying for the league lead in that category. The Braves' first three losses came on late-inning blasts—Spencer's on opening day, a two-run shot in the ninth by the Cubs' Sammy Taylor on April 14, and a two-out grand slam in the ninth by Chicago's Al Heist on April 15. Milwaukee wound up leading the National League in home runs, but in the season's first month the Braves were out-homered, 36-16, while compiling the worst team earned run average in either league.

The Braves' 6-6 April, good for fourth place but just two games back, gave way to a 13-14 May that left them five and a half out of first. Their inept bullpen, their proclivity toward gopher balls, the sudden loss of Del Crandall, and their unsettled outfield prevented them from winning more than three straight or rising more than two games above .500 (a level they reached only once before July 22).

In June the Braves really started to hit—not win, just hit. In Cincinnati's Crosley Field on June 8 the Milwaukee sluggers produced six home runs, including one by Spahn and a pair by Mathews, and a major-league first: four consecutive homers, by Mathews, Aaron, Adcock, and Thomas. The explosion was not enough, though, as Dressen's charges lost, 10-8. The next day in Chicago's Wrigley Field the Braves hit four more, including a grand slam by Lee Maye, but seven Milwaukee hurlers could not prevent an 11-10 loss to the Cubbies with Spahn, in relief, suffering his second defeat in two days. The following day Braves' bats clubbed four more four-baggers, including one by Burdette, to tie the three-game record of fourteen. Finally in Wrigley on June 11, in the first of a twin-bill, Milwaukee bombers added two more round-trippers, tying another record with sixteen in four games. The record-tying blast was hit, appropriately, by Spahn, whose homer on June 8 began the streak, and the victory in the fourth game also went to the indefatigable Spahn, his third decision in four days.

Of course the long-ball hitting did not stop when that four-game surge ended. On June 18 in the L.A. Coliseum the Milwaukee musclemen supported the mound staff with five homers, two by Adcock, one of which was a 500-foot suborbital launch to centerfield. Through the game on June 24 Braves' hitters had posted 39 homers in fifteen games; by July 2 they had 46 in 21 games. Even as they continued to explode at the plate, though, the team stumbled along near or below .500, bottoming out on July 15 in St. Louis (after the Cardinals won 12-4 with eight runs

New doubleplay tandem Roy McMillan and Frank Bolling

in their last at-bat) in fifth place, fourteen and one-half games distant from the Redlegs.

Beginning the next day the Braves won nine of ten (averaging better than seven runs per game), gaining six games in the standings. After that they lost three of four to the Reds, though, and by the second All-Star game on July 31 (a 1-1 yawner ended by rain after nine innings) Milwaukee trailed Cincinnati by eleven games, despite a one-hitter by Bob Buhl two days before, broken up by Ken Boyer's single with two out in the seventh.

Once August got started, though, so did the Braves. They won their first four post-All-Star contests, then lost three straight on the West Coast. Returning home, Dressen's club began to play the way their fans had always believed they could. Combining timely hitting with solid pitching, Spahn and company won ten straight starting with Spahn's 300th win on August 11, and concluding with Spahn's 302nd win on August 20. They ended with a 20-9 mark for August, in third place, six and one-half out.

With 27 games still to be played, Dressen thought his boys had a chance.

Dressen was wrong. Within 48 hours, while Spahn was on the mound shutting out the Dodgers, the Braves' front office hastily called a postgame press conference to announce that Executive Vice-President George "Birdie" Tebbetts would replace Dressen as the team's manager, effective immediately. With no forewarning, Dressen was told to pack his possessions and clear out. He was not even told who his successor would be, and he did not ask. He stoically accepted the decision and left without any acrimonious comment.

Under Tebbetts' direction the Braves split a doubleheader with the Cubs the next day, then won two of the next three to crawl within six of Cincinnati. That was their last hurrah— beginning on September 11 Birdie's team went into a batting swoon, lost eight straight, and was officially declared dead on September 17. The Braves completed their season with an eight-game home stand, six games of which they won, but few people saw them and probably even fewer cared. After eight years of pennants or at least pennant contention, the Milwaukee Braves had become also-rans.

1961 Nemesis - Willie Mays

"Joe Louis, Jascha Heifetz, Sammy Davis, and Nashua rolled into one."

—Leo Durocher, describing Willie Mays

Many people considered Willie Mays the most exciting ballplayer of the 1950's and '60's. He could beat you with his glove, his arm, his baserunning, and his bat. He was destined for the Hall of Fame from the time he joined the New York Giants in 1951. He hit more career home runs than anyone except Henry Aaron and Babe Ruth, but even in a career like his, what he did to the Braves pitching staff in 1961 stands out.

What he did was hit twelve home runs, two of them grand slams, in 21 games with Milwaukee, driving in 31 runs. His batting average against the Braves was "only" .309, a fraction of a point higher than against the rest of the league, but his power was exceptional. Mays finished second in home runs for the year with 40, trailing teammate Orlando Cepeda; with the same success against the other six teams that he enjoyed against Dressen's team, Mays would have hit 84 for the season.

Four games in particular deserve mention. On May 13 in Candlestick Park, the "Say Hey Kid" smashed his fifth career grand slam in the third inning, then hit a two-run encore two innings later to spearhead an 8-5 San Francisco victory. On June 22 at County Stadium he clubbed two singles and two homers, driving in three runs in an 8-6 losing effort saved for Milwaukee by five homers of their own. (At that point Mays had hit sixteen home runs, ten against the Braves.) On September 19 his grand slam was the biggest blow in an 11-10 slugfest won at home by the Giants over the Braves. Mays' greatest outburst of the season, though, had come early.

On April 30 in Milwaukee, two days after being held hitless

along with everyone else in Spahn's second no-hitter, Mays rose from a sick bed to blast a record-tying four home runs, driving in eight, in a 14-4 San Francisco triumph. Despite being unable to consume solid food all day, the amazing Mays found the strength to hit two homers off starter Lew Burdette and one each against Seth Morehead and Don McMahon. Mays' only failure to belt the ball over the fence came in the fifth inning against Moe Drabowsky, when he hit a long fly that Aaron snagged in center. The Giants' final out of the game was registered with Mays in the on-deck circle; if Jim Davenport had reached base, Mays might have become the first to hit five homers in a game rather than the ninth to hit four.

The twelve home runs Mays slugged against the Braves in 1961 fell one short of the National League record against one team: Hank Sauer of the Cubs established the mark in 1954 against Pittsburgh, and Joe Adcock equaled it in 1956 against the Brooklyn Dodgers. Mays' failure to attain the record was small consolation for the Braves' pitchers.

Milwaukee Sentinel Photo

Willie Mays robs Johnny DeMerit of extra bases, April 29, 1961.

1961 Feat of Clay

"The relief pitcher is the one man on a team that can make a manager look like a genius."

—Birdie Tebbetts

The poor start of the 1961 Braves can be attributed as much to a lack of relief pitching as to any one factor. Don McMahon and Ron Piche both returned from the previous season, but neither inspired much confidence in Charlie Dressen. Piche had been spotty, and McMahon's 5.94 earned run average, on the Richter scale, would have caused devastating damage, perhaps loss of life. Dressen also wanted to test the recent additions to his staff, including farm system products Ken MacKenzie and Don Nottebart and recent trade acquisitions Moe Drabowsky and Seth Morehead.

As early as April 15 the signs of impending bullpen doom were evident. On that day Nottebart pitched well in long relief for four innings, then gave up a grand slam to Al Heist with two out in the ninth and lost 9-5. On May 2 MacKenzie allowed five runs, four earned, in so-called relief, gaining his only decision of the year, a loss. Three days later the relief corps failed even more egregiously.

On May 5 against the Redlegs, Lew Burdette took a 4-1 lead into the ninth inning before faltering, allowing one run in and leaving two men on base. Morehead was summoned to record the final two outs, but the first man he faced, Wally Post, slammed a three-run homer to put Cincinnati ahead. Milwaukee tied the game with a run in the bottom of the ninth, but eventually Piche yielded a run in the twelfth and the Braves lost, 6-5.

On May 14 Dressen's club fought back after trailing the Giants 5-2 by scoring four times against their old nemesis, Billy Loes. Starter Carl Willey gave up two hits to start the sixth inning, so

Dressen replaced him with MacKenzie. In his final act as a Brave before receiving a one-way ticket to Louisville, MacKenzie gave up a single to Harvey Kuenn to tie the game. Exit MacKenzie, enter Drabowsky. He was touched for a base hit by Chuck Hiller to put the Giants ahead. The Braves scored in the ninth to tie the game, but in the last of the ninth an error by Roy McMillan, the league's leading shortstop, put the winning run on base. Ron Piche did the rest. After a sacrifice, Piche intentionally walked Ed Bailey, then proceeded to walk Jose Pagan and Matty Alou and force in the winning run.

Three days later Seth Morehead, not wanting to be outflopped by Piche, walked in the winning run in the eleventh inning against the Dodgers to spoil a great performance by Warren Spahn. On June 5 Federico "Chi Chi" Olivo made his debut and immediately entered the competition for the relief pitchers' hall of shame by succumbing to a Jerry Lynch home run on his second big-league pitch. Then the next day he tried to outdo that performance by issuing a double and three walks while retiring just one batter, sending his earned run average to a nice round 36.00.

As futile as the relievers were individually, they probably reached their collective nadir on Friday, June 9 at Wrigley Field. Seven Milwaukee hurlers—Buhl, McMahon, George Brunet (five days short of being farmed out), Claude Raymond, Olivo, Spahn, and Willey—failed to check the lowly Cubs and ultimately lost, 11-10, despite four home runs, including a grand slam. Combined with the previous game, the loss gave the Braves back-to-back defeats in which they scored a total of eighteen runs and blasted ten homers.

No matter where Charlie Dressen looked in 1961, there was no relief in sight.

Time Capsule - April 28, 1961

"It was so easy, it was pathetic."

—Warren Spahn

His manager called it "the most perfect game I ever saw." His catcher said, "He made one bad pitch all night," a high screwball that Willie Mays topped weakly to the mound. Spahn himself said he "didn't have as good stuff" as in his first no-hitter against the Phillies. Good stuff or not, on a frigid Friday night at County Stadium, April 28, 1961, Warren Spahn, at age 40, hurled his second no-hitter in his last six starts. Only one pitcher in major league history, the immortal Cy Young, had achieved a no-hitter at a more advanced age (41). The New York team that Young held hitless back in 1908, though, was an impotent last-place bunch that hit a collective .236 with eleven total home runs all year.

In contrast, the San Francisco Giants that Spahn dominated entered the game in first place and boasted a murderers' row that included Harvey Kuenn, Willie Mays, Willie McCovey, Orlando Cepeda, Felipe Alou, and Ed Bailey. The 1961 Giants smashed 183 home runs, led by Cepeda's 46 and Mays' 40. Spahn's fastball was no longer a match for such sluggers, but using a mixture of screwballs to the righthand hitters and his recently-developed slider to the lefties, along with pinpoint control, the ageless southpaw kept the powerful Giants off balance and off the bases all night.

Spahn needed to be every bit as tough as he was in order to win. His mound adversary was Toothpick Sam Jones, a fearsome righthander who had won 39 ballgames for the Giants over the previous two seasons and who had himself spun a no-hitter in 1955 while employed by the Cubs. On this night Jones had his usual live fastball, his sweeping curveball, and his customary, unsettling uncertainty of where his pitches were going. He allowed only five hits by the uneasy Milwaukee batters, all singles, but he also hit one and walked five. He struck out ten, seven in the first three innings, and despite having Braves on the bases all night, he did not allow an earned run.

Milwaukee's only score, the only one Spahn would need, came in the bottom of the first inning. With one out the Braves' new second baseman, Frank Bolling, looped a base hit to centerfield, extending his hitting streak to nine games. Then came a crucial play. With Eddie Mathews at bat, Giants' catcher Ed Bailey, acquired only the day before from Cincinnati, let one of Jones' wicked breaking balls bounce away from him and Bolling took second. Mathews then struck out, but a two-out single to right by Hank Aaron scored Bolling with the game's only run, unearned because of the passed ball.

Spahn kept the bases empty until the fourth inning, when he walked leadoff batter Chuck Hiller on four pitches. The rookie second baseman had little time to enjoy the view from first base, though. Next batter Harvey Kuenn, a Milwaukee native making

Milwaukee Journal Photo

Burdette and Spahn shared good times on and off the field.

his first hometown appearance in a league game, bounced one back to Spahn, who threw to McMillan to force Hiller. McMillan fired to Adcock to beat Kuenn and put Spahn back on the three-batters-per-inning track.

In the fifth Spahn again walked the leadoff batter, McCovey, again on four pitches. Once again Spahn induced the next hitter, this time Cepeda, to ground the ball back to him. Spahn picked it up and again threw to McMillan, who again fired to Adcock to complete the doubleplay.

Against Jones the Milwaukee hitters had several chances to provide their star southpaw with some insurance runs. In the third inning they put two men on with two out, but Mel Roach went down swinging. In the sixth Roach and Adcock each singled after one out, but Charlie Lau, a replacement for the injured Del Crandall, and Johnny DeMerit, a former $100,000 bonus player who lived up to his name, not his salary, both failed to advance the runners.

Then in the home seventh Spahn was safe at first on a McCovey fumble. McMillan did his duty and sacrificed. Bolling lined a single up the middle that might have scored Spahn, but Mays' peg to the plate was, as usual, perfect, so the pitcher with the 40-year-old wheels wisely held third, with Bolling taking second on the throw. Mathews was purposely passed to load the bases for Aaron. The Braves' leading hitter struck out on three straight curveballs, though, and Roach grounded to the first baseman. Spahn had to make do with his one-run lead.

For just a moment at the start of the eighth it appeared the no-hitter might be in jeopardy. First batter McCovey golfed a slider into short rightcenter field that Aaron had to run a long way to reach, but with his characteristic and deceptively fast lope Aaron arrived in time to make the catch. After that, Cepeda and Alou were cupcakes.

The top of the ninth brought the 8518 shivering fans to the edge of their seats and several times to their feet. Spahn put Bailey in the hole with a slider and a fastball, both strikes, then missed twice with breaking balls. On the 2-2 pitch Bailey lofted a high popup in front of the third-base dugout. Lau, the catcher, called off Mathews, who probably had an easier play. The ball struck Lau's mitt and bounced to the ground. Giving new life to a good hitter like Bailey was the kiss of death; everyone in the stadium except Spahn knew it. Bailey prolonged the agony by fouling off two more pitches, then struck out. The crowd breathed a huge sigh of relief, drowned out by that of Charlie Lau.

Shortstop Jose Pagan was due next, but manager Alvin Dark

(the Braves' leftfielder in Spahn's first no-hitter) sent Matty Alou to pinch-hit. Alou drag-bunted the first pitch down the first-base line. Spahn sprang from the mound, ran toward first, backhanded the ball to Adcock, and got Alou by a step for the second out.

For the final chance at spoiling Spahn's masterpiece, Dark sent Joe Amalfitano to bat for the pitcher. Spahn fell behind by missing with two screwballs, but Amalfitano hit the third pitch on the ground toward McMillan. The shortstop was in perfect fielding position, but the ball took a bad hop and struck him in the groin. ("Don't think my knees didn't buckle," he said after the game.) McMillan scrambled after the ball, picked it up and rifled it to Adcock, just ahead of the runner. Spahn had his once-in-a-lifetime moment for the second time.

The victory was Spahn's 290th of his career, and his 52nd shutout. The win pushed the Braves into first place, by percentage points, for what would be the only day of the 1961 season.

Milwaukee Journal Photo

Gino Cimoli misses George Altman's inside-the-park home run.

Time Capsule - August 11, 1961

"It was destiny, that homer." —Gino Cimoli

After sixteen years of playing professional baseball in front of big crowds he was nervous before the game, anxious to get it over with. He had won World Series and All-Star games and hurled no-hitters and seemingly done everything a pitcher could do, but somehow another milestone remained. And what made it nerve-wracking was that, unlike the other accomplishments, which were done spontaneously (no pun there), this one had been foreseen for months, even years.

That was why his phone kept ringing all day and why people were sending him congratulatory telegrams before the fact. That was why two devout hero-worshippers had sent him 102 four-leaf clovers before the game. That was why a throng of 40,775 delirious fans had gathered on a Friday night to see the fourth-place Braves, the largest crowd at County Stadium in nearly two years, since the all-time record 48,642 that watched Milwaukee tie the Dodgers for the pennant on the final day of the regular season in 1959.

What all the baseball world was awaiting was Warren Spahn's 300th victory. The kid from Buffalo, the young southpaw that Casey Stengel had farmed out for refusing to throw at Pee Wee Reese, was now a baseball centenarian on the brink of joining the immortals of the game—men like Cy Young, Walter Johnson, Grover Cleveland Alexander, Christy Mathewson, most recently (1941) Lefty Grove, all Hall of Famers—among the distinguished group of 300-game winners.

The anticipation and pregame hoopla were vexing, but once Spahn got onto the pitching rubber he was fine. He was so fine that fans began to wonder if they might witness their idol's third no-hitter—for three and two-thirds innings no Chicago Cubs

302

batter managed a base hit. With two out in the fourth, though, clean-up hitter George Altman lined a single to centerfield to dispel those hopes. Once more the goal at hand was the victory.

Spahn continued to shut out the Cubs, but rookie Jack Curtis kept the Braves scoreless too, until the last of the fifth, and then his defense betrayed him. Joe Torre hit a line drive to left that Billy Williams ran in for, but as Williams was about to make the catch, he slipped on the wet grass, the ball caromed off his glove, and Torre was at second on the error. The next batter, Roy McMillan, singled to short rightfield, with Torre taking third. Spahn then belted a sacrifice fly and the Braves led, 1-0.

The Cubs only accomplished six hits against Spahn, all singles, but half of them were bunched in the sixth inning. Second baseman Don Zimmer led off with a sharp liner to leftcenter. Ron Santo grounded to McMillan, who tossed to Bolling for a forceout. Spahn retired Altman on a popup, but Williams singled to right. Andre Rodgers, whom the Braves had obtained for Al Dark the previous Halloween, then traded to Chicago for two pitchers, lined a base hit up the middle to bring home the tying run. Jerry Kindall then fouled out to end the rally, leaving the score tied at one.

Spahn's teammates continued to be baffled by the slow curves, changes, and lobs of Jack Curtis, while the Cubs continued to put men on base, as they did in every inning beginning with the third. In the seventh Al Heist was safe on an error by Frank Bolling, but Spahn used his patented pickoff move to first to erase him. In the eighth Zimmer slashed his second base hit of the night to lead off. Santo bunted him to second. Altman flied out to rightcenter, Zimmer tagging and moving to third. Again Spahn worked out of danger, though, getting Williams on a grounder to Bolling.

And then in the last of the eighth it was Gino Cimoli's moment. The journeyman outfielder, obtained from the Pittsburgh Pirates two months earlier in exchange for local favorite Johnny Logan, was playing for his fourth team in as many years, mostly without distinction. He was not a bad ballplayer—he had hit .293 as a regular with the Dodgers in 1957—but he had only medium speed, an average arm, and little power. Entering the game, in fact, he had the same number of career home runs, 29, as Spahn. In the previous five weeks with Milwaukee he had started exactly one game (and after tonight's ballgame would be back on the bench). Nevertheless, on one of those managerial whims that lead either to unemployment or, as in Casey Stengel's case, a permanent place in baseball's folklore, Charlie Dressen elected to pencil Cimoli into the lineup.

Cimoli had contributed a single in his first at-bat, but he reserved his piece de resistance for the eighth inning—he ripped one of Curtis' tosses high into the leftfield bleachers, his third home run of the year, to give Spahn and the Braves a 2-1 lead with an inning to go.

The crowd was hushed as Andre Rodgers stepped into the batter's box to start the ninth. They erupted when Rodgers looked at strike three, a fastball at the knees. Next came Jerry Kindall. The Cub shortstop lined the ball to centerfield. Cimoli charged the ball, lunged, skidded along the ground on his knees, and caught the ball inches above the grass, robbing Kindall of a base hit, or more if it had bounced past Cimoli. Again the crowd went wild. The next batter scheduled was Dick Bertell, but he was called back. In his place Ernie Banks, withheld from the lineup because of an eye injury, strode to the plate. Spahn quickly got two strikes on the slugger. The next offering was hit on the ground to Mathews, who scooped it up and fired across to first. The crowd gasped as the ball sailed over Adcock's outstretched glove and banked off the box seat railing.

With the tying run at first, Jim McAnany was sent to bat for the Cubs pitcher. Spahn fell behind with two outside pitches. McAnany lifted the third pitch to Aaron in shallow rightfield, and the game was over.

Spahn met Aaron at the edge of the infield to retrieve the baseball as a memento of the game that was "my biggest thrill." He then jogged over for a quick radio interview with the Cubs' announcer Lou Boudreau, waved a final time to the huge crowd standing and paying him tribute, and disappeared into the clubhouse for a champagne celebration, followed by a raucous party with his teammates at Ray Jackson's restaurant.

304

Time Capsule - August 20, 1961

"Whew, I'm sure glad to get that monkey off my back."

—Phillies Manager Gene Mauch

As the saying goes, "When you're hot, you're hot," and the Braves were. After stumbling along at two games above .500 up to the second All-Star Game, Dressen's uninspired automatons had finally caught fire. They had now won fourteen of seventeen, including their last nine in a row, all at home, beginning with Spahn's 300th win. The Milwaukee bombers were still hitting home runs, but the big improvement was the pitching, both starting and relief. The Braves had far out-distanced the fifth-place Cardinals and were rapidly closing in on the Giants and Dodgers. With six weeks to go even the leading Redlegs appeared catchable.

Yes, when you're hot, you're hot; and when you're not, you're the Philadelphia Phillies. Gene Mauch's sorry bunch from the City of Brotherly Love had come to Milwaukee on August 17 strapped to a nineteen-game losing streak, tied for the longest chain of defeats in modern National League history. It took eleven innings, but the Braves extended the Phillies' skein of failures to twenty in the series opener, then 21 behind a Lew Burdette six-hitter, then 22 behind Tony Cloninger. Having demolished the twentieth-century record for serial losing, the Phillies now had a chance in the series-ending Sunday double-header to equal the all-time continuous failure mark, 24 straight, woven by the Cleveland (N.L.) Spiders in 1899.

The first game matched the Phillies' Chris Short, laboring under a 4-9 record, against Warren Spahn, sub-par at 13-12 but winner of four straight and one of the driving forces of the recent Milwaukee renaissance. Spahn yielded a second-inning homer to

305

Bobby Malkmus after a base on balls to Pancho Herrera, temporarily putting Philadelphia in front, but the Braves tied the score in the fourth on an infield hit by Aaron, a walk to Adcock, and a long double by Frank Thomas.

In the bottom of the fifth the visitors demonstrated why they were record-setting losers. After two were out Eddie Mathews sliced a home run to the opposite field, a legitimate run by any standard, but then the Phillies took over. Hank Aaron singled and moved to second on a passed ball by catcher Albert Daniel George Kenders, who retired from major league baseball with more middle names than runs batted in. A wild pitch put Aaron on third, where he remained while Adcock drew a walk. Frank Thomas hit an easy popup to the pitcher, but Short dropped the ball and Aaron scored. Another wild pitch put Adcock on third, whence he promptly scored as shortstop Malkmus mishandled McMillan's ground ball. After that the Braves failed to score against rookie reliever Jack Baldschun, but there was no need. Spahn prevailed, 5-2.

With their 23rd straight loss safely under their belts, the Phillies sent Johnny Buzhardt against Carl Willey and the rampaging Braves, now boasting ten straight victories. Buzhardt was no world-beater, sporting a 3-13 record coming in, but one of his trio of successes had been a 4-3 win over the San Francisco Giants in the second game of a doubleheader on July 28—the last game Philadelphia had won. Now three weeks into the month, Mauch's team was 0 for August.

For the first two innings Willey was perfect; Buzhardt was not, but the game remained nothing-nothing. In the top of the third, catcher Clayton Dalrymple stroked a leadoff single off Willey. The Braves' righthander retired Malkmus, but Buzhardt, determined to earn a victory one way or another, crashed a two-base hit. Tony Taylor walked to load the bases. Willey got Johnny Callison to ground to Adcock, who threw to the plate to force Dalrymple for the second out. Tony Gonzalez then bounced to McMillan to end the Phillie threat. In the last of the third McMillan banged a home run off the leftfield foul pole to give Milwaukee a 1-0 head start.

In the next round the Phillies got to Willey. Former Brave (also White Sock and Athletic) Wes Covington greeted his old teammate with a home run. Lee Walls doubled, Dalrymple singled, and Buzhardt had a 2-1 lead to protect. The lead became 3-1 in the sixth when Walls and Dalrymple got hits again and Malkmus hit a sacrifice fly. The Braves halved the margin in the seventh on singles by Aaron and Adcock and a forceout by Frank Thomas, with Aaron scoring.

The Phillies put the game out of reach, though, and put their losing streak in the past tense, with a four-run outburst in the eighth against Bob Hendley, who had entered in the seventh after Willey went out for a pinch-hitter. Don Demeter singled to lead off. Righthand batter Ken Walters pinch-hit for Covington against the southpaw Hendley, and he also singled. Walls forced Walters at second and Dalrymple walked to load the bases. Dressen replaced Hendley with Don Nottebart. Malkmus welcomed him with a short single, driving in Walls and leaving the bases loaded and the score 4-2.

The batter due up was pitcher Buzhardt with one out; Mauch faced the choice, pinch-hitter or no pinch-hitter. He chose to let his pitcher hit—sort of. What he actually chose was one of baseball's most spectacular plays, a suicide squeeze. Walls broke from third and sprinted hellbent for home plate. That meant Buzhardt must bunt the ball or the runner was an easy out. The Braves had anticipated the squeeze, though, so Nottebart did what baseball protocol demands in that situation—he threw at the batter's head! This forces the hitter to duck out of the way or get beaned. Incredibly, Buzhardt did neither. He held up his bat, almost vertically, and somehow made sufficient contact to poke the ball into fair territory. In doing so he fell backward and was an easy out at first, but Walls scored to make it a 5-2 game. Tony Taylor then singled home two more, and the game was all but over.

The Braves tried to come back, scoring on a walk, an out, and a hit in the eighth and on an Adcock home run in the ninth, but 7-4 was as close as they could get. The streaks were over.

After the game it was pointed out to manager Mauch that the 23-game losing streak had been ended by Buzhardt, whose uniform number was 23. Mauch's reply was, "I should have started (pitching coach) Bob Lemon a long time ago. He wears number 2."

1961 Swan Songs

"And put some ice cream on it."

—Johnny Logan, after ordering pie a la mode

The Milwaukee Braves' second bonus player, signed a week after Joey Jay, was Mel Roach. Like Jay, Roach was hampered by his premature introduction to the National League and lack of minor league training. As a result his contribution to the Braves was minimal in six-plus seasons. For a time in early 1958 he was the apparent answer to the Braves' second base problem, hitting over .300, but a knee injury finished his season and, effectively, his career. His greatest value to the team came in leaving it, in exchange for Frank Thomas in May, 1961.

Roach's final day as a Brave was a Sunday doubleheader at County Stadium against the Cincinnati Reds on May 7, 1961. The day was a disaster for Charlie Dressen's club, a double loss by the Braves (5-4 and 4-0) that plunged them into sixth place in the standings, their lowest point in seven years. Roach played both games in leftfield, going 0 for 3 in the opener with a run scored and a sacrifice, and one for four, a single, in the nightcap. He left for Chicago the next day with a meager .167 batting average.

Five weeks later the Braves traded another player, this one with much deeper roots in the history of the franchise. Johnny Logan had been Milwaukee's regular shortstop from the beginning until the acquisition of Roy McMillan in mid-December, 1960. He had been a solid hitter and, in 1953 and 1954, the best fielding shortstop in the National League. To the fans, though, he was much more—a blue-collar ballplayer, a scrapper, a fighter willing to tackle Hal Jeffcoat of the Reds or Don Drysdale of the Dodgers or, perhaps most memorably of all, Vern Bickford of his own team.

The last participation of Logan's Milwaukee affiliation occurred on June 6, 1961, in Cincinnati's Crosley Field. The Braves lost the ballgame, 7-3, and again dropped back into sixth place. Milwaukee hitters produced thirteen base hits in the game, but sloppy baserunning held them to three runs, and Chi Chi Olivo's second consecutive relief pitching failure doomed the Braves to their second straight loss. Logan batted for Claude Raymond in the eighth inning with runners on second and third and one out. He hit a slow-bouncing ball that winning pitcher Bob Purkey grabbed and threw to the catcher to tag Joe Torre for the second out. Purkey got out of the inning, and nine days later Logan was traded to the Pirates for Gino Cimoli.

Milwaukee Journal Photo

Battling Johnny Logan anchored the infield throughout the 50's.

1962

"I will definitely never manage again."

—Birdie Tebbetts, October 11, 1958

The National League ran amok in 1962. After 86 years of relative sanity, the league expanded, creating new clubs for Houston and New York. The transplanted Dodgers settled into their new showplace in Los Angeles' Chavez Ravine after a protracted legal fight. The co-transplanted Giants entered their third season in the wind tunnel that is San Francisco's Candlestick Park. The newborn Houston Colt .45's sweltered in the subtropical Texas humidity in a mosquito-ridden minor league playground. The New York Mets, baseball's answer to the Keystone Kops, performed their vaudevillian shenanigans in upper Manhattan's venerable Polo Grounds.

The traditions of the national pastime continued to be chiseled away. The National League's eight-team, 154-game format, a fixture since the turn of the century, was distorted into a ten-team, 162-game structure, following by one year the example of the American League. In the process the westward migration begun by the Braves took another giant step, and most portentous of all to a baseball purist, the seeds were sown which would grow into Sunday night games, indoor baseball, and "artificial turf."

In a scheme concocted both to fill the rosters of the league's new entrants and to enrich the owners of the existing ballclubs, the league held a "draft" (sale) of ballplayers the day after the Yankees finished beating the Reds in the 1961 World Series. Each team was allowed to protect its nucleus of regulars, then make available for purchase by the Mets and Colts a group of has-beens, never-wases, minor league prospects, and bench-warmers.

310

The Braves' contributions to the fledgling teams were modest but not insignificant. The Mets bought outfielder John DeMerit, a fizzled Milwaukee bonus phenom who appeared in just fourteen games with the New York, hit .188, and retired from baseball at the start of June. However, the Mets also purchased utility man Felix Mantilla, who played three infield positions (not all at once) acceptably and batted a solid .275 with eleven home runs.

To the Houston club the Braves lost (sold) three players: minor league pitcher Paul Roof, who had played the previous year at Cedar Rapids and who would never work an inning in the big leagues; Merritt Ranew, a catcher from the Louisville farm club who would hit .234 for Houston as a back-up backstop; and Al Spangler, a once-promising leftfielder who had played intermittently in Milwaukee for two seasons but who became a starter with the Colts and batted .285, second-high on the team.

Houston's group of cast-offs surprised the baseball world by finishing in eighth place, higher than the 86-year-old Chicago Cubs. They were helped considerably by the fine pitching of Dick Farrell, a reliever-turned-starter whom the Braves had coveted for two years for their bullpen. The Colt .45's also obtained a top-notch fireman on May 8 when they purchased Don McMahon from the Braves. McMahon had become disgruntled and asked to be traded because manager Birdie Tebbetts was not using him often and because Tebbetts thought McMahon's fastball was gone. McMahon appeared 51 times for Houston, winning five games, saving eight, and compiling an earned run average of 1.53, best in the majors. On June 7 McMahon gained revenge for what he perceived as unfair treatment by beating the Braves, 3-2, pitching one perfect inning and striking out the last two batters with the fastball Tebbetts told him he had lost.

If the performance of the Colt .45's was a surprise, the performance of the New York Mets was a shock, but in the other direction. People expected the Mets to be bad, but they overestimated them. Under the guidance of Casey Stengel, released by the Yankees after the 1960 World Series as being too old ("I'll never make the mistake of being seventy again," Stengel said at the time), New York's replacement for the absconded Giants and Dodgers turned out to be an awful ballclub, setting new standards for losing. They lost a record 120 games, finished sixty and one-half games out of first, and achieved elimination from pennant contention on August 7, the earliest ever.

The Mets' futility was best represented by "Marvelous Marv" Throneberry, their first baseman who ran the bases without

Birdie Tebbetts (on right) with coaches (clockwise from Tebbetts)
Bill Adair, Andy Pafko, Jimmy Dykes, and Whit Wyatt

touching them, ran down a baserunner while the winning run scored, and dropped the ball with sufficient frequency to edge out Pittsburgh's Dick "Dr. Strangeglove" Stuart as the league's worst-fielding first sacker. (On Throneberry's birthday Stengel told him, "We was going to get you a birthday cake, but we figured you'd drop it.")

The Mets were inept, but their front office was ept enough to inveigle the Braves' front office into giving up Frank Thomas, the slugger who was one of the bright spots of the 1961 season after his acquisition from the Chicago Cubs. The Mets obtained Thomas for a player to be named later who turned out to be Gus Bell, an over-the-hill outfielder who hit for a respectable average for Milwaukee for a half-season but who paled beside Thomas, who led New York with 34 home runs and 94 RBI's. The loss of Thomas left a three-year void in the Braves' outfield.

Milwaukee's decisions to part with McMahon and Thomas were part of their charge to Tebbetts to rebuild. After standing

312

pat with the same core of veterans for nearly a decade, the Braves clearly needed fresh blood. Unfortunately, the new plasma that was transfused was inferior to the old team's lifeblood that it replaced. Even the choice of Tebbetts as field manager was a curious one. Before being named Milwaukee's Executive Vice-President following the 1958 World Series, Birdie had been a hated rival of the Braves. He was constantly squawking about Lew Burdette's alleged spitball, and his team often fought and exchanged beanballs with the Braves. Some Milwaukee ballplayers and most Milwaukee fans despised him, and his managing background offered little to suggest that his replacing the tyrannical Dressen would be either popular or successful. As history records, it was neither.

The refurbishing of the Braves included the continuing erosion of the original Milwaukee unit. On April 30 the Braves swapped hard-throwing righthander Bob Buhl, age 33, to the Cubs for Jack Curtis, a 25-year-old lefthanded junk pitcher. As in the Frank Thomas deal, the Braves came up short—Buhl won a dozen games for Chicago, four of them against his former team, while Curtis earned just four victories, although he pitched well in relief a number of times.

One deal that helped the Braves was the December, 1961, exchange of three minor leaguers—Manny Jiminez, Ed Charles, and Joe Azcue—for pitcher Bob Shaw (and throw-in Lou Klimchock) from the Kansas City A's. Shaw had the best control in the league, won fifteen and lost nine, and finished second with a 2.80 earned run average. The price for Shaw was not cheap, though. Jiminez hit .301 in the Kansas City outfield, Charles played third base regularly and batted .288 with seventeen home runs, and Azcue served as an adequate second-string catcher. As part of the youth movement, the Shaw trade was a step backward—Shaw was nearly 29, while the three ex-farmhands were 23, 26, and 22 respectively. As far as long-term pitching help, Shaw was not it. The following year he was a relief man; the year after that he was gone in a trade to San Francisco.

The Braves' other roster additions came primarily from their farm system. Mack Jones received another try in rightfield but was disappointing, striking out 100 times in 91 games. Howie Bedell started in leftfield in the season opener but hit only .196 in a part-time role. Mike Krsnich played in left three times but managed just one hit. Henry Aaron's younger brother Tommie was utilized as a part-time first baseman and sometime outfielder, but his skills never approached those of his brother. Amado Samuel fielded adequately as a substitute shortstop and second baseman but hit for neither power nor average. Milwaukee native Bob Uecker made his major league bow at catcher but proved more adept at comedy than baseball.

Denis Menke, the former Iowa high school star who had signed for a bonus higher than the salary of the President of the United States, sampled major league pitching for the first time, without distinction. In mid-season the Braves acquired Cleveland infielder Ken Aspromonte to shore up their injury-riddled lineup, and he batted .291 for them in a reserve role. In mid-summer they also obtained outfielder Lou Johnson, who proved to be an above-average hitter but one without power. By the following spring both Aspromonte and Johnson were playing elsewhere.

Besides Bob Shaw and Jack Curtis, the other pitchers the Braves added all came from their minor league affiliates. Cecil Butler showed promise but was plagued by a bone spur on his elbow, allowing him just nine pitching chances. Hank Fischer appeared 29 times in relief and demonstrated a good fastball but little else, especially the control a short reliever needs. The most impressive rookie pitcher was Denver Lemaster, like Bob Hendley a southpaw heir-apparent to Warren Spahn. Working primarily as a starter, Lemaster compiled a 3.01 ERA in 86 and two-thirds innings, with his best effort a six-hit shutout of the Phillies on September 12.

Finally in mid-September the Braves called up Jim Constable, a 29-year-old lefty with mostly minor league experience. Constable saved a win for Carl Willey; threw a spectacular five-hit, no-walk shutout at the Pirates for his only complete game in the big leagues; and lost an 8-2 decision to Pittsburgh in a game in which Bob Uecker's dropped popup off the bat of former Brave Johnny Logan led to three unearned runs. Constable never pitched for the Braves again.

As a group the Milwaukee pitching staff was in a state of flux. Spahn still anchored the starting rotation, but the other members of the Braves' old reliable triumvirate were essentially absent. Lew Burdette still started some games, but only about half his typical allotment, and Buhl now toiled with the Cubs. Bob Shaw proved a capable substitute for most of the season, although his last victory occurred on August 17. The third spot, though, assumed by Hendley because there was no one else, was rather weak (Hendley was 11-13), and the other young starters—Cloninger and Lemaster, occasionally Ron Piche—were unseasoned and bothered by illness or minor injuries.

The bullpen was sometimes effective , often not. Second- year man Claude Raymond and ex-Cub Jack Curtis provided good relief most often, but the others—Don Nottebart, Carl Willey, Hank Fischer, sometimes Piche—were not reliable. No one adequately filled the shoes of the departed Don McMahon, as the Braves' 32 one-run losses illustrate.

For the first time in seven years, Warren Spahn failed to win twenty or more games, but the fault was not entirely his. He led the league in complete games, as usual, with 22; his ratio of walks

Warren Spahn hurls to Orlando Cepeda.

315

per innings pitched was third-best in the league, the second-best of his career; and his earned run average was 3.04, nearly the same as his career average. The problem was lack of hitting support. Eight of Spahn's fourteen losses were games he deserved to win. Six of those were complete games, another was lost with two out in the ninth, and the other was an eight-inning job. Three of the games were lost 3-2, three were lost 2-1, one was 3-1, and the other was 2-0. With ordinary run production by his team-mates, Spahn could well have had his biggest winning season ever.

Milwaukee Journal Photo

Eddie Mathews fields a grounder.

The problem for Spahn and all the Milwaukee hurlers was that the Braves simply did not get on base enough to win. Led by Hank Aaron with 45, the Braves slammed 181 home runs, second to San Francisco's 204, but too often the bases were empty at the time. The Milwaukee team average was an anemic .252, the lowest since their Boston residency and the lowest among National League teams in 1962 except for the two expansion clubs.

316

Aaron was as usual among the league leaders at .323, and Del Crandall made a strong comeback from his shoulder injury to hit a career-high .297. Most of the team, however, slumped. Ed Mathews averaged only .265, Joe Adcock dropped to .248, and Lee Maye struggled at .244, the lowest he would ever hit. The Braves' pinch-hitting was also terrible, so bad that pitcher Jack Curtis was twice called on to pinch-hit (once successfully). Milwaukee's fielding was the best in the National League for the second straight year, but the offense was not sufficient to propel the team higher than fifth place.

One other aspect of the game in which Tebbetts' club was inadequate was baserunning. They lacked the team speed to take the extra base, to put pressure on opponents' fielders, and most of all to steal bases. The game was evolving into one of speed, hard-throwing starting pitchers, and relief specialists. The prime example of this evolution was the Los Angeles Dodgers, led by fireballing hurlers Don Drysdale and Sandy Koufax, bullpen artist Ron Perranoski, and fleet-footed Maury Wills and Willie Davis. Wills rewrote the record book with 104 steals, more than any other team in the majors and nearly twice the total stolen by Milwaukee's flatfoots, who ranked eighth in the league.

The Braves' bench was clearly deficient, evidenced by their poor pinch-hitting, making them all the more vulnerable to crippling injuries. In 1962 their injuries were all comparatively minor—no season-ending fractures or muscle tears occurred—but a series of nagging hurts and illnesses kept the Braves struggling most of the year. Spahn had the first sore arm of his career. Only Aaron was able to start as many as 150 games, and only he and Mathews and McMillan started as many as 120. The injuries were minor, but collectively they were devastating.

The team's on-field difficulties predictably led to a continued decline in attendance. The opening day turnout of 30,001, smallest for a Milwaukee season premiere, was a clear indicator, and "crowds" under 10,000 became the rule rather than the exception. An Easter gathering of 6571 set a new low for a Sunday contest, and a cozy enrollment of 2746 rattled around County Stadium on May 10 to set a new standard for avoidance of Milwaukee's ballclub.

The front office tried special promotions and events, and the County Board rescinded the ban on beer carry-ins on June 8. On August 3 the management stationed TV sets around the stadium so fans attending the Braves game could also watch the football game between the Green Bay Packers and the College All-Stars (the Braves game was rained out, but many fans stayed to watch television). Lou Perini even joined the twentieth century and allowed fifteen road contests to be televised. Nothing, however, could lure people into the stands until September 3 when a Family Night sponsored by a local grocery chain enticed 33,228 smart shoppers at 39 cents a head to watch Joey Jay shut out the home team, 3-0.

Actually the Braves' season was doomed even before the team played a home game. They suffered five straight losses on the West Coast, three to the Giants and two to the Dodgers, before finally experiencing victory, the worst start in their franchise history. Then they lost a game in Cincinnati, so when Spahn took the mound for the home opener, his team was 1-6, in eighth place, five games out of first. They were to get closer to first only once, on April 28, when Cecil Butler earned his first big-league victory as the Braves defeated Houston for their fifth win in a row. The surge left Milwaukee four and one-half games out of first, but the next day they lost to the Colts, beginning a four-game losing streak that dropped them nine and one-half behind. After May 18 that was as close as they got. They did not achieve a .500 record until July 2, after 78 games, and it was July 22 before they edged above the .500 level. After that it was August 29 before they climbed briefly into the league's first division, and September 17 before they reached the upper division to stay.

After the first All-Star Game, won by the National League, 3-1, on July 10, the Braves did finally play respectable baseball. Led by a resurgent Warren Spahn (who won ten of thirteen decisions beginning on July 21) and the slugging of Henry Aaron (who put together a 25-game hitting streak in August), Milwaukee won seven straight, their longest string of successes, beginning July 21, and won eight of nine between August 4 and August 11. Their horrendous start, however, had precluded any serious thoughts of pennant contention. The Braves bottomed out on September 13, 21 and one-half games behind the league leaders. Only a closing rush of eleven wins in the last fourteen games enabled Tebbetts' ballclub to finish with a deceptive 86-76 record and avoid the club's first finish out of the first division.

Five days after the 1962 season ended, Birdie Tebbetts resigned as Milwaukee manager to take the manager's job with the Cleveland Indians. Two weeks later Braves' President John McHale announced the signing of Bobby Bragan, the former Pittsburgh Pirates manager, as the new skipper of the Braves. Bragan had previously been set to join Tebbetts' coaching staff. As had been the case when Tebbetts was hired, the Braves were getting a former National League manager whom the Milwaukee

318

fans did not particularly like. Moreover they thought of him as a buffoon, remembering his orange juice incident at County Stadium the night before Pittsburgh fired him [see Time Capsule, July 31, 1957].

The year's *coup de grace* for Milwaukee baseball fans occurred on November 16 when it was announced that Lou Perini had sold the Milwaukee Braves to a syndicate of Chicago investors, plus John McHale, for $5,500,000. Perini retained a ten percent share of the club, but the controlling interest now belonged to a group of young, aggressive Illinois businessmen. On that day no one could have foreseen the ramifications the club's sale would ultimately have. Perini, however, offered his assurance to Milwaukee fans that the new owners were "your kind of people." These reassuring words came from the same man who, on July 5, 1951, told a reporter, "The Braves are going to stay right here in Boston." And that fount of wisdom known as Warren Giles, President of the National League, proclaimed that it was his belief that the team's sale was "for the good of the club." Giles further said, "I know Lou Perini would not sell baseball interests to anyone who would not be a credit to our league."

Milwaukee Journal Photo

Bob Buhl and Billy Martin at Elks Club dinner

319

1962 Nemesis - Bob Buhl

"There's no reason for me to blast the Braves and I'm not going to."

—Bob Buhl

And then there were five. On April 30, 1962, the Braves traded Bob Buhl to the Cubs, leaving just five members of the original cast. Buhl had returned from military service to join Charlie Grimm's new Milwaukee edition in spring of 1953. He threw a two-hitter in his first start and followed it up with a shutout. For nearly the next decade he was a key part of the Braves' rotation of starting pitchers, winning 109 ballgames. For his first eight seasons in Milwaukee he compiled a .621 winning percentage, the best among active league hurlers.

Buhl was not a subtle pitcher. He threw hard and challenged the hitters, walking nearly as many as he struck out. Six times in nine years with the Braves his earned run average was among the league's ten best. He fired a one-hitter and four two-hitters as a Brave, and in the world championship year of 1957, he was arguably the best pitcher in the National League, with an 18-7 record and a 2.74 ERA.

Some teams could hit Buhl and some could not. The Dodgers, from 1953 through 1959 especially, could not. Buhl compiled a 19-8 record against the Bums of Brooklyn and Los Angeles during those years, tying a record by beating them eight times in 1956. The Redlegs, on the other hand, used Buhl for batting practice. So futile was Buhl against Cincinnati that he rarely faced them, losing to them seven times in nine-plus seasons with the Braves while winning just once, on August 14, 1957, in a game in which the Braves scored eight runs in the ninth inning at Crosley Field.

After Buhl was traded to the Cubs, he found a new team to

320

torment—the Braves. He started six games against his former team in 1962 and beat them four times, fashioning a 2.49 ERA against them. Had he been with a team less pathetic than the ninth-place Chicagoans, he might conceivably have won all six attempts. His two losses derived from lack of team support: on May 29 Buhl lasted only three innings in an 11-9 defeat, but his stone-fingered accomplices let in six unearned runs; on August 9 Buhl allowed just one run on six hits, with no walks, but lost 1-0 to Tony Cloninger, with a save by Claude Raymond.

Buhl's four triumphs over the Tebbetts version of the Braves were well-deserved. On May 24 he worked eight innings and allowed three runs, two of them earned, in beating Bob Hendley, 4-3, with a ninth-inning assist from knuckleballer Barney Schultz. On June 29 Buhl and Don Elston combined for a 4-0 win, the Cubs' first shutout of the year. On July 8 Buhl outpitched Lew Burdette, 7-5, taking a 7-2 lead into the ninth before requiring relief. Finally on August 24 Buhl avenged his 1-0 loss to Cloninger by beating him 7-2 while striking out seven Milwaukee batters.

Besides earning a large measure of satisfaction in 1962 by beating his ex-teammates with regularity, Buhl earned a place in baseball's record book with his bat, or rather his inability to use it. In 70 official times at bat, once as a Brave and 69 times as a Cub, Buhl failed to get even one base hit. When it came to not hitting, nobody did it better than Bob Buhl.

Time Capsule - May 12, 1962

"[I drafted Hobie Landrith first because] you gotta have a catcher. If you don't have a catcher, you'll have all passed balls."

—Casey Stengel

In 1962 the Milwaukee Braves began playing "Requiem for a Heavyweight." After nearly a decade of main events, they began consorting with stumblebums and castoffs, part of the permanent undercard. Braves fans were reluctant to admit it, but the signs clearly indicated that the heroes of Beertown had fallen from their pedestal and landed in the low-rent district. On Saturday, May 12, 1962, at New York's decrepit Polo Grounds, the evidence became incontrovertible—the Braves were swept in a doubleheader by the month-old collection of remnants called the New York Mets.

Casey Stengel's misfits had begun their existence with nine straight losses before achieving a victory. Their terrible start had enabled the Braves, experiencing their own worst start, to avoid the cellar despite winning only two of their first ten games. A month into the season, Birdie Tebbetts and his club were looking to take a pair from the Mets, now 5-17, and surpass the .500 barrier for the first time. Milwaukee ace Warren Spahn, off to a characteristically slow start at 3-3, was the Braves' starter in the opener, opposing Roger Craig, on his way to a league-high 24 losses.

In the second inning Del Crandall put the Braves in front with a long home run that cleared the second deck in leftfield. The score stayed 1-0 until the fifth when Milwaukee added a second run on a base hit by Frank Bolling, a stolen base on which Bolling took third because of a bad throw from catcher Harry Chiti, and a run-scoring single to center by Spahn.

322

"The Great Profile" poses for photos.

New York got one back in the sixth as shortstop Elio Chacon singled with one out, advanced on a ground out, and scored on a double by ex-Brave Frank Thomas. The Braves had two more scoring chances, but neither one reached fruition. Spahn led off the eighth with a double but was left stranded at second; Hank Aaron walked to start the ninth, moved up on a grounder, but expired at second as Bolling and Menke failed. Spahn took a 2-1 lead to the last of the ninth.

Gil Hodges singled to open the Mets' final stanza. With relief pitcher Craig Anderson due to hit, Stengel sent Cliff Cook to pinch-hit. Spahn struck him out. Johnny DeMerit, the ex-Braves' bonus baby, was scheduled next, but Gus Bell batted in his place and popped up for the second out. Needing one more out, Spahn faced substitute catcher Hobie Landrith, whom the Mets had unaccountably made their first pick in the October, 1961 draft to stock their team. A lefthand batter and a lifetime .230's hitter,

Landrith seemed a likely candidate to be replaced by a pinch-hitter. Stengel, however, let him hit. The veteran catcher swatted a 280-foot pop fly down the rightfield line, fair by a few feet. In nine ballparks in the National League, Landrith's lazy fly was a putout for the rightfielder to end the game; in the Polo Grounds, with a 275-foot rightfield line, it was a game-winning two-run home run that looked like a 400-foot wallop in the box score. The crowd of 19,748, nearly the season's largest for a Mets home game, celebrated in World Series fashion.

In the nightcap the Braves sent Carl Willey, in the throes of a three-year slump, against the Mets' Bob Moorhead, a rookie destined to appear in 47 big-league games but never earn a victory. Willey wasted no time in continuing his slump, giving up a home run to Jim Hickman, the leadoff man; walking Chacon; and yielding a single to ex-teammate Felix Mantilla. Birdie Tebbetts quickly sent for Tony Cloninger, who closed down the rally without further damage but gave up a run in the second on a walk to Landrith, a sacrifice, and a single.

Meanwhile the Milwaukee hitters were taking a long time to figure out Moorhead. For three and two-thirds innings the New York rookie had a no-hitter, although in true Mets form, his teammates had allowed the Braves to score a run. Mack Jones drew a base on balls, then went to third as a pickoff attempt eluded Marvelous Marv Throneberry, the first baseman. Henry Aaron drove Jones in with a sacrifice fly to make the score 2-1 Mets. Frank Bolling ended the incipient no-hitter with a single but did not score.

In the last of the fourth the Mets added to their lead with a leadoff single by Landrith, a walk, and a bloop single behind second by Mantilla, which either centerfielder Aaron or second baseman Bolling could have caught but which neither one did. Mantilla's hit gave New York a 4-1 lead.

Milwaukee fought back to take the lead in the fifth. With one out McMillan singled. Then as an illustration of the Braves' woeful pinch-hitting corps (depleted further because of a shoulder injury to Eddie Mathews), pitcher Jack Curtis batted for Cloninger—and singled. (Tebbetts knew that Curtis had hit two homers with the Cubs the previous year; he had no way of knowing that in 1966 Cloninger would hit two grand slams in the same game.) Tommie Aaron scored McMillan with a sacrifice fly. Jones tripled home Aaron, and Aaron's older brother homered to put his team ahead 5-4 and send Moorhead to the showers.

Pinch-hitter Curtis stayed on to pitch and gave up two runs in the sixth on a walk, a triple by Chacon, and a base hit by Thomas.

The Braves regained the lead, 7-6, with two runs in the eighth. Jones and Hank Aaron hit back-to-back doubles, Joe Adcock made a perfect sacrifice bunt, and Bolling hit a sacrifice fly. Don Nottebart came in to pitch the eighth for Milwaukee and gave up the tying run on a walk, a sacrifice, and a base hit by Chacon.

The Braves failed to score in the ninth, and Nottebart, for whom Mike Krsnich had batted, was replaced by hard-throwing Hank Fischer. The rookie reliever retired the dangerous Thomas, but Gil Hodges swung late on a fastball and hit an opposite-field home run to give New York an 8-7 win and their first sweep of a doubleheader.

The twin loss to the team already acclaimed as one of the worst of all time not only kept the Braves from passing the .500 mark. It also dispelled any of the team's delusions of adequacy and served notice to Milwaukee fans that this 162-game season would be the longest their heroes had ever played, in more ways than one.

Time Capsule - May 20, 1962

"You don't mind so much when [Frank] Thomas hurts you with his bat...but Mantilla beating you with a homer..."

—Birdie Tebbetts

They did it again. On Sunday, May 20, 1962, eight days after losing a doubleheader to Casey Stengel's Mets in the Polo Grounds, the Braves dropped another twin-bill to the New Yorkers, again taking an early lead, then collapsing in the late innings. This time a County Stadium crowd of 12,672, the largest gathering since opening day, was in attendance to witness first-hand why their idols were mired in the second division. By the middle of the second game most of the fans had seen enough and had fled, leaving the Milwaukee ballplayers to endure another humiliation in relative seclusion.

What the diehard patrons saw merely confirmed what they had already known—the Braves' front office had made a big mistake by dealing leftfielder Frank Thomas to the Mets. Thomas had represented one of the Braves' shrewdest trades ever when they obtained him from the Cubs in May of 1961 for Mel Roach. Thomas had slugged 25 homers for Milwaukee and plugged the enormous leak in the outfield. Unfortunately he arrived just before Tebbetts and the "youth movement" to which the Braves were committed. Emulating the Dodgers, the Milwaukee brain trust decided they needed younger, faster ballplayers, so Thomas became expendable. His subsequent absence hurt the Braves throughout 1962, a fact demonstrated on this dismal day.

In the doubleheader Thomas produced four hits, two in each game, including a home run, and drove in five runs. Those contributions gave him three home runs, a triple, a double, and three singles in the four-game Milwaukee-New York series and raised his season totals (for six weeks) to eleven home runs and

326

27 RBI's, statistics surpassing those of any player on the Braves' roster. The Braves, meanwhile, started two leftfielders in the doubleheader—Howie Bedell and Tommie Aaron—whose combined career home run total would never exceed thirteen.

The first ballgame of the afternoon pitted the Mets' Bob Miller (on his way to a record-tying 0-12 start) against Milwaukee's Jack Curtis, starting his first game since his acquisition from the Cubs. Curtis gave up a run-scoring double to Thomas in the first inning but settled down after that while his mates built him a lead. The Braves did so at once, scoring four times in the bottom of the first on an infield scratch by Bedell, a base on balls by Roy McMillan, an RBI single by Henry Aaron, and a three-run homer by Mack Jones. In the sixth the home club added another run after two were out. Denis Menke was hit by a Miller pitch, advanced on a single by second baseman Amado Samuel, and scored on a base hit by Curtis, giving the Braves' lefty a 5-1 lead to carry to the eighth inning.

New York halved the margin in the eighth on two singles, a double, and a fielder's choice, but Curtis still boasted a 5-3 advantage with just three outs to go. Then the Mets got nasty. Pinch-hitter Richie Ashburn singled, Jim Hickman doubled, pinch-hitter Ed Bouchee walked, and Thomas brought two men home with a single off reliever Hank Fischer, tying the score, 5-5. A few moments later Roy McMillan, the National League's best fielding shortstop in 1961, let a grounder go through his legs, two more runs scored, and the Mets led 7-5. The Braves got a run in the last of the ninth when Tommie Aaron walked and stole second and brother Henry doubled him in, but Del Crandall flied out to end the game and give ex-Milwaukee relief specialist Ken MacKenzie his second straight win against his former employer.

In the nightcap Tony Cloninger, in his first starting assignment of the year, gave up a run in the first inning, and once again the culprit was Frank Thomas. After Hickman doubled to lead off, Elio Chacon sacrificed him to third. Cloninger retired Felix Mantilla, but Thomas pushed a bunt past the mound and beat it out for a run-scoring single—this from the man deemed too old and slow to play in the Milwaukee outfield!

In the Milwaukee first a walk to McMillan, a base hit by Mathews, and a fielder's choice grounder by Henry Aaron tied the score. In the second Menke hit a home run with Joe Torre aboard to give Cloninger a 3-1 lead that lasted until the fourth. Then Charlie Neal doubled home Mantilla and Bouchee to knot the score at three. The game stayed at that score until the top of the seventh.

First Neal struck again, driving a Cloninger pitch into the bleachers for a 4-3 New York lead. The Braves' righthander retired two batters and should have escaped without further damage, but a walk and two singles, one of them an easy fly that Tommie Aaron (in Frank Thomas' old position) lost in the sun, added another run and drove Cloninger out in favor of Bob Hendley. The reliever was met with a three-run homer by Mantilla. With the game as good as over, Thomas added the final insult with another home run, making the score 9-3. The Braves tried to make a game of it, scoring once in the seventh off starter Al Jackson and twice in the ninth against Bob Moorhead, but with the bases loaded Roger Craig came in and retired Hank Aaron on a deep fly to end the game.

The ignominy of two doubleheader losses in eight days to the 1962 New York Mets defies description. Casey Stengel's club lost more games that year than any major league team before or since. The combined season record of the six pitchers who faced the Braves on May 20 and May 27 was 27 wins and 79 losses.

Immediately following the second double defeat the Mets completed the Frank Thomas deal by sending outfielder Gus Bell to the Braves. Bell was to perform quite well for Milwaukee, batting .285 in 79 games, but he was no Frank Thomas, hitting six home runs for the year compared to Thomas' 34. The final irony of the trade was that the departure of Thomas in the "youth movement" made room for Bell—who was older than Thomas by seven months.

Time Capsule - June 12, 1962

"I had good stuff and I made the pitches I wanted to make."

—Lew Burdette

Trivia Question: Which brother combination hit more home runs than any other? Answer: The Aarons, Henry and Tommie, a total of 768. Tommie, the younger, larger, and lesser, contributed thirteen of that number, eight in his rookie season of 1962. Three times that year the siblings Aaron homered in the same game: the last time on August 14 in Cincinnati in a 5-4 Milwaukee victory; the second time on July 12 at home, both in a five-run ninth-inning rally (Tommie's a pinch hit, Henry's a grand slam) to beat the Cardinals, 8-6; and initially at County Stadium on Tuesday night, June 12, in a 15-2 blowout of the Los Angeles Dodgers.

In the last instance the league-leading Dodgers came to town fourteen games ahead of the sixth-place Braves. The home team had spent the weekend splitting back-to-back doubleheaders with the third-pace Pittsburgh Pirates, winning a pair on Saturday, losing twice on Sunday. After two months of struggling the Braves had yet to achieve a .500 record, even for one day. The pitching, except for the work of new member Bob Shaw, had been spotty, frequently awful, and the hitting had not been timely.

The Dodgers, in contrast, were riding high. They had beaten the Milwaukeeans in four of six previous meetings and showed every sign of returning to the World Series after a two-year absence. Walter Alston's club had been extensively renovated since its Brooklyn tenure, replacing the "Boys of Summer" with a new breed of athletes. Except for the pitching staff, the only vestige of the Flatbush era still in the lineup was third baseman Junior Gilliam. On the mound the Dodgers had a number of notable holdovers—Don Drysdale, Ed Roebuck, Sandy Koufax, and the elder statesman in years of service, lefty Johnny Podres, matched this night against Lew Burdette.

The contrast between the Braves and Dodgers was stark. Alston's team was mostly young, with only Gilliam among the regulars topping age 30. Birdie Tebbetts' club, meanwhile, was dominated by the post-30 generation. While the Dodgers were led by emerging youngsters—Frank Howard, 25; Tommy Davis, 23; Maury Wills, 29; Willie Davis, 22—the Braves had only Henry Aaron, at 28, as an under-thirty star. On the mound Alston had only reliever Ed Roebuck at 30; Tebbetts had Spahn, 41, and Burdette, 35. The Dodgers were a team on their ascendancy; the Braves were on the wane.

Another striking difference between the teams was that the Dodgers were characterized by speed, both afoot and on the mound. Wills was the greatest basestealer since Ty Cobb, perhaps the greatest ever, and Willie Davis was not far behind. For either man a slow grounder was as good as a double. For Dodger pitchers the fastball was the principal tool, with Drysdale and Koufax ranking one-two in league strikeouts and Stan Williams having ranked second in 1961 in strikeouts per inning. For the plodding Braves, though, the stolen base was an aberration—they ranked eighth in the league in 1962—and they also finished eighth in strikeouts, relying rather on breaking balls and control.

Despite the fact that the Dodgers were in first place, their visit to County Stadium drew only 10,376 fans, a far cry from five years before when their arrival guaranteed four times that number. The loyal burghers who did turn out on this night were treated to an immediate display of batting pyrotechnics. In the top of the first Los Angeles appeared ready to dismiss Burdette early. Wills led off by legging a triple to centerfield; Gilliam promptly doubled him home with a drive to rightcenter. Burdette retired Willie Davis but then hit Tommy Davis with a breaking ball. Fidgety Lew worked out of the inning, though, and in the bottom half his mates repaid the Dodgers many times over.

Podres retired the first two Milwaukee hitters, Tommie Aaron and Roy McMillan. (Tebbetts' batting order defies belief—the younger Aaron, barely a .200 hitter, was leading off, and McMillan, a .220 hitter the year before, was second. Small wonder the Braves hit so many bases-empty home runs.) Number three hitter Eddie Mathews bounced a fluke single off the bag at first. Henry Aaron singled, Jones and Crandall singled, and Gus Bell smashed his first home run as a Brave, a three-run shot that gave Burdette a 5-1 lead.

In the bottom of the second the Braves struck again. With a man on and two out, Mathews connected for a two-run home run

330

that ended Podres' evening and brought in Filomena Ortega. Hank Aaron greeted the new pitcher with another home run and Milwaukee enjoyed an 8-1 lead. The Braves added three more runs off Ortega in the third without benefit of a home run, and in the fourth Frank Bolling nicked Ortega for another circuit blast, a two-run job, to put the Braves in front 13-1.

With such lusty hitting support Burdette could have succeeded with a mediocre showing, but instead he was at his sharpest of the season. He had lost his place in the rotation for three weeks, regaining it only six days earlier against the Colt .45's, but on this evening his fastball was alive, his control was acute, and he retired nineteen Dodgers in a row from the time he hit Davis in the first until Wally Moon singled with two out in the seventh.

In a gesture akin to Red Auerbach's lighting of a victory cigar, Tebbetts sent in Lee Maye to bat for Henry Aaron in the last of the seventh. The Dodgers managed one more run off Burdette in the eighth, but in the home eighth Tommie Aaron poled a two-run homer off third Dodger hurler Ed Roebuck, making the score 15-2, the Braves' largest outpouring of runs since September 2, 1957, when they pulverized the Cubs, 23-10.

Burdette's easy outing, punctuated by eight strikeouts, earned him his fourth straight win of the season (after four initial losses) and broke a personal streak of ten straight defeats by the Dodgers at County Stadium, going back to July 13, 1956. Sadly for Tebbetts and his team, though, the 15-2 shellacking of the National League leaders did not signal the beginning of a trend—the following night they reverted to form and lost a heartbreaker (behind the unfortunate Spahn) to Los Angeles, 2-1, as Sandy Koufax belted the first home run of his eight-year career.

1962 Feat of Clay

"Isn't Crandall supposed to bat eighth?"

—Bob Hendley

From 1960 through 1962 the Chicago Cubs lost more games than any other team in baseball, but they led the league in managers. Seven men, beginning with recycled Charlie Grimm and ending with Charles Moreskonich (a.k.a. Charlie Metro), out of Nanty Glo, Pennsylvania, held the reins as the Cubbies tried to substitute quantity for quality in a revolving-door "head coach" scheme. With that kind of turnover it would have been understandable for the Cubs to be confused, but in Wrigley Field on July 6, 1962, it was the Braves who reached the pinnacle of confusion—they batted out of order.

With two out and nobody on base in the top of the second, outfielder Mack Jones was scheduled to bat next. He was not in the on-deck circle, though; Del Crandall had told him " I'm after Adcock," and Jones took the word of the all-star catcher. Neither bothered to check the lineup card, and neither did anyone in the dugout. Crandall took his place on deck, then stepped in against hurler Don Cardwell and drew a base on balls. Jones hit next and drilled a single to right, moving Crandall around to third. Cubs skipper Metro recognized what had happened and charged out of the dugout to inform umpire Stan Landes.

After a brief confab near home plate, Landes signaled Bob Hendley, due up next, out without even taking a pitch. He was the batter subsequent to the appeal, so he was the one out of order. Because Jones was the player who had advanced before the appeal, his single was nullified. Only Crandall's walk, because it was not appealed under rule 6.07(c), was allowed to stand.

Crandall's faux pas was finally rendered harmless in the tenth inning when Eddie Mathews followed an Ernie Banks error with a

332

two-run homer onto Sheffield Avenue, his third game-winning blast in five games, to give the Braves and Claude Raymond a 5-3 victory. Nevertheless, the blunder earned a unique place in Milwaukee baseball annals.

Milwaukee Journal Photo

Henry Aaron nimbly avoids an inside fastball.

1962 Swan Songs

"He's a pitcher now. There was a time when Bob [Buhl] was just a thrower."

—Pee Wee Reese

The Milwaukee Braves stayed in serious pennant contention from their arrival until late in 1960, primarily on the strength of their starting pitchers. Bob Buhl was a key part of that pitching rotation, winning 100 games during that time. His control could not match that of his counterparts Spahn and Burdette, but Buhl had a live fastball and a competitive nature that made him one of the best in the league. In addition, he could consistently beat the Dodgers, eight times in 1956 alone.

Buhl pitched for the Braves only once in 1962 before being traded to the Chicago Cubs. On April 12 in San Francisco, in the Braves' third game of the season, Buhl opposed the powerful Giants and lasted only two innings plus three batters, allowing five runs on six hits and four walks. In Buhl's defense it should be noted that three of the runs scored in the first inning on a triple that a rightfielder of major league abilities would have caught; unfortunately for Buhl, Mack Jones was stationed in rightfield. Nonetheless, Buhl left with a 5-0 deficit that ended in an 8-4 loss.

The four Milwaukee runs in that game scored on the ninth career grand slam by Joe Adcock, the Louisiana slugger who also played his last game for the Braves in 1962. Adcock's performance with the Braves was always marked by the spectacular: home runs of prodigious proportions, home runs in record bunches, home runs on auspicious occasions. The big first baseman with the squeaky voice and the inflexible batting stance possessed an affinity for the unusual and a flair for excitement that fans loved.

334

Big Joe took his leave from the Milwaukee ballclub on September 29, 1962, in a 7-3 win over the Pirates at County Stadium. The rival manager of the day was ex-teammate Johnny Logan, appointed by Pirate skipper Danny Murtaugh to give the veteran ballplayer a taste of managing. (Four and a half years later, Adcock himself would be managing the Cleveland Indians.) Adcock finished his Milwaukee residency with style, getting two hits in four tries in support of Warren Spahn's eighteenth victory. Fittingly, in his final plate appearance as a Brave, Adcock blasted his 29th home run of the year.

Hard-throwing Bob Buhl came back to haunt his former team.

1963

"I can't imagine the Braves anywhere but in Milwaukee."

—William Bartholomay, September 12, 1963

More than anything else, 1963 was the year the pitchers gained control of the National League. The league earned run average plummeted to 3.28 (from 3.94 the previous year, 4.03 the season before that), lower than the best team in 1962 and the lowest league figure since the dead-ball year of 1920. (In 1920 Babe Ruth, in the other league, became the first major league hitter ever to exceed 30 home runs in a season; the National League was led that year by Cy Williams with 15.) In 1961 Warren Spahn had achieved the league's lowest ERA—3.02; in 1963 that same figure earned Dick Farrell eighteenth place among league starting pitchers. National League pitchers recorded 154 shutouts in 1963, the most since pre-World War I days, even adjusting for the expanded schedule and number of teams.

The dramatic improvement in pitching statistics was in part legislated—the strike zone was expanded upward from the armpit to the top of the shoulder, and downward from the top to the bottom of the knee. Another factor was a change in philosophy, with teams relying less on complete games and more on relief specialists. Whatever the causes, the 1963 season ushered in a period of pitching dominance that caused run production to drop by more than 1000 throughout the league. When the trend had not abated in six years, baseball officials diminished the strike zone and lowered the pitching mound. Fans pay to see home runs hit and runs scored.

It is axiomatic in baseball that pitching wins ballgames, and in 1963 the Los Angeles Dodgers proved it. Walt Alston's team cruised to the pennant and a World Series sweep of the Yankees with a team of swift-footed banjo-hitters: twenty points below the

336

Cardinals in team batting, sixth in runs scored, seventh in home runs, eighth in doubles and slugging, last in triples.

What the Dodgers had was the league's best pitching and base-stealing. Maury Wills again led in base thefts, with Willie Davis also among the leaders. On the mound Don Drysdale was excellent, winning nineteen games, but he was overshadowed by two men who were better. Relief man Ron Perranoski won sixteen, lost three, and compiled a 1.67 ERA. Even he, though, was outshone. Sandy Koufax won 25 and lost 5, struck out 306 batters (a National League record), hurled eleven shutouts (most since Grover Cleveland Alexander in 1916), and led the league with a 1.88 earned run average, lowest in the league in twenty years.

Against such pitching prowess the Braves were simply over-matched. Their team earned run average of 3.26 would have led the league the year before, but in 1963 it ranked fifth. Thanks primarily to Spahn, Milwaukee led in complete games, but in games saved they ranked eighth. The changeover to younger ballplayers left only Spahn and, for a brief period, Lew Burdette among the old guard. Recently-acquired veteran Bob Shaw worked mostly in relief, providing the only real relief the Braves received, and the other hurlers were youngsters: Denny Lemaster, Bob Hendley, Tony Cloninger, Claude Raymond, and after mid-June, Bob Sadowski. All showed ability but lacked the consistency that had marked the Milwaukee staff during the glory years.

The man who pitched like the old days was the man who had always done so—Warren Spahn, still magnificent at age 42. Pitching again for a manager who allowed him to work with three days' rest, Spahn matched his career-best record with a 23-7 slate, the same as in his first year in Milwaukee, and achieved a 2.60 ERA, his best since that first year in County Stadium. By now his fastball was largely a memory, but the crafty southpaw's screwball and slider more than compensated, and his control was actually the best of his life. The wily veteran also equalled his highest number of shutouts, seven, set in 1947.

Spahnie's start in 1963 was uncharacteristically strong, with four victories in five decisions in April. On May 3 he had his first bad outing, allowing four runs in two innings in a no-decision effort that the Cubs eventually won, 10-7. Twice more in May, on the 9th and again on the 24th, Spahn was hit hard and suffered defeats. In June he won four times without a loss, although on June 18 he was pounded by the Pirates and failed to complete the second inning, but his teammates rallied and won the game to keep Spahn's June slate clean.

Then in one incredible two-and-a-half month stretch from June 23 through September 8, the great lefthander pitched thirteen brilliant games in a row, completing twelve and winning eleven of them. Three of those games were shutouts, one a 1-0 masterpiece that began with six and one-third perfect innings [see Time Capsule, June 28]. The only non-victories in the streak were his eight-inning, 3-1 loss to Lew Burdette [see Time Capsule, July 25] and a heartbreaking 1-0 loss to Juan Marichal and the Giants in sixteen innings [see Time Capsule, July 2]. Spahn's streak was twice interrupted by an elbow ailment, from July 7 to July 25 and again from July 29 to August 14, but when he did pitch, he was outstanding.

Perhaps the most remarkable facet of Spahn's amazing season was his sudden mastery of the Dodgers. After nearly two decades of being live bait for the former denizens of Brooklyn, Spahn vanquished his former tormentors four times in as many tries, twice in their home park, where he had not beaten them in fifteen years. For Spahn, it was a season for settling an old score.

Despite his personal success, 1963 was a bittersweet season for Spahn. His longtime compatriot, roommate, and partner in high jinks, Lew Burdette, was dealt to the St. Louis Cardinals just minutes before the June 15 trading deadline. The trade left Spahn without his alter ego, the Braves' pitching staff without one of its mainstays, and Milwaukee fans without one of the four remaining heroes from the original Milwaukee Braves team.

One of the two players the Braves received for Burdette was 25-year-old minor league pitcher Bob Sadowski, the youngest (and most talented) of three baseball-playing brothers. Sadowski quickly earned the nickname "Lucky" for the same reason a tall man is called "Shorty"; no matter how well he pitched, he seemed unable to win. The unfortunate righthander lost his first four starts despite an ERA well below 3.00. On July 1 in Los Angeles, his second start as a Brave, Sadowski took a two-hitter and a 1-1 tie into the ninth, then lost on a single by Maury Wills and a pinch double by Wally Moon. On July 16 at Wrigley Field, Sadowski hurled a three-hitter but lost 1-0 to the second-place Cubs (no, that is not a misprint) as Ken Hubbs (seven months before his tragic death in a Utah car crash) poled a fifth-inning homer and ex-Brave Bob Buhl pitched six and two-thirds innings of no-hit ball.

Sadowski finally earned his first big-league victory on July 21 in the first game of a Sunday doubleheader against the first-place Dodgers, before the largest County Stadium crowd of the season

338

up to that date: 28,534. The rookie allowed just two runs in seven and two-thirds innings as his eighth-place mates pasted Los Angeles twice behind a 26-hit barrage. On August 2 in another twin-bill, Sadowski labored ten innings against the Mets, allowing just one run on five hits before giving way to a pinch-hitter. The Braves and Bob Shaw then lost in the eleventh. On August 8 Sadowski pitched a complete game, allowing no walks and five singles until the ninth, when a single and a double gave Bob Friend and the Pirates a 1-0 triumph over the luckless hurler. On August 25 he allowed a run in seven innings, dueling Sandy Koufax to a draw, but failed to earn a decision. Finally on September 14 Sadowski gave up only one earned run against the Cardinals but lost 3-2 as surehanded Roy McMillan erred twice. Sadowski's season record of 5-7 could easily have been 11-2.

No less a victim of non-support was sophomore Denny Lemaster. The young southpaw carved out a 3.04 earned run average and struck out 190 batters, sixth highest in the league, but his

Roy McMillan legs to first, April 16, 1963, but where are the fans?

record was a pedestrian 11-14. Seven times when Lemaster started, the Braves were shut out. Six times Lemaster allowed one run or less and failed to earn a victory, including five losses and a twelve and two-thirds inning no-decision against the Colt .45's on June 2. On that day his ERA dipped to 1.32, belying his 2-3 record. The hardluck lefty lost all six of his starts in September, three of them to shutouts.

The problem for Milwaukee pitchers, Sadowski and Lemaster in particular, was simple—the Braves did not hit. Like the rest of the National League teams, the Braves produced fewer runs, nearly one hundred fewer than in 1962 and at a lower average per game than in any season since the impotent Boston years. Only Henry Aaron had a truly productive year, tying for the league home run crown with 44, leading in runs batted in with 130 and runs scored with 121, leading in total bases (370) and slugging percentage (.586), finishing second in hits (201) and stolen bases (31) and third in bases on balls (78) and batting average (.319). Only the stolen base total marked a career high for Aaron, but all the statistics taken collectively, especially in relation to the rest of the league, indicate that 1963 may have been Aaron's finest year. If five more of his line drives had fallen for base hits, he would have become the only National League hitter since Ducky Medwick in 1937 to win the triple crown (home runs, runs batted in, batting average).

Besides Aaron, though, offensive highlights were few. Only Eddie Mathews exceeded twenty home runs, with a new career-low 23. Mathews' major contribution was his career-best 124 bases on balls, half-again as many as anyone else in the league. His 84 RBI's were the team's second-high total. Catcher Joe Torre, now the regular backstop in place of Del Crandall, hit .293 with fourteen homers and 71 runs batted in, but no other Milwaukee player hit .275 or contributed a dozen home runs or drove in more than 50 runs. The team batting average of .244 set a new low for the franchise; the home run total of 139 lagged far behind San Francisco's 197 and equalled the Milwaukee low set in 1954, when rookie Aaron hit only thirteen.

As good an illustration as any of the Braves' sorry offense was their performance against the Chicago Cubs. From the time the Braves arrived in Milwaukee the Cubbies were their "cousins," nearby geographically and a soft touch on the field. The Braves had always finished higher in the standings, always won the season series, and always compiled a better team earned run average than their cousins—until 1963.

Thanks to a four-hit shutout by Spahn on the season's final

day, Milwaukee did finish ahead of Chicago atop the National League's second division, but the Cubs dominated Bobby Bragan's club, winning twelve of the eighteen games between them, and they did it with superior pitching. In ten of the Cub victories their pitchers held the Braves to two earned runs or fewer, twice shutting them out 1-0. The Chicagoans' team ERA was a remarkable 3.08, second best behind the Dodgers and well ahead of Spahn and company (especially the company). The Cubs victimized Tony Cloninger three times by identical 3-2 scores and also beat Denny Lemaster three times and Shaw and Sadowski twice each.

One reason the Braves lacked offensive punch was that old reliable slugger Joe Adcock, another of the Milwaukee Originals, had been traded during the off-season, along with Jack Curtis, to the Cleveland Indians. In return the Braves received relief pitcher Frank Funk and a pair of young outfielders, Ty Cline and Don Dillard, who between them produced one home run. Cline started the season as the regular centerfielder and seemed promising, earning praise as the best at his position since Billy Bruton. Manager Bobby Bragan soon realized, though, that he could not afford the luxury of a non-hitting outfielder. Dillard received a brief trial in the outfield, then settled into a pinch-hitting role.

Other additions to the Braves' roster included former Dodger and Colt .45 first baseman Norm Larker, outfielder Bubba Morton, first baseman-catcher-outfielder Gene Oliver, and pitchers Dan Schneider and Bob Tiefenauer. Larker, the villain who had knocked out Johnny Logan with a body block in the 1959 playoff with the Dodgers, arrived from Houston before the season, played sparingly, hit below his weight, got pummeled by Bob Shaw in a fight in the dugout on July 13, and was sold to San Francisco on August 8. Morton was purchased from the Detroit Tigers in a waiver deal on May 4, appeared in fifteen games, and returned to the minors. Oliver arrived from St. Louis as part of the Lew Burdette deal in mid-June and became the starting first baseman, contributing eleven home runs to the enfeebled Milwaukee lineup. Schneider, a gangling 20-year-old southpaw phenom, worked in 30 ballgames, all but three in relief, and showed signs of a bright future, winning his only decision of the season on August 4 by pitching six shutout innings against the Mets. Tiefenauer, a 33-year-old knuckleball artist who had popped in and out of the big leagues since 1952, popped back in on August 8 and pitched amazingly well in twelve relief chances, allowing just four walks and four earned runs in 29 and two-thirds innings for a 1.21 earned run average.

Norm Larker took out Logan and the Braves in '59 playoff with a rolling block.

A Braves fan returning to County Stadium after, say, a four-year absence would have been hard-pressed to identify the Milwaukee players. Fortunately for that fan and others like him, the Braves began wearing their names on the back of their uniforms in 1963. Manager Bragan's proclivity for lineup juggling made that identification near-mandatory, but the parade of new faces added to the problem. Many of the shifts resulted from a dearth of outfielders and a plethora of catchers. The inability of Mack Jones to hit National League pitching consistently, the lack of batting prowess displayed by Cline and Dillard, and an injury to Gus Bell made the outfield a festering sore all season. Bell's injury, which effectively ended his career, was suffered on April 18 while the veteran was shagging flies before a game at County Stadium against the Phillies.

Among the outfielders attempting to man the outfield slots, along with regulars Hank Aaron and Lee Maye, were Mack Jones, Ty Cline, Don Dillard, Bubba Morton, Len Gabrielson, and Gene

Manager Bobby Bragan was a continual target of fans' booing.

Oliver. In addition, several strangers to the position tried as well: Mathews, who had failed miserably as a leftfielder in 1954; jack-of-all-trades Denis Menke; and even catcher Joe Torre. On July 15 Bragan actually entered four catchers in the starting lineup—Del Crandall behind the plate, Torre at first base, Oliver in leftfield, and Hawk Taylor in center. The experiment failed as the Braves lost to the Reds, 4-3, in twelve innings.

343

At the start of the season the only position seemingly in doubt had been first base. Larker's ability to fill Adcock's spikes was problematic; otherwise the team looked solid, with veterans at every spot. Bragan's team lost its first two ballgames, both 3-2 in Pittsburgh, but then returned home and won seven straight, taking over first place for the first time in two years. Among the heroes in the surge to the top were Gabrielson, Cline, Jones, and Larker. Alas, the Braves' sojourn at the top was short-lived—they went back on the road and lost four straight to the Mets.

On May 13 the Braves struck bottom—they were tied for ninth (last) place, the nadir of the Milwaukee Braves' existence. They finally crawled above the .500 mark on June 25 but did not permanently pass that barrier until August 13. Before that time a new crisis had emerged.

On July 21 sports editor Bob Broeg of the St. Louis *Post-Dispatch* predicted that the Braves would leave Milwaukee and move to Atlanta if attendance did not improve. Attendance at County Stadium had fallen off dramatically, averaging about one-third of its peak figures, and the Braves did have new owners, a cadre of aggressive young entrepreneurs. Nevertheless, the response of Chairman of the Board William Bartholomay was immediate and predictable: "We didn't buy the Milwaukee franchise to move it to Atlanta. How do these things get started?" Despite repeated denials, rumors continued to spread like jock itch during the following months.

On August 11, with a 58-59 record and mired in eighth place, the Braves came to life. Over the next four weeks they won 22 of 28 games, Spahn leading the way with seven consecutive victories. On September 9 they swept a doubleheader in Cincinnati, putting them fifteen games above .500, in third place, seven games out of first with seventeen remaining. Then, as suddenly as they had been resurrected, they died. They left eleven on base, lost to the Reds, 4-3, and began a plunge back into the abyss of the second division, losing thirteen of sixteen.

The Braves' only highlights in the final three weeks of the season belonged to Warren Spahn. On Tuesday night, September 17, Warren Spahn Night at County Stadium attracted a crowd of 33,676 to pay tribute to baseball's greatest lefthander. It was the largest crowd in Milwaukee since August 11, 1961, the night Spahn notched his 300th career victory. Spahn received gifts and accolades and a congratulatory telegram from President John F. Kennedy. Even this occasion, though, was tinged with unhappiness. Spahn was belted mercilessly by the San Francisco Giants, allowing four runs in three innings before being relieved in an

344

11-3 loss. The defeat was the Braves' eighth straight, tying the longest losing string in their eleven-year history.

Spahn's last three starts of the season were complete game victories, two of them shutouts of the Chicago Cubs, giving Spahn 62 shutouts in his illustrious career and a 23-7 season mark. The team, under Bobby Bragan's guidance, was not so successful, finishing out of the first division for the only time in their history, with their poorest record ever: 84-78. In games that Spahn did not pitch, the Braves had a 59-70 record.

In the waning days of the 1963 season the rumors of the Braves' imminent flight to Atlanta continued. Every columnist, reporter, and announcer around the country seemed to have inside information that the Braves would reside in Georgia in the immediate future. Finally on September 23 Braves President John McHale made the official announcement concerning the team's future: "The Braves will be in Milwaukee today, tomorrow, next year, and as long as we are welcome."

Many baseball fans in Wisconsin believed him.

Milwaukee Journal Photo

"The Rover Boys" —from left, Thomas A. Reynolds, James B. McCahey, jr., John J. Louis, jr., Daniel C. Searle, William C. Bartholomay, Delbert Coleman, and (seated) John McHale

1963 Feat of Clay

"The umpires are ruining the game." —Bob Shaw

Beginning in 1950, National League rules required that a pitcher must remain in a set position for one full second before delivering a pitch. Failure to do so with a runner or runners on base constituted a balk. The rule caused no controversy because, like the rule requiring the pivotman on a doubleplay to be on the bag when receiving the throw, it was ignored. Then in spring training of 1963, following two years of complaining by Dodger manager Walter Alston, National League President Warren Giles ordered umpires to start enforcing the one-second provision. The result was chaos.

By April 25, scarcely two weeks into the season, 68 balks had been called by obedient league umpires, compared with two balks called in the American League. Giles instructed the umpires to stop enforcing the one-second requirement, but his new edict was disregarded. By the end of April the league had broken the all-time season record for balks, with no let-up in sight.

On Friday night, May 3, in County Stadium, the Braves opened a three-game series with the Cubs. Chicago won the opener, 10-7, but new Cubs' manager Bob Kennedy did not stay around to see the conclusion; he was ejected for arguing a balk called against Jim Brewer, Kennedy's first disqualification in nineteen years as a player, coach, and manager. Two other balks were called against Milwaukee's Claude Raymond, but this merely served as preliminary to the main balk event on Saturday, May 4.

The game shaped up as a pitchers' battle between longtime Milwaukee nemesis Glen Hobbie and Bob Shaw, the Braves' best pitcher the previous season. With the score tied 1-1 in the top of the third inning, the game left the realm of the ordinary. Shaw walked Billy Williams, then was called for a balk, advancing

346

Bob Shaw explains the balk concept to umpire.

Williams to second. Presently Shaw again failed to pause long enough to suit umpire Al Barlick; another balk was called, and Williams moved to third. When Shaw repeated the action on his next delivery, Barlick called his third balk of the inning, scoring the bemused Williams. With no one else on base, Shaw was able to avoid further balk calls and retire the side.

After the Braves tied the score with a run in the bottom of the fourth, Shaw again got into difficulty. Williams hit a grounder to first baseman Norm Larker and narrowly beat the fielder to the base. The call so incensed Larker that he was thrown out for arguing with umpire Ed Vargo. Tommie Aaron came in to replace Larker. Shaw retired Ron Santo, but Ernie Banks singled. Shaw then balked again, his fifth of the game, and the runners advanced to second and third. Andre Rodgers drew a base on balls, loading the bases. Nelson Mathews, an outfielder unrelated to Eddie Mathews either by birth or ability, also drew a walk from Shaw, forcing in the lead run. The call on ball four enraged

347

the frustrated hurler, and before Braves skipper Bobby Bragan could remove his pitcher, Barlick did it for him. Shaw left with a 3-2 deficit, responsibility for all three baserunners, and a place in the record book.

Relief man Ron Piche immediately wild-pitched another run home, singles by Merritt Ranew and Lou Brock drove in three more, and the Cubs had a five-run inning and an insurmountable 7-2 lead. The Braves tried to fight back with a run in the sixth and two in the seventh, but Lindy McDaniel shut them down completely to preserve the win and push the Cubs ahead of Milwaukee into fourth place in the standings.

Shaw's ignominious performance earned him two major league records—most balks in a game, 5; most balks in a season, 8—and a share of another record: most balks in an inning, 3. Ten days later the league rule on balks was officially amended, eliminating the requirement to pause one full second. Relative sanity returned to the National League. Bob Shaw managed to pitch 43 more times during the season without incurring another balk call.

1963 Nemesis - Jim Maloney

"He just overpowered us." —Bobby Bragan

It was lefthanders that gave the Braves fits in the early sixties, but in 1963 a 22-year-old righthander with a blazing fastball set Milwaukee hitters on their collective ear. Cincinnati's Jim Maloney, who the Braves thought was as fast as Sandy Koufax, beat Bragan's team four straight times. He did not just beat them, though; he blew them away.

Maloney's first opportunity came on May 21 in a night game at County Stadium. He hooked up in a pitchers' duel with Milwaukee's Bob Hendley, but Maloney made two early runs stand up for a 2-0 victory. Along the way the young Redleg fanned sixteen Braves hitters, striking out every man in the starting lineup, including Eddie Mathews three times and five others twice each. Eight of Maloney's strikeouts occurred in succession (every starter except Hank Aaron) in the first through fourth innings, tying the post-1900 record set by Milwaukee's Max Surkont in 1953 and equalled in 1962 by Johnny Podres of the Dodgers. Maloney yielded just two singles before giving way to relief ace Bill Henry with one out in the ninth.

On July 28 in Milwaukee the young Cincinnati star again outpitched Hendley, striking out seven in seven innings and allowing just four hits, two of which were home runs by Aaron and Menke, in a 4-3 win. After seven innings the heat did what Milwaukee hitters could not—forced Maloney out of the ballgame.

In Cincinnati on September 11 Maloney breezed to a 14-3 laugher over the hapless Braves as Cincinnati batters produced nine runs in the fourth inning. Staked to a huge lead, Maloney coasted to a complete-game victory punctuated by eight strikeouts, with just one of the Milwaukee runs earned.

Finally on a cold autumn evening in Milwaukee, September 25, the date on which the Dodgers clinched the National League pennant, Maloney worked seven innings, striking out fourteen and allowing only three hits before his arm stiffened. Once again Bill Henry mopped up, preserving a 4-2 victory for Maloney.

The 1963 season was the finest of Jim Maloney's excellent career. He won 23, lost 7, had an earned run average of 2.77, and set a Cincinnati record by striking out 265 batters, leading the league in strikeouts per nine innings. As impressive as those figures are, his performance against Milwaukee was even more impressive: in four starts, in 31 and one-third innings, he won four games, struck out 45, and allowed only six earned runs, an earned run average of 1.72.

Milwaukee Sentinel Photo

Bob Shaw, Warren Spahn, and Lew Burdette

Time Capsule - June 28, 1963

"Maybe it's true that you don't need much sleep when you get old."

—Warren Spahn

The Braves checked into their Los Angeles hotel at 4:00 A.M. on June 28 after a flight from Denver, where they had lost to their Triple-A farm club by an embarrassing 16-1 score. Six hours later a group of them, Warren Spahn included, set off to tour a Hollywood movie and TV studio, where they met Bob Hope and the stars of the television show "Combat," Rick Jason and Vic Morrow. That evening the weary ballplayers, led by 42-year-old Spahn, opened a four-game series with the Dodgers at Chavez Ravine, the beginning of a 21-day, six-city road trip, the longest of the season.

In taking on the Dodgers on their home turf, Spahn was going against a long history of failure. Against the Dodgers anywhere he was an odds-on favorite to lose, having beaten the former Brooklynites just 19 times in his career while losing 34. In the Dodgers' ballpark, though, the task was even more formidable. He had lost to them on the road fourteen straight times: nine in Ebbets Field, four in the L.A. Coliseum, and once in Chavez Ravine. Spahn's last victory on the Dodgers' home field had been achieved nearly fifteen years earlier, on August 21, 1948, the year Spahn and Sain and the Boston Braves won the pennant.

Aside from Spahn's other challenges, his mound opponent this night was Don Drysdale, one of the Braves' prime nemeses. The big righthander sported only a 9-8 record on the year, but that figure was misleading—his earned run average was below 3.00, he was not far behind super teammate Sandy Koufax in strike-outs, and he was as wickedly intimidating as ever.

The first batter of the game, leftfielder Lee Maye, swung late

351

on a Drysdale fastball and poked it to left for a single. Drysdale pitched carefully to second hitter Eddie Mathews, respecting his power, and walked him. Henry Aaron lined a single to right. Maye held up, unsure of whether the ball would be caught, so he failed to score on the hit, leaving the bases loaded for Joe Torre with nobody out. Torre slammed a long flyball to rightcenter that easily scored Maye and allowed both Mathews and Aaron to advance. Drysdale worked his way out of the jam, though, getting both Mack Jones and Frank Bolling on infield popups. In the bottom of the first Spahn retired Maury Wills, Jim Gilliam, and Willie Davis in succession, so Milwaukee led, 1-0.

The Braves put two runners on base in the second, but with two out Drysdale retired Mathews to quell the uprising. In the Los Angeles half Spahn set down Tommy Davis, Frank Howard, and Ron Fairly without difficulty. His control was less than pin-point, but his fastball was humming as it had when he was a young man, say, mid to late thirties. Spahn's teammates threatened again in the third with base hits by Torre and Jones, but again Drysdale worked out of it. Spahn ignored the lack of support and routinely dispatched Doug Camilli, Dick Tracewski, and rival hurler Drysdale.

In the fifth inning Aaron blasted a long triple off the centerfield fence, but two were out at the time, and clean-up batter Joe Torre failed to bring Aaron home, leaving the score 1-0. Spahn then extended his string of perfect innings to five. The Braves went hitless in the sixth, providing interest only when Mack Jones protested a called third strike and earned an expulsion. Once again Spahn got by all three batters in the Dodger turn.

After Drysdale blanked the Braves in the seventh, Maury Wills tried to end Spahn's incipient perfect game by laying a bunt down the third-base line. Mathews charged the ball, picked it up cleanly, and threw out Wills by a step. The next hitter, though, Jim Gilliam, bounced a clean single past Mathews into leftfield. Willie Davis slapped a grounder to Frank Bolling, but the normally surehanded second baseman, hurrying to double up the speedy Davis, bobbled the ball and both runners were safe. Unperturbed, Spahn threw a doubleplay ball to Tommy Davis, the league's leading hitter two years in a row, with Bolling making the play unassisted at second and throwing to Norm Larker to complete the play.

In the visitors' eighth the Milwaukee batsmen not only failed to produce any runs for Spahn but tied a record for futility—all three of their outs were called strikeouts. The first, by Mathews, so infuriated the Braves dugout that Gene Oliver, a non-participant, and Bobby Bragan, for the first time as Milwaukee's manager, were banished. Next Aaron watched strike three with his Louisville Slugger on his shoulder. Torre doubled to right, but Don Dillard joined his more renowned predecessors in passively watching a third strike.

Still protecting his slim lead, Spahn yielded a leadoff single to Frank Howard. Nate Oliver ran for Howard and advanced on a perfect sacrifice by Fairly. Spahn bore down and got Camilli to foul out, then induced pinch-hitter Lee Walls to ground out. Again in the ninth Milwaukee's hitters were helpless against Drysdale, requiring Spahn to complete his shutout if he were to win the ballgame.

Moose Skowron grounded out batting for Drysdale to begin the final frame. The pesky Wills singled to right, though, setting up a likely stolen base to put the tying run in scoring position. At that point Spahn received the help his hitters had failed to provide. With Gilliam at bat, catcher Joe Torre fired a throw down to first and caught the league's top baserunner off the base. Spahn then wrapped up his long-awaited road win against the Dodgers by forcing Gilliam to bounce out to shortstop Denis Menke.

The great lefthander's brilliant three-hit, no-walk performance earned him his 338th career victory, his 58th shutout, the Braves' third shutout in the last four games, but most of all, a satisfying triumph over his career-long tormentors.

353

Time Capsule - July 2, 1963

"He [Willie Mays] hit a screwball that hung."

—Warren Spahn

Three times in August of 1903, Joe "Iron Man" McGinnity pitched and won two complete games in the same day for John McGraw's New York Giants; he came by his nickname honestly. Sixty years later an amazing 42-year-old lefthander performed a similar feat of endurance—but lost.

On a cold night in San Francisco's Candlestick Park (that may be redundant), July 2, 1963, a crowd of 15,921 witnessed a classic pitchers' duel between Warren Spahn, the Braves' superannuated southpaw, and Juan Marichal, the Giants' 25-year-old right-hander from the Dominican Republic. Marichal, whose high-kicking motion was reminiscent of Spahn's except with the opposite leg, had won eight straight games, including a no-hitter against Houston just seventeen days previous. En route to 25 wins in his third full big-league season, blessed with a live fastball and extraordinary control, Marichal was one of the hard-throwing young hurlers who were dominating National League batters.

Spahn, of course, was not doing badly himself. He was 11-3 for the season, having won five in a row. His previous outing four nights earlier and 300 miles to the south had been a three-hit shutout of the Dodgers. Five days before that he had beaten these same Giants in Milwaukee, 10-4, allowing ten hits but walking nobody and even contributing a home run (the 33rd of his career) to start a seven-run inning that insured his victory.

The San Francisco batting order that Spahn had to face this night was the league's most fearsome of the 1960's. Leadoff man Harvey Kuenn, an eight-time .300 hitter, was followed by a murderers' row of five sluggers who in their careers produced a total of 1921 home runs: Willie Mays, 660; Willie McCovey, 521;

354

Felipe Alou, 206; Orlando Cepeda, 379; and Ed Bailey, 155. Manager Alvin Dark's crew of musclemen not only led the National League in homers in 1963 with 197, but they hit 58 more than Milwaukee, who finished second in that department.

The early innings gave no indication that either Spahn or Marichal or the game itself would be in any way exceptional. Milwaukee had a failed opportunity in the top of the second after Del Crandall reached second base on a throwing error by Kuenn, the unaccustomed third baseman. In the same inning San Francisco muffed a chance after Cepeda singled, stole second, tagged and moved to third on a long flyball.

In the top of the fourth Hank Aaron led off with a long fly to left, an apparent home run, but the stiff San Francisco Bay breeze returned it to the playing field and McCovey made the catch. Next up was Eddie Mathews, returned to the lineup after missing three games with an injury to his right wrist. Still feeling the effects, Mathews struck out for the second time in the ballgame (and was subsequently replaced at third by Denis Menke). Larker drew a base on balls, and Mack Jones singled him to second. Next up was Crandall, no longer the regular catcher, behind the plate for the first time in over two weeks. Crandall dropped a single into short centerfield. Larker rounded third and headed for home. Mays charged the ball, grabbed it on a hop, and fired to the plate to gun down Larker. The game remained scoreless.

Spahn continued to hold the Giants at bay (pun intentional), but his mates could not cash in either. In the sixth Menke singled and stole second with one out, but Marichal got both Larker and Jones to pop up and leave Menke stranded.

The Braves made their last menacing gesture in the top of the seventh. Crandall led off with a single. Manager Bragan then called for a hit-and-run with McMillan at bat. McMillan swung and missed, and Crandall, no speed merchant even as a rookie in 1949, was an easy out at second. McMillan then popped up for the second out. Spahn was up next. The always-dangerous hurler got around on a Marichal fastball and ripped it toward the rightfield corner. The ball struck the top of the fence, inches from being a home run. It rebounded toward the infield, and Spahn pulled in with a double. He died there, though, as Lee Maye grounded out. For all practical purposes, that was it for the Braves—they never threatened again.

After the seventh-inning stretch the home club put runners on first and second, but Spahn escaped without a run scoring. The eighth inning was routine for him, but in the last of the ninth McCovey crushed a towering blast deep into the rightfield

355

seats—just foul. McCovey and Dark and assorted others argued vehemently, but the call stood. McCovey was retired, the Giants were retired, and the scoreless game moved into extra innings.

In the extra frames the two mound opponents remained invulnerable. Through the tenth, the eleventh, the twelfth, the thirteenth inning, neither team could accomplish a run. In the last of the fourteenth, Milwaukee centerfielder Don Dillard, who had pinch-hit for and replaced Jones earlier in the ·inning, misplayed Kuenn's short flyball, allowing it to drop for a leadoff double. Immediately Spahn was in trouble. He walked Mays intentionally to set up a force or a doubleplay, ending a personal string of 31 and two-thirds innings without a base on balls. He then pitched to and retired McCovey and Alou, keeping the runners at first and second. Next he got Cepeda to ground to Menke, but the substitute third baseman booted it to load the bases for Ed Bailey. Undaunted, Spahn retired Bailey on an easy flyball to end the inning.

Both pitchers had an easy time in the fifteenth; Marichal did again in the first half of the sixteenth. In the last of the sixteenth, however, the end came suddenly. The first batter, Kuenn, flied out. Then at 12:25 A.M. (2:25 in Milwaukee), after four hours and ten minutes of incredible pitching by two of baseball's premier pitchers, Willie Mays blasted a ball far over the leftfield fence and Spahn was a loser.

Spahn was not a stranger to long, bitter defeats. In 1951 he had lost to the Dodgers, 2-1, in sixteen innings, and the following season he had lost to the Cubs, 3-1, in fifteen innings in a game in which he struck out a record eighteen batters (and the only run for his team scored on Spahn's home run). Considering his age and the competition, though, this one was even more remarkable. After 201 pitches, the equivalent of a doubleheader, and after 27 and one-third consecutive shutout innings, the courageous Spahn had only his fourth defeat to show for his night's labor.

Time Capsule - July 25, 1963

"He's probably the best friend I've ever had."

—Lew Burdette, of Warren Spahn

On August 29, 1951, the New York Yankees acquired pitcher Johnny Sain from the Boston Braves. In exchange the Braves received $50,000 and a 24-year-old righthander who had pitched all season for the San Francisco Seals of the Pacific Coast League. His name was Lew Burdette. When he joined the Braves in early September of 1951, he began a teammate-partnership with Warren Spahn that lasted until the pre-dawn hours of June 16, 1963, when Burdette was traded to the St. Louis Cardinals.

In their nearly twelve years together, Burdette and Spahn were road roommates, kindred spirits, collaborators in practical jokes and gags, and the best one-two mound combination in baseball. Spahn was already an established star; Burdette became one after the transfer to Milwaukee. They won 412 games as teammates, Spahn 233 and Burdette 179, and hurled three no-hitters, Burdette the first and Spahn the next two. They combined for 385 complete games and 66 shutouts, figures rivaling some entire pitching staffs during the same period. For the first decade the Braves were in Milwaukee, Burdette and Spahn were indomitable, indefatigable, and inseparable.

Two days after Burdette was traded to the Cardinals, he beat the New York Mets, 6-2. In the five weeks after that he lost all three of his decisions. In the same time span, Spahn pitched two of the greatest games of his career, shutting out the Dodgers in L.A. on June 28, 1-0, and dueling Juan Marichal for sixteen innings on July 2 before losing, also by 1-0. During that same period, though, Spahn also endured the first extended arm trouble of his life (he had missed one start in late July, 1962, with tendinitis), missing eighteen days with a sore left elbow begin-

357

ning, perhaps not coincidentally, five days after his marathon performance in San Francisco.

At County Stadium on Thursday afternoon, July 25, 1963, Spahn made his first appearance since developing elbow trouble two and a half weeks earlier. His opponent was ex-crony Lew Burdette. In anticipation of the historic face-off between the former Damon and Pythias of the Braves, a crowd of 22,331 fans (15,019 paid), the third-largest gathering of the season, turned out to watch their seventh-place ballclub battle the second-place Cardinals.

Before the game Bobby Bragan, the manager who had traded Burdette, made a prediction: "Spahn will finish and win this game. Burdette won't go all the way." As it happened, Bragan's talent for prognostication matched his talent for managing—and not one of his teams ever finished higher than fifth place.

In the top of the first the Cardinals scored a cheap run against the obviously struggling Spahn. Curt Flood beat out a slow chopper in the infield to lead off. He moved to second on a line single by Dick Groat, tagged and went to third on Ken Boyer's long fly, and scored on a grounder to the right side by Bill White. The Braves got the run back in their half of the inning when shortstop Denis Menke doubled and Henry Aaron bounced a single up the middle past Burdette, the kind of play Burdette made routinely when younger ("I thought I had it all the way, but it skipped right over my glove.")

The ballgame stayed tied until the top of the fourth. Spahn retired Boyer to start the inning, but White timed a curveball and ripped it to the gap in rightcenter for a double. Spahn put away Charlie James, but with two down, Stan Musial, the greatest hitter in the National League during Spahn's tenure and the only player on the field older than Spahn, came to bat. Spahn had retired "The Man" at the start of the second inning, but this time Musial stroked a base hit to drive in White with the lead run. Julian Javier hit a grounder to Menke that should have ended the inning, but the shortstop failed to pick it up. St. Louis catcher Tim McCarver then singled home Musial with an unearned run to make the score 3-1 for the Cardinals.

Burdette, meanwhile, was mowing down the Milwaukee hitters with an assortment of breaking balls and excellent control. His fastball was now mostly a memory ("You couldn't even tell what his pitch was. His breaking balls didn't break enough to tell them from his fastballs," Bragan said later), but from the time he hit Joe Torre in the back with a pitch in the second inning until Spahn beat out an infield hit in the sixth, the bases stayed empty

358

with the Braves at bat. After Spahn's hit, Menke struck out, but Mathews doubled to the fence in rightcenter to put the tying runs in scoring position. Burdette worked out of it, though, getting Aaron to foul out and Lee Maye to ground out to the first baseman unassisted.

The remainder of the ballgame belonged to the pitchers. Burdette gave up one more hit, a leadoff single by Torre in the seventh, but he erased him with a doubleplay ball. St. Louis put a runner in scoring position in the seventh and again in the eighth, but neither scored. In the last of the eighth, Spahn gave way to a pinch-hitter, Norm Larker, who grounded out. Bob Shaw replaced Spahn in the ninth and gave up a walk and a hit but no runs. Burdette took his 3-1 lead into the ninth and held it, striking out Mathews, getting Aaron on a weak pop fly, and retiring Maye on a grounder. The loss evened Milwaukee's season record at 50 wins, 50 losses, and dropped them into eighth place.

In the postgame locker room Bragan was not about to concede anything to the winning pitcher. "Burdette won that game with less than anybody I've ever seen on a major league mound," said the ever-gracious skipper. He may not have been far wrong, though; Burdette would win only one more game in 1963, a six-hit, no-walk, complete-game win over the Braves in St. Louis on September 15, with only a two-run homer by Aaron averting a shutout. The vanquished Spahn, meanwhile, was pleased to have pitched effectively against his old friend, if not victoriously, after more than two weeks' layoff. Spahn would go on to win eleven of his last thirteen decisions.

1963 Swan Songs

"I'm not accusing him, understand, but he's got the best spitter I've ever seen."

—Jackie Robinson

As the 1963 trade deadline approached, the rumors of Lew Burdette's departure were fast and furious. Manager Bobby Bragan had lost confidence in the veteran righthander and clearly hoped to exchange him for someone younger. Burdette's exit would leave just three of the Braves' Originals and would deprive Milwaukee fans of a ballplayer who had pitched some of the most memorable games in franchise history. For longtime fans it was hard to imagine the Braves without their accused spitballer from Nitro, West Virginia.

On the evening of June 12, 1963, the Braves opened a long homestand by taking on the New York Mets. Pitching his last game for the Braves, although his performance must have given them second thoughts, was 36-year-old Lew Burdette. His first starting assignment for the Milwaukee Braves in 1953 had been a gem, a tough 2-1 loss at Ebbets Field; his final starting assignment surpassed it. He limited the Mets to three singles and a walk, retiring the first fourteen batters he faced, and only one Met reached second base as Burdette breezed to a 9-0 victory, his 30th career shutout. Three nights later he was traded to the St. Louis Cardinals.

Burdette's catcher in his Milwaukee finale, as in so many games before, was Del Crandall, who homered to provide one of the nine Braves' tallies. Crandall too made his last appearance in a Milwaukee uniform in 1963, concluding his stay on September 28 at County Stadium in a 4-1 loss to the Cubs. The veteran catcher had been so good at his job that he was taken for granted, earning All-Star honors year after year. He had served as team

360

captain and taken charge of the Braves' pitching staff. He was truly a ballplayer's ballplayer.

The last appearance by Del Crandall for Bragan's Braves was in an incidental role on a cold, damp football Saturday. With the Braves trailing Dick Ellsworth by a score of 2-1 in the fifth inning, Crandall batted for starting pitcher Denny Lemaster. Crandall grounded out, trotted to the dugout, and never again performed for the Braves. The following season he was a member of the San Francisco Giants.

Leaping Del Crandall was a perennial all-star catcher.

"I don't think the players or somebody isn't doing something right here."

—County Board Chairman Eugene Grobschmidt

"Grobschmidt had better have proof...or be prepared to retract that statement...If not we would probably take the next step—presumably a lawsuit."

—President John McHale

For most of the first decade of the Braves' stay in Milwaukee, pitching had been their hallmark. It was their marvelous pitching staff that had lifted them from the nether regions of the National League to immediate respectability and pennant contention upon reaching the shores of Lake Michigan. In 1964 even a faint semblance of that mound magic of years past would have been sufficient to achieve the pennant. Unfortunately for manager Bobby Bragan and his ballclub, the cupboard was bare. Only the laughable New York Mets surpassed the Braves in pitching futility.

Paramount among Milwaukee's pitching problems was the inevitable yet sudden failure of Warren Spahn [see Feat of Clay]. Considering that Spahn was 43 years old, though, one is hard-pressed to explain why the Braves' management would have consummated the deal it made on December 3, 1963, with the San Francisco Giants. The Milwaukee brain trust peddled catcher Del Crandall (whose future, at age 34, was clearly behind him) and pitchers Bob Shaw and Bob Hendley to the West Coast club, receiving in exchange catcher Ed Bailey (at age 33, on the same side of the hill as Crandall), pitcher Billy Hoeft, and outfielder Felipe Alou.

Crandall, now a Giant, slides past his successor Joe Torre.

The Crandall-Bailey switch was essentially even, both being former All-Stars now gone to seed. In the exchange of relief men Shaw and Hoeft, the Braves definitely came up short. Shaw had performed well in Milwaukee for two years, winning fifteen games as a starter in 1962, saving thirteen and winning seven in 1963 as a relief man, both years compiling an ERA well below 3.00. Hoeft, on the other hand (left vs. right), a native of Oshkosh, had had one successful season since 1956, the year he managed to win twenty games with a 4.06 earned run average, the highest by a twenty-game winner since Bobo Newsom's 5.08 in 1938. Hoeft was an especially dubious acquisition because of shoulder problems the year before. He would win three fewer games than Shaw in 1964 and save seven fewer.

Most damaging to the Braves, however, was the loss of Hendley, the heir apparent to Spahn. Hendley's first two-plus years with the Braves had been unspectacular, but at age 25, the young Georgian had already won 25 games at an age at which

363

Spahn had yet to win his first. As San Francisco's number four, and least effective, starter in 1964, Hendley won 10 and lost 11 with an ERA of 3.64; those same figures with the Braves would have made him the second-most effective starting pitcher. What is more, in a season in which six victories more would have won the pennant, Hendley might well have made the critical difference. The offense the Braves received from Alou, hobbled by a knee injury in June and July, was minimal: a .253 batting average with just nine home runs and 51 runs batted in. Hendley's value would have been far greater.

Besides the trade with San Francisco, the Braves made numerous roster moves in an attempt to find a winning combination. Bragan, a notorious juggler of lineups anyway, was very much in his element, starting 29 different configurations by the end of May. Most notable among the departed were former regulars Mack Jones, now catching flies in Syracuse of the International League, and shortstop Roy McMillan, swapped on May 8 to the Mets for $100,000 and lefthander Jay Hook. Former relief ace Claude Raymond went to Houston. Milwaukee native Bob Uecker, a catcher-comedian whose only home run had come on the final day of the 1962 season, was sold to the St. Louis Cardinals. Occasional outfielder Len Gabrielson was dealt to the Cubs on June 3 for cash plus catcher Merritt Ranew, who had been drafted from the Braves' farm system in October, 1961, by the newly-created Houston Colts. Gus Bell, once a good reserve outfielder, pinch-hit three times, produced nothing, and retired. Finally, perhaps most noticeable of all, radio announcer Earl Gillespie, the most recognizable voice in the state of Wisconsin, resigned from the Braves' broadcast booth to join a Milwaukee TV station.

The Braves dipped frequently into their farm system in search of pitching help. A few of the hurlers barely had time to unpack—Dave Eilers stayed long enough to appear six times in relief; Dick Kelly worked twice in relief; and Arnie Umbach pitched once, on October 3, went eight and one-third innings and beat the Pirates for the only major league victory he would ever achieve. Rookie Phil Niekro relieved in ten games in the early season, Clay Carroll in eleven games after September began. Dick Smith, obtained from the Dodgers, came out of the bullpen 22 times, winning two and losing two. Chi Chi Olivo, a veteran of two innings in 1961, performed respectably as a fireman, compiling a 3.75 earned run average in 60 innings of work. Even Frank Lary, the former Yankee killer obtained from Detroit on August 8, pitched five times, winning his only decision.

364

The prize mound addition of the season was Wade Blasingame, a 20-year-old southpaw who won nine games and lost five, as a starter and a reliever, despite a hefty 4.24 ERA. Contributing needed relief was knuckleballer Bob Tiefenauer, a late-season recruit from 1963, who saved thirteen games and compiled the team's best earned run average, 3.21, in 73 innings. Most disappointing of the Milwaukee pitchers, next to Spahn, was Bob Sadowski, who, after pitching brilliantly but unluckily in 1963, saw his earned run average soar from 2.62 the year before to 4.10 in 1964.

The team's best won-lost percentage was attained by Denny Lemaster at 17-11 as the hard-luck hurler of the year before became the recipient of strong batting support to compensate for a 4.15 ERA. The club's biggest winner and new ace was Tony Cloninger, 19-14, who, with a little support from his hitters and fielders, might have won 25 games. Of all the Braves' pitchers, though, the most puzzling was definitely Hank Fischer.

The hard-throwing 24-year-old righthander became a starter in 1964 after two years in the Milwaukee bullpen. The result of the changeover was Dr. Jekyll and Mr. Hyde. At his best, Fischer was incredible and unhittable—he tossed five shutouts, including a two-hitter, two three-hitters, and a pair of four-hitters. In the two-hitter, a 1-0 win on May 3, Fischer even singled home the only run. In his nine complete games he allowed an average of 1.00 earned runs and won every game. In seven of his starts, though, he failed to survive the third inning, five times failing to finish even the second inning. In the first half of August in four consecutive starting assignments, Fischer lasted a total of four innings. On August 6 and 7 he started in two straight games, one in Cincinnati amd one in Milwaukee, each time retiring just one batter, exiting each game behind 4-0, and losing both. When he was good he was very, very good, but when he was bad....

Besides pitchers, the Braves also gave the once-over to an assortment of hopefuls. Gary Kolb, a versatile young player obtained from the Cardinals, played outfield, third base, second base, even catcher, but failed to hit at any position. Lou Klimchock came back for a second time and appeared in ten games as an infielder and pinch-hitter. Phil Roof, a veteran of one game in 1961 (as a catcher, no plate appearances), returned to appear in one game (this time batting twice, unsuccessfully) behind the plate, then was shipped back to the minors. Ethan Blackaby, the former University of Illinois running back with three games of outfield experience in 1962, closed out his major league career by appearing in the outfield five times, garnering one base hit.

Twenty-year-old Sandy Alomar joined the ballclub for the final three weeks and played acceptably at shortstop.

Eighteen-year-old Bill Southworth crammed his entire big-league career into the final weekend of the season, pinch-hitting and playing third base a couple times, driving in two runs with a homer in the last game. Woody Woodward, age 21, played every infield position but proved to be another good-field, no-hit ballplayer. Mike de la Hoz, a jug-eared Cuban who had come over from Cleveland in exchange for Panamanian prospect Chico Salmon, hit .291 as a utility player and pinch-hitter. Without question, though, the Braves' most valuable new player of 1964 was Ricardo Adolfo Jacabo Carty.

Milwaukee Journal Photo

Popular Rico Carty greets his fans.

Rico Carty had earned his shot at the big time with a good season at Austin in the Texas League in 1963. Nevertheless, his hitting with the Braves surpassed anyone's expectations. Carty led the team in average with .330, second only to Roberto Clemente's .339; he slugged 22 home runs, two behind team leader Henry Aaron; he drove in 88 runs, the most among league regulars per time at bat; and he finished fourth in the league in slugging percentage.

Led by Carty, the Braves tore up National League pitching, leading the league in runs scored with 803, the highest total by a Braves team in the twentieth century. Three of the top four batters in the league were Braves: Carty, .330; Aaron, .328; and Joe Torre, .321. Centerfielder Lee Maye hit .304 and led the league with 44 doubles. Every player in the starting lineup except second baseman Frank Bolling finished in double figures in home runs, five of them belting twenty or more.

Team leader Henry Aaron hit only 24 homers, his lowest output since his rookie year and the fewest he would hit in a year from 1955 through 1973. His RBI total also dipped, to 95, but he still scored 103, his tenth straight year over the century mark. Eddie Mathews homered 23 times, tying his career low set the previous season, and slumped to a career-low .233 average. All-Star catcher (and first baseman) Joe Torre took up the slack, though, with career-bests of 36 doubles, 193 base hits, 20 home runs, and 109 runs batted in. Shortstop Denis Menke contributed 20 home runs, sometime first baseman Gene Oliver added thirteen more, and Maye hit ten. Outfielder Felipe Alou, hindered by knee problems, had a disappointing year but provided nine more. The Braves' murderous batting order was a nightmare for opposing pitchers, offering only one weak spot—Frank Bolling.

The veteran second sacker did his customary good job in the field, leading his position in fielding for the third time in four years. His bat, however, was pitiful, producing career lows in every offensive category, most notably a .199 batting average, the league's worst among regular players. Particularly galling to some fans was the fact that the league's All-Star second baseman, Ron Hunt of the New York Mets (a .303 hitter in 1964), was a former Braves farmhand who had been let go after the 1962 campaign because Milwaukee was solid at his position.

The serious problems of Bragan's pitching staff were evident from opening day in San Francisco. Spahn was cuffed for six runs on three gopher balls, and relief man Fischer was touched for two more in an 8-4 loss to the Giants. The loss left the Braves a game

Sluggers Felipe Alou, Henry Aaron, Gene Oliver, Eddie Mathews

out of first, and they never got any closer. The following day Bob Sadowski received a preview of his season. With two out in the third inning he walked pitcher Jack Sanford; then the Giants scored ten runs. Five days later Sadowski pitched brilliantly in beating the Dodgers, retiring 21 batters in a row at one point, but he experienced a different kind of failure. As a batter he tied a league mark by striking out five times in the game. In his next start, also against the Dodgers, Sadowski gave up just three hits in eight innings but lost 1-0. His next assignment was also promising, a shutout until the Phillies scored two meaningless runs in the ninth, but after that game Sadowski struggled. His fortunes mirrored those of the Braves.

As late as May 5, a date on which Spahn shut out the Mets on four hits to end the first homestand, Bragan's ballclub was in second place, just a game out of first. The next night in Philadelphia, though, Sadowski was bombed in the opening inning, the Braves lost, and the skid was on. They stumbled through a mediocre May and first half of June. Beginning on June 16 they started a string of seven losses that carried them firmly into ninth place, where for a week they trailed the entire National League except Stengel's New York bunch. At the All-Star break on July 5, the Braves were 38-40, ten and one-half games behind and in seventh place. The pennant race was hardly on people's minds in Milwaukee.

Milwaukee Sentinel Photo

County Board Chairman Eugene Grobschmidt, county official John Doyne, and sportswriter Lloyd Larson

What was on their minds was Georgia—to be specific, Atlanta. The Braves' rumored move to that city had been a hot topic of discussion for nearly a year, but by All-Star time, 1964, the transfer was a foregone conclusion. The Braves' executives continued to deny their intention to leave, but their words were hollow. Meanwhile every baseball mogul and elected public official felt duty-bound to put in his two cents' worth. Baseball Commissioner Ford Frick took his usual position, saying his hands were tied. Congressman Henry Reuss suggested the possibility of anti-trust action against major league baseball. Milwau-

369

kee aldermen proposed a resolution with essentially the same message. Milwaukee County's Corporation Counsel said the county could force the team to stay through the end of 1965. County Board Chairman Eugene Grobschmidt, in a television interview, offered his observation that someone was apparently "trying to make the team look bad for Milwaukee." Braves President John McHale thought Grobschmidt's remarks were slanderous and threatened to sue. It was that kind of summer. The consensus among Milwaukee fans was that General Sherman had been too lenient with the future Georgia capital.

Back on the baseball diamond the Braves began to play winning baseball, taking 16 of 24 games after the All-Star break through the first of August, drawing within six and a half games of the league leaders in the process. During that stretch they received a few good pitching performances, but mostly they won by bludgeoning their opponents: 11-6 and 9-8 over the Pirates, 8-7 over the Giants, 11-7 and 15-10 in a doubleheader sweep of the Mets in their new home, Shea Stadium.

On July 31, euphoric after winning three straight and five of six, scoring fifty runs in the six games, Bobby Bragan announced that he had finally found his perfect and permanent lineup. It was: Mathews at third base, leading off despite his power and low batting average (.228 at the time); Maye in centerfield; Aaron in right; Carty in leftfield, batting clean-up; Torre catching; Alou at first base; Menke at shortstop; de la Hoz at second base; and the pitcher. After winning August 1, the Braves lost six of their next seven and fell to seventh place again, ten games out of first place on August 8. So much for the perfect lineup.

The rest of August was no improvement. On August 23, after losing their third straight game in Houston, the Braves were just two games above .500 and thirteen and one-half games behind the league-leading Phillies. By Labor Day they were exactly at .500, 68-68, in sixth place, fourteen and one-half out. Then in a Labor Day doubleheader in Wrigley Field, the Braves began a remarkable turnaround, too late to rescue their pennant hopes but remarkable nonetheless. They swept the Cubs in a twin-slug-fest, 10-9 and 8-7, beating alumni Lew Burdette and Bob Buhl. Then they took two straight from the Mets at Shea and two straight from the Reds in County Stadium before losing there to Cincinnati in Spahn's final start as a Brave. A doubleheader loss to the Cardinals put their comeback on hold, but from September 16 through the season finale on October 4 they won fourteen of seventeen games.

In that stretch run they gained nine games on first place, but of

370

course the streak did little more than boost morale. They were mathematically eliminated from pennant contention on September 23 and finished fifth, five games behind champion St. Louis, which sneaked into the pennant in the final scramble, a game ahead of Cincinnati and Philadelphia. The Phillies lost ten straight and turned a sure World Series appearance into a legendary failure by Gene Mauch and his ballplayers.

Milwaukee fans were probably gratified to see their team's September renaissance, but their pleasure did not induce many of them to attend the ballgames. The final six-date homestand attracted only about 36,000 loyalists, bringing the season total to 910,911, an improvement over the previous two seasons but a far cry from the glory years. A lame duck team simply does not generate fan interest, and the Braves were clearly a lame duck. In early September C.C. Spink of the conservative *Sporting News* reported that the ballclub would be leaving Milwaukee. Talk of injunctive legal action proliferated, but the only question seemed to be how soon the team would be able to make the switch. As late as September 30 President John McHale still had the unmitigated effrontery to say that the Braves "have never had an offer as such to go anywhere," but the statement was as transparent as it was disingenuous. Milwaukee was obviously the temporary home of the Atlanta Braves.

1964 Nemesis - The Houston Colt .45's

"I've actually got more incentive against the Braves on account of Bragan, and so have the rest of us."

—Hal Woodeshick, June 21, 1964

In their third year of existence, the Houston Colt .45's remained a sure bet for the depths of the National League's second division. They had shocked the baseball world in 1962 by finishing above the Chicago Cubs in eighth place, far above the equally-new Mets. In 1963, though, they had sunk a notch, thanks to the impotence of their batting order of castoffs, the most pathetic group of run-producers since the Philadelphia Phillie team of 1942 on which Bobby Bragan played shortstop (and hit a rousing .218). The 1964 Houston team still produced runs at a rate well below any other team in the majors, but their pitching staff far excelled the Braves' mound corps with a 3.41 staff earned run average, the league's fifth best.

Despite good pitching, the Colts again finished ninth in 1964, losing 96 games and enjoying success against only one team—the Milwaukee Braves. The lowly Texans beat Bragan's Braves twelve times while losing only six. The Milwaukee club won only three of nine at home amd the same number in the Lone Star State.

On Friday night, June 19, the Braves returned home from a western road trip in fifth place, five and one-half games out of first. Forty-eight hours later when the Houston Colts left town, the Milwaukeeans were in ninth place, nine and one-half games back, having lost four straight to the expansion team. On their next western swing the Braves reached Houston after sweeping a doubleheader from the second-place Giants and two of three from the Dodgers in Chavez Ravine. The Braves promptly dropped three in a row to the Colt .45's.

Actually the Braves' record against Houston might have been worse, but they found one Colt pitcher they could beat— Hector "Skinny" Brown, a 39-year-old transplanted American Leaguer in his final season in the big leagues. Brown ended the year with a 3-15 slate, and four of the defeats were administered by the Braves.

Against other Houston hurlers the story was different. Ken Johnson, a tall righthander who had thrown a no-hitter at the Cincinnati Reds on April 23, beat Milwaukee four times in five tries. Dick Farrell, always a thorn in the Braves' side, won twice without a loss, as did former Brave Don Nottebart (who had pitched a no-hitter against the Phillies two months after the Braves got rid of him). Even Don Larsen, the 35-year-old former perfect-game thrower of the Yankees, beat the Braves with a five-hitter, his first complete game in five years.

The Braves also made stars out of several weak hitters from Houston. Third baseman Bob Aspromonte, younger brother of a former Braves infielder, hit four home runs, half his previous year's total, against Milwaukee pitching. Rookie catcher Jerry Grote, a .181 hitter for the season, hit .286 against the Braves. Bob Lillis, a .198 hitter the previous year, batted .306 against the Braves. Finally Walt Bond, an enormous (6'7") outfielder who hit .245 against the rest of the league in 1964, stroked Milwaukee hurlers for a .348 average in fourteen games.

The Braves dominated the Houston Colts in 1963 and 1965, with respective records of 13-5 and 14-4. If Bragan's club had achieved either of those marks in 1964, rather than their 6-12 result, they would have won the National League pennant.

Time Capsule - July 9, 1964

"Do the Braves hit like that all the time?"

—Danny Murtaugh

Warren Spahn gained his first victory as a Braves pitcher in the opening game of a Sunday doubleheader in Forbes Field on July 14, 1946, at the age of 25. His career had been postponed more than three years by serving with the combat engineers in World War II, receiving a shrapnel wound in the neck and earning a Silver Star. In his initial triumph Spahn outpitched 38-year-old Fritz Ostermueller and beat the Pirates, 4-1, allowing seven singles, three walks, and a solo home run by Frankie Gustine. Spahn retired rookie Ralph Kiner, in the first of his seven consecutive seasons leading the National League in home runs, four straight times. He also proved adept with his bat, singling once and sacrificing twice in four at-bats.

Eighteen years later less five days, on July 9, 1964, Spahn won his last game as a Brave, again beating the Pirates at Forbes Field, this time on a rainy evening on which Milwaukee batters, not Spahn's pitching prowess, were responsible for the victory. Two days earlier the 35th edition of baseball's All-Star Game had been played in New York's Shea Stadium—without Spahn, a rare occurrence after the great lefthander's fifteen selections to the classic from 1947 through 1963. On this night, though, Spahn illustrated why he had not been chosen to face the American League.

This game also was Bobby Bragan's team's first contest since Milwaukee County Board Chairman Eugene Grobschmidt had insinuated in a television interview that the Braves were not playing up to their capabilities. Bragan used Grobschmidt's bit of innuendo in his pregame pep talk to fire up his players, and they responded with a batting explosion.

Vern Law, alias "The Deacon," started on the mound for the Pirates, but he never had a prayer. The game's first batter, Eddie Mathews, drilled a single to right. Shortstop Denis Menke also singled, Mathews moving to second. Henry Aaron hit a sinking liner that fell for the third straight hit, loading the bases. Lee Maye also singled, scoring Mathews and Menke, sending Aaron to third, and driving Law out of the ballgame. Righthander Bob Priddy came in to pitch, and Joe Torre greeted him with a double that scored two more runs. Rico Carty added to the carnage with a single that scored Torre with the fifth run. Priddy then retired Ed Bailey, Frank Bolling, and Spahn to end the half-inning.

In the home first Spahn gave two runs back, with help from Aaron. Leadoff man Bob Bailey singled. Next batter Manny Mota doubled off the screen, and when Aaron could not pick up the ball, Bailey scored and Mota motored to third. Spahn got Roberto Clemente to hit a flyball, but Mota tagged and scored on the sacrifice fly.

Dejected Warren Spahn and Eddie Mathews

In the second inning Mathews again led off with a single, and Menke again followed with a single. Pittsburgh manager Danny Murtaugh, experiencing a queasy sense of *deja vu*, yanked Priddy and brought in Tom Sisk to pitch to Aaron, who singled home Mathews with the sixth Milwaukee score. Maye then belted a triple to deep center to bring in Menke and Aaron, and the Braves led 8-2.

Spahn shut the Pirates down in the last of the second, and in the next inning Mathews hit his tenth homer of the season to give the old lefthander a commanding 9-2 bulge. As it turned out, though, even that was not enough to allow Spahn to break his string of nine unfinished games. In the fourth the doubleplay combination of Bill Mazeroski and Gene Alley slammed back-to-back home runs over the rightfield fence to narrow the margin to 9-4. Spahn escaped trouble in the fifth, but three balls were hit hard in that inning—it was not Spahn's night, as it had not been since May 19, his most recent complete game.

Through the first five innings Spahn had struggled to find the plate, to stay ahead in the count. In those five innings he had walked three batters, but in the sixth his lack of control became intolerable. He walked catcher Jim Pagliaroni to start the inning, then did the same for leftfielder Willie Stargell, and he was through. With five innings completed, making Spahn the pitcher of record, Bragan summoned Bob Sadowski to preserve the victory. Sadowski promptly fanned previous sluggers Mazeroski and Alley, then worked too cautiously to pinch-hitter Jerry Lynch and walked him to load the bases. Bailey singled in the runners from second and third, both charged to Spahn, giving him six earned runs allowed in five official innings and raising his already substantial season earned run average above 5.00.

In the seventh the Braves utilized two singles, two Pittsburgh errors, a fielder's choice, and a wild pitch to pad the lead to 11-6, where it stayed as Sadowski worked three perfect innings to close out Spahn's victory. At least in the record book it was a victory.

As he trudged head-down toward the visitors' dugout after being relieved in the sixth, Spahn was not thinking victorious thoughts. Neither was he aware of the significance of the moment—after 356 victories in a Braves uniform, he had reached the end of the line. He would pitch for the Braves again; he would start for them again; he would even, four days later, pitch a complete game for them again. Unhappily, what he would never again do in a Braves uniform was pitch and win.

1964 Feat of Clay

"I honestly believe that our staff is as tough as anybody's...We don't need any outside help."

—Warren Spahn, May 5, 1964

According to the Bible, the *Sporting News* of religion, Methuselah lived 969 years, and Noah reached the ripe old age of 950. Eventually, though, both died. The eternal flame on the grave of John F. Kennedy goes out sometimes and needs to be relighted. Nothing lasts forever...not even the good left arm of Warren Spahn.

After becoming the winningest southpaw in baseball history with 350 victories in eighteen seasons, after thirteen seasons of twenty or more wins, after tying his best season record at age 42, Spahn finally lost it in 1964. The change was not immediately apparent—he pitched well in five of his first ten starts of the season, and on June 11 his record was 5-4, giving him more wins on that date than in 1955, 1956, or 1960, and in the latter two campaigns he had won his customary twenty games. This year, however, was different.

This year after June 11 Spahn lost seven of his next eight starts, winning only on July 9, his final victory as a Milwaukee Brave [see Time Capsule]. In his next start, on July 13, he pitched well for nine innings against the Phillies, his last complete game in a Milwaukee uniform, but lost, 3-2. Two starts later, on July 22, Spahn was, in his words, "as good as I've been all year," again against the Phillies, but again he lost, this time by 4-1 with two of the runs unearned. On July 26 in New York he started the first game of a doubleheader, got bombed in the second inning, and immediately lost his place in Bragan's starting pitching rotation. Spahn worked two innings of relief in the nightcap of the doubleheader and remained a bullpen specialist until August 11, when he pitched four innings against Houston without earning a decision.

During the last eight weeks of the season Spahn started only two games. On August 23 he lasted seven innings against Houston, allowing three runs, but lost. Finally on September 13 against the Cincinnati Reds he survived only until one out in the third inning, allowing eight hits and five runs to earn his thirteenth and final loss of the year. In the final three weeks he was relegated to mop-up relief duty. He actually pitched well in his final appearances, earning four saves. Nevertheless, it was a case of a five-star general policing the latrines.

And so it goes. The greatest lefthanded pitcher in major league history ended his last year as a Milwaukee Brave with the highest earned run average among all National League starting hurlers: 5.29. As a starter only, his ERA was 5.45. The most regrettable part was that, with even a mediocre season by his personal standards, Spahn could have led the Braves to one more pennant.

Milwaukee Journal Photo

Warren Spahn watches a Gordy Coleman home run.

Time Capsule - September 11, 1964

"This had to be the best game of my baseball career."

—Denny Lemaster

Denny Lemaster was sick. In New York the previous afternoon he had developed a sore throat and swollen glands. His temperature reached 101 degrees. Team trainer Doc Feron gave the young southpaw some pills, and by Friday he felt well enough to pitch against the Cincinnati Reds as the Braves opened a ten-day homestand.

The chilly evening and the team's now-obvious intention to flee Milwaukee had held the crowd to 6,715 faithful followers. The ballclub had won four in a row, sweeping a doubleheader from the Cubs on Labor Day and winning back-to-back games from the Mets. Even so, Bragan's team remained in fifth place, twelve games behind the front-running Phillies with just over three weeks to go. The Reds, meanwhile, were tied for second place with the Cardinals, six games behind Philadelphia. Making Lemaster's job even tougher in this game was the Cincinnati mound choice—fireballing nemesis Jim Maloney.

The visiting team was under the interim direction of coach Dick Sisler, replacing rugged manager Fred Hutchinson, ailing with cancer and only two months from his tragic death at age 45. Sisler, son of Hall of Fame first baseman George Sisler, had chosen to play the percentages by starting eight righthanded hitters against lefty Lemaster, the only exception being pitcher Maloney.

To accomplish this, Sisler benched regular centerfielder Vada Pinson and catcher Johnny Edwards, inserted catcher (and Milwaukee native) Don Pavletich at first base for the only time all year, moved leftfielder Tommy Harper to Pinson's spot in center, and shifted first baseman Deron Johnson to leftfield, a position

379

he had seldom played in the past three years. Sisler's strategy failed doubly: not only did his dextrous lineup fail to hit, but the fielding switches cost his club the ballgame.

The second batter to face Lemaster, sophomore second baseman Pete Rose, slashed a grounder near third base for an apparent hit, but Eddie Mathews stabbed the ball and threw out the hustling Rose. Lemaster then retired Frank Robinson. In the home first Mathews drew a base on balls with two out, and Torre did the same. Maloney threw a wild pitch to advance both men to scoring position, but Rico Carty looked at strike three to end the inning.

Neither pitcher allowed a baserunner in the second, but catcher Jim Coker led off the Reds' third with a walk. He advanced on a flyball, but Lemaster fanned Maloney and Chico Ruiz to nullify the threat. Maloney, in the process of retiring seventeen straight batters, kept the Braves off the bases in the third, and the fourth, and the fifth. Through five innings, neither team had achieved a base hit, and some students of the game hearkened back to the 1917 double no-hitter of Fred Toney and Hippo Vaughn.

In the Cincinnati sixth, though, leadoff hitter Chico Cardenas slapped a solid single to leftfield. Lemaster uncorked a wild pitch that sent the runner to second with nobody out. Next batter Maloney, however, surprised the Braves by disdaining the bunt and swinging away, driving a sinking liner into centerfield. Lee Maye charged the ball, caught it at knee level, and fired to second base to double up Cardenas who, thinking the ball would drop, had run to third. The Reds' scoring chance died with Cardenas.

The Braves failed to hit in the sixth; the Reds did likewise against Lemaster in the seventh. Finally after the seventh inning stretch, with one down, Joe Torre grounded a single to left for the first Milwaukee hit. Like Cardenas, though, Torre was quickly erased as Carty bounced into a doubleplay, and the game remained scoreless.

The top of the eighth was easy for Lemaster; the bottom of the eighth proved Maloney's undoing. First batter Gene Oliver hit a sinking line drive toward the leftfielder. Deron Johnson started in for the ball, then hesitated as he lost the ball in the glare of the lights. When he located it, the ball grazed the fingertips of his glove and skipped past him to the fence. Oliver chugged into second base standing up, and the scoreboard signalled "error." Maloney bore down and fanned Denis Menke, his eleventh strikeout victim of the night. Second baseman Gary Kolb was walked intentionally to set up a force or doubleplay and bring up light-hitting Lemaster.

380

The Milwaukee pitcher tried to sacrifice but missed the ball. Then with Lemaster still batting came the play of the game—Oliver and Kolb, neither one a baserunning star, executed a perfect double steal. The twin theft so unnerved Maloney that he walked Lemaster and loaded the bases. Felipe Alou followed with a fly to left, deep enough to score Oliver. Maloney got Maye for the third out, but Milwaukee led, 1-0, thanks to an unearned run.

Lemaster walked Cardenas to open the ninth, then compounded the mistake by walking Steve Boros, batting for Maloney. Chico Ruiz tried to bunt the runners into scoring position but instead popped out to Mathews outside the third base line for the first out. Switch-hitting Pete Rose, batting righthanded against Lemaster, worked the count to three and two. With both runners on the move, Rose took Lemaster's pitch for a called strike three. Torre fired down to Mathews, who scooped the ball out of the dirt and tagged the sliding Cardenas to complete a doubleplay and end the ballgame. A contingent of Cincinnati players and coaches descended on plate umpire Tom Gorman, claiming the pitch was out of the strike zone and should have been ball four to load the bases. As usual, the complaint was ignored, and Lemaster had his one-hit shutout victory.

After the game the official scorer, Lou Smith of the *Cincinnati Enquirer*, reconsidered his earlier decision and awarded Oliver a two-base hit in the eighth inning, negating Deron Johnson's error and making the winning score an earned run. Two facts remained unalterable: an experienced outfielder would most likely have caught Oliver's drive, and the Lemaster-Maloney performance qualified as one of the finest pitching duels during the Braves' Milwaukee residency.

Time Capsule - September 27, 1964

"It's great to win, but you have to feel sorry for those guys."

—Bobby Bragan

During the first six decades of the twentieth century, the worst record in the National League belonged to the Philadelphia Phillies. They captured the fewest pennants (two), won the fewest games, finished in the first division the fewest times, and during one thirteen-year stretch (1933-1945) never finished higher than seventh in the eight-team league. Even their two World Series appearances were disasters: after Grover Cleveland Alexander won their first Series game in 1915, they dropped the next four in a row to the Red Sox; in 1950 they scored just five runs in a four-game Yankee sweep, and two of those runs scored on a dropped flyball with two out in the ninth inning of the final game. In Philadelphia, losing came naturally.

Two weeks before the end of the 1964 season, though, with just twelve games left, Gene Mauch's Phillies led the senior circuit by six and one-half games. Mauch's team could not score runs like the Braves or field like the Reds or match pitchers with the Dodgers, but led by sluggers Johnny Callison and Richie Allen, the latter the Rookie of the Year, they were winning sixty percent of their games and enjoying a comfortable lead in the standings. Then beginning on September 21 they lost three straight games, and when the Braves arrived at Connie Mack Stadium on September 24 to start a four-game series, the Philadelphia lead had dwindled to three and one-half games.

By losing to the Pirates the day before, the Braves had been mathematically eliminated from pennant contention. They arrived in the City of Brotherly Love in the role of potential spoilers, and they succeeded magnificently. They took the series opener, 5-3, behind the pitching of Wade Blasingame and the

Milwaukee Sentinel Photo

Gene Mauch will forever be remembered for the collapse of the 1964 Phillies.

slugging of Joe Torre. The next night the Braves nipped the Phils in twelve innings on Eddie Mathews' clutch base hit and Clay Carroll's strong relief for his first big-league victory. In the third game the Phillies pounded Denny Lemaster early, but the Braves rallied for a comeback 6-4 victory on Rico Carty's bases-loaded triple in the ninth and Warren Spahn's perfect inning of relief.

So it was that on Sunday, September 27, the Phillies entered their final home game of the season before an anxious crowd of 20,569, leading the second-place Cincinnati Reds by only a half-game. Both teams were starting their ace pitchers—Tony Cloninger for Milwaukee, seeking his eighteenth win, and eighteen-game winner Jim Bunning for Philadelphia, working on two days' rest after pitching the series opener.

The Braves attacked at once, scoring twice in the first inning on a single by Felipe Alou, a double by Lee Maye, and a two-run double by Hank Aaron. The Phillies got one back in the bottom of the first on a double by Tony Gonzalez and a single by Richie

Allen. Then in the second the Phillies took a 3-2 lead and nearly drove Cloninger out with a double, a triple, and a sacrifice fly by Bunning.

Cloninger got through the third inning unharmed, and in the top of the fourth his teammates all but wrapped up his victory by scoring six times on seven straight hits, four of which were fluky. Torre led off with an infield hit. Carty hit a doubleplay ball that bounced crazily away from the infielder at the last moment for a hit. Denis Menke smashed a single off the shortstop's glove, scoring Torre. Ty Cline pinch-hit for Sandy Alomar and doubled home Carty. When Cloninger blooped a single beyond the infield, scoring Menke, Mauch had seen enough and jerked Bunning in favor of Dallas Green. Alou then doubled Cline across with the fourth run of the inning. Maye singled, bringing in Cloninger, and Aaron topped off the scoring by grounding into a doubleplay, with Alou tallying the sixth run.

As if the 8-3 lead were not sufficient for Cloninger, he and his mates added four more to his lead in the next inning. With two out and nobody on base, Menke singled and Cline walked. Cloninger then singled home Menke with the eventual winning run. Alou slammed his second double of the day, driving in two runs, and Maye capped the outburst with his third straight hit of the afternoon, scoring Alou and making the count 12-3.

The ballgame was only half over, but in point of fact, the season was over for the forlorn Phillies. They tried gamely to come back—Callison homered in the last of the sixth—but the Braves matched that with two singles and a Rick Wise wild pitch in the seventh. A Torre home run in the eighth off relief star Jack Baldschun made it 14-4 for Milwaukee.

While the Braves were batting in the eighth, Cloninger's arm stiffened up, so Chi Chi Olivo came in to work the last two innings. His first pitch was belted out of the park by Callison, and a subsequent double and single brought the Phillies back to 14-6. After two were out in the last of the ninth, Allen doubled and Callison blasted his third home run in four innings, making the score 14-8. Finally Olivo caught former Brave Wes Covington looking at strike three to end the ballgame and, simultaneously, the Phillies' grasp on first place. Mauch's club had led the league since July 17, but their fourth straight loss to Milwaukee and seventh in a row overall dropped them a half-game below the streaking Cincinnati Reds, winners of their last nine ballgames.

The Braves' incipient win streak, thus at four, would reach eight, and ten of eleven, narrowing the space between them and first place to five games at season's end. The unfortunate Phillies' skid would extend to ten straight, a fatal lapse that left them tantalizingly close but one game shy of the top. Their 10-0 thrashing of Cincinnati on the final day of the season drew them even with the Reds but allowed the St. Louis Cardinals, victors over the Mets in their finale, to sneak away with the pennant by one game.

Warren Spahn, Hank Aaron, and Bob Sadowski at 1964 Diamond Dinner

1964 Swan Song

"I may have pitched the first and last innings ever in Milwaukee. But let's hope not."

—Warren Spahn

Warren Spahn began his big-league pitching career with the Boston Braves as a reliever in April, 1942; he threw his last pitch as a Brave on October 4, 1964, at County Stadium. In between he won 356 games, pitched two no-hitters, won four World Series games and an All-Star Game, and generally established himself as the greatest lefthanded pitcher ever in major league baseball.

The final inning of Spahn's career with the Braves occurred in a game with the Pittsburgh Pirates on the last day of the 1964 season, in front of 10,079 fans. With the pennant race over, Eddie Mathews was designated manager by Bobby Bragan, who sat in the grandstand and observed the proceedings. Bob Sadowski was pitching for the Braves and led, 6-0, after eight innings, having allowed only two infield hits. The Milwaukee lineup consisted mostly of rookies and ballplayers who rarely got a chance to play.

As a gesture of farewell, though, especially considering the uncertainty of the Braves' home city for 1965, manager Mathews inserted Henry Aaron, Ed Bailey, Frank Bolling, Denis Menke, and himself into the lineup for the ninth inning. Mathews even took the unusual measure of replacing Sadowski, in the process of pitching a shutout, with Warren Spahn. The great lefty faced four batters, allowing a single by Gene Alley and retiring Bob Bailey before striking out first baseman Donn Clendenon. Finally, in a moment of triumph for older citizens everywhere, the 43-year-old Spahn ended the game, the season, and his Milwaukee career by striking out 20-year-old Pirate catcher Jerry May.

386

1965

"Milwaukee can get its baseball henceforth by going to Chicago 75 miles away or to the Twin Cities 200 miles away."

—National League President Warren Giles

What had begun in ecstasy in the spring of 1953 ended in the early autumn of 1965 in rancor, acrimony, and litigation. Like a marriage gone bad, the love affair between the Braves baseball club and the Wisconsin fans had turned ugly, with both parties trying to outdo the other in inflicting pain and suffering. There were the usual charges and countercharges, each side blaming the other for the breakup. Infidelity, alienation of affection, irreconcilable differences, mental cruelty—they were all part of the record. In the end a judge made his ruling, but it was superfluous—the thirteen-year union was damaged beyond repair. As usual, the lawyers made out like bandits. Afterwards the two combatants each found a new partner—one right away, the other five years later. Life goes on.

Indicative of the animosity surrounding the lame-duck Braves and their management were charges by two departing pitchers— Warren Spahn at the time of his sale to the Mets in November, and Oshkosh-native Billy Hoeft after his release in spring—that in 1964 Bobby Bragan had tried to lose ballgames. As evidence they cited the 110 different starting lineup combinations Bragan had concocted during the season.

"We should have won the pennant," Hoeft asserted. " But they [Braves' management] didn't want to win." The reason he offered, of course, was that moving a pennant-winner would have embarrassed the owners. As further support for his claim, Hoeft pointed out that in a Labor Day doubleheader with the Cubs, with 26 games left on the schedule, Bragan had used as starting pitchers Clay Carroll and Dan Schneider. Carroll was making only his second big-league appearance and his first start, while Schneider had two big-league wins to his credit in his two seasons (he never won another). Hoeft failed to mention that Milwaukee was in sixth place at the time, fourteen and one-half games behind the Phillies, but his point was clear. He also criticized Bragan for shifting players around in the field, such as putting Hank Aaron at second base, Lee Maye at third, and Eddie Mathews at first.

Again in 1965 Bragan had ample opportunity to maneuver his players around like chess pieces, both because of injuries and because of new acquisitions. At the start of the season Aaron was absent, recovering from ankle surgery on March 17. During the year Maye, Denis Menke, Felipe Alou, Gene Oliver, and Rico Carty all were unavailable for periods of time.

Other possibilities were created by the return from the minors of outfielder Mack Jones, the elevation to semi-regular status of shortstop Woody Woodward, the brief recall of Tommie Aaron, and the increased use of infielder Sandy Alomar. On July 20 the Braves exchanged little-used Gary Kolb for third-string Mets catcher Jesse Gonder. Near the end of the campaign they also acquired outfielder Billy Cowan from the Mets and former Yankee pinch-hitting star Johnny Blanchard from Kansas City. At the end of August they made two interesting deals, neither important. They got Frank Thomas from the Astros (the third former Brave to be reacquired, along with Johnny Antonelli and Alvin Dark), and they purchased aging Harvey Haddix from Baltimore. The coincidence of Haddix returning to the scene of his twelve-inning perfect game was mildly intriguing, but the little lefthander, a few weeks short of 40 and plagued by arm trouble, chose instead to retire.

Three deals, two pre-season and one mid-season, vastly improved the performance of the Braves' pitching staff, from dreadful to mediocre. Thirty-one-year-old Dan Osinski came over from the Dodgers and worked 61 ballgames in short relief, saving six games and compiling a 2.82 earned run average. Lefthander Billy O'Dell, obtained from the Giants for catcher Ed Bailey, did even better, appearing in 62 games, winning ten in relief and saving eighteen. Best of all, though, was Ken Johnson, for whom the Braves traded Lee Maye to Houston on May 23. Beginning on June 3, Johnson won twelve games in a three-month period while losing six. He faltered a bit in the final month, but from June through August his addition to the starting rotation was a key factor in Milwaukee's rise to the top of the

388

standings.

Another important ingredient in the Braves' resurgence was the return to form of two veterans who had experienced subpar years in 1964: Frank Bolling and Felipe Alou. Bolling increased his previous year's batting average by 65 points, especially in the first half of the season when he batted over .300 and narrowly missed (by ten votes) election to the starting All-Star squad. Alou, meanwhile, raised his average 44 points and hit fourteen more home runs, making Lee Maye expendable and enabling the Braves to trade for Ken Johnson.

Even with the addition of Johnson, unfortunately, the Braves' pitching staff was not of pennant caliber. Their relief corps of O'Dell, Osinski, and Phil Niekro was solid, but the starting contingent was not sufficient. Ace Tony Cloninger lowered his ERA to a respectable 3.29 and won 24 games, most ever by a Milwaukee hurler. Youngster Wade Blasingame won sixteen games and lost ten. Denny Lemaster had a terrible year, though, at 7-13, and Bob Sadowski and Hank Fischer were not much better. What the Braves needed to return to the World Series was what had gotten them there twice before, and nearly two other times: Warren Spahn.

After more than two decades as a Brave, going back to Casey Stengel's seventh-place Boston club in 1942, Spahn was sold to the New York Mets on November 23, 1964, thereby reuniting him with Stengel and with the depths of the second division. Bobby Bragan had given up on Spahn as a starter the previous August, but the Mets were willing to take a chance on him as a starting pitcher and pitching coach. Spahn performed well for the first month and a half, winning four games and losing a couple tough ones. After that, however, he lost eight straight decisions and was given his release by the Mets on July 14. And how did Stengel feel Spahn had done with New York? "All right, except when he pitched."

Five days later the pennant-contending San Francisco Giants signed Spahn for the stretch run. The 44-year-old lefty started eleven games for the Giants, winning three and dropping four, twice pitching complete games but losing as his team was shut out, including a 2-0 loss to Lew Burdette and the Phillies on August 31. Spahn's 7-16 final record and 4.01 ERA would indicate that his superannuated arm would not have been sufficient to propel Milwaukee to one final pennant. Any of his seventeen seasons from 1947 through 1963 would have, though. With no one around to fill the void in 1965, the Braves fell one pitcher shy of the pennant.

389

Felipe Alou regained his skills in 1965.

Until the final month of the season, the Braves appeared capable of achieving the top spot by brute force. Among the regulars only Henry Aaron hit above .300 (he hit .318, second best in the league), but Milwaukee batters claimed a National League record as six of them hit more than twenty home runs (Mathews 32, Aaron 32, Mack Jones 31, Torre 27, Alou 23, and Gene Oliver 21). The Braves' total of 196 homers led both leagues, and one of the fans' chief pleasures of the season was arriving early to watch batting practice as the Milwaukee sluggers launched one baseball after another beyond the fence.

The Braves produced nearly 100 fewer runs than in 1964, but when they did score, it was frequently in bunches. For example on June 3, after being held to two runs twice in a row by Houston, the Milwaukee bats exploded for nine runs in the third inning against Bob Shaw and the Giants. Five days later in Wrigley Field the Cubs and Braves were tied 2-2 after nine innings; in the tenth the Braves went wild. After Bolling singled, pinch-hitter Joe

Torre, limping from a pulled hamstring, slammed a home run. Alou followed with another home run. Mathews walked, then Aaron crashed a home run. Finally Gene Oliver completed the parade, smashing the fourth homer of the inning for an 8-2 lead and victory. A week later Bragan's batters smacked 21 hits, including three home runs, in a 12-7 win over the Phillies. On July 20 Aaron's three-run homer highlighted a seven-run seventh inning in a 7-1 victory over the Mets. Yet this same explosive Milwaukee lineup was shut out a dozen times, compared with a major league low four whitewash jobs by Braves hurlers. It was that kind of team.

Another feature of the powerful Braves in 1965 was that the Mathews-Aaron tandem set career records for home runs by two teammates. On May 2 they surpassed the Duke Snider-Gil Hodges duo to establish a new National League record of 746. On August 20 in Pittsburgh, Mathews slammed his 28th home run of the season, one more than Aaron, the 794th home run by the Braves' pair of sluggers, putting them ahead of the former home run standard-bearers, a couple of guys named Babe Ruth and Lou Gehrig. By the end of the season, the Mathews-Aaron combination had extended their record to 803.

The Braves' final Milwaukee season saw the birth of a new National League team, or more correctly, the rechristening of a three-year-old team—the Houston Colt .45's became the Houston Astros. Regardless of their name, they were a thoroughly forgettable ninth-place ballclub. Along with their new name, though, they acquired a new ballpark—an incredible structure, the eighth wonder of the world, an ultramodern monstrosity destined to change the face (and character) of America's national pastime. They acquired the Houston Astrodome.

The world's original indoor ballpark, the Astrodome offered the baseball world immunity to weather and, more important in the muggy Texas summer, sanctuary from the ravenous mosquitoes that had tormented ballplayers for three years. The indoor playfield boasted a 208-foot-high lucite dome, a constant temperature of 72 degrees, and a glare from reflected sunlight that blinded outfielders and made every flyball an adventure. The dome had to be made opaque to cure the problem, creating a new dilemma—the grass on the playing field died. That challenge was met with a new variety of synthetic grass, dubbed "Astroturf," and suddenly the sporting world had a new fad—artificial turf— and its attendant difficulties: a new breed of injuries and a different style of baseball. The Braves adjusted easily to the strange new environment, winning seven of nine games there, but the athletic world has yet to recover from the mania for plastic grass and the claustrophobia of the great indoors.

Of course the inauguration of a covered baseball diamond was by no means the only extraordinary aspect of the Braves' farewell season in Milwaukee. After years of allowing fans to bring their own beer to ballgames, then disallowing it, then reallowing it, the County Board rescinded its reallowance and redisallowed it. The chairman of that board, Eugene Grobschmidt, again charged publicly that Bragan's team was not doing its best to succeed. Further, board members introduced a resolution calling for an investigation of the team management's "apparent ineptitude" and possible contract violations in the selling of tickets at a June 6 doubleheader with the Dodgers.

On a much grander scale, the county filed suit to keep the Braves in Milwaukee, accusing them and major league baseball of antitrust violations. In a pre-emptive strike, however, the Braves sued Milwaukee County for its actions in "harrassing or requiring" them to "schedule baseball games in 1966" in Milwaukee. That was a month and a half after the Braves failed to buy their way out of Milwaukee, offering $500,000 if they could be permitted to move to Atlanta at once. Four-hundred thousand dollars of that amount would have been paid to the county; the other portion would have gone to Teams, Inc., an organization set up to bring a baseball club to Milwaukee after the Braves absconded. The offer was refused, however, on a 24-0 vote of the County Board. On July 28 in Madison, corporation papers were filed for the Milwaukee Brewers Baseball Club, Inc., and the search for a new team began in earnest.

One way in which the Braves were able to pour salt in Milwaukee's wound was by playing exhibition games in Atlanta on off-days. They played pre-season exhibitions in the Georgia capital on the three days prior to opening day, drawing 106,188 for the weekend. In June they played charity games on consecutive Mondays against the White Sox and the Minnesota Twins. After the latter, on June 21, the Braves' front office gleefully announced that their five Atlanta appearances had drawn more customers than their first 28 home games at County Stadium. This exercise in propaganda clearly indicated that the Atlanta-Milwaukee rivalry had taken on many aspects of the Cold War.

Two other incidents are illustrative of the uneasy state of affairs between Milwaukee and the Braves and their National League cohorts, and both involve newspaper writers. On June 20 Lou Chapman, the *Milwaukee Sentinel*'s longtime baseball reporter, was barred from the Braves' locker room for writing

392

stories quoting visiting players criticizing the team's impending move to Atlanta. Chapman was told he had a "disquieting effect...on the players in the clubhouse, the employes in the ticket office and throughout the stadium."

Then on October 1, testimony relating to Milwaukee County's antitrust suit revealed that the only reason Houston Astros' owner Judge Roy Hofheinz had voted to allow the Braves' move to Atlanta was *Milwaukee Journal* sports editor Oliver E. Kuechle. "Whenever a newspaper man or radio-television man takes it upon himself to be hostile, it's up to me to speak out," the judge was quoted as saying. Apparently the judge was a sensitive man.

While the real action of the Braves' 1965 season occurred in smoke-filled rooms, the ballclub did take part in a pennant race, and it very nearly had a storybook ending. The Braves won their opener in Cincinnati behind the two-hit pitching of Tony Cloninger. Three days later they won their home opener behind the

Reunion of "Originals" at 1965 opener: Pafko, Mathews, Logan,
Gordon, Burdette (hidden, above Gordon), Spahn, Surkont, and Buhl

four-hit pitching of Bob Sadowski. At the end of April, Bragan's ballclub was at 6-6, in fifth place but only two and one-half games out of first.

During the first half of May the Braves were alternately good and bad. On May 16 they were six games back, wallowing in seventh place, but by winning seven of ten they reached fourth place, three and one-half out of first, on May 26. When they returned from a western road trip on June 3 and beat the Giants, they climbed all the way to second in the closely-bunched National League standings. They stayed second behind the Dodgers for more than two weeks, but in late June they began another slide. On June 27 and 28 the Braves' pitching collapsed; they were swept in back-to-back doubleheaders by the Reds and the Mets, hitting fifth place in the process. By the Fourth of July the Braganites had sunk to the second division, six and one-half games behind, and at the All-Star break they stood fifth, only two games above .500 at 41-39.

Milwaukee's baseball fortunes seemed to shift in the All-Star contest. Henry Aaron, in his eleventh classic appearance, contributed one hit, and Joe Torre, playing in his second classic, smashed a two-run homer as the Nationals triumphed, 6-5, in Minnesota. The next day in Chicago the Braves lost the first game of a doubleheader with the Cubs, but in the nightcap, despite hitting into a triple play, the Braves won 6-3 and began a ten-game winning streak, their longest in four years. During the streak Aaron and Mathews each slammed four home runs, Oliver hit three, and Alou and Carty each blasted a pair as the Milwaukee sluggers made easy work for the pitchers, four of whom won two games each during that stretch. The streak lifted the club to third place. Another hot streak, beginning August 1, during which the Braves won fifteen of nineteen, propelled them into first place on August 18, the first time since 1960 that the Braves had led the league later in the season than April.

The next eleven days, though, were disastrous. The Milwaukee club dropped nine of eleven, including six in a row at County Stadium. Beginning in late August the Braves' booming bats fell silent, and the team plunged to fourth. In early September the pitching staff began to perform heroically, keeping the team in the pennant scramble. In New York on September 10 through 12, Braves hurlers pitched back-to-back one-hitters, then lost a heartbreaking 1-0 ten-inning game that signalled the beginning of the end for pennant aspirations. Just two and one-half games out of first on September 12, the Braves lost 14 of their final 21 games to finish fifth, eleven games back. Without a home run threat or a hitter above .286, the Dodgers ran and pitched their way to a 14-1 finish to overtake the Giants and sneak into the World Series.

Fittingly, the Dodgers wrapped up their pennant at home in Chavez Ravine by beating the nearly-extinct Milwaukee Braves three out of four times. In the series the Milwaukee sluggers, the most powerful lineup in baseball, scored a total of three runs. Don Drysdale shut them out on three hits. In the pennant-clinching game, Sandy Koufax, now the best pitcher in baseball but a wild flamethrower back when he had debuted at County Stadium on June 24, 1955, struck out thirteen and required just two hits from his teammates to gain the victory.

In the season finale a group of ballplayers in Milwaukee Braves uniforms took the field, but they were not the Milwaukee Braves. These were impostors. Their names were Cowan, Cline, Gonder, Thomas, de la Hoz, Beauchamp, Woodward, and Alomar. The Milwaukee Braves had already passed into history. The Milwaukee Braves had been Eddie Mathews and Billy Bruton. The Milwaukee Braves had been Johnny Logan and Andy Pafko and Warren Spahn and Bob Buhl and Lew Burdette and Joe Adcock and Del Crandall...and Sid Gordon and Jack Dittmer...and Max Surkont...and Henry Aaron...and Red Schoendienst and...and many others, but not these masqueraders. Milwaukee had loved the Braves, and the Braves had loved Milwaukee. The Braves had loved Milwaukee.

1965 Feat of Clay

"If the people don't want to come out to the park, nobody's going to stop them."

—Yogi Berra

From the time of the Braves' arrival in Milwaukee from Boston, attendance at County Stadium was a matter of civic pride. Local newspapers trumpeted the impressive figures as the Braves set an all-time National League record for attendance in their first season. The next year they far surpassed that mark, becoming the first league team to draw over two million spectators. From 1954 through 1957 they attracted over two million annually, peaking in 1957 with 2,215,404 paid admissions. As the team dipped in the standings, attendance mirrored the ballclub's performance. In the lame duck season of 1965, local resentment at the abandonment of the city caused attendance to plummet.

Thanks to a vigorous promotional effort by civic leaders, the home opener drew 33,874 paying customers. Two days later the second home game of the season attracted only 3,362 diehards in frigid weather as the Cubs walloped the Braves, 9-4. The next day the 3,391 assembled followers set a record low for a Sunday ballgame at County Stadium. The next day 2,804 paid to see their former heroes, the second lowest crowd in Stadium history.

The season low stood only until the Braves returned from a weekend series in Chicago. On a chilly Tuesday evening, April 27, the stadium turnstiles recorded the smallest crowd ever for a Braves game—1,677 paid, plus 166 Ladies' Night guests. That milestone of ignominy lasted just 24 hours, though; the following game, a 5-0 shutout by Bob Gibson of the Cardinals, was witnessed by only 1,324 loyalists.

On Tuesday evening, May 4, the Houston Astros visited Milwaukee for a two-game series. They left town the following

396

night having been seen by 2,304 fans in two games. The nadir was reached in the opener—913 (nine hundred thirteen) baseball fanatics poured into County Stadium and watched Eddie Mathews hit a home run and Henry Aaron slam two.

As warm weather arrived and the Braves moved into pennant contention, attendance did rise to a level of respectability. On June 6 a crowd of 17,175 showed up for a doubleheader with the first-place Dodgers and set a record for the Braves' largest gate sale ever. The month of August saw a Bat Day crowd of over 20,000 on the 8th and another of 20,000-plus on the 27th against the Cubs (won by Bob Buhl). A similar-sized turnout witnessed the Braves-Pirates contest on September 5.

The crowning touch, however, still remained. On Monday afternoon, September 20, in a makeup game of a rainout earlier in the month, 812 people sat through a rain-delayed 4-1 Phillie victory over Wade Blasingame and witnessed Henry Aaron's last home run as a Milwaukee Brave. As sparse a gathering as it was, it was not the day's smallest—537 patrons saw the Twins lose to the Athletics in Minnesota in a similar makeup game.

The Braves' final attendance figure for their final campaign in Milwaukee was 555,584, an average of 7,610 fans per game. Civic pride could be solaced only by the fact that, in a year when the Braves remained in Milwaukee only under legal restraint, season attendance nearly doubled that of the Braves in their last Boston year.

Time Capsule - May 20, 1965

"He's the greatest lefthander of all time and we're grateful to him for the extra 15,000 fans he brought to the ballpark."

—Bobby Bragan

After opening day, in thirteen home dates, the Braves' biggest crowd was 8,630 for a Sunday doubleheader with the Phillies; the next largest was under 3,400. On May 20, though, a Thursday night, enough people showed up at County Stadium to necessitate opening the upper grandstand for the first time since the opener. The attraction was not free bats or nickel beers—the enthusiastic crowd of more than 19,000 (17,433 paid) came out for one final chance to watch old number 21, the greatest lefty of them all.

It was just like the old days except old number 21, Warren Spahn, was now wearing a gray uniform with the words "New York" emblazoned across the chest. Spahn's Milwaukee mound foe was also a lefty, 21-year-old Wade Blasingame, Spahn's heir apparent. When Spahn started his first game as a Brave, Blasingame had not yet been conceived. Before Blasingame made his big-league debut, Spahn had won 347 games. Blasingame's debut had come in two innings of clean-up relief on September 17, 1963—Warren Spahn Night at County Stadium. Blasingame had truly begun his tutelage in 1964, as Spahn's road roommate.

Now, however, their roles were different. Spahn was a pitching coach and starter, sporting a 3-3 record, for the worst team in baseball; Blasingame was the number two starter, sporting a 2-4 mark, for the National League's third-place team, a team with a three-game winning streak, including two over the Mets. Despite the Braves' position near the top of the standings, the crowd's loyalties were undividedly with Spahn. They carried banners welcoming and encouraging him; they cheered his every move; they lustily booed the home club. Probably the greatest outpour-

398

ing of emotion occurred when Spahn came to bat with two out in the third—the fans rose and awarded their longtime hero a sustained standing ovation.

Through the first four and one-half innings the two southpaws gave every indication of a classic pitchers' duel, Spahn allowing only harmless singles by Felipe Alou and Gene Oliver, and Blasingame allowing nothing, although Roy McMillan had reached on an error by Mathews in the fourth. The idea of the 44-year-old veteran pitching his heart out and beating his upstart rival was a scriptwriter's dream, but in the last of the fifth the dream was shattered.

Rico Carty led off with a double. Oliver drove him home with another double to break the scoreless tie. Frank Bolling singled, but plodding Oliver held third. Sandy Alomar, playing shortstop in place of injured Denis Menke, singled to drive in Oliver and make the score 2-0. The next batter, Blasingame, tried to sacrifice the runners into scoring position but failed, striking out while

Milwaukee Sentinel Photo

Braves' Mathews, Mets' Spahn, and Cubs' Buhl and Burdette

399

bunting with two strikes. Alou walked to load the bases. Spahn obviously was in need of relief, but Mets' manager Casey Stengel, who 23 years earlier had sent Spahn to the minors because he lacked the guts to throw at Pee Wee Reese, did his pitcher the honor of letting him get out of the jam himself.

With the bases loaded, one out, and the game still close at 2-0, Spahn worked carefully to his former compatriot Eddie Mathews. With the count at one ball and one strike, Spahn tried to get cute by throwing a fastball outside, setting him up for a slider on the next pitch. Instead the fastball came over the plate in the strike zone and Mathews crushed it, far over the rightfield fence for the 453rd home run of his career and the seventh grand slam. As Spahn kicked the dirt in disgust, four runs scored to make it 6-0. In an uncharacteristic display of sentiment, Stengel still let his pitcher stay in, not wishing to embarrass him in front of nearly 20,000 friends.

Next batter Henry Aaron topped a grounder and beat it out for the sixth hit of the inning. Spahn retired Joe Torre, but Aaron stole second with two out and scored on Carty's record-tying second double of the inning, making it 7-0. Finally Oliver grounded to the shortstop to end the blood-letting. Spahn trudged to the third-base dugout, this time not to wild cheering but to polite, respectful applause. In the top of the sixth Joe Christopher pinch-hit for Spahn, allowing him to leave the game from the dugout. It was a dignified, merciful exit for the great lefthander.

With Spahn gone, the tenor of the crowd changed. They sensed the possibility of witnessing history in the form of a no-hitter by Blasingame, so their shift of allegiance, though not universal, was immediate and overwhelming. In the sixth inning Blasingame fulfilled their hopes, retiring the side without a base hit. In the seventh, however, after disposing of the leadoff batter, Blasingame walked Billy Cowan. Perhaps upset by the sight of a baserunner, he then unleashed a wild pitch, with Cowan taking second. Charlie Smith was retired for the second out, but Ron Swoboda bounced a ball back up the middle. A better-fielding pitcher might have made the play, but Blasingame merely waved his glove as the ball bounded into centerfield, ending the no-hit performance. Cowan scored from second to end the shutout. Catcher Joe Torre shuffled to the mound and told the young pitcher, "You're too young to pitch a no-hitter anyway."

Blasingame regained his composure and got out of the inning. He breezed through the eighth and ninth to earn a 7-1 victory, the twelfth of his major league career; Spahn was saddled with his 233rd loss.

This game did not mark Spahn's farewell to County Stadium, although he never started another game there. After being released by the Mets on July 14, he signed with the pennant-contending San Francisco Giants. Along with Willie Mays and company, Spahn made his final Stadium appearance in relief in the first game of a doubleheader on August 1, pitching the seventh and eighth innings in a 4-2 Giant loss. Spahn allowed one run, but it was tainted by his own error, a passed ball, and a wild pitch. The Braves also won the nightcap that day, and the winning pitcher, earning his thirteenth win of the year, was Wade Blasingame.

Milwaukee Sentinel Photo

Henry Aaron earned many awards and honors before and after leaving Milwaukee.

1965 Nemesis - Tony Perez

"How could anyone who runs as slow as you pull a muscle?"

—Pete Rose, to Tony Perez

The Cincinnati Reds killed the Braves in 1965, winning twelve games and losing just six. In addition to Jim Maloney, who beat Milwaukee five times in a row, the Reds boasted the second (behind the Braves) most powerful lineup in baseball, with nine men hitting over ten home runs. One of those was a part-time first baseman from Cuba, rookie Atanasio Rigal Perez, better known as Tony. The lanky youngster had a promising, if unspectacular, first season, but against the Braves he was murder incarnate.

Perez made his season debut in Cincinnati in the year's second ballgame, against Milwaukee. In the fifth inning he smashed a Denny Lemaster pitch over the centerfield wall with the bases loaded, making his first big-league hit a memorable one. To show it was no fluke, he added a double two innings later. The Reds won the game, 8-3.

On June 27 in the first game of a doubleheader in Milwaukee, Perez again contributed a home run, this one a two-run job, in Cincinnati's 10-9 victory. On July 9 at Crosley Field he singled home a run the Reds did not really need in a 6-2 win, but the next day he chipped in a single and a double and drove in the eventual winning in a 9-8 Cincy triumph.

When the Redlegs visited County Stadium for four games in late August, Perez was on the bench, hobbled by a pulled hamstring. The teams split the first two contests, and the third game was tied 4-4 in the ninth inning. Two Cincinnati runners were on base with two out. Gordy Coleman was announced as a pinch-hitter, but before he reached the plate, a downpour of rain caused a fifteen-minute delay. When play resumed, Perez was

402

sent to bat for Coleman. The injured first sacker limped to the plate and blasted a three-run homer to give his team a 7-4 victory.

One week later, on September 1, Perez made his final appearance against Milwaukee in a doubleheader in Cincinnati. He contributed a double in a 7-6 victory in the opener, then smacked a second-inning home run that gave Maloney all the support he needed to win the nightcap, 2-0. The next day, with Perez on the bench, the Braves defeated the Reds in their final meeting.

Perez finished the season with a .244 average against the other eight clubs in the National League; against the Braves he batted .407. He played first base in nine games against Milwaukee—and the Reds won every one.

Milwaukee Sentinel Photo

The banner speaks for itself.

Time Capsule - August 18, 1965

"It was either a grudge call or he [umpire Chris Pelekoudas] just wanted to get his name in the papers."

—Bobby Bragan

Busch Stadium in St. Louis was called Sportsmen's Park and was shared with Bill Veeck's Browns when the Milwaukee Braves began playing there in 1953. As home to the Gashouse Gang in the thirties, one-armed Pete Gray in 1945, and midget Eddie Gaedel in 1951, the venerable ballpark had seen its share of peculiarities. On the night of August 18, 1965, in its final year of existence, the cramped and creaky home of the Cardinals witnessed another bizarre event—Henry Aaron slammed a home run onto the roof of the rightfield pavilion but was called out because of the position of his left foot.

The Braves were the hottest team in baseball, having won 27 of 37 since the All-Star Game, nine of their last ten, and six in a row. Their turnaround had lifted them from fifth place to second, only a half-game behind the Dodgers in the five-team National League pennant scramble. Bragan's team had won the first two games of this four-game series; Tony Cloninger (17-8) was trying to make it three straight over the Cardinals, opposed by veteran southpaw Curt Simmons.

As he seemed to do often, Cloninger experienced a rocky first inning. Leadoff man Lou Brock singled and stole second, tying a 38-year-old team record for thefts. Dick Groat walked. Curt Flood singled home Brock. Bill White grounded into a force play at second as Groat scored, and the Cardinals led, 2-0. Cloninger walked Ken Boyer, but he retired the next two batters, Bob Skinner and Tim McCarver, beginning a string of fifteen consecutive Cardinal outs that extended into the sixth inning.

By the time St. Louis put another runner on base, the Braves had taken the lead. They got on the scoreboard in the fourth when Aaron singled, stole second, and came home on Joe Torre's double. Then in the top of the sixth they went ahead when Boyer misplayed a grounder by Felipe Alou and Mack Jones followed with a prodigious home run off a light standard on top of the roof in rightfield.

Cloninger retired Groat to start the home sixth, but Flood got a base hit. White grounded out to Frank Bolling at second, with Flood reaching second. A moment later Boyer singled, driving home Flood to tie the game, 3-3.

Neither team scored in the seventh. With one out in the top of the eighth, though, Milwaukee apparently took the lead. Henry Aaron was at bat against aging Curt Simmons. Aaron had been subjected all evening to offspeed pitches from the veteran, whose fastball had lost its zip, leaving him an assortment of slow breaking balls and, in the case of Aaron, lobs and blooper pitches. The tantalizing tosses had drawn numerous chuckles earlier in the game from the 13,902 Cardinal rooters, to the chagrin of Milwaukee's hitters. This time, Aaron had seen enough—he carefully timed one of Simmons' balloons, stutter-stepped sideways toward the mound, took a giant step with his left foot, and blasted the ball well beyond the wall in rightcenter. Aaron loped around the bases, undoubtedly pleased with his 28th home run of the season, until he reached home plate and learned that he had been called out.

Plate umpire Chris Pelekoudas had ruled that Aaron, in moving forward to meet the pitch, had stepped out of the batter's box and was automatically out. The Braves, especially manager Bragan, were livid. None had ever seen or heard of such a call before. Bragan's ire was exacerbated by the fact that, in the eighth inning, the chalk lines of the batter's box had long since been obliterated, making the umpire's judgment of Aaron's step highly speculative. The furious manager argued long enough and hard enough to earn an ejection, his fourth of the season and his second by the same umpire crew in four days. When he left, he informed the arbiters that he was playing the game under protest.

With Aaron's run nullified, neither team scored in the eighth. Simmons gave way to a pinch-hitter in that inning, so Ray Washburn replaced him to work the ninth. Gene Oliver greeted him by beating out an infield hit. Next batter Denis Menke, starting at third base because Eddie Mathews had bruised his glove hand the night before, bunted Oliver into scoring position. Frank Bolling was retired for the second out, bringing up Woody Woodward as Milwaukee's last hope in regulation time. With a righthander throwing, however, lefthand-swinging Don Dillard was sent to hit in Woodward's place.

Dillard had spent most of the previous two seasons in the minors, returning in July from Syracuse. He had managed just one single in eight pinch-hitting attempts since his return, although he had driven in the winning run in the twelfth inning the previous Sunday by grounding into a fielder's choice. Against Washburn his result was more positive—he belted a long flyball to the wall in rightcenter. Outfielder Curt Flood leaped for the ball, and for a moment no one knew what had happened. Oliver crossed home plate, and Dillard pulled up at second base. A few seconds later umpire Bill Jackowski gave the home run signal, Dillard trotted home, and the Braves led 5-3. Jackowski ruled that a fan had touched the ball above the wall and knocked it back into the playing field. The Cardinals disputed the decision, but with success equal to Bragan's.

Bill White gave St. Louis hope with an infield hit to start the ninth, but Boyer grounded into a doubleplay and Bob Skinner looked at a called third strike to end the ballgame. A few hours later the Braves learned that the Dodgers had lost to the Phillies, and for the first time since 1959 the Milwaukee Braves led the league later in the year than August 1.

Aaron's nullified home run, then, made no difference. The Mobile slugger had another four-bagger washed away by rain in Cincinnati thirteen days later, but even so he eventually outdistanced Babe Ruth in career homers. Don Dillard stayed with the Braves through the end of the season, achieving one pinch single in ten trips, then disappeared from major league baseball forever. Neighborly Busch Stadium also disappeared shortly. The next time the Braves visited St. Louis (representing a different city, of course) they inaugurated a shiny new Busch Memorial Stadium next to the Mississippi River, near the magnificently arching "Gateway to the West."

Time Capsule - September 22, 1965

"This may be the end of the thirteen best years of my life."

—Eddie Mathews

The 12,577 mourners who attended the graveside ceremony did not wear black arm bands or veils, but they may as well have. The corpse had been dead for well over a year. On a pleasant evening in early autumn of 1965, the remains of the Milwaukee Braves Baseball Club were finally laid to rest in ground formerly occupied by the Old Soldiers' Home. The stadium bugler, after years of playing "Charge" to activate the crowd, played instead a solemn rendition of "Taps." In lieu of a eulogy, the grieving friends of the deceased showed their respect with standing ovations.

The team's brief tenancy at County Stadium, which had begun thirteen years earlier in extra innings, ended in extra innings, not in thrilling victory as it had begun, but in agonizing defeat. The Stadium's first game had ended with the Braves' centerfielder crashing a game-winning home run; the final game ended with the Braves' centerfielder being doubled off first base on a flyball. The hero of each game was the league's leading basestealer, the former for the home team, the latter for the visitors. The Braves' first home game augured a wonderful future; their 1016th home game offered only wonderful memories.

As the Braves and Dodgers squared off for the final National League contest in Milwaukee, the home team was simply running out the string, eagerly awaiting nirvana in the Land of the Pecan. The visitors, meanwhile, were locked in a struggle for the pennant, fighting desperately to overtake the San Francisco Giants. Milwaukee had lost its past four games, all due to lack of hitting. Los Angeles had won five straight with strong pitching and had moved within three games of the leaders. For the

Milwaukee farewell each team had its star lefthanded pitcher working: Wade Blasingame, with a 16-10 season mark, for the Braves; Sandy Koufax, a 23-game winner and baseball's current best hurler, for the Dodgers.

The Dodgers' hitting for the year bordered on feeble; the Braves were facing a pitcher in the process of setting a record for strikeouts in a season. On paper the game threatened to be scoreless. Naturally, then, it quickly turned into a slugfest, Koufax retiring only six batters and Blasingame leaving in the fifth inning. The Dodger first inning was a typical Los Angeles rally: Maury Wills singled, stole second, moved to third on a hit by Jim Gilliam, and scored on a fielder's choice.

Koufax struck out the first two Milwaukee batters and breezed through the opening inning unscathed. In the second, though, the Braves' awesome power resurfaced, this time from an unlikely source. Clean-up batter Joe Torre singled, as did Gene Oliver. Eddie Mathews looped a base hit that loaded the bases. Then against baseball's premier pitcher, second baseman Frank Bolling, who in eleven big-league seasons had never homered with the bases loaded, poked a grand slam over the leftfield fence to put Milwaukee ahead, 4-1.

Clearly this was not Koufax' night, a fact Dodger manager Walt Alston finally acknowledged in the last of the third inning. Mack Jones led off with his 29th homer of the year, and after Hank Aaron lined a single, Koufax was replaced by Howie Reed. Torre promptly bounced into a doubleplay, but Oliver hit a ball in the gap that rolled to the fence. Willie Davis displayed no skill in fielding the ball, and Oliver chugged all the way around the bases for an inside-the-park home run. The Braves had a comfortable 6-1 lead.

The lead, however, was short-lived. In the next inning Al "The Bull" Ferrara singled and scored ahead of Jim Lefebvre on the latter's home run. Like Koufax, Blasingame showed little "stuff," plus he had felt ill before the game, but Bragan left him in. The Braves' southpaw got through the inning, but the Dodger fifth began with a base on balls to pinch-hitter Dick Tracewski, batting for the pitcher. Wills forced the runner at second, then stole second. Jim Gilliam walked, an obvious signal that a pitching change was required. Still Bragan stayed in the dugout, perhaps unwilling to incite the boos that had greeted his every appearance throughout most of the year. Davis singled, scoring Wills. Lou Johnson grounded out; on the play Gilliam scored from third. Ferrara drew the third walk of the inning; Bragan remained inert. Lefebvre then singled home Davis. Finally Bragan emerged to

408

remove Blasingame and summon relief ace Billy O'Dell. The change came far too late, though; the 6-1 lead had dissolved into a 6-6 tie.

From the last of the fifth through the last of the ninth, relief pitchers predominated. For the Dodgers, Ron Perranoski was nearly untouchable, giving up only three harmless singles and allowing no serious threats. For the Braves, O'Dell worked an inning and a third before straining his elbow while batting in the sixth and departing in the seventh. Dan Osinski and Phil Niekro each checked the Los Angeles hitters for two innings after that.

The most memorable occurrences of the Braves' County Stadium finale came in the eighth and ninth innings. In the eighth, Eddie Mathews, the last of the original Milwaukee Braves, came to bat and received a tumultuous, three-minute standing ovation from the appreciative crowd. In the ninth, Henry Aaron and Joe Torre received similar, if somewhat lesser, tributes.

In the last of the tenth the Braves had a chance to score against Perranoski and win the game. Oliver started with a walk and was advanced to second by Mathews' first sacrifice bunt of the year. Bolling was passed intentionally. With two on, one out, and weak-hitting Sandy Alomar scheduled to hit, Bragan had a chance to end his Milwaukee stint with a smart decision. He had slugger Rico Carty warming the bench, a winning RBI waiting to happen. Carty, though, had publicly criticized Bragan's managerial skills earlier in the season. Instead Bragan let Alomar swing, and he popped out. Bragan still had a chance with two gone, but he sent Denis Menke to hit for the pitcher. Menke hit the ball hard, but Ron Fairly ran in and caught it in rightfield to kill the rally.

Chi Chi Olivo retired Don Drysdale, batting for Perranoski, on a grounder to start the eleventh. The beginning of the end followed, though; Wills beat out a bunt and (what else?) stole second. Gilliam was walked intentionally. Olivo left, replaced by Dick Kelley. The new pitcher got Davis on a popup for the second out, but Lou Johnson, released by the Braves in 1962, singled to score Wills with the lead run.

Bob Miller came in to save the game for the Dodgers. He retired Don Dillard, but Mack Jones singled in the infield. Representing the tying run, Jones strayed too far from first on Aaron's line drive to center. Willie Davis made the catch and threw to first, doubling Jones off base and ending the Braves' occupancy of County Stadium. The Dodgers' victory moved them within two games of the slumping Giants, en route to a National League pennant for Los Angeles.

1965 Swan Song

"Mathews would be a bargain at $500,000."

—Frank Lane, April 22, 1953

Eddie Mathews was a star from the beginning. He hit 25 home runs in the big leagues before he was old enough to vote. At first he struck out too much and played third base with more courage than finesse, but he quickly became the best ballplayer in the league at his position; he may have been the best ever at his position, all factors considered. When he led the majors with 47 homers in the Milwaukee Braves' first season, at age 21, his Hall of Fame future was already virtually assured. He went on to hit 452 home runs in a Milwaukee uniform. He also became the only ballplayer ever to represent three different cities as a member of the same team. The Braves' tribal designation was never specified, but Mathews was "The Last of the Mohicans."

The great third sacker first greeted Milwaukee baseball followers in the summer of 1951 when, just discharged from the Navy, he joined the Brewers for a dozen games. His first hit for the Braves' top farm club was an auspicious one—a game-winning, pinch-hit, grand slam home run at Borchert Field on July 22. That spectacular introduction gave fans high hopes for the young strongman when he returned as a major leaguer two years later. Mathews did not disappoint them.

Just as the Braves' final campaign was of the lame duck variety, however, Mathews' last appearance as a Milwaukee Brave was an anticlimax. The veteran slugger had enjoyed a return to power in 1965, belting 32 home runs and driving in 95 runs, his highest totals since 1960. In Los Angeles on October 1, though, on the day when the Dodgers clinched a tie for the National League pennant despite losing 2-0 to the Braves, Mathews appeared only as a pinch-hitter in the ninth inning for Mike

410

de la Hoz. Mathews failed to get a hit against Bob Miller, played third base in the bottom of the ninth without incident, and then disappeared into the Georgia sunset.

Mathews at bat in last Milwaukee Braves opener, April 15,1965

411

Epilogue

"There is as much chance of the Braves playing in Milwaukee this summer as there is of the New York Yankees."

—William Bartholomay, April 13, 1966

And so they fled, like thieves in the night, only during daylight hours. They took their bat and ball and absconded to their gleaming new stadium in the capital of the Peachtree State, trailing behind them an antitrust suit filed in Wisconsin Circuit Court, the first serious challenge to the baseball monopoly in 44 years.

Armed with a 25-year lease on their new ballpark, the Chicago-based owners of the Braves set up shop in Dixie and began peddling season tickets. The state of Wisconsin's antitrust action festered until March 1, 1966, when it finally went to trial. On Wednesday night, April 13, 1966, while the Braves were playing their second game in their most recent home, Circuit Judge Elmer W. Roller rendered his verdict: The Braves and the National League had violated Wisconsin's antitrust laws and must either 1) give Milwaukee a major league franchise through expansion in 1967, or 2) return the Braves to Milwaukee, effective May 18, 1966.

Testimony in the trial had revealed that, contrary to ownership's claims that the team had lost $3.5 million in 1963 and 1964, the club had actually showed a profit during those years. Nevertheless, evidence and judicial decision not withstanding, National League moguls met the verdict with their customary disdain.

Speaking of Judge Roller, Bobby Bragan said, "He saved a lot of lives. If he had ruled the other way, a lot of people might have died of shock."

412

Judge Roller's courtroom, with Bowie Kuhn, facing, at right

Dodger owner and de facto commissioner of baseball Walter O'Malley called the decision "an order that is impossible to obey."

National League President Warren Giles pronounced the court order "Preposterous," and National League attorney Bowie Kuhn, the future commissioner still in his larval stage, announced that the league would appeal.

Subsequently, and probably predictably, the Wisconsin Supreme Court overturned Judge Roller's verdict, saying in effect that baseball had a legal monopoly status. The state appealed that decision, but on December 13, 1966, the United States Supreme Court had the last word by saying nothing—by a 4-3 vote, the high court refused to review the decision of the Wisconsin Supreme Court. Case closed.

In the ensuing years, three members of the Milwaukee Braves were voted into the Baseball Hall of Fame. In 1973 Warren Spahn became only the sixth ballplayer to be elected in his first year of eligibility. In 1978 Eddie Mathews joined Spahn, and Mathews' slugging partner Henry Aaron was enshrined in 1982. Aaron, of course, played long enough and well enough to surpass baseball's most coveted milestone, Babe Ruth's seemingly unreachable total of 714 home runs. Aaron broke the record in Atlanta, 1974, then concluded his career in Milwaukee with the Brewers in 1975 and 1976, finishing with 755 homers.

Baseball's leading home run duo, Mathews and Aaron, after their final Milwaukee appearance

The last Milwaukee Braves crowd, September 22, 1965

And the Atlanta Braves? They made their debut on April 12, 1966, in a game fraught with irony. As in their County Stadium debut thirteen years earlier, the game went into extra innings; the Braves' pitcher hurled a complete game; the Braves scored first, but the visitors tied it late in regulation; the game was won on a home run in the last inning by a lefthand-hitting outfielder; and the final score was 3-2. The differences, though, were striking: the Atlanta version and Tony Cloninger lost in thirteen innings on a home run by Willie Stargell of the Pirates. For the season the Braves, led by Aaron, hit a ton of home runs but finished fifth, Bobby Bragan's maximum. Bragan was replaced as skipper in mid-season by Billy Hitchcock.

At this writing, more than 22 years later, the Braves have yet to win a pennant in Atlanta. Milwaukee Braves fans can only take perverse pleasure in the fact that Milwaukee returned to the World Series (in 1982, with the Brewers) before the Braves did.

415

Douglas American Sports Publications
P.O. Box 21619
Milwaukee, Wisconsin 53221-0619